MONSIGNOR TAYLOR
of CARFIN

MONSIGNOR TAYLOR
of CARFIN

---

by Susan McGhee

GLASGOW:
JOHN S. BURNS & SONS
1972

Printed in Scotland by
JOHN S. BURNS & SONS
25 Finlas Street, Glasgow. G22 5DS

PREFACE

This is a book that is wide in its appeal, timely in its publication, and fortunate in its authorship. It is the golden jubilee of the foundation of the famous Carfin Grotto: it is nine years since the death of Monsignor Taylor who initiated it: and the writer of this biography has had the good fortune to have been a member of Carfin parish for most of her life, as well as being academically qualified to undertake the varied and often laborious tasks of research by which the details of his engrossing life might be brought to light.

Monsignor Taylor was, in many ways, unique. People meeting him for the first time were struck by that direct, searching look which seemed to reach their very soul; that aura of sanctity which marked him off from the ordinary man; and the deep spirituality and sacred guidance which inspired his judgment on any problems submitted to him for his opinion. Though serious of mien, yet he had a rich sense of humour which made him a most lovable companion. He had, moreover, a wonderful faith. Without that, he could never have accomplished the many seemingly impossible tasks which he readily undertook, and which many willing co-operators helped to realise. Men felt it was a privilege to be allowed to help.

A turning point in his life was when, in 1901, he learned about the sanctity of the little nun of Lisieux who died in 1897. His translation from the French of her Autobiography went through many editions and helped to make her widely known; also he led pilgrimages to her shrine, where he was always most welcome.

I was fortunate enough to become very intimate with him, and again and again, I was astounded at the answer to his fervent prayers. In particular, he espoused the cause of the Missions. Not only did he gather enormous sums of money on their behalf, but he won for them many vocations both from his own parish and from his wide circle of acquaintances, as well as from among the many pilgrims from all parts who flocked to the Grotto.

One notable example of his readiness to help a good cause was when I was asked to help in trying to re-organise the Catholic Teachers' Federation, which had been gradually losing members in our Scottish dioceses. It was decided that it should henceforth, from 1934, be called a Guild and dedicated to St. John Bosco. On Canon Taylor's suggestion, hard-pressed though we both were for time, we decided that one of the best ways to secure the help of our Patron was to visit his shrine at Turin and beg his blessing on the new venture. There, we received a warm welcome from the Salesian Fathers, who assured us of the Saint's help in such a sacred cause. To mark the occasion, among other things, they presented us with a first-class relic of St. John Bosco, for the Guild. Clearly our Patron has done his work well, for since then, similar Guilds with the same dedication have spread over Scotland.

No matter how busy he might be, he was always at the disposal of any who called to consult him about their problems. He had great powers of concentration and gave himself up to the problems of the moment. This was a great asset when so many were calling from all parts to seek his prayers and guidance in most serious and confidential matters.

Monsignor Taylor was completely dedicated to the service of his Master. To him might well be applied the wholehearted appeal of St. John Bosco: *Da mihi animas, cetera tolle.* For the one great object of his life was the saving of souls.

I congratulate Susan McGhee most warmly on the result of her devoted labours and wish her volume a full measure of success.

PATRICK McGLYNN K.S.G., M.A., D.Litt.

CONTENTS

ACKNOWLEDGEMENTS

When Monsignor McRoberts first suggested that I should consider writing Monsignor Taylor's biography, I was not greatly enamoured with the idea. Primarily, I suppose, because I was convinced then, as I am still, that I had neither the ability nor the literary experience required for such a vast undertaking. Now, with close on seven years of absorbing research behind me, my first duty is to thank Monsignor McRoberts, not only because he thought me worthy of the task, but also for his constant interest, and the practical help he so willingly provided over the years.

Many sources of information were made available to me, most of them through the good offices of the executors of Monsignor Taylor's estate: letters, diaries, copies of articles which appeared in periodicals or press, as well as Monsignor Taylor's own extensive writings. The information from these sources was at times confirmed or added to by Mrs. D. Harvey, Monsignor Taylor's niece, and by Dr. Patrick McGlynn, for many years his closest friend. To Mrs. Harvey I am also indebted for a few of the family photographs appearing in this book; to Dr. McGlynn I offer my sincere thanks for a worthy preface to the biography, one which reveals aspects of Monsignor Taylor's deep spiritual character which could be understood only by an intimate friend. To the names of Mrs. Harvey and Dr. McGlynn I add a third, Mr. W. Murphy, news editor of the *Scottish Catholic Observer,* whose professional advice when sought was always freely given.

Of great value too, were the letters sent to me after Monsignor's death by so many of his friends—lay, clerical and religious. To all of these I offer my sincere thanks for the information they contributed and for their assurance of prayers. Not less worthy of my thanks are the archivists who consulted college records, the translators, typists, script readers and general factotums, all of whom helped in the production of this biography: from among their number I beg leave to mention only my sister and brother and my friend Elizabeth, since these three only were always at my beck and call.

My final acknowledgement goes to the publishers of this biography, Messrs. John S. Burns & Sons of Glasgow, the firm which for many years published Monsignor Taylor's books. The manner in which they have arranged and set up this book is a tribute not only to their skill as craftsmen, but to the respect and esteem in which they held Monsignor Taylor.

Many generous tributes have been paid to Monsignor Taylor, both before and after his death, but perhaps the one which epitomises them all is to be found in the simple words expressed recently by His Eminence Gordon J. Cardinal Gray, Archbishop of St. Andrews and Edinburgh: "Monsignor Taylor was a great priest."

EASTER SUNDAY, 1972.

Golden Jubilee year of the founding at Carfin of the Grotto of Our Lady of Lourdes and St. Thérèse of the Child Jesus.

RIGHT REVEREND MONSIGNOR THOMAS N. CANON TAYLOR

CHAPTER I

ANGLO-IRISH ROOTS

A fading entry in an old diary, covering more than half a century, records that on Tuesday, 16th December, 1873,

"Mrs. James Taylor got a son at 8.15 a.m."

Thus, James Taylor, the diarist, who at that time was Headmaster of the local school of St. Laurence's parish, Greenock, made mention of the birth of his first born, Thomas Nimmo Taylor. The stark simplicity of the entry was scarcely an augury of the infant's future, for during the ninety years of his natural life, Thomas Nimmo Taylor's manifold interests were often widespread and complex; his priestly duties and his many and varied occupations brought him into contact with a heterogeneous multitude of people, of varied class, colour and creed, many of whom shared only the common factor of being in search of Divine Truth. By the turn of the century the recently ordained Father Thomas N. Taylor was already well-known in the older parishes existing on the lower stretches of the Clyde; by 1912 throughout the English-speaking world, his name was more than familiar to devotees of Saint Thérèse of the Child Jesus, the wonder-worker French Carmelite nun, who had died in 1897, the year of Father Taylor's ordination to the priesthood; fifteen years later the Grotto at Carfin, founded by him in 1922, in honour of our Lady of Lourdes, roused the fervour of the Catholics of the West of Scotland: this in turn gave rise to the unsought publicity of the press, which made the name of Father Taylor a household word throughout the British Isles.

But, of the parents, neither the twenty-five year old James Taylor nor his twenty-eight year old wife, Roseanne, had cause to believe that their young son would, in later years, differ in any respect, from the average Catholic young man, the son of staunch Catholic parents. Certainly, further entries in the father's diary were not auspicious of an unusual future. We learn only that a Mrs. McCallum, who nursed the mother and child, was paid the sum of £1 for her week's services—a fair payment for her task at that time; also the notice of the birth appeared in the local *Telegraph*, on the 23rd December, 1873, and a copy of the paper was sent to Mrs. Anne Taylor, the widowed paternal grandmother, who resided at the family home of the Taylors in St.

[1]

B

Helens, Lancashire. This, in effect, is all the information at present available from family records, concerning the first few weeks of the life of Monsignor Thomas Nimmo Canon Taylor, priest in charge of St. Francis Xavier's Catholic Mission at Carfin, Scotland, from 1915 until his death on 1st December, 1963; and founder and administrator of the Grotto of Our Lady of Lourdes and Saint Thérèse, built adjacent to the parish church.

*   *   *   *

A healthy tree almost invariably grows from healthy roots. How much truth lies in this dictum when it is applied to human stock, and in particular when it is applicable to Monsignor Taylor's forebears, the reader may well judge for himself.

James Taylor (Monsignor's father), had come north to Greenock on the 7th January, 1871, to take up the post of Headmaster at St. Laurence's Catholic School. He was a scion of Lancashire Catholic stock, small land owners, who in spite of opposition over the centuries since the Reformation, had remained staunch to the old Faith. In the first half of the nineteenth century, another James Taylor, paternal grandfather of the young Greenock dominie, had then been in a position to provide his family with the necessities of life, and a little of its luxuries, from income accruing from his various properties in Lancashire. The chief of these seems to have been at Longshaw, near Wigan, where, at the age of 88, the patriarchal grandfather died, in March 1874, just three months after the birth at Greenock, of his great-grandson, Thomas Nimmo Taylor.

In addition to the income from their estates, the Taylor family fortunes were sustained by weaving, which was still a lucrative home occupation. With the advance of the Industrial Revolution came the decline of " cottage industries "; and with the further division and sub-division of land at marriage and death, we find that the Taylor family were compelled to adapt themselves to other skills and crafts, although a small, but fairly regular amount still obtained from the family estates.

Henry Taylor, the eldest son of James Taylor of Longshaw, worked as a quarryman at Billinge, near Wigan, and it was here he met and married Anne Green, daughter of a Catholic family of weavers, who it is believed " has come from Manchester "* and " was of Irish extraction."* Five children were born of this marriage, three boys and two girls, the Benjamin of the family being James Taylor, who was born at Westfield Street, St. Helens,

---

* Information from family records.

on the 29th November, 1848. This last named son was to become the father of Monsignor Taylor.

Since their twenty-year-old son had shown a certain aptitude for academic study, Mr. and Mrs. Henry Taylor decided, in January 1868, to send him to St. Mary's College, Hammersmith, London, to pursue a two years' course of training for a school teacher's certificate. During the student's first year at college his father died at St. Helens and the widowed mother, Mrs. Anne Taylor, then 63 years of age, insisted that James should continue and complete his course of training at the college.

Of his second year in college James records in his diary that in October 1869, he received " 2nd prize, money, £2." A further £2 received from the Public School Committee, subsidised by an occasional " quid from mother," made college days fairly agreeable. In addition to renewing his wardrobe, and procuring an extensive supply of books ("old ones at Holywell Lane "), he still had the wherewithal to visit Lord's Cricket Ground on numerous occasions. Cricket, skating, walking and fishing were to be his favourite forms of outdoor recreation for many years after he had set up his home in Greenock, and one of the great joys of the eldest son Thomas was to accompany his father on the frequent boating and fishing expeditions on the numerous lochs near their home.

In 1869, armed with a teacher's certificate and a prize for excellence in drawing, James Taylor bade farewell to Fr. Graham, Rector of St. Mary's College, Hammersmith. Of the twenty-four students who had trained with James, three hailed from Lancashire and with these for company, the newly fledged teacher travelled northwards to arrive at his home at St. Helens a few days before Christmas 1869.

An assistantship in Manchester at an annual salary of £50 was declined in favour of the more remunerative offer of £65 from Rev. Dr. McCann, Manager at Holy Trinity School, Bilston. Unsuitable accommodation, at a considerable distance from the school, too many unpaid evening classes and a " shortage of female staff " for the girls, caused the young principal teacher to offer his resignation as soon as a more tempting post became available elsewhere.

In Greenock, Scotland, the headmaster of St. Laurence's Catholic School had been seriously ill, and when the Manager, Rev. Michael Condon, advertised for a replacement, James Taylor, a head teacher of one year's experience, holding a School Report of " Satisfactory in instruction and discipline," applied for and was appointed to the post.

Thus was forged the first link in the chain of events which brought James Taylor, the Englishman born and bred at St. Helens, Lancashire, into close proximity with the Nimmo family residing at Greenock, on the Firth of Clyde, a little over twenty miles west from Glasgow. Of the eleven-hour, fifteen shilling railway journey north across the Border, the newly appointed headmaster had little to record, except that " the scenery was good but the journey was cold." Whether the latter part of the remark was a reflection on the more northerly climate or the lack of heating on the train is a matter of conjecture.

His arrival at Greenock coincided with Father Condon's hours for Confession so that Miss Garty, the priest's housekeeper, was entrusted with the task of directing the young man to 15 Hope Street, Greenock, home of Thomas Nimmo and his daughters, Roseanne and her step-sister Teresa. For the next two years Mr. Taylor was to board with the Nimmo family, until Mr. Nimmo's tragic death on 1st January, 1873.

Hence the evidence available from family archives indicates that James Taylor's ancestors were from Lancashire Catholic stock, with an admixture of Irish blood on the distaff side, in earlier generations. Roseanne Nimmo, future mother of Thomas Nimmo Taylor, for her part, could claim that she was of indigenous Irish Catholic extraction on the distaff side, although on the spear side her forbears were Irish Presbyterians. The latter may have crossed from Scotland to the North of Ireland during the plantations of the seventeenth century. At any rate the surname Nimmo is not generally classified as indigenous to Ireland. When this was pointed out to Monsignor Taylor on one occasion, his reply was:

" That may well be so." And then with a touch of his own inimitable humour he added, " If God had not directed Cupid to intervene, I might well have been a Presbyterian minister."

At the rejoinder, " Or a whisky distiller," he laughed heartily.

The latter remark referred to the fact that the Nimmo family were wealthy Irish distillers and spirit merchants, who, at the beginning of the nineteenth century, resided at or near Coleraine, County Derry, Northern Ireland. Here, one of the family, a Thomas Nimmo (great grandfather of Monsignor Taylor), had married a Miss Hendry (or Henry) of Grangemore, and after their marriage they settled in the district. There is reason to believe that the couple were in a fairly affluent position and were able to provide their family with a good education as well as the material comforts of life. A son, Thomas, born about 1818, having completed his education, assisted in the clerical department of the family distillery business. When the lad was in his late 'teens, his mother employed as one of her domestic staff, Roseanne Lafferty, an eighteen-year-old servant girl, who hailed from the adjoining County of Donegal. Roseanne's parents, typical of the majority of country people from that region, were staunch Catholics. Opinions conflict on the question of whether the girl's home was Letterkenny or Moville, but for want of more direct evidence, it might be assumed that the Lafferty family lived somewhere in the hinterland of uplands, east of Letterkenny and west of the upper reaches of Lough Foyle, a district claimed to be the traditional place of origin of the O'Laverty (Lafferty) families. Support is given to the claim of the first-named by the fact that Monsignor Taylor's mother, Roseanne Nimmo, was sent over from Greenock to be educated at Loreto Convent, Letterkenny, and that Monsignor's cousin, Kitty Nimmo, home on a visit from South America, at the beginning of the present century, visited " relations " at Letterkenny. Monsignor Taylor himself was unable to state conclusively the exact place of birth of his maternal grandmother, Roseanne Lafferty.

In spite of strong opposition from his parents, the son of the Coleraine distillers, Thomas Nimmo, as yet not twenty years of age, became attached to his mother's maid-servant and determined to marry her, with or without his parents' consent. Monsignor Taylor, referring to his grandfather's dilemma, related that in spite of pleas and the persuasions of material rewards, the young man remained adamant in his decision to marry the eighteen-year-old Roseanne Lafferty, even though the consequences would be disinheritance by his parents: she, on her part, convinced of his sincerity and of his promise not to interfere with the practice of her religion, accepted the young man's proposal of marriage.

In all probability the marriage was no more popular with the bride's parents than with the groom's, for in the Ireland of that era, marrying out of the family class was suspect, all the more so when the marriage partners were of different creeds. Possibly for these reasons, the young couple decided to leave their native land and start their married life in the busy port of Greenock, which, even before the Irish influx of emigrants, brought on by the potato famine of the " hungry " forties, attracted a large number of Irish labourers; some were to seek casual seasonal work on the West coast farms, others employment as " navvies " in the heavy work entailed at the wharves or in the building of the fast-expanding railways.

For ten years, Thomas Nimmo worked as a clerk, often for a meagre pittance, until the year 1847, when his wife Roseanne died, at the age of twenty-eight. Of the five children born of the marriage, two had died before the age of two; of the surviving three, James, a marine engineer, emigrated to Colonia, near Montevideo in South America, and John, a tailor to trade, settled in Pennsylvania, U.S.A. The youngest of the family, a girl born on the 25th August, 1845, also named Roseanne, was but two years old when her mother died.

Although Thomas Nimmo in no way hindered his wife from rearing their children in the Catholic religion, it was not until the year 1846, prior to his wife's death, that he surrendered his allegiance to the Presbyterian faith and was formally received into the Catholic Church at St. Mary's, Greenock. For the exemplary and assiduous practice of his adopted religion, his descendants have just reason to revere his memory. To be an emigrant Irishman in the days of the " hungry " forties was to invite rebuffs from many quarters; to be a " turncoat " from the religion of the majority in Greenock, was to antagonise the supporters of the Orange Lodge; to be in addition the chief henchman of the local parish priest, in those non-ecumenical days, was tantamount to begging for trouble. Of the latter, Thomas Nimmo had more than his share during several decades, following his reception into the Catholic Church.

Relating to these difficulties, notes recorded after Mr. Nimmo's death, by his son-in-law, James Taylor (who in the interval had married Roseanne Nimmo, daughter of the deceased), are, happily, still available; these notes were affirmed and added to in 1898 by the newly ordained Father Thomas Nimmo Taylor and the seminarist Alexander Taylor, both grandsons of the deceased Thomas Nimmo. The information provided therein may explain, to some extent, a remark made by Canon Taylor many years later:

" After my parents, I owe my vocation more to my grandfather Thomas Nimmo than to anyone else."

The testimony recorded by Reverend Alexander Taylor about his grandfather is as follows:

" His (Thomas Nimmo's) reception took place in St. Mary's Church, Greenock, in the year 1846. He became one of the most zealous and influential Catholics of the town. (He) Was for a long time President of the St. Vincent de Paul Society and (by ringing a bell in the streets), was accustomed to collect the parish children on Sunday and bring them to Sunday School. His zeal drew down upon him the hatred of the Orangemen, with whom Greenock was then filled, and twice he was compelled to fly for refuge to woods at Port Glasgow, his house being only saved from wreckage by the mob, through the intervention of some Protestant neighbours.

Thomas Nimmo was a man of truly Christian piety. For many years he was a weekly communicant; and never omitted hearing two Masses on Sunday.

His zeal in assisting the parish priest (Rev. William Gordon) procured for him, among the Orangemen of the town, the nickname, ' Holy Tammy Nimmock, the Pope's Granny.'

He died in Greenock Infirmary, 2nd January, 1873, lamented alike by the Catholic clergy and the laity of the town, and fortified by all the rites of the Church.

" Beati omnes qui timent Dominum, qui ambulant in viis ejus. Labores manuum suarum quia manducabis beatus es et bene tibi erit.' "

A further note adds:

"Thomas Nimmo had for mother one of the Henry's of Grangemore. The Nimmos are believed to have emigrated to Australia. Thomas, not yet twenty, was expelled and disinherited; hence settled in Greenock as clerk."

After the death of his wife in 1847, Thomas Nimmo remarried, possibly about 1854, and from this marriage another daughter was born in 1855. In the ensuing years, and certainly before 1870, his second wife died, and after his two surviving sons had emigrated he lived with and maintained his two daughters, Roseanne and her step sister Teresa, the former a dressmaker, who seems to have acquired much of her skill from the nuns at Loreto Convent Boarding School, Letterkenny, where she had studied for a time.

The decades between 1846 and 1866, after Thomas Nimmo's reception into the Catholic Church, were turbulent and trying years for Irish immigrant Catholics, not only in Greenock but in the colonies of squalid hovels and slums, where they settled elsewhere throughout the Lowland towns of Scotland. It is but just to say in defence of the average church-going, God-fearing Greenockian that while suspecting the increase of the so-called " Irish menace," he kept himself aloof from the skirmishes and attacks which served as a pastime for the extremist element of the town.

The latter, left to themselves, might have come to tolerate the immigrants, whose heavy manual labour served as a deterrent to convivial bouts in the town, except for the traditional visit on the evening of " pay day." When, however, pay day coincided occasionally with the peregrinations of one of the many itinerant preachers, who moved from town to town, wherever he might have a hearing for a truculent papist harangue, invariably there were clashes. As Greenock was on the circuit of towns which provided a venue for charlatans, so-called ex-priests and de-frocked monks, it is hardly surprising that faction-fights between conflicting parties became serious. It may have been during a serious riot brought on by the outbursts of the frenzied John Sayers Orr, familiarly known by the sobriquet of "Angel Gabriel," that Catholic public buildings were damaged and the rabble mob, beyond police control, moved on to attack Catholic homes, the Nimmo home being one of these.*

Nor did the attacks and opposition from those outside the Catholic Church provide the only test to Mr. Nimmo's fortitude and loyalty to the Faith. Domestic strife had existed for some time between the "Highland clergy" and the *Glasgow Free Press*—the latter, allegedly the organ of the Irish Catholic clergy and laity. The vituperative attacks of the *Free Press* caused Bishop Murdoch of the Western District, to denounce the editor of the paper for the slanderous charges made not only against him, but against the Reverend William Gordon of St. Mary's, Greenock. In this case, as in others, the serious charges made by the *Free Press* were without foundation, although it is idle to deny that the Irish missionary did suffer from a sense of grievance, which was not allayed until the Restoration of the Hierarchy in 1878. In the intervening years, Archbishop Manning was sent north to investigate the causes of tension in the Western District, and as a result a joint pastoral letter was issued through-out the Districts of Scotland, banning the *Free Press* to clerics and laity alike.†

The domestic troubles of the Western District do not seem to have daunted Thomas Nimmo. With the foundation of the new mission of St. Laurence, also in Greenock, his support of the pastor of his new parish (Rev. Michael Condon, an official of the Committee of Irish Clergy), was as zealous as it had been hitherto on behalf of the Scottish priest, Rev. William Gordon, of St. Mary's.

When the young Englishman, James Taylor, arrived in Greenock on the 7th January, 1871, to take charge of St. Laurence's School, there was an air of tranquillity about Greenock. A second generation of Irish had reached a com-promise with their brethren and only on rare occasions did religious strife become apparent and faction fights develop. The

---

* Information in this paragraph is derived from *The Irish in Scotland*, by James Handley (Cork University Press); and from Taylor family records.
† From *The Irish in Scotland*, by James Handley (Cork University Press).

Nimmo household, to which Mr. Taylor had been directed by Reverend Michael Condon, manager of the school, was clean and comfortable. The astuteness of an Irish lawyer had procured for the disinherited Thomas Nimmo a three hundred pound legacy, a small portion of his father's estate at Coleraine. For the next two years James Taylor lived with the Nimmo family, during which time a mutual regard developed into strong affection between him and twenty-five years old Roseanne. At Christmas, 1872, James had returned to his own home at St. Helens in order to be present at the wedding of his sister Mary, on the 2nd January, 1873. The wedding ceremony, which took place at historic Lowe House Church, St. Helens, was scarcely finished when a telegram was delivered at St. Helens bearing the sad news that Thomas Nimmo had died that morning, following on an injury received when he was crushed between the buffers of two railway carriages at the Caledonian Station, where he was employed.

Without delay, Mr. Taylor hurried to Greenock and helped the distraught daughters make the necessary arrangements for the burial of their father in Greenock cemetery on Sunday, 5th January. Of the funeral itself Mr. Taylor records, " Father Condon and a great many gentlemen, mostly strangers to me, followed the hearse and two cabs."

Mr. Nimmo's tragic death meant that the young head teacher of St. Laurence's School had lost not only a friend, whom he had cherished and respected, but also a home, for propriety demanded that he leave the house which had been home to him during the two years since he had arrived in Greenock. The sketchy notes recorded on that day suggest that he intended leaving immediately but Roseanne deemed it more expedient that he should not. At any rate, the problem seems to have been resolved by what James Taylor referred to in jest as " R.A.N.'s proposal." As he makes it quite clear that he himself was not averse to an immediate marriage, it causes us no great surprise to learn that on the following morning, after Mass, the young couple sought out Father Condon. The latter, though sympathetic, advised postponement of the wedding, but once the formalities had been completed, Mr. Taylor noted in his diary on Monday, 13th January, that he was " resolved to be married to-morrow, as Father Condon is going to Glasgow on Wednesday. This is Miss Nimmo's wish as well."

And marry they did, on Tuesday, 14th January, in spite of many obstacles and last minute difficulties, the chief being that the groomsman failed to turn up, due to the sudden death of his mother, prior to the time scheduled for the wedding ceremony. Eventually the much delayed marriage ceremony did take place, with the young curate, Father John Crawford, officiating as witness. Father Crawford was to remain a family friend and counsellor until his death many years later. He it was who baptised the first child, Thomas Nimmo Taylor, and who acted as godfather to Henry James, the second child.

Unavoidable delays in the morning caused the newly-married couple to spend the remainder of their wedding-day in Glasgow, instead of in Edinburgh as previously planned. In the evening, Mr. and Mrs. James Taylor returned to their home in Greenock, where commenced a married life stretching over half-a-century. During this time the couple remained steadfast in their affection for each other; and during which, too, their trust and confidence in God increased and strengthened, in face of the heavy crosses and trials which they suffered in the early death of their only daughter and many years later, in the deaths of two of their priest sons.

Chapter II

EARLY CHILDHOOD

A few months after marriage, Mr. and Mrs. Taylor moved their home from 15 Hope Street to a nearby house at 36 Lyndoch Street, where they remained for the next seven years, until in turn this house proved unsuitable for their increasing family, when they took a larger home a few yards along the same street, at number 15 Lyndoch Street.

In August 1873, James Taylor brought his wife to St. Helens to be introduced to his mother, Mrs. Anne Taylor, and his patriarchal grandfather, James Taylor, who at that time was still living at Longshaw. At the outset, the visit was somewhat of an ordeal for Mrs. Taylor, junior, for her husband, due to the pressures of a funeral and a hasty wedding, had failed to communicate with his mother at St. Helens until a letter of enquiry arrived from her, concerning the rumour of his marriage. The momentary annoyance was soon forgotten by the mother, for family ties were strong with the Taylor clan; and without nursing any grievance, the English mother and other relations from St. Helens were generous in their gifts to the young couple. The visit was a great success and Mrs. James Taylor had reason to be grateful to her newly-acquired English relations, with whom she stood in high esteem during her married life.

On returning home from St. Helens, Mr. and Mrs. Taylor devoted their energies to making their new home as comfortable as possible in anticipation of the birth of their first child in mid-December of that year, 1873.

In the absence of evidence to the contrary, and taking into consideration the notes shown in Mr. Taylor's diary, and recorded at the beginning of this book, it can be safely assumed that the health of the infant, Thomas Nimmo Taylor, was completely satisfactory during the first twelve months. It is remarkable, therefore, that his baptism did not take place until 4th January, 1874, three weeks after his birth. Although deploring the three weeks' delay, Monsignor Taylor cherished the 4th January, not only because it was the day on which he himself became a Child of God, but because, by unusual coincidence, it was the first anniversary of the date on which little Marie Thérèse

[11]

Martin—the Little Flower, who was to have such a marked influence on his life—had been baptised at Alençon, in France.

The delay between the birth and baptism of each of the Taylor children is hard to understand, unless we accept the fact that it was common practice in Scotland at the time. In the reception of other Sacraments and indeed in fulfilling the demands of the Church, Mr. and Mrs. Taylor were most assiduous in their duty. Indeed, they seemed to have modelled themselves on the life of the deceased Thomas Nimmo, who had been such a shining example to the whole parish of St. Laurence.

Realising the danger in delay of the baptism of children, Monsignor Taylor himself regularly exhorted his parishioners to bring babies to Church to be baptised as soon after birth as possible; or if there were any reasons for alarm, he directed that a priest should be sent for immediately, to administer Baptism. On this subject an elderly midwife, now deceased, remarked on how insistent Father Taylor was that in Catholic families, she should take every care to baptise the child when the delivery was prolonged and there was likelihood of danger to the child; also in the case where the foetus only was present after a miscarriage and there was a possibility of living organism, she must also administer the Sacrament of Baptism. Father Taylor's earnestness in the matter impressed her so greatly that she could clearly recall his instructions in one particular case after the passage of half-a-century.

But no thought of these future matters was present in the minds of the chief participants in the joyful ceremony on Sunday, 4th January. It is probable that Father Crawford, who officiated at the Baptism, and Miss McEwan, a family friend from Helensburgh, who acted as sponsor, as well as the parents, recalled the memory of the admirable grandfather, Thomas Nimmo, whose name was being honoured in this ceremony, which was taking place almost exactly two years after his untimely death.

When baby Thomas was three months old, his great-grandfather, James Taylor, died at Billinge at the venerable age of 88 years. As a legacy, each of his grandchildren received a bequest of three pounds, with the proviso that the interest accruing from all his properties should be shared among them twice a year.

The first six months of Thomas's life found him a thriving baby and on Easter Sunday, the 5th April, he was " shortened " from long infant robes to the shorter dresses, which baby boys continued to wear until they were able to walk. In early May he was vaccinated and in the following month, having recovered from his first mild upset, he was hoisted into a " high chair " which had cost his father 4/6. In the ensuing months, until his first birthday, nothing untoward happened in the boy's life except a minor cold and a slight convulsion fit from which he " rallied shortly." He suffered again from more prolonged attacks of convulsion during his second year while he was teething, but the attacks ceased after his gums were lanced by Dr. Stewart.

When Thomas was thirteen months old a second son, Henry John, was born, and he was followed in July 1876 by Alexander. In May 1878 a little girl, named Roseanne after her mother Roseanne Nimmo, and her grandmother Roseanne Lafferty, increased the family to four. To the great distress of the parents, Roseanne, a delicate child from birth, contracted pneumonia and in spite of attentive ministrations from two medical practitioners, died before she was one year old. Monsignor Taylor recalled the memory of these three, more than half-a-century after the death of his baby sister, when he wrote to a nun in South America who had made it possible for him to have in his Chapel of Relics at Carfin, a relic of St. Rose of Lima. On the 22nd February, 1880, the anniversary of the little girl's death, another son, James Bede, was born. This boy completed the family of four boys, three of whom were to become priests and the fourth, Henry John, was destined to become the father of a priest, the Reverend Thomas Taylor, junior, who died at his sister's home in 1956, after a prolonged illness.

While the children were still young and even after they had reached maturity, Mrs. Taylor kept herself fully occupied sewing clothes for them. In her teens she had trained as a dressmaker, and she made full use of the Singer sewing machine which her father, Thomas Nimmo, had purchased for her a few years before his death. Judged by the material she bought, the yardage and cost carefully noted in Mr. Taylor's diary, the amount of sewing she did for her own family and others was enormous. Every type of garment was tackled, from shirts to suits and top-coats; each of the boys was fitted out in turn for school or college, with garments made mostly by the mother. A source of constant worry to Mr. Taylor was that, "Ma was knocking herself out with overwork." Forever industrious, Mrs. Taylor felt that she could ease the family budget in this way and provide the children with extra comforts which they might not otherwise have been able to enjoy on Mr. Taylor's monthly salary of eight pounds, which included evening school salary and an additional bonus payment for drawing, which was granted to him on the successful passing of an annual external examination.

By careful budgeting, the parents and children were able to enjoy annually a summer vacation away from home. During the early years of marriage, Largs or Rothesay was the venue; but these resorts soon lost favour to Portobello, which had the added attraction of being on the doorstep of the Capital City, with all its historical and cultural interest. Periodically there were visits to St. Helens, where the children were always popular with their grandmother and their Aunt Mary, a Mrs. Hewitt, who lived at Gilders Green until her death in 1922, at the age of eighty-two.

During one of these visits to his Aunt Mary's farm, the five-year-old Thomas was so entranced with a litter of twelve piglets, whose strange dull eyes and quizzical tails held him fascinated, that it was only with difficulty that his father dragged him away. Fortunately, the child was too young to understand that the succulent pork joint enjoyed by the Greenock Taylors at Christmas—thanks to Aunt Mary Hewitt's kindness—was, no doubt, a cut from one of the chubby little animals which had attracted the boy so strongly at Gilders Green.

Examples are legion, if one had the space to relate them, showing how God's creatures in the animal world, attracted and held the love and interest of the boy Thomas and the mature priest Monsignor Taylor. He himself related the embarrassing tale of one of the first gifts his father made to the young lady he was eventually to marry.

On one occasion, when returning from St. Helens to Greenock railway station, Mr. Taylor proudly carried with him a lively young canary in its cage, a present for his future wife. As soon as he had left the station, he realised that the streets were teeming with school children, all enjoying the last few days of their summer holidays. Seldom or ever did such an interesting diversion present itself to a group of mischievous children, as the vision of the headmaster of the local school emerging from the railway station carrying a beautiful and active bird in a handsome new cage. Discretion, always the better part of valour, encouraged the headmaster to withdraw once more to the station, rather than be the unwilling leader of a triumphal procession through the streets, homewards. Hastily wrapping his raincoat round the cage and bird, he summoned a cab, paid half-a-crown, a just price for privacy, and with dignity preserved arrived safely at Hope Street; but not too soon for Joey the canary, which was already half dead with shock and lack of ventilation. Joey survived the ordeal and was succeeded by a dynasty of Joeys, each in turn giving joy to the growing boys. Joey the fifth suffered an interloper to share his realm for a time, in the person of a canary, bearing the pontifical name of Leo. James Bede, at that time in his early 'teens, brought the bird to the Taylor home, while its owner, young Father Thomas N. Taylor, then stationed at St. Patrick's, Dumbarton, was undergoing surgical treatment in a Glasgow nursing home.

Another delightful story has been told by one of the Grotto "volunteers"—the workers who helped to build the Grotto of Our Lady and St. Thérèse. The volunteers were busy pruning trees in the vicinity of the Calvary Shrine, when a thrush's nest was discovered in the branches of one of the trees. Canon Taylor's attention was drawn to the nest, but try as he might, he was unable to stretch his five feet five inches of height up far enough to peer into the nest. Nothing daunted, he nodded to two of his stalwart volunteers, and even before the thought was expressed, the pair had crossed hands, and there in the presence of his friends, the Canon was hoisted to a position of vantage, from which he gazed to his heart's delight at the five blue-green, ink-spotted eggs. Never could twelve-year-old schoolboy have been so enraptured with his unexpected "find." It goes without saying that "operation pruning" in that area, was suspended until the young fledglings had left the nest.

More than sixty years prior to the delightful incident just related, on the morning of the 3rd August, 1880, an air of excitement prevailed in the Taylor household, for on this day six-and-a-half-year-old Thomas was due to enrol at the local Franciscan Convent School. Nearby, at Belville Street, final preparations were being made for the ceremony of laying the foundation stone of the new St. Laurence's parish school, by Archbishop Eyre of Glasgow Archdiocese. It was in this new school that Mr. Taylor was to continue as principal teacher until he eventually retired in 1914. At the Convent school, where Thomas was now a pupil, he met a number of boys with whom he associated until his teenage years when he attended St. Aloysius' College, Glasgow. Two of these were the McBrearty brothers, one of whom, Father Denis McBrearty, was destined to be Father Taylor's predecessor at St. Francis Xavier's, Carfin.

Each of the four brothers attended the Franciscan school for a few years before they transferred to their father's school at Belville Street, where they completed their primary education. Likewise, each in turn won class prizes at the Convent, and on one occasion Thomas, Henry and Alexander approached the official table to receive their respective prizes from the hands of Reverend Alexander Taylor, of St. Mary's Church, Greenock. The latter was particularly pleased, and the tumultuous applause of the audience demonstrated their pleasure also, when Alexander the youngest of the trio, not yet six years of age, and bearing the same name as the presiding priest, stepped forward to accept his reward for diligence. During his years of study at St. Mary's College, Blairs, at St. Peter's, Bearsden, and later at the Scots College, Rome, Alexander was to maintain his high standards of diligence. After his ordination in Rome, he studied for his Doctorate in Divinity, and having succeeded, he was eventually appointed to St. Anthony's Mission at Govan. Here in the Clydeside parish the people quickly grew to know and respect the devoted Dr. Taylor, whose engaging and boyish frankness won the hearts of parents and children alike. His early death within two years of ordination was a great sorrow to his parents and brothers, and to all the parishioners.

During Thomas's initial year at school, two events occurred to upset the even tenor of his schooldays. The first, an attack of diphtheria which kept him away from school for the greater part of a term, but the buoyancy of his small but wiry body enabled him to return, fully recovered, in the second term; the second event which touched his childish sensitivity more deeply was the death at St. Helens of his seventy-five year old grandmother, Mrs. Anne Taylor. She was the only one of his grandparents whom Thomas had known—the others had died before or shortly after his birth—and the unfailing sympathy and kindness shown by the old lady to the young boys was not easily forgotten. Thomas's father and mother, too, had reason to grieve, for though separated by a distance of many miles, a close family kinship existed between them. There was a constant exchange of letters and gifts between Greenock and St. Helens and although this was natural between members of the same family, something that was less usual was that Mrs. Taylor, senior, already recognised for her charitable generosity in St. Helens, on more than one occasion subscribed to the redecoration of St. Laurence's Church, Greenock. It is not to be wondered at that Monsignor Taylor inherited through his own parents goodness and generosity of heart, qualities abundantly apparent in the character of his grandparents, and about which he had heard so much, especially in the case of his grandfather, Thomas Nimmo, and his grandmother, Mrs. Anne Taylor.

Other memories of these early days, confused at times, were revived occasionally by Monsignor Taylor. As an octogenarian, he laughingly recalled that for almost a lifetime he had believed it was His Eminence Cardinal Manning who had, in 1881, blessed and opened the new school in Belville Street, where his father was headmaster.

This lapse in memories of childhood was corrected when on reading through his father's diary, he learned that Archbishop Eyre had performed the opening ceremony in the new school on the 1st May, 1881. On the 1st June in the same year, Cardinal Manning* had preached in Greenock Town Hall, and four and a half months later a Synod of Bishops was held at Glasgow under the aegis of Archbishop Eyre. From this galaxy of dignitaries one can appreciate that a six-year-old child would naturally associate the most exalted of the prelates with the opening of his father's school.

Exciting as was Thomas's first day at school, the event palls compared to the day of his first Holy Communion and Confirmation. For some weeks, the Sisters at the Franciscan Convent had been preparing Thomas for the first reception of Confession and Communion. As Archbishop Eyre had intimated that he intended administering the Sacrament of Confirmation on Sunday, 25th February, the third Sunday in Lent of that year 1883, it was arranged that the Sisters should prepare the First Communicants to receive the three Sacraments on the same day. Thomas was then nine years old and must have been well aware of the importance of the day when he first received his Divine Lord from the hands of His Grace Archbishop Eyre. Among the treasured mementoes which he preserved until his death was the brightly coloured Communion Card given to him by the Franciscan Sister who had prepared him for the reception of the Sacrament.

A quarter of a century later, at the Eucharistic Congress held in London, in 1908, Father Taylor was to address the dignitaries of the Church assembled there on the PRIESTS' COMMUNION LEAGUE FOR THE PROMOTION OF DAILY COMMUNION among the laity, and the early reception of the Eucharist by children. The precepts he preached so eloquently at Westminster were the inviolable tenets from which he never deviated during more than sixty years of sacerdotal practice.

During his own childhood, it would appear that fortnightly confession seemed to be the practice of the family, although Mr. Taylor did not mention it in his diary as a rule of life. In addition

* It may be of interest to the Catholics of Greenock, although not necessarily connected with the event, that on the Sunday after Cardinal Manning addressed the joint congregations of the Catholic parishes of Greenock, the League of the Cross was set up in both parishes to combat the evils of drunkenness then prevalent in Scotland. On Sunday, 19th May, 1889, by order of the Archbishop, the League was to be revived, or founded in every parish in the Archdiocese of Glasgow.

to the entry, " Pa and the children, confession," there is repeated mention of Confession for feasts, festivals and anniversaries of deceased relatives, followed by the usual "Early Mass" on Sundays, for in these years Holy Communion was not received at later Masses. On Christmas day, the parents, whenever possible, assisted at three Masses, a practice followed by the children as they grew older. It is interesting to note also, that on various occasions Mr. Taylor specifically mentioned that all the family went to Confession on the last day of the year and attended early Mass on New Year's Day. This may be an indication that the father deplored the excess of drunkenness so much that he wished to offer reparation; on the other hand, it may suggest that the festival of Christmas was still shrouded in the gloom into which it had been pushed by three centuries of Presbyterianism. This suggestion is borne out by a remark made by Canon John McKay —sometimes affectionately referred to as "Jock the builder" because of the number of churches he founded in Lanarkshire— that shortly after he came to St. Ignatius' Mission in Wishaw, in 1859, Catholics would stop him in the street and ask, "When is Christmas, Father?" Three years later at the village of Carfin, about some three miles south of Wishaw, Canon McKay founded the Mission of St. Francis Xavier. For a number of years this Mission, the offspring of Wishaw, served as the sole Mass Centre for the area circumscribed by the parishes of St. Mary's, Abercromby Street; St. Ignatius', Wishaw, St. Mary's, Hamilton, and St. Aloysius', Chapelhall.*

In 1884, the Taylor home was a crowded and busy one. Mrs. Taylor's step-sister had died shortly after the birth of her daughter Mary Teresa. As the baby's father was not well-placed for caring properly for the child, Mr. and Mrs. Taylor, without hesitation, offered to look after her. To help her with the children, Mrs. Taylor employed a country girl, Maggie Livingstone, to act as nursemaid. During this year all the children, Mary Teresa included, contracted whooping cough, and ten-year-old Thomas was Maggie's chief helper, while Mr. Taylor was occupied with other duties. Eventually, during the summer vacation, the whole of the Taylor family, with Mary Teresa and her father, went off to Rothesay for a holiday, while Maggie Livingstone took herself off to her own family home. Maggie is of unique interest in this respect, that she was the first recipient of a letter from one who

---

* The Missions at Mossend (1868), Motherwell (1873), Cleland (1874) and Uddingston (1883) were set up in quick succession and before the turn of the century the limits of Carfin Mission covered only the villages of Newarthill, New Stevenston, Jerviston and Cleekhimin.

perhaps in a single year wrote as many, if not more, letters than does the average person in a lifetime; and who in spite of spending half the night writing was always faced with a mound of letters put aside for further attention. It is true to say that during about thirty years of his ministry at Carfin, the only time left to Monsignor Taylor for answering letters, were the hours snatched from sleep. His lamp was still burning on most nights until three o'clock, and at times even later in the morning. He was the torment of everyone who helped him with secretarial work, for he personally read every letter he received and drafted a rough reply to each when he had time. As time was a precious commodity, letters piled up unanswered. Reverend William Smith, senior curate at Carfin for many years, took great delight in lessening the pile of unanswered letters, while Canon Taylor was on Retreat or at Lourdes, by giving instructions to the acting secretary to acknowledge each letter as briefly as possible, and then to enter them in the posting book. Father Smith's motto, " A brief reply is better than none," paid dividends, when dealing with an " In-tray " well in arrears, although he was conscious of the fact that his replies did not provide the comfort and consolation of Monsignor Taylor's letters. An anecdote contributed by Monsignor David McRoberts has relevance here:

" A friend of Father Taylor recalls how his addiction to letter writing occasioned an incident at the Redemptorist retreat house at Kinnoull during the Second World War. The nation lived in constant fear of air-raids and a strict black-out was enforced everywhere lest any glimmer of light should guide the enemy bombers. The Civil Defence personnel in Perth were alarmed one dark autumn night to see a strong steady beam of light shining out over the town from a window in St. Mary's monastery, high up on Kinnoull Hill. Several cars were rushed to the spot to investigate the matter. The Civil Defence wardens found the monastery locked up and everyone asleep, while one uncovered window shone like a lighthouse out over the countryside. The wardens demanded admittance and everyone in the retreat house was wakened by the noise. When the wardens were finally led by the Father Rector of Kinnoull to the source of the trouble, they found T.N.T. in his room, engrossed in writing a great pile of letters to correspondents, quite oblivious of the fact that it was well past midnight and he had not drawn the curtains on his windows and as a result the whole neighbourhood was in a state of alarm."

While still a pupil at the Franciscan Convent school, Thomas was tutored on the piano by one of the Sisters. These lessons in piano theory and practice were to continue until he commenced as a seminarist at St. Mary's College, Blairs, near Aberdeen.

As the boys grew older and friends dropped in—visitors were always made welcome in the Taylor home—the evenings often ended in musical sessions, with Tom, as the boys called him, playing the piano and Alick the violin. Bede, the youngest boy, studied music seriously and eventually became an accomplished pianist.

Although neither Thomas nor his brothers experienced in their home the drab austerity and extreme poverty which was the lot of many of their contemporaries, this was not the result of great affluence or high incomes to the family; rather it was the result of careful economy on the part of Mr. Taylor and hard working industriousness by his wife. Every penny was carefully budgeted and whenever surplus was available, Mr. Taylor went off to the Provident Bank and deposited the extra cash there, to be withdrawn when exigency demanded. This indeed often happened, for the mid-eighties were years of depression on Clydeside. This was early reflected in payment of "Church dues"; and as Catholic schools were built and maintained by the parish—although they were helped also by a government grant paid *per capita* on pupils attending the school, and who attained a recognised standard—the task of school Manager (in effect the Parish Priest), was, more often than not, an unenviable one. The never-ending problem of teachers' salary was a matter of grave concern for Canon Michael Condon and for Father Alexander Grant who succeeded him in April 1885. On the receiving end of the scale, Mr. Taylor, with the majority of his Catholic colleagues elsewhere, could gauge the "condition of labour" in their district by the delay in the payment of salaries. On one occasion Mr. Taylor's salary was paid a fortnight late and was made up of silver and copper coins of various denominations, no doubt straight from the Sunday offerings collection plates.

The wolf never did succeed in reaching the front door of the Taylor household, although at times he could be heard howling in the distance. But renewed effort and careful economy on the part of the parents, provided for the four boys a comfortable—and happy—home life, even though they were, to quote Alexander's words, " as poor as mice " for most of the time.

CHAPTER III

ST. ALOYSIUS' COLLEGE (1885-89)

Since the completion of the extensions to St. Aloysius' College at Garnethill at the beginning of 1885, Mr. and Mrs. Taylor had given serious consideration to the thought of sending their eldest son there for his secondary education. Unfortunately, there had been a threatened cut in teachers' salaries and as the College fees, in addition to the cost of railway travel, were prohibitive, the boy's parents were hesitant about arriving at an early decision. For some years Thomas had been showing signs of a potential vocation to the religious life. In many indefinable ways he differed from the average boy of his age; he was more withdrawn, more studious and generally less inclined to take part in the thoughtless pranks with which boys enliven their leisure hours. Not that high spirits are by any means the negation of spirituality; if this were so, Thomas's younger brother, Alick, would not have become an ordained priest. In the event of a window-pane being broken during boyish horse-play, Alick was always the culprit; in a dare-devil, bareback escapade on a borrowed horse, Alick was the victim with injured ribs. During the visit of friends two of the boys—Alick and Henry—were dismissed from the parlour for boyish misdemeanours. Never once during the fifty-odd years he kept a diary did Mr. Taylor make mention of a single incident where he considered a reproof of his eldest son to be necessary. Of course, it may well have been possible, but highly improbable, that Mr. Taylor favoured his eldest son to the extent of refraining from noting traits in the boy's character which displeased him. In the interests of justice, however, the writer of this book suggests that, from available evidence, it seems entirely contrary to Mr. Taylor's character to attempt evasive action in his diary. If he were unwilling to make reference by name to any subject, his practice was: " Spoke to ' X ' about a certain matter." Further information was withheld.

This aspect of Thomas's character is quite in keeping with an opinion expressed by an Irish priest during a conversation with the writer before going in to lunch in a hotel in Limerick. Noticing the Scots accent, the good priest asked the visitors which part of Scotland they had come from. On being told, " Carfin," he inquired further about Canon Taylor's health; and

[21]

then he added as an afterthought: " Tommy Taylor, the student who never broke a rule." The gong sounded for lunch, and on this unfinished note the conversation ended.

This incident took place during Marian Year, 1954, and the thought of the biography of Canon Taylor was far from the minds of those present during the conversation. The story is repeated now with an appendage—in case the unknown Irish priest was making a wry jest about a colleague—" There is seldom smoke without fire."

Providence stepped in to help Mr. and Mrs. Taylor arrive at a decision on their son's future, for on August 25th, 1885, a " Jesuit Father arrived from St. Aloysius' to ask for Thomas (now eleven years nine months), to be sent to the College, kindly offering to take him for half fees." The boy was to commence his studies there on 7th September, and was to procure a nine months' rail ticket costing £4 . 2 . 6. For travelling companions, Thomas would have the two McBrearty brothers, a boy named Cook and a few others from the Greenock district. Several of these boys were later to become priests, and one, Father Denis McBrearty, was to serve at Carfin until 1915, after which he was transferred to St. Aloysius', Springburn, where he was to remain as pastor for over thirty years.

Stories have been told of the " high jinks " the young Aloysians enjoyed on their daily journey to and from the College. Realising that something was amiss, Mr. Taylor questioned his son and the story of the pranks came to light. Sensible co-operation from the parents of all the young travellers soon put an end to pranks, and Thomas settled down to a steady routine. In recent years, a younger relation of one of Thomas's schoolmates recalls how the boys nicknamed him " Pious Tommy." This seems to bear out the remark of the Irish priest in Limerick and Mr. Taylor's lack of criticism of his eldest son throughout his diary.

At any rate, Father Chandlery, S.J., who seems to have taken a great interest in the welfare of the boy, assured the parents that Thomas had settled down and was progressing satisfactorily at the College now that the boisterous high spirits of one or two of his travelling companions had been curbed.

During the next three years, until July 1888, Father Chandlery's estimation of Thomas's intellectual ability was more than justified. In addition to gaining class prizes on each occasion, he gained the scholarship award in two successive years, while in the third year he failed to gain it only by a slight margin. In the Local Schools examination, a competitive one associated with

Glasgow University, he was successful in gaining the Junior Certificate in 1887 and the Senior in 1888. The latter showed passes in five subjects, and at the presentation ceremony which took place at Glasgow University, Thomas was awarded a book prize in addition to his certificate.

In the month of April 1888, Father Chandlery, who had been the boy's spiritual adviser while he was a student at St. Aloysius' College, advised Mr. Taylor to apply to Rev. Dr. Maguire, V.G., for approval for Thomas's admission to the national seminary at St. Mary's College, Blairs. When the reply to the application was received, the Archbishop's terms were quoted as twenty pounds, to be paid in instalments of five pounds per annum, the first instalment to be paid at once. In effect, this latter amount, in that era, was more than half a month's salary. To make matters worse, the letter of intimation arrived on the 7th April, at a time when the payment of Mr. Taylor's monthly salary was already a week overdue. The diary's entry in this connection is the remark of any individual who lives on a close budget, " Where is it to come from?" After a further delay, when eventually salaries were paid at St. Laurence's School, Mr. Taylor settled his monthly accounts and sent off the instalment of five pounds. The resulting confusion, whereby Thomas's admission to Blairs College was delayed until the following year, is not adequately explained. Since a reply to Mr. Taylor's letter had not been received by the month of July, there was every hope that Thomas's application had been accepted. One may well understand the disappointment experienced by the boy and his parents when prospective candidates received notification at the beginning of August that the date of entry to Blairs College was the 13th August. Thomas had not been notified! Investigation by Father Chandlery served no useful purpose except to confirm that the fees were " paid late." An unfinished entry in the diary—" Fr. Chandlery thinks . . ." —leaves us with the impression that rather than record an implication of carelessness at the Vicariate, a fact about which he was not certain, Mr. Taylor preferred to leave the sentence unfinished, and instead added only the official reason, " Paid late." Similar instances, where there was reason for doubt, are treated in like fashion throughout the diary.

Undaunted by this keen disappointment, Thomas resumed his studies at St. Aloysius' College in the specialised Syntax class, under Father Chandlery. The latter, perhaps, more than other priests, had a very marked influence on the boy's spiritual development in the early adolescent years. Not only did he know the boy as a pupil in the College, but from occasional visits to his home in Greenock, he was able to assess his character in the natural setting of his parents' home. In 1890, Father Chandlery was transferred to other duties in Wales, and five years later he seems to have been stationed in Rome from where he wrote as follows to Thomas, then in his second last year of study at the Seminary of St. Sulpice, Paris:

> 8 Via S. Nicola da Tolentino,
> Rome.
> 15th March, 1895.

My dear Thomas Taylor,

". . . In my memory I have a picture gallery of all my old friends, which I often look at, and among them is the picture of a bright, innocent little boy, who came all the way from Greenock to school every day. I have often asked Our Lord that He would make that boy one of His chosen and most devoted friends.

You are very privileged in being allowed to make your studies at St. Sulpice. The secular priests I have known, that came from there, always struck me as wonderfully edifying, and as having a spirit of piety, recollection and fervour quite above what one sees in many priests.

I was very pleased to hear of your brother at Blairs (Alexander), and I hope you will both, in course of time, become *model* priests, ' SACERDOTES SECUNDUM COR DEI.'

When you write home, remember me kindly to your father and mother. They must be very happy in having such good sons, whom God has favoured with so many natural and supernatural gifts.

Good-bye, my dear Tom. Often say to yourself with St. John Berchmans, ' I am determined to become a Saint and that as soon as possible.'

> Pray for me.
> Yours affectionately in Christ,
> P. I. Chandlery, S.J."

During the four years Thomas attended St. Aloysius' College, he spent what free time was available to him at the Franciscan Convent, Greenock, where the Sisters found him very willing to help in every way he could. It was Thomas and Alick who served as acolytes during solemn ceremonies, or who acted as messengers when letters or packages had to be delivered at the Franciscan Convent, Charlotte Street, Glasgow. His respect and affection for the Sisters fostered in Thomas a love for their founder, " Il poverello " of Assisi, which lasted throughout his life, and which led him to become a Tertiary of St. Francis in 1896, and after his ordination in 1897 to encourage others to join the ranks of the Third Order. Other Societies and Orders in his parish at Carfin were founded and fostered, but the Third Order of St. Francis might claim to be the only one set up in the first half-dozen years of Father Taylor's pastorate at Carfin which survived the founder's death. Like the Legionaries of Mary and the Knights of St. Columba, the Tertiaries were often called upon to exercise the virtues of Charity and Patience, while Canon Taylor was their Chaplain. Invariably during the summer months proceedings were held up while their chaplain was occupied with the many pilgrims who attended the Grotto on Sundays and almost as regularly on weekdays. Eventually, when his eyesight began to fail in the 'fifties, he was compelled to delegate his duties to his curates. Before this happened he spoke on one occasion at the Third Order monthly meeting, to this effect:

"My dear Tertiaries, you are the first to be told this news publicly. My doctors have told me that my eyesight will continue to deteriorate and that eventually I will be blind. Pray, my dear Brothers and Sisters, pray that my successor, when the time comes, will have a great love of Our Blessed Lord, His beloved Mother and her ' Little Queen.' "

God alone can judge his private and personal thoughts, but at that moment " his dear Tertiaries " could only wonder at Monsignor Taylor's complete resignation in face of such a heavy cross.

Almost an average lifetime before the event just related occurred, the fifteen-year-old Thomas was experiencing for the first time the novelty of wearing a tailored suit of long trousers. Already, in the spring of 1889, the industrious Mrs. Taylor was preparing the various garments required by her son for the Seminary at Blairs. A period of illness interrupted her work and, as happened on similar occasions, a seamstress was employed to complete the work on hand. It would seem that on this occasion the seamstress's standard was not as high as Mrs. Taylor's, for after the employee had gone, Mrs. Taylor unpicked a topcoat that had been made for Thomas, and herself refitted and finished it to her own satisfaction.

Chapter IV

SEMINARY LIFE — ST. MARY'S AND ST. SULPICE

On the 6th August, 1889, final confirmation was received that Thomas was to enter Blairs College at the beginning of the new term on the 16th August. The fees stated for admission in 1889 were ten pounds, double that of the previous year. It is obvious that Mr. Taylor used up all his available resources in sending Thomas to the Seminary, for the entry against Sunday, 11th August, 1889, records, " Drew the whole of my money out of the Bank to pay for Tom's admittance." It is interesting to note that banks did not at that time abide by the Presbyterian Sabbath observance; clients rather than bank clerks received consideration, when it was a question of hours of business.

Hurried last minute preparations having been completed, on Friday, 16th August, at 7.50 a.m., Mr. Taylor travelled to Glasgow to see his eldest son set out on the five-hour railway journey to Aberdeen. There were to be many more good-byes as the three boys travelled to and from the various seminaries in the next twenty-odd years; but for every family, perhaps, the wrench is greatest when the eldest leaves home for the first time.

The first few months in the Seminary were uneventful. Letters arrived saying Thomas was safely settled; these were soon followed by requests for additional text books for study, all indicating that the seminarian was tackling his work seriously. About the time of his sixteenth birthday in December, he was laid up for a week or so, but soon recovered although, between then and the spring of 1890, he experienced recurring attacks of indifferent health. In spite of his bouts of illness, he still could experience the excitement of the average lad, when he received from his parents for a birthday gift a much appreciated penknife.

At home in Greenock, the other boys of the family at various stages, were growing up. James Bede, the youngest, not yet ten years of age, had made his First Communion in December 1889. Alexander, recently left school, started on his first clerical job with a local firm at one pound per month.

Three months later, he applied for and was appointed to the accounting department of the Greenock branch of the Provident Bank, where he remained until he too decided to offer his life in the service of God. About the time Alick started his job as clerk, Henry John, the second eldest of the family, commenced an apprenticeship in engineering at the South Western Railway station, Glasgow. There were changes, too, affecting Mr. Taylor's work. In the autumn of 1889, Catholics received the welcome news that school fees were to be abolished for the first five standards of the Primary school; henceforth, the Government undertook to pay an equivalent amount from probate grant. Two years later, all children under the age of fourteen were to receive free education. This legislation removed a constant worry from the shoulders of many headmasters who were expected to collect fees from the pupils attending school. Since many Catholic parents were often unable to pay the fees, low as they might be, they kept their children away from school, or in some cases sent them to Board Schools. As the annual Education grant to the school was based on attendance and attainment, the financial difficulties experienced by Headmasters, Managers of schools, and Catholics generally when school attendance was low, was a constant source of distress. The improved school code, at the beginning of 1890, brought a further alleviation of tensions, when payment of grants to schools, based on results (as it had existed since 1870), was abolished. Mr. Taylor and the Manager of St. Laurence's school, the recently appointed Father Murphy, welcomed the changes, as did all Catholic Managers and Headmasters.

In the Taylor home, now that two of the boys were, in a small way, helping the family income, the balancing of the family budget no longer proved as difficult as in preceding years. With some pride, Mr. Taylor records, " Ma at last got some new clothes." The new pastor of St. Laurence's could not report a like affluence in his parish, for the amount paid by his parishioners at the Christmas collections amounted to thirty pounds only, a drop of seventy pounds from the one hundred pounds received by Father O'Reilly in 1889.

Meanwhile, at St. Mary's College, Blairs, Thomas had commenced his second year of studies. His health seems to have improved during the summer and autumn of 1890, but early in the new year his health again gave cause for concern. The period of indifferent health was prolonged, lasting until the summer months of 1891. In a letter to his father, the seminarian admits that his illness was affecting his ability to study. His parents, at their wits' end with the problem of how best to help their son, were relieved when Thomas wrote at the beginning of July, saying there was a possibility he might be sent home. A further letter received on the 17th July, informed them "leave of absence could be granted by the Archbishop, if sought." On the same date, Alexander hastened to Skelmorlie and received the necessary permission from the Archbishop. Four days later, Thomas arrived at his home in Greenock. Of his general condition of health, nothing is recorded by the father except that he " had not grown as his brothers have; and his eyesight is defective at a distance."

Although the fact was not realised at the time, Thomas was destined not to continue his studies at St. Mary's, Blairs, but instead was to be transferred to the senior seminary of St. Sulpice and thence to Issy, where he was to be raised to the priesthood six years later, in 1897. Transfer to the seminary at Paris may have been prompted by the spell of ill-health experienced at St. Mary's College. It could be assumed that the milder and drier climate of Paris would mitigate the recurring bouts of colds which had afflicted him in his second year at St. Mary's. A disturbing echo of this spell of malaise crops up again when Archbishop Eyre gave " health reasons " for refusing Thomas permission to pursue higher studies in Rome in 1896, the year before he was ordained. Instead, he was given permission to study for the Baccalaureate at the Catholic Institute of Paris, which he attended for a year until he was old enough to be ordained.

On Thomas's return from Blairs College in 1891, it soon became apparent that there was nothing wrong which a period of rest and his mother's attention and care could not cure. Within a week or so his father records that the boy was free from tension and strain, and with his natural resilience he was able to enjoy three months' unexpected vacation. A week of this time he spent with the Haley family in Hamilton, a visit which was returned by Charles Haley, one of the boys of that family. Another family at whose home he stayed for a week was that of the Brotherhoods. Mr. Thomas Brotherhood, Master of an Industrial School at Dalbeth, seems to have been one of Mr. Taylor's friends since the latter's student days at Hammersmith.

In the middle of September, Thomas's trunk was sent from Aberdeen to Greenock and shortly afterwards he received definite instructions about going to Paris. On October 9th, 1891, this time accompanied by all the Taylor family and several friends, including Mrs. Brotherhood, Thomas set out from Greenock railway station on the first lap of the journey to Paris. At Glasgow, Thomas was joined by fourteen other students, who, like him, were travelling to the seminary in Paris. It says much for postal communications in the last decade of the nineteenth century, that a short note from Paris was delivered at Lyndoch Street within three days of Thomas's departure stating that he had arrived safely at his destination. Thereafter, every three or four weeks, a letter was received with " great eagerness " by his parents. From these letters his parents were relieved to find that their son's health remained sound, and indeed it was not until a few months prior to his ordination, that he had occasion to consult a doctor, " the first time in six years." His father did not report any complaint on his son's part, either, about food or any of the other discomforts which often afflict young people staying away from home.

It is obvious Thomas had retained his avid interest in books for study, for shortly before the approach of his first Christmas in Paris, he wrote to his father requesting that a hamper of food should not be sent to him; he " would prefer to have money to buy books." He, the eldest son, was fully aware how difficult it was for his parents to meet the extra expense involved in keeping him at College; also he probably already knew that the third son, Alick (as Thomas invariably called him), also intended, if he was accepted by the ageing Archbishop Eyre, to apply for admission to St. Mary's College, Blairs. Alick did commence his studies at St. Mary's, and in two years' time he was transferred to St. Peter's College, Partickhill.*

In 1900 Alexander was sent to Rome to continue his studies at the Scots College and Gregorian University, where he received a Doctorate in Divinity. On his return to Scotland in July 1904— the year following his ordination—Rev. Dr. Taylor served as supply for a week in the parish of St. Mary's, Cleland, prior to his appointment as assistant priest at St. Anthony's Mission, Govan. Here he ministered only for nine months, before his untimely death on 29th May, 1905, after a serious attack of pneumonia.

Even during his first year at the seminary in Paris, Thomas does not seem to have suffered from the pangs of home sickness which are normally the lot of young students in a foreign land. In later years, Monsignor Taylor recalled with affection two older seminarians, Patrice and Henri Flynn, who " had taken him by the hand " and helped him to feel at home at St. Sulpice. These two, sons of an Irish father and French mother, had their

---

* This was the Seminary which was founded in 1874 by Archbishop Eyre and paid for from his own personal resources, while he was still Vicar Apostolic of the Western District of Scotland. As a jubilee testimonial, the Catholics of the Glasgow Archdiocese presented their prelate with a gift of £2,600, which he immediately transferred to the College he had founded, to be used as bursaries for the students.

home in Paris; in course of time one was to become Administrator of one of the larger churches in Paris; the other, Patrice,
was to be elevated to the Hierarchy, as Bishop of Nevers. The
friendship continued over the years and was cemented when the
French prelate, Monsignor Flynn, visited Our Lady's Shrine at
Carfin; in return, Canon Taylor was invited to preach on St.
Thérèse to a congregation of seminarians in Paris. A further link
of friendship was forged when an Irish relation of the French
prelates donated to the Grotto the beautiful bas-relief shrine of
Our Lady and Saint Dominic.

Another story, this time about Madame Flynn, the mother of
his two friends, is one which seems to have made a life-long
impression on the seminarian Thomas Taylor. Early one stormy
morning, while Madame was making her way along the deserted
streets of Paris, to assist at Holy Mass in a nearby church, for no
reason obvious to the good lady she was suddenly halted in her
tracks, and was unable to take one step further forward. Undaunted by this strange impasse, she took a few steps to one side
and to her great relief she realised how she had been preserved
from certain death. Within seconds a huge slab of stone came
hurtling down from a nearby building and crashed to the ground
across her original pathway. Madame Flynn attributed her miraculous escape to constant devotion to her Guardian Angel and
the Holy Souls, whose meditation she sought daily in her prayers.
The providential escape impressed Thomas Taylor very much,
and as we shall learn from the following story, Monsignor Taylor
had his own reasons, more than half a century later, for acknowledging the intervention of the Holy Souls on his own behalf.

Autumn of Holy Year, 1950, found Monsignor Taylor seated
in Rome's central station waiting for a train that would take him
north to France—and Lourdes. The sultry mid-day sun bore
down on the seventy-six year old Monsignor as he prayed that
someone would turn up to help carry his luggage to a distant
platform, or even help him further on his journey to France.

On this occasion his prayer was addressed to his own deceased
father, whom he remembered daily when he prayed for the Holy
Souls. The answer to his prayer was prompt:

" Hello, Canon! What are you doing here?"

The voice was that of a former curate from Monsignor's native
parish—the curate who had administered the last Sacraments to
his father during Mr. Taylor's last illness, some time previously at
Greenock.

When Monsignor Taylor returned from France, he told the
story to the one who writes these lines (she was helping him with

his correspondence at that time); and as far as she can now recall the priest from Greenock not only helped Monsignor with his luggage at the Rome station, but also travelled north with him to his destination in France.

During his second year of study at Issy College, on May 26th, 1893, Thomas experienced the great joy of receiving the tonsure at the hands of the saintly Cardinal Richard of Paris. Many students experience doubts about their true vocation at some stage during their long years of preparation for the priesthood. These doubt do not seem to have assailed Thomas at any time: if they did, he has not noted them in his diary nor in personal notes recorded during his student years. In a notebook of personal reflections commenced in 1892, and entitled " Mes Pensées," he dwells on many and varied subjects, from the evil effects of excessive drink to the higher sanctification of the soul; but nowhere does he express doubt about his abiding desire to be raised to the priesthood. Throughout his long life, Monsignor Taylor on many occasions publicly gave thanks to Almighty God for raising him to this exalted dignity. But, as he pointed out in his writings, the solemn day of ordination, perhaps the happiest day in the life of a young man, is not the day on which a miracle of perfection is created in the ordinand's soul:

" Perfection," he wrote, " could be achieved only by prayer and the constant sublimation of self, with its personal aims and ambitions, to the omnipotent wisdom of the Divine Plan. In this lay the path towards Perfection.'

Again, he wrote, possibly on the model of St. Augustine:

" We are commanded in our transitory sojourn in this vale of tears, to strive unceasingly after Perfection, never to rest stationary on the ladder, under pain of being borne downwards; and if not to be really perfect, which is above human nature, to have at least the intention of becoming so. Let us say with St. Augustine, ' I am not perfect, but I desire to be so.' "

On the eve of receiving his tonsure, he refers once more to the same ideal:

" God's title for imposing such a charge (the aim of perfection), upon us, is triple in its nature: He is almighty; He is our benefactor; He is God. Under these three appellations, He lays claim on our homage, our gratitude and our Love."

Finally, on the same theme, he wrote:

" Were man able to create a being endowed with life, would he not, and with reason, exact from it a scrupulous obedience and attention to his orders in their smallest particular? . . . How much more then ought not we to give attention to the slightest intimation of what may be our Master's will? It is in this that we should strive to be perfect."

Following on the above, the next reflection in " Mes Pensées " is in the form of a meditation on the reception of the tonsure, and ends with a supplication to the Holy Spirit:

> " My talents, miserable as they are, are no more to be employed in procuring the enjoyment and the pleasures of the transitory world . . . O Truth, ever ancient and ever new, open to me the floodgates of Thy knowledge; impart to me some portion of the wisdom which belongs to Thee as the Vestal of the Most High. Give to me, O Holy Spirit, those seven gifts which you reserve for those docile to your inspirations."*

The advent of his twenty-first birthday on 16th December, 1894, finds Thomas a young man, deeply involved in his studies and in the spiritual exercises which take up a great part of the seminarian's life. Already he had received minor orders, from Cardinal Richard, and as the venerable Cardinal was, in this year, celebrating the golden jubilee of his own ordination, his fervour and sanctity made a strong impact on the students on whom he conferred orders. For Thomas in particular, the year 1894 ended on the note of revival of spiritual energy. " Mes Pensées " was discontinued and in its place he kept a rough diary, which briefly recorded important events during the remaining years of his time in Paris.

This diary opens on his twenty-first birthday with the Latin quotation:

> " Apud Deum praeterita; pro Eo futura. Age quod agis. Quid haec ad aeternitatem."†

Following on the opening Latin quotation, comes a few histrionic exclamations which betray his immaturity, but the final prayer was to remain his motto for the remainder of his life:

> " My twenty-first birthday! Will the new life be like the old? Good-bye childhood and youth. May God grant me the grace of a holy life spent for His glory and for souls. Xavier's motto: ' Jésus et les âmes.' "‡

---

* The notebooks from which the above extracts have been taken were among Monsignor Taylor's private and personal papers and, as far as the Editor knows, they have not been published, nor even read by anyone else during his lifetime. Most of the writing is in longhand, with frequent abbreviations and a few words in shorthand. It can be safely assumed that the reflections express the hopes and ideals of a sincere seminarian seeking the lofty paths of perfection.

† " The past belongs to God: the future is for Him. Do what you may. What are these things compared to eternity?"

‡ " For Jesus and for souls."

THE TAYLOR BOYS:

Back row, l. to r.:
Future priests, James Bede,
Thomas Nimmo, Alexander.

Front:
Henry (father of Rev. Thos.
F. Taylor).

THE TAYLOR FAMILY:

Standing, l. to r.:
Henry, Mr. James Taylor,
Thomas Nimmo.

Seated, l. to r.:
Alexander, Mrs. Roseanne
Taylor, James Bede.

Father Taylor Blesses the Grotto of Our Lady of Lourdes,
Sunday, 1st October, 1922.

Thomas could not have suspected on that day when he had left his youth behind him and in the privacy of his diary had sought from God the precious gift of a holy life spent in his service, that his priestly life was to stretch beyond the diamond jubilee of his ordination; nor could he at that time have imagined that for close on half a century his priestly endeavours for the sanctification of souls were to be carried out in a parish placed under the patronage of St. Francis Xavier, the zealous missionary apostle whose motto, " Jésus et les âmes," he had adopted on his twenty-first birthday, in December 1894.

It is the prerogative of the Almighty to judge the success or failure of human effort in this world, but nevertheless the human mind may presume to assess the positive results of actions done in the spirit of Christian charity. From far-flung missionary outposts in India, Africa, China, and elsewhere; from priests and sisters struggling against heart-breaking odds in jungle and desert there is testimony in abundance that Monsignor Taylor never forgot Xavier's motto. It is literally true that he gave of his utmost to the Foreign Missions, not only financial help, but what his missionary friends considered equally important, his constant spiritual aid. Few of Monsignor Taylor's parishioners are likely to forget the ejaculation which he invariably added to the thanksgiving prayers after Mass or the reception of Holy Communion: "Holy Virgin Mary, pray for us and the poor heathen children."*

The following schedule entitled, in the diary, " A Sketch for the Day," demonstrates clearly that Thomas and the Sulpician collegiate led a fully occupied life:

Rise at 5 a.m.	Visit to the Blessed Sacrament.
5.30 a.m.	Meditation.
6.15 a.m.	Mass and Communion.
7.15 a.m.	English (Milton), with Father Touzard.
7.30—8 a.m.	Breakfast and recreation. (*Interim*: German with Father Many).
8.00—9.30 a.m.	Preparation for class.
9.30—10.45 a.m.	Dogma and Philosophy (alternating).
11.0—11.45 a.m.	Hebrew, Liturgy, Chant.
11.45—12 noon	New Testament and particular examination.
12 noon—1.45 p.m.	Dinner and recreation.
1.45 p.m.	Rosary.
2.00—3.30 p.m.	Preparation for class.

* This was referred to as the prayer for " The Holy Childhood," or in Father Taylor's language with the younger generation, " For the Black Babies." The term covered all unbaptised children in Missionary lands.

3.30—4.15 p.m.	Canon Law and Theology (alternating).
4.15—4.30 p.m.	Recreation. (*Interim*: German with Seiler).
4.30—5.15 p.m.	Scripture and History (alternating).
5.15 p.m.	Visit to the Blessed Sacrament.
5.30—7.00 p.m.	Private Study and Scripture.
7.00 p.m.	Spiritual Lecture.
7.30—8.45 p.m.	Supper and recreation. (*Interim*: German).
8.45 p.m.	Prayers and visit to Blessed Sacrament.
9.00 p.m.	Retire.
9.20 p.m.	Light out.

Interruptions to this full time-table were welcomed by the students as on feasts and festivals and during ordinations; but on the whole there was little room for idle moments. The study of German during the years 1895 and 1896, and in the latter year an additional study period of Italian, was a voluntary choice on the part of Thomas Taylor; as we learn from his diary, the study of these languages was suspended at times due to the pressure of more essential work. Even with the curtailment of non-essential study, Thomas admits that he was pushed for time for private study, especially during the 1896 term. Undaunted by the long occupations of the day, however, he surmounted this obstacle by rising an hour earlier in the morning at 4 a.m., while his friends were still abed. It is not surprising that on Good Friday of 1895, he felt faint during the exacting fast; this led him to note that " Study and fasting do not go well together."

This year, 1895, the young man's fourth year in Paris, brought the joyous anticipation of the sub-diaconate and diaconate. His prayer for that year was:

" Qu'elle soit pour Dieu! Qu'elle soit sainte et faite pour sa gloire. Ce qu'on fait en dehors est—nul."*

Although the seminarian's life was of necessity geared to the passing of examinations, Thomas always found the time to interest himself in the welfare of his ailing friends; this good habit formed in childhood and encouraged by his charitable parents, was to set its seal on the young man's character and to remain there during the whole of his adult life. Early in 1895, Father Grey, a clerical friend, died at St. Joseph's Hospital, after a prolonged and painful illness. The invalid priest's spirit of resignation to God's will and his stoical patience made a profound impression

---

* " (I pray that) This year may be for God. That it may be holy and for His Glory. What one does beyond that is worth nothing."

on Thomas. The resolution recorded in his diary after Father Grey's death was, " Be kind to the sick." The promise proved to be no empty vaunt on the part of the twenty-two year old seminarian, for in later years one could scarcely find a priest more devoted or attentive to the sick. During the years when he was parish priest in Carfin, excluding regular chaplains, there was no more frequent nor more welcome clerical visitor to hospitals in the west of Scotland than Father Taylor of Carfin.

An amusing story is told of one of these visits to a hospital some miles distant from the village. A certain parish priest noted for his brusqueness and sharp repartee had occasion to visit one of his parishioners in a neighbouring hospital. While chatting to the patient, the good priest became aware of unusual excitement in the hospital ward. On peeping through the screens around the patient's bed, he noticed at the foot of the ward a little figure enveloped in a long cloak being ushered in by the ward sister. There was little doubt about the welcome being accorded to the smiling Canon Taylor as he moved from one bed to the next. Realising the patient behind the screens was as anxious to greet the unexpected visitor as were others in the ward, the disconcerted priest hurriedly collected his hat and coat and with a disgruntled remark to Canon Taylor that there was not room in one hospital ward for two parish priests, he withdrew from the ward as gracefully as was possible in the circumstances. A sardonic Jove must have hovered near, for after his death this worthy priest was to share with Monsignor Taylor the limited confines of the same grave, in the plot reserved for clerics, in St. Patrick's Cemetery, New Stevenston.

At the end of the academic term, most of the Sulpician students went home for the long summer vacations; a few spent the first few weeks widening their knowledge and experience by visiting places of cultural and religious interest in Europe. During his first two years in Paris, Thomas had no alternative but to return home for the whole of his vacation, as straitened financial circumstances did not allow for the additional money required for a holiday abroad. Two sons in seminaries, a third serving an apprenticeship in engineering, and the fourth son still a student at day school, left little for holidays for any one of them. However, in the beginning of 1894, Mr. Taylor was pleased to receive his share of the proceeds from the sale at St. Helens, of the home and property of his deceased mother, Mrs. Anne Taylor. For the next few years, Thomas was enabled to spend a few weeks on the Continent before returning home for his summer vacation. Thus it happened that in July, 1894, he was able to make a prolonged

pilgrimage to the shrine of Our Lady at Lourdes; his first visit
to the Shrine had been in the previous year, 1893.

In the short notes which Thomas recorded at the time of the
1894 visit, we see clearly the changelessness and timelessness of
the devotion to our Mother on the spot where she appeared to
the Child Bernadette over a century ago.

Saturday, 7th July, 1894.

". . . at 2.50 p.m. we got on the road (from Bayonne) to Lourdes
at last. The scenery towards the end became very attractive, with
the railway running along the surging waters of the Gave and
between hills all swathed in mist. Impossible to forget the first
glimpse of the Basilica, as we rounded the base of the hill and
circled round into Lourdes. After a short delay we made our way
to the private lodgings recommended to us, at the home of
Madame Abadie, 39 Rue de la Grotte. Supper over, we hastened
to pay our first visit to the Grotto.

Who can describe his first impression of this hallowed spot?
The long rows of crutches hanging from the roof or lying out
against the rock, the innumerable candles in pyramid form, the
blackened walls, the flowing waters of the Gave on the other side
of the road, the Basilica towering overhead; but above all, the
hushed crowd of worshippers and the statue of our Queen, may
never be forgotten . . ."

Further notes deal with the spiritual exercises that followed
on the next day—the Rosary and Benediction given by a Bishop
from Mexico, the Stations of the Cross along the face of the hill
adjoining the Basilica, the torchlight procession of the Mont-
pellier pilgrims . . . which looked superb from the square in front
of the Basilica.

A reference to the stiff climb " up the hill with the three
crosses " and then up a higher one with one cross is fitting testimony to the vigour of the two seminarians (Taylor and MacKay),
who made the ascent. The final note on this expedition raises a
smile:

"The climb was hard, especially in soutanes, which we had
donned in the train just before entering Lourdes. We fairly slid
down the hill home; it was steep."

Of the remaining ten days which Thomas spent at Lourdes,
little can be said. Scribbled notes are still extant, but the hieroglyphics are difficult to decipher. It is clear he visited the village
of Bartrès, so closely associated with St. Bernadette's childhood,
and on that night, during the torchlight procession, there was a
" deluge of rain and heavy thunderstorm "; also, he visited
Gavarnie, and enjoyed the beauty of the mountainous scenery,

but his daily routine was Mass in the morning and " visit to the Grotto morning, afternoon and night as usual."

During the last few days of the visit, he made the acquaintance of an American Bishop and a Monsignor from Wisconsin who were leading a group of pilgrims. Apart from these diversions, Thomas seemed to have explored every spot of interest in the neighbourhood, as well as writing numerous letters and finishing the reading of *East Lynne*. One could hardly say that his first fortnight at Lourdes was solely one of quiet meditation and prayer. Be this as it may, it can safely be averred that Father Taylor visited Lourdes more frequently than most people from Britain did—lay or clerical—up to the period of the outbreak of World War II. His farewell visit to Our Lady's Shrine was in June, 1957, on the occasion of the diamond jubilee of his ordination to the priesthood. A span of sixty-three years bridges the gap between Father Taylor's first visit to Lourdes and his last, a life span for many.

It would be invidious to imagine that Thomas, in spite of his obvious interest in places of religious interest, was a goody-goody plaster-saint type of young man. Small in stature and lightly built, he was no match for the more brawny students in competitive games. He did note in his diary on one occasion that he enjoyed a game of handball now and again. His real interest, however, was in walking, boating and fishing, and while at home in 1894 he learned to cycle—at least he had reached the stage of remaining erect on a bicycle. Of this he relates an amusing anecdote which befell his friend Mr. McKay in the summer of 1896. The two had set out on a cycling holiday in Switzerland and Bavaria. Undaunted by the fact that Thomas had not ridden since his week's practice at home the previous summer, nor by the more perilous risk resulting from the fact that his worthy Scots friend was a " veteran " cyclist of only four days' cycling experience, in high spirits the two young men set out on their adventure through the tortuous mountain passes of the Bavarian Alps. A few weeks later Mr. and Mrs. Taylor, at Greenock, were startled by an unexpected telegraphic appeal for money. Understanding that an emergency must have arisen, for Thomas had previously acknowledged money received from them for the cycling holiday, the anxious parents immediately telegraphed £3 to their wandering son. A postcard from Tauberbischofsheim, dated 25th September, 1896, covered with their son's microscopic hieroglyphics, briefly explained the reason for the untoward financial embarrassment. It seems that Thomas had been cycling gaily alongside his friend, when suddenly the latter " rode

furiously down a hill, went off the road, cleared two somersaults
in ten yards over the machine and smashed the latter, to the tune
of twenty francs." Succinctly, Tom added—no doubt to the great
relief of his parents—" We have not ridden since."

This incident by no means spoiled their holiday, although they
were compelled to seek alternative means of transport, when the
mountainous paths proved too much for their inexperienced
trekking efforts. It was during this holiday, as Father Taylor himself explained many years later to pilgrims at the Carfin Grotto,
that he had " discovered Our Lady had a birthday." Unexpectedly the two students had come to a small convent church where
they were transported with joy at the sight of a procession of
small girls, tastefully dressed for the occasion in long white
dresses with blue sashes. When the little processionists had
reached a statue of Our Lady, erected outside the church, one of
the leaders stepped forward and placed a garland of flowers on
the statue. " Until that occasion," Father Taylor informed his
listeners, " I did not fully realise the significance of the 8th
September in the Church Calendar. That incident brought home
to me the striking fact that in Scotland we do not know how to
honour the birthday of Our Mother in Heaven. Since then," he
added, " I have tried to ensure that every pilgrim coming to the
Grotto is made aware that the Church has set aside one day in
the year to remember the nativity of our Blessed Lady."

It goes without saying that the 8th September was always celebrated as a special feastday in the Grotto of Our Lady of Lourdes
at Carfin.

Although the normal means of travel for long distances was by
railway, Thomas learned in the autumn of 1895 that neither time
nor trains wait for a dreamy young man. While at home on vacation he had received a telegram from one of his professors
inviting him to join the priest in a sight-seeing tour of London.
Thereafter they crossed the Channel to Normandy where Thomas
was to stay at the priest's home for a week, during which time
the seminarian hoped to visit many of the places of interest for
which Normandy is renowned. It was arranged that Thomas
should travel one day by a particular train to a certain railway
station where he was to join his host and together they would
continue their journey. Having an hour or two free before setting
out for his rendezvous, Thomas decided to explore on his own
account. His absorbed interest in a medieval shrine caused him
to lose count of time and to his horror he discovered that he had
already missed the only train which would bring him to the
meeting-place in time. A quick enquiry elicited the information

that a dog-cart, which might cover the distance in time, was available. The result—an exultant seminarian seated precariously on the back of a dog-cart, arrived at the station in a flurry of excitement. One can well imagine what a clerical professor, with a Gallic temperament, might have had to say to an over ebullient and unrepentant young man who had almost caused him to miss the train. For the benefit of posterity, Thomas recorded only " The road was lovely; so long and white."

The exuberance and *joie de vivre* shown on this occasion is noteworthy in that when he arrived home at Greenock two and a half months earlier, Mr. Taylor had noted in his own diary, " Thomas is nearly knocked up."

Thomas himself on this occasion wrote, " Feel very exhausted "; yet within a few weeks during a holiday with his family at Port Bannatyne on the Isle of Bute, he was able to say that he did " eighteen miles in a row boat," not to mention the long hikes he had daily with his father and brothers. This remarkable resiliency, mental as well as physical, was characteristic of Monsignor Taylor even when he was an octogenarian.

CHAPTER V

ORDINATION 1897

On his return to St. Sulpice in October 1895 the young seminarian expected that this year, his fifth, would culminate in his long looked for ordination to the priesthood. On Tuesday, 1st October, he noted in his diary:

"Another and last year of preparation. I pray that God and His Holy Mother bless it and strengthen me for the duties of the year."

Now he started work in earnest for the diaconate course, and finding himself "hard pressed for time" that autumn, he made a practice of "rising at 4.30 a.m.," thus gaining an extra half-hour for study. Pressure of work, however, did not prevent him from reading Newman and discussing at length with Father Touzard "the beauties of the Second Spring" of the restored Church, in England.

Nor did the extra study interfere with his plans for instituting what was probably his brain-child, the seminarian's society, which eventually became "Our Lady's English Circle." Several attempts had already been made to establish the Circle, but now (November 1895) Thomas notes "At last (it seems to be) upon a sure footing . . . after its stormy foundations by the two of us" (i.e. seminarian Mr. Harig and himself). The particular significance of this Society was that, unlike other literary societies, it had a deeper aim, namely "To raise Catholic standards of science, in Scotland; to raise the people to a higher level of Catholicity."

Tentative efforts were made to interest seminarians in other colleges in the project, and to this effect propaganda was disseminated at the College of St. Peter, Bearsden, and the Scots College, Rome. Alexander Taylor, at that time a seminarist at St. Peter's College, was interested in the idea of such a society, until by some mischance (before permission had been granted), his religious superiors gained possession of a copy of the constitution of the Circle. To Alexander's chagrin, he was compelled to acquiesce in the decision to have nothing further to do with the projected plans. In rather an amusing letter to his brother Thomas, he relates how his activities had been discovered, in spite of extravagant efforts at secrecy; very philosophically, he decided that his future actions must be governed by his superiors at St. Peter's and not at long-distance range by his brother Thomas and the latter's worthy Sulpician friends. " Our Lady's English Circle " flourished throughout the remaining years Thomas spent in Paris, but whether the vigorous roots grew to verdant growth or died a natural death thereafter, is not known to the author.

From November 1895 until early spring 1896, the students had little or no time for other diversions. Thomas's diary records a fervent " Maria Gratias " for success in the canonical examination for diaconate. On his twenty-second birthday, his heart-felt prayer was:

" May this year of the diaconate and the priesthood be blessed by the Sacred Heart. Oh, my God, make me a holy priest."

On receipt of his demissional letter, on his birthday on the 16th December, telegraphic communication was made with Rome for dispensation—on the account of age—for " interstices." Two days later, Bishop Maguire of the student's home diocese, telegraphed permission for the reception of the diaconate, which was administered by Monsignor Desforges on the 21st December.

During these days when the thought of ordination to the priesthood must have occupied his mind greatly, Thomas seems to have wavered slightly as to where he should best accomplish his mission as a priest. On the 30th November, 1895, his prayer, on the feast day of St. Andrew, patron Saint of Scotland, was, " Make me a true disciple of Jesus, in our dear country." It would appear that up until then, the real desire in the heart of the young man was to minister among his own people in Scotland. And yet, as he himself revealed during a conversation he had with the writer on this very subject, for some time he had had the secret urge to offer himself for service on foreign missions.

This is borne out by reference to an interview he had with Father Many, Director of Vocations, on the 17th December, 1895, when the Director " settled that my vocation lay in Scotland." The recorded " Fiat voluntas tua " is in keeping with the manner in which Monsignor Taylor accepted many and varied tribulations in later life.

His New Year resolution of 1st January, 1896, was:

" It (the year) must be one long retreat in preparation for that solemn event (Ordination) . . . In the words of Père Eudes, ' Mass requires an eternity for preparation; a second for offering up; a third for thanksgiving.' "

Part of the deacon's preparation, prior to being ordained priest, was to help with various clerical duties in neighbouring parishes; to assist at Benediction of the Most Blessed Sacrament; to preach sermons; and generally to learn a little of the practical side of a priest's duties. During this time, too, Thomas endeavoured to spend more time in private meditation before the Blessed Sacrament. As a lay member of the Eucharist League, whenever possible he spent the prescribed monthly hour of adoration at his favourite shrine of Our Lady, the Church of Our Lady of Victories.* This was the church visited by Thérèse Martin on the 4th November, 1887, and of which she spoke in her autobiography, *L'Histoire d'une Ame*, when referring to her visit to Paris, at the commencement of her pilgrimage to Rome, with the Bayeux diocesan pilgrimage. Sister Thérèse wrote of this visit:

" Papa took us to see all its wonders (i.e. of Paris), but for me the sole attraction was the Church of Our Lady of Victories. I can never tell you what I felt at her shrine; the graces she granted me there were like those of my First Communion Day, and I was filled with happiness and peace. In this holy spot the Blessed Virgin, my Mother, told me plainly that it was really she who smiled on me and cured me."

While Thomas was a student in Paris, it is hardly likely that he would have had any inkling of Sister Thérèse's great veneration for the shrine of " Our Lady of Victories," since it was not until some time after her death, which took place on the 30th September, 1897, that her autobiography was made public. Thomas Taylor was ordained priest in June 1897 and was already serving as curate at St. Patrick's, Dumbarton, at the time of Thérèse's death. His great love for this church of Our Lady may well be because it was here that the saintly Abbé Desgenettes was inspired by Our Lady, in 1836, to establish the Confraternity of the Immaculate Heart of Mary for the conversion of sinners. Monsignor Taylor's perennial devotion to the Immaculate Heart of Mary for this cause, must have stemmed from the devotion fostered at the shrine during his College days.

---

* In *Saint Thérèse of Lisieux*, by Very Rev. Canon T. N. Taylor, we learn that a Novena of Masses was offered at this shrine for Thérèse's recovery from a serious malady in the spring of 1883. During the Novena, when the pain the sick child was experiencing became unbearable, she turned towards the statue of our Heavenly Mother and begged her to have pity on her. The statue (now known as " Our Lady of the Smile ") seemed to " become animated and radiantly beautiful " and in Thérèse's words, " What penetrated to the very depths of my soul was her gracious smile." On that instant, Marie (later Sister Mary of the Sacred Heart) who was a silent witness of the scene, realised that Thérèse was cured. Thérèse later explained to Marie what had actually happened.

Excluding the consideration of the spiritual and devotional side of his training, the seminarian's immediate concern before his anticipated ordination in June 1896 was his final examination. Information taken from the Register of Marks for the year 1893 to June 1896 showed that Thomas scored an overall average of 72.8 per cent in the seminary of Theology. The archivist of St. Sulpice, who so kindly sent the information in his letter on 26th January, 1966, pointed out that though the results did not indicate that Thomas was a " student of exceptional capacity," nevertheless, " it is true that the results are good."

We may consider further that in June 1896, Thomas was only twenty-two and a half years of age and had then completed his course of studies at a standard above that of the average student; and even after a year's postponement he, nevertheless, in 1897 still required exemption on the grounds of age before he was admitted to ordination to the priesthood.

Whether final examinations caused undue worry or not to the students, we find that on a " rest day " on the 20th February, Thomas joined a number of his English-speaking friends at the home of Miss Shortt,* in Paris, where they " enjoyed themselves with music and singing "; as usual, Thomas was the pianist at the self-styled " Glee Club."

This soirée was prefixed, on Thomas's part, by an hour spent in Our Lady of Victories.

A few weeks later, on 2nd March, we learn that Thomas was " in a state of perplexity "; he had been told that his superiors had been considering the advisability of recommending him for further study in Rome. Such a transfer would cause the day for which he had been yearning to be postponed. During the trying interval of indecision, Thomas, with his fellow students, continued with his preparations for ordination : " An altar had been installed in (his) room " and he had said his " first Mass of preparation."

On Thursday, 12th March, he noted in his diary, " Directed by Father Many (Director of Studies) to write to the Bishop for permission to go to Rome." On the feast of the Annunciation Bishop Maguire replied granting permission for another year at St. Sulpice, but without reference to Rome. A fortnight later, on the 8th April, to his great surprise the " perplexed " young man " received (his) call to the priesthood." Fully convinced that he was to receive holy orders at Trinity, he set his heart and mind

---

* Miss Shortt was a convert from the Anglican Church. Her chief concern was to make her home a place of relaxation for the English-speaking students at St. Sulpice, a kindness which was deeply appreciated by the students and College authorities.

to the serious preparation ahead of him. But this was not to be.
In spite of representations from the Sulpician authorities that
Thomas should be ordained and then continue his studies in
Rome, the Glasgow Archdiocesan authorities remained adamant;
Bishop Maguire wrote, " The Archbishop (Eyre) does not wish
to send for dispensation to Rome." Also his wishes were that
Thomas should not go to Rome for advanced studies, on the
grounds of the risk to health, but that he should remain in Paris
for a further study.

One can understand the natural reluctance of the Glasgow
authorities to seek a dispensation for the ordination of one so
young, but it is not clear why permission to study in Rome should
be refused on the grounds of health, for Thomas was able to
record in his diary in the following year that it was his " first visit
to a doctor " since his illness in St. Mary's College, Blairs.

The entire blame for the disappointment caused to Thomas
and to his family does not rest entirely on the Scottish authorities.
No doubt the young man was eager to reach his lofty aim, but it
is difficult to see why he should have been allowed to make his
final preparations without being decisively warned about the
difficulties over his youth. He himself sums up his disappointment
briefly and with resignation on the 1st May, 1896: " Mary, I had
hoped to be ordained this month. Jesus has willed it otherwise.
Non sum dignus! Fiat!"

The decision once made, Thomas was not one to worry himself with useless regrets. His close friends, Fathers Harig, Flynn,
Slattery, and others of his course, were ordained priests as had
been anticipated, at Trinity. After rejoicing with his friends, he
had now the unusual experience of having free time on his hands.

The summer vacation was imminent and since his hopes for
ordination had been upset, he along with Mr. MacKay, proceeded
with arrangements for the earlier mentioned cycling holiday in
Switzerland and Bavaria, before returning to Scotland to visit his
parents.

Pending the official break-up of College, Thomas relaxed and
for the first time in his diary he refers to the activity of a ball
game in College. Not for him any form of football, but a " first
game of basket-ball," a game which was, in those days, played
with a bat and ball. He enjoyed the game but did not find it as
interesting as handball.

During the last weeks of term he still rose early in the morning
to take advantage of the opportunity of serving Masses for his
newly ordained friends. A day on which he must have had a
surfeit of religious ceremonies was Wednesday, 24th June, 1896.

His timetable on that day bears some resemblance to the crowded hours endured by the pilgrims coming from south of the border to the Grotto, prior to the outbreak of World War II. Thomas's diary reads:

"Rose at 4 a.m. Mass at 4.30, preceded by Communion. Walked to the "Gard de L'Est" immediately: soon *en route* for Reims Cathedral for Mass: plain chant exquisite."

This Mass seems to have been followed by prolonged ceremonies, attended by two cardinals, an archbishop and 2,000 pilgrims, all of whom took part in a procession of relics and solemn Benediction of the Blessed Sacrament. The sermon which followed was "too long"; this was an unexpected complaint from Thomas, for in later years he was known to "sit in" continually during long services and sermons—much to the discomfiture of some of the preachers, who preferred to preach to the laity only.

The aftermath of the services in the streets of Rheims, late that evening, must have reminded Thomas of the tales told of his grandfather's experiences in 19th century Greenock. There were "one or two quarrels in the street, where the banner-man was insulted and a local seminarist was arrested." After supper, Thomas and a few Sulpicians who had joined him for the procession, left by train for Paris, and had "a noisy homecoming in a heavy thunderstorm." If true to the form which he showed in later years, no doubt his friends would find him serving their Masses as usual in the morning.

One last event of importance remains to be mentioned for this year. On the 1st July, 1896, a few days before he set out for the planned cycling holiday, Thomas was received by Father Vigouril, " at Issy, into the Third Order of St. Francis, under the name of Frère Marie Antoine." Other associations and societies were to claim him as a member, often for lengthy periods, but he was to remain a loyal member of the Franciscan Tertiary Congregation for the remainder of his life.

A blank in his diary, between July and November 1896, leaves us with lack of information except for that provided on a number of postcards sent home; these were preserved by his father during his lifetime, after which an old friend of the family retrieved them from destruction in the incinerator. In remarkable fashion, and by devious means, the correspondence came into the possession of the present writer, with the gracious consent of the good Greenock lady who had preserved them from destruction. The text on one of these postcards, referring to MacKay's bicycle accident, has been reproduced earlier in this book.

In early November, 1896, Thomas and another student were studying for the Baccalaureate which would enable them to study at the Catholic Institute of Paris. The three-hour written and oral examination did not prove an obstacle to Thomas, although his friend failed to pass; a few days later, he commenced what he described as " splendid classes " at the Institute.

No longer kept fully occupied by the normal routine of classes at the Institute, Thomas found that he could now devote more leisure time than in previous years to the dissertation and argumentation circles; the members of these circles were so noted for their profundity of thought and fecundity of expression, that in the ensuing years the students of the 1896-97 course were known as the " Intellectuals." *Our Lady's Circle* and the *Association of English Students* provided the platform from which the students from Britain and the U.S.A. expressed their views. Thomas, as co-founder of the first, devoted to it much attention and care; he was elected president of the latter in 1896.

In mid-November, the question of his ordination again came up for discussion. Father Many advised Thomas not to seek ordination at Christmas as he might be recalled to Scotland immediately afterwards, without having finished his course of lectures at the Institute. An appeal for advice to the Bishop of Glasgow brought the reply that Thomas had the choice of two things : either accept ordination at Christmas and return to Scotland and the ministry, or continue classes at the Institute and prepare for ordination at Trinity 1897. The personal wish of the young ordinand was to receive holy orders as soon as possible, but acting on "the unanimous advice of superiors" at St. Sulpice, eventually, on the 27th November, he decided to stay until Trinity.

On two occasions he had been within a few weeks of ordination and twice the reception of the Sacrament was postponed; the first time on the instigation of Archbishop Eyre in Glasgow, and the second time on the advice of his College superiors. Throughout all these deliberations, he had not as yet reached his twenty-third birthday, and time was on his side.

This, however, did not lessen the distress and concern of his parents and his friends at home. Telegrams and postcards sped like gunfire across the Channel, enquiring whether the ordination was to be or not to be on the 19th December of that year. It was with some regret that Thomas eventually wrote to his parents giving them the full details. Once more it was Thomas's lot to stand aside and watch twenty of his classmates leave him behind.

Among them was his fellow patriot and cycling friend, Father MacKay.

With natural hesitancy and much humility, he notes on 1st January, 1897: " Probably the year of my ordination! Fiat Voluntas Tua! Faites de moi un prêtre saint, humble, chaste, zélé."* The following day he visited Our Lady of Victories for one hour to entrust his future to Our Lady's care, after which he joined some friends for " dinner, toasts, music, tea, and songs, at Miss Shortts."

About this time, too, he contributed his first article, " Les Anglais at St. Sulpice," to the *Bulletins of the Anciens Elèves de St. Sulpice*. A further literary effort on his part was to collaborate with a Sulpician Father in the translation of the Gospel of St. Luke, for publication in English.

In preparation for his long delayed ordination, in the spring, Thomas commenced a series of Novenas, the first in honour of the Blessed Sacrament, and this was followed in turn by others in honour of Our Lady, St. Joseph, the Holy Souls, and his own patron, Saint Thomas. Not content with this, he resumed the practice of reciting the Rosary privately, in addition to the public Rosary in the College chapel, at which most students assisted. This time Thomas left nothing to chance; the whole armoury of Heaven was engaged on his side.

The classes at the Institute can scarcely be blamed for the indisposition from which Thomas suffered in April and early May, for he did not consider his studies as over-taxing his strength. Rather, it must have been that the vexing postponements of his ordination on the two earlier occasions had brought on a spell of debility, marked by a recurrence of abscesses on his cheek. His dejection at being confined to his room for a week was dissipated by the long-sought for news that his day of ordination was the 12th June. The good news cheered him and helped him towards recovery, although the septic condition was to return periodically (for the next few years), until eventually he had to undergo surgical treatment in hospital.

In letters sent to his brothers, Alick and James Bede, in May, he expressed " sentiments of fear at the terrible onus of the ministry." His doubts were, not that he had chosen the wrong vocation, but that he himself might not be sufficiently worthy. His prayer on the 1st June was:

" O Heart of Jesus, give me a heart meek and humble like Thine, that I may be an ' alter Christus ' whose life is hidden in

---

* ". . . Thy Will be done! Make me a holy priest, humble, chaste and zealous."

Thee. Mary, Joseph, make me an apostle of the Blessed Sacrament."

A great disappointment was the news that none of the Taylor family could be present at the ordination ceremony. The expenses involved in two sons attending seminaries, and another at high school, had proved a heavy load on domestic economy; and, as Mr. Taylor told Thomas, although he and Mrs. Taylor might have been able to manage the travel expenses, they would have been unable to pay for the other joyous festivities which would crop up after the ceremony; Thomas concealed his keen disappointment from his parents, but his brother Alick sensing it, tried to console him with the remark that this was the price of " being as poor as mice."

Alick himself was to suffer in the same way at his ordination in Rome, although he had the joy of meeting his two brothers, Father Thomas and James Bede, just prior to receiving holy orders, while they were there during the Scottish pilgrimage in honour of the jubilee of the aged pontiff Leo XIII. It must have been during this meeting that plans were finalised by the three brothers concerning the entry of the youngest, James Bede, to the Vincentian Order at Blackrock, in Dublin.

If circumstances prevented members of the Taylor family from being present at St. Sulpice on the 12th June, it did not prevent Heaven from being bombarded by the constant prayers of the family and their friends from all over Scotland. In the treasure box of souvenirs of the ceremony, preserved by Monsignor Taylor, were many letters from clerical friends who remembered him during the Sacrifice of the Mass, on that day. Similarly, the Religious of the many convents in the Greenock and Glasgow area, with which the family had been associated over the years, joined in a union of prayer beseeching God's blessing on the future priest.

Among the numerous gifts he received—sets of vestments, stoles, stocks, a breviary and a missal from three of the professors at St. Sulpice, and various gifts of money—the " chief souvenir " was his chalice. At the cost of £10, it may not have been the most beautiful or in material value the most expensive gift, but the money contributed came mostly from the meagre savings of his own family: £5 from his parents; £1 from his brother Harry; £2 he had assiduously saved up himself, and the remaining £2 from his former classmate, Father Harig.

The Pentecostal retreat for the priesthood began amid a whirlpool of excited preparation, on Saturday, 5th June. Naively he propounds a method of overcoming distractions and excitement during prayer: " I spent a delightful hour before the Blessed Sacrament ' speaking Latin ' (which is) an excellent method of avoiding distractions."

The wheels of time grind slowly for those who wait, but at last Saturday, 12th June, 1896—the solemn day of ordination—arrived. After the ceremonies were over and the newly ordained Father Taylor had sent off a telegram conferring his blessing on his family, he wrote, among other things, in his diary:

" Hundreds were praying for me. Grant, O God, that their intercession obtain for me my conversion into Thee, ' Alter Christus,' not for the few days after my ordination, but till the blessed day when our union will be consummated in heaven."

On Sunday, 13th June, he celebrated his first Mass at 8.30, at Issy, assisted by his class friends, Father Harig, deacon, and Father MacKay, Subdeacon, both of whom with another friend, Father Payne, had crossed over from Britain for the ceremony. After the long ceremonies of the previous day, the friends were again up early on Sunday morning, for Father Taylor insisted on serving Father MacKay's Mass at 6 a.m. Present among special friends at the breakfast after Mass was Miss Shortt, who had showered so much kindness on Thomas and his Sulpician friends over the years. In the absence of his own family, Miss Shortt was Father Taylor's closest lay friend in Paris; in token of this, on Monday, 14th June, as he tells us in his diary, he called by cab for Miss Shortt and together they drove to his favourite church, Our Lady of Victories where, assisted by Fathers Payne and Cleary, Father Taylor celebrated his second Mass and where Miss Shortt was honoured by being the first to receive Holy Communion from the young priest's hands. Having remained for his friends' Masses at 11 a.m., Father Taylor " said good-bye to the sweet shrine."

After celebrating his third Mass, this Mass for the community of St. Sulpice, Father Taylor took a final farewell of his friends and advisers on the College Staff. Father Basil's admonition, " Love Mary and the Blessed Sacrament," impressed him greatly, for it merited a heavy double underlining in his diary. His priestly life shows how much he endeavoured to obey this injunction during the subsequent sixty-five years.

When writing to his father before his ordination, Father Taylor had expressed the wish to celebrate his first Mass at home, at St. Laurence's Church on the feast of Corpus Christi (17 June).

The wish was easier in the request than in the granting, and Mr. Taylor, reluctantly, was compelled to inform his son that he was unable to obtain this favour from Rev. Doctor Fox, the incumbent then at St. Laurence's Church. Hence the young priest was compelled to delay his return home until Sunday, 20th June, when his first Mass in his home parish was due to take place. The intervening days were spent in London, where he had been invited to break his journey to visit several friends of long standing, who were anxious to meet him and receive his blessing.

While in the metropolis, Father Taylor was presented to His Lordship Monsignor Bourne, the recently appointed Bishop of Southwark. After his consecration in April, Monsignor Bourne had travelled to his old seminary at St. Sulpice to seek recruits among the ordinands for the Philosophy department of his own seminary at Wonersh. On the occasion of this visit, Thomas, confined to his room through illness, did not meet the Bishop; but now, in London, Monsignor Bourne asked Father Taylor if he would be willing to join his staff. Father Taylor's reply, no doubt with tongue in cheek, was " I'll go, if you can get me." A few months later, Bishop Bourne did apply to Archbishop Eyre for Father Taylor's release, but as the latter had anticipated, permission was refused by the Glasgow Archdiocesan authorities. But this refusal did not interfere with the friendship between prelate and priest, a friendship which grew stronger over the years and which was marked especially by Cardinal Bourne's visit to Carfin in July 1924.

After eight years of seminary life—in Scotland and in France —Father Thomas, now free from the cares of study, was able to relax in his own home, in the company of his overjoyed parents and his three brothers. Only on rare occasions during these years had it been possible for all the boys to be at home together; now conscious of the honour conferred on the family in having a priest among them, all were content to spend the few days quietly in his company before he commenced his first curacy at St. Patrick's Church, Dumbarton, as " supply for Father Linster," then absent from his parish.

CHAPTER VI

CURATE AND PROFESSOR

Dumbarton, the modern town built near the fortress rock of that name, marks the southern exit of one of the ancient passes along the River Leven to Loch Lomond and the North. Across the winding river Clyde from Dumbarton Rock and some miles west, at the Tail of the Bank, rises the port of Greenock. From his home in Greenock to his new parish in Dumbarton was little more than a thirty-five minute sail by steam-boat for Father Taylor when he left to take up his new appointment on 2nd July, 1897.

Like his native town of Greenock, Dumbarton was a town with a well established Catholic tradition, and as the name of the patron saint suggests, with a strong mixture of emigrant Irish. St. Patrick's parish, Dumbarton, set up in 1830, straggled far beyond the limits of the present town, taking in several small hamlets on the banks of the Clyde.

There is no sound reason for believing that, over seventy years ago, work in an active parish, as St. Patrick's must have been then—all the more so since one of the two priests serving there was absent on leave—was less strenuous than in any parish of relative population today. Whether this assumption be true or not, immediately after lunch on the day of his arrival the new curate was bustled, without stay or ceremony, into the community life of St. Patrick's. He was kept " very busy with societies," he writes, and he gave the parochial Friday evening Benediction, after which he assisted with Confessions. The fact that he was " very nervous " did not prevent him from speaking to the penitents on the " Precious Blood, the Agony and the Pillar and Cross." The timetable for Sunday strikes strangely on modern ears: " Said 10.30 and 11.30 Masses. Heard Confessions morning and evening. Gave Benediction at seven o'clock and took Drama Class afterwards." One wonders about Confessions on a Sunday evening, for one presumes that the usual practice for the majority in these days was to go to Confession either on Friday or Saturday prior to receiving Communion on Sunday morning. Could it be that there were a number of the faithful who wished to receive daily Communion, even before the practice became common generally? As with his " first " confessions, the administration of other sacraments caused the young curate some trepidation: two children, by name Jane McFall and Catherine Macauley (or McIvor), received the sacrament of Baptism and Mrs. McLafferty from the village of Milton was the first to receive the last Sacraments from his hands. Three days of preparation went into his first sermon, on the Holy Eucharist, but the candid diary tells us that Mr. Grant (believed to be a young seminarian friend), criticised the sermon as " too flowery; apt to be monotonous in delivery; too quick sometimes." The diary does not record that anything favourable was said by the candid friend. Either one or the other is true: Father Taylor's humility was great or his sermon was very poor.

Other " firsts " he mentions were his first convert for instruction in the Catholic faith and his first official visitation in the parish. Of the former it can be truly said that this work became a very important part of his priestly apostolate. Before he was many weeks in St. Patrick's, Dumbarton, the " first " convert became two per week, and in his second year there he notes " Converts all week." Whichever alchemy had been infused into Father Taylor's soul by the Holy Spirit, and which had endowed him with the power of attracting to himself persons of divers religions or of none, it is clear that he had an instinctive power of discerning when a soul was troubled or in doubt. Letters exist which indicate that he conducted an extensive correspondence with persons dissatisfied with their particular way of life. On occasion he referred some of these to other priests who might understand more fully the soul in doubt.

One case in point was that of the young Protestant lady of high academic attainment, who was sent by Father Taylor to his friend, Father H. G. Graham (later Bishop), then serving at Our Lady of Good Aid, Motherwell. Doctor Graham, himself a convert from Presbyterianism, was able to put his finger on the lady's difficulties and thereafter Father Taylor proceeded with the instruction. The result of this distinctive branch of his sacerdotal apostolate, commenced shortly after ordination, increased and fructified over the years. Only the wisdom of Eternal Providence may gauge the result of Father Taylor's work in the souls of his legion of " spiritual children."

It is the lot of most junior curates to serve their apprenticeship in the time-consuming task of visitation, around the most distant parts of the parish, this distribution being based, it seems, on a scale-weighted justice which favours the seniors on the score of age and previous experience. Father Taylor was no exception to the general rule. Towards the end of his second week in the parish, gaily, the slightly built priest, mounted on the bicycle which was now indispensable to his duties, set out on his rounds. Soon, his rosy illusions were shattered and he was compelled to admit that although he was " welcomed by the people," he found that " only a minority attended Church or made their Easter duties "; for some it was a case of the farther away from the Church, the farther away from God. For the first time in his life he came face to face with harrowing and " pitiful cases reduced to misery by drink and worse." As drink was the curse of the times, Father Taylor's experience was no different from that of doctors, priests and ministers throughout the industrial belt of Scotland. Alcohol was the panacea, the elixir of life, which temporarily alleviated the misery of the downtrodden; but, once caught in its grip, it was difficult for the victim to struggle free.

One of several cases the sympathetic young priest noted was that of a " poor woman suffering from *delirium tremens* "; this lady suffered also from the added indignity of a black eye. It seems that while in a slightly convivial state she had felt a maudlin sympathy for her self-righteous husband, who had " taken the pledge after a bout of drinking the previous weekend." Pushing her sympathy too far, she offered him a glass of beer; the thankless reward was that " she got the glass and its contents " thrown at her face. The ensuing fight was fast and furious, and as often happens, the priest, in this case Father Taylor, was sent for to arbitrate in the dispute. How Solomon judged the case is not stated.

From spasmodic entries in the diary, spread over a number of months, emerges the story of a man, who for the sake of anonymity we will refer to as Mr. X; Father Taylor, preserving charity, uses an initial also. This man, although an inveterate drunkard, seems to have gained the priest's affection. Time and again Mr. X was visited at his home by Father Taylor, and it was with some satisfaction that the latter noted that " X was sober again." This was all the more gratifying since it was also noted earlier that for some reason not stated " X hit the Bishop during a bout," while His Lordship was visiting the parish church.

For this heinous crime, committed against episcopal dignity, Father Taylor gave his erstwhile friend " a severe raking up." As X does not seem to have retaliated against Father Taylor's " raking up," we can only assume that he was more fortunate on that occasion than he was many years later when he reprimanded a noisy " drunk " for his profanity. Possibly for the first and only time in his life, he was manhandled for doing his duty. But in youth or old age, Father Taylor never shirked his responsibilities.

His lack of stature was not at any time symbolic of intellectual timidity or physical cowardice; on the contrary, he showed the courage of his convictions in situations which might have daunted a more stalwart man.

The priest on ministry in a busy parish is more—much more—than the celebrant at the Sacrifice of the Mass and the administrator of the Sacraments; he takes on, when the need arises, the duties of parent, teacher, physician, philosopher and friend. Over and above these manifold duties, the priest of past generations was the organiser and leader in the Catholic community and in this capacity he was often director of vocations, spiritual and lay. In all these activities Father Taylor was quickly immersed. The innocence of young children attracted him then and later, and he took immense joy in visiting the schools. His initial venture in drama production, however, convinced his parish priest that the young priest would be more successful as choirmaster, a change with which Father Taylor agreed.

A reminder of Father Taylor's work as chaplain to the Children of Mary is found in a letter sent from Africa by a nun, who for twenty years treasured the rosary given to her by Father Taylor while she was a member of the society. Men's societies too, in particular the Young Men's Society, inaugurated in St. Patrick's, Dumbarton, in January 1898, claimed much of Father Taylor's time and attention. It was with some pride that he noted that about 150 members were initiated at the imposing opening ceremony on Sunday, 16th January, 1898. The older members of the congregation were not to be outdone by the enthusiasm of the young men, for on the same day at 2.30 the Sacred Heart Society held its first meeting.

A quarter of a century later, as pastor in St. Francis Xavier's at Carfin, Father Taylor introduced the C.Y.M.S. to his own parish. Now a busy man, heavily preoccupied with the cares of the Grotto of Our Lady of Lourdes, he handed over the care of the Young Men's Society to his very competent assistant curate, Rev. John J. Murphy, under whose aegis these young men performed wonders in the running of the parish and the Grotto.

The silver jubilee of the Franciscan Convent in January 1898 brought about a reunion of many of the former pupils of the convent, Father Denis McBrearty, predecessor of Father Taylor at Carfin, being one of these. Always a faithful friend to the good Franciscan sisters, Father Taylor undertook all the arrangements for the ceremonies and celebrated the Jubilee Mass on the feast of the Epiphany.

These additional activities did not prevent the active priest from being persuaded on the following week to enter a chess tournament at which he gained for first prize a handsome set of valuable books. Towards the end of the month, he travelled north, to Kingussie, on retreat, in the company of Fathers Lynch and Ritchie. Father Lynch, as we shall see later, is important not only as a friend of Father Taylor, but because he was to be the instrument by which the name of Sister Thérèse of the Child Jesus was brought to Father Taylor's notice in the first instance.

At Aberdeen they interrupted their journey to attend the consecration of Bishop Chisholm. Sulpician priests were well represented at the celebrations, and the close college friends, Fathers MacKay, Payne and Taylor enjoyed a happy reunion.

A return to Dumbarton brought no respite to Father Taylor's activities. Unheeding the warning of a week's illness in the autumn of the preceding year, he persisted in doing more than was required of him. James Bede, his younger brother, reported to Mr. Taylor after a visit to St. Patrick's, that " T.N.T. was not at all well : in fact he was laying himself up with overwork."

In May, Father Taylor arrived home on sick leave and was compelled to go off to Ballater for three weeks' convalescence. His health restored, he returned to his parish, but the recurring septic condition in his cheek continued to undermine his health and in September 1899, he found it necessary to consult Professor McEwan of St. Elizabeth's Nursing Home, Glasgow. The latter advised surgical treatment as an in-patient. Seemingly in good health after his operation, on the 18th November Father Taylor was given permission to return to duty in the parish. However, in May of the following year, he was back in the nursing home once more, but thereafter for the rest of his life he does not seem to have been troubled again by a similar complaint.

The dying months of the nineteenth century slipped away with the threat and rumours of war rumbling in the background. These did not deter the arrangements for special celebrations for the end-of-the-century Hogmanay in Scotland. The Church made her own more Christian arrangements, and at the request of His Holiness Pope Leo XIII, a Midnight Mass was to be celebrated in churches, wherever possible, on the last night of the year, to seek God's blessing on the new century. It would seem that times were still troubled in certain parts of Scotland, for in some Catholic parishes, Greenock being one, it was deemed unsafe to have Catholics assist at Mass at the hour when the Scots revellers were celebrating their traditional Hogmanay, by " first footing " their neighbours' homes. By an ironical turn of fate, less than three months later, Queen Victoria granted permission to all soldiers in her service to wear the shamrock on St. Patrick's Day, this as a reward for bravery of Irish regiments in the Transvaal fighting.

The first year of the twentieth century saw several important changes in the Taylor family. James Bede, the youngest boy, had applied to Glasgow and Edinburgh Archdioceses for permission to enter their respective seminaries; he was refused by both. There was talk of him joining the Franciscan Order, but again he was refused. Dissatisfied with his post as pupil teacher in his father's school, he took his eldest brother's advice and studied for a bursary to allow him to train for a teacher's certificate at St. Mary's College, Hammersmith, his father's " Alma Mater." Less gifted intellectually than his elder brothers he, nevertheless, succeeded in achieving his aim, and gained a favourable place in the bursary list. He started his two years' course of study in the autumn of 1900. A month earlier, in August, Mr. and Mrs. Taylor moved their home from 15 Lyndoch Street, where they had been living for twenty years, to 35 Regent Street, which was to be their home for the remaining years of their lives. A few weeks after James Bede had set out for Hammersmith, Alexander was transferred to the senior seminary at the Scots College, Rome. In effect, Mr. and Mrs. Taylor were now left alone in their new home as Henry, the second eldest son, was working with an engineering firm in Kilmarnock and returned home only at weekends.

But more relevant to this story was the change which most directly affected Father Taylor himself. In early March 1900, he received word that on the 23rd of the month he was to be transferred to the teaching staff of St. Peter's College, Bearsden. It is not clear whether the appointment to the College came as a result of his indifferent health on mission work in the previous year, or whether it was because his academic record fitted him for the post of Professor of Sacred Scripture. At any rate Father Taylor's ecclesiastical superiors were soon to realise that the regular routine of the college curriculum and longer holidays did not *ipso facto* mean more leisure time for the young priest.

In his personal diary we find evidence that he tried to occupy himself profitably throughout every hour of day. On 1st January, 1898, he wrote:

" First New Year of my new life. Have tried to return to the old by rising at 6 a.m. and getting through meditation, Office and Rosary by 8.30 a.m. Mass."

Later, he wrote: "I must be careful not to dissipate my time when I retire to my own room."

In later years still, he was to tell his parishioners that "the devil finds work for idle hands." This, in Father Taylor's case, was not a meaningless admonition; his own life story shows that he practised what he preached, and it soon became increasingly clear to the staff of St. Peter's that Father Taylor's priestly apostolate was not to be bounded by the confining walls of the College. During the fifteen years he remained there, his interests increased in many directions; but foremost and constant was his love for Christ in the Eucharist. This devotion flowed over to God's Mother and to all God's saints. If at times it seemed to some that St. Thérèse of the Child Jesus—the Little Flower of Jesus, as she is popularly known—monopolised his heart even to the exclusion of our Blessed Mother, this was because he believed that "The Little Way of spiritual childhood," taught by St. Thérèse, was the shortest way to the throne of God. This devotion did not, and was not intended to obviate due honour and reverence to God's mother—Father Taylor's lifetime of rosaries makes this clear; he used St. Thérèse as the magnet which was to draw souls closer to God. Who among us would care to say that his fervour and zeal were misdirected?

CHAPTER VII

LOVE OF THE EUCHARIST

The major seminary of St. Peter's College, to which Father Taylor was appointed Professor of Sacred Scripture and Church History in the spring of 1900, was at that time situated at New Kilpatrick, to which place it had been transferred from its original foundation at Partickhill in 1892. Archbishop Charles Eyre, first Archbishop of the restored See of Glasgow, and founder of the college in 1874, had achieved success in welding the archdiocese into a united and loyal See, no longer disturbed by the domestic dissensions of the previous half-century. Six years earlier, in May 1894, while Thomas Taylor was a student at St. Sulpice, Bishop John A. Maguire was to relieve the ageing Archbishop of much of the heavy routine of his episcopate. But one interest remained close to the Archbishop's heart, even in the last difficult decade of his long life; this was his dream child, St. Peter's Seminary, founded twenty years earlier to satisfy the clamant need for a major seminary for senior students in the Western District of Scotland.

Nor did the Archbishop's magnanimity end with the building of the college, which was largely financed from his own personal resources: in 1892 on the occasion of the silver jubilee of his episcopate, the benign Archbishop transferred to the new college, for the purpose of providing bursaries to the seminarians, the handsome sum of £2,600, presented to him as a jubilee gift by the people of the Archdiocese. His foresight in providing a major seminary for the future priests of Scotland and his constant and fatherly interest in its progress, was to help realise his dream, that of seeing a steady stream of native priests ordained annually for home missions.

It was to the staff of this energetic young college that Father Taylor was appointed on the 24th March, 1900, in his twenty-seventh year. His slim build and boyish features made him look younger than many of the students who were to be his charge; but there the resemblance ended. From snippets of information gleaned from the few students (now ageing priests) who have survived him, it can be assumed that the young professor of Sacred Scripture was endowed with a spiritual maturity well above the average. Of his intellectual ability, his academic records and his writings over the years give ample testimony. The absence of evidence on his prowess as a teacher suggests that Professor Taylor's influence over his students gained strength from the example of his practice rather than from his teaching.

Two priests, both students under him at St. Peter's College and both now living in retirement outside Scotland, recall him with affection. One conjures up a picture of the young professor, as he addressed his students. " His air of sanctity," he writes, " was apparent to all." Also it was known to the seminarians that Professor Taylor " always seemed fully occupied and was known to work on, in his own room, until the early hours of the morning."

This was all the more remarkable as " none of the students had ever seen a fire burning in the Professor's room." The reminiscence bears the stamp of truth, for Monsignor Taylor's hardiness, even in his declining years, was remarkable. It was well known that he frowned on too many creature comforts in his own parochial house and that at times this was a bone of contention among his less ascetically attuned assistant curates.

A second priest writes of " his dear Professor and friend " and pays generous tribute " to the one who introduced *Sancta Teresia* to the English-speaking world." This good priest regretted that he was not well enough to write a fitting testimony on a worthy priest, who had been his friend since college days.

A third priest,* a student under Professor Taylor and for a number of years a fellow professor in the college, remained a staunch friend to Monsignor Taylor until the latter's death in 1963. Smilingly he recalled how the lightly-built young priest entered the lecture room " as quietly as a mouse, almost hidden behind the mound of books he invariably carried." Other memories revived were that of a young priest deeply engrossed in every aspect of the spiritual life of the seminary. In his capacity of college choir master, Father Taylor travelled south to the Isle of Wight to attend a course on liturgical music, the better to help raise the standard of singing in church. When questioned on this, the one who was supplying the information and who was himself a fair expert on liturgical plain chant, admitted generously that

---

* The lately deceased Monsignor A. Canon Hamilton, St. Mary's, Hamilton.

whatever expertise he could claim to have, he owed to the training of his college choirmaster.

From the same source we learn of Professor Taylor's unceasing and untiring zeal to inculcate in the hearts of the young men, who were to be future shepherds of the flock in the Archdiocese of Glasgow, a deep and abiding love of Our Lord in the Eucharist. This apostolate, prepared for during his own student years at St. Sulpice, was fostered during the fifteen years he spent at St. Peter's College and bore abundant fruit in the parish of St. Francis Xavier's at Carfin, where he was pastor for close on half-a-century.

The decree of Leo XIII, 1902, and more especially the " *Sacra Tridentina Synodus* " of Pius X, in 1905, marked a clear step forward in the history of the Blessed Sacrament. The teaching of the latter decree made it clear that " a right intention, excluding pride, routine and human respect, was the sole necessary condition, together with the state of grace for daily participation in the Eucharistic Banquet . . . What had hitherto been the daily food of the shepherds was henceforth to be the daily sustenance of their flocks, as far as circumstances might permit. In seminaries and in religious institutes, the practice was to be especially promoted."

These words, taken from an address given by Father Taylor to the dignitaries of the Church, assembled at Westminster for the nineteenth Eucharistic Congress in September 1908, expressed clearly the apostolate of the Holy Eucharist he preached and practised during sixty-six years of ministry in the Church. At the beginning of the twentieth century, when Father Taylor was appointed to St. Peter's Seminary, the fabric of Jansenism was still strong and the fallacies attending it could be found lurking insidiously in the teachings of some theologians. As a result, the faithful often refrained from Holy Communion, unless they had received the Sacrament of Penance almost on the day prior to the reception of the Eucharist; and indeed, according to the custom and habit of the time, even innocent children were considered unworthy to receive the Sacrament, except after Confession. It was in an attempt to cure this malaise in the Church that the papal decrees were promulgated; and it was in the spirit of love of our Lord in the Eucharist and as a loyal supporter of Pope Pius X, well named the " Pope of the Eucharist," that Father Taylor by word, pen and example, devoted his utmost energy to the propagation of the teachings of the Church. Three years before his ordination to the priesthood,

Thomas Taylor, then a seminarian at St. Sulpice, had been attracted by the work of the Congregation of the Most Holy Sacrament, an order of priests founded in 1856 by Blessed Julien Eymard. Père Eymard's main object in founding this religious order was to observe within the congregation perpetual adoration of the Blessed Sacrament. A natural development of this devotion was the limited extension of this practice among secular priests and laity. In 1894, after a visit to the College of St. Sulpice, by one of the Fathers of the Congregation, Thomas Taylor became a member of the Eucharistic League for Lay People, a membership which imposed on the participant the promise to observe each month one hour of adoration before the Tabernacle. This obligation was far from being irksome to the seminarian, for on several occasions in his writings he refers to the tranquillity and strength of soul acquired by those who seek the company of the forgotten Prisoner of the Tabernacle.

Shortly after his ordination in 1897, Father Taylor became a member of The Priest-Adorers, which had been canonically approved in 1887; in 1908 the name was changed to The Priests' Eucharistic League, by which name it is still known. Among several conditions of membership, the most binding was to make weekly, at least, one full and uninterrupted hour of adoration before the most Holy Sacrament of the altar.

Almost the first to take up the banner on behalf of the papal encyclicals on the Eucharist were the Fathers of the Blessed Sacrament, and in the vanguard of the adherents to their cause they found Father Taylor one of their most energetic supporters.

In 1903 he was appointed National Director for the League in Scotland, and later he held a similar position for The Priests' Communion League for the Promotion of Daily Communion, among the laity. Like the Priests' Eucharistic League, the Priests' Daily Communion League came into being under the aegis of the Fathers of the Blessed Sacrament, about seven months after Pope Pius X's decree. But, whereas the primary task of the Priest-Adorers was the weekly hour of Adoration, the paramount aim of the Communion League was to inculcate, in season and out of season, the teaching of the Decree, *Sacra Tridentina Synodus*, which advocated frequent and whenever possible daily Communion.

Thus Father Taylor, in the first decade of the century, and until the outbreak of the 1914-18 World War, found himself fully

committed in three directions to increasing among the faithful—
lay and religious—a deeper love of our Blessed Lord in the
Eucharist. As a priest-member of the Daily Communion League,
he directed his immediate attention to his students. Daily reception of Holy Communion in the early years of the present
century was the rare exception rather than the rule, even in
seminaries and convents. With patience and assiduous care, we
are told by a former student of St. Peter's College,* Professor
Taylor made arrangements which ensured that at least one from
among the more faithful of the seminarians would approach the
Communion rails each morning; thereby an example would be
set for those who were still hesitant about their worthiness to
receive the Sacrament daily, or even frequently, without a recent
Confession.

Simultaneously with his campaign to encourage more frequent
reception of the Holy Eucharist among the laity, Father Taylor,
in his capacity of National Director of the Priest-Adorers, conducted an extensive correspondence with the Director General
of the Association in Belgium, as well as with the few scattered
priest members for whom he was responsible in Scotland. The
inertia among some priests, isolated from their colleagues for
months on end, often gave cause for concern; these were the
priests whom Father Taylor wished to rouse from their lethargy
by making them interested in the Association of Priest-Adorers,
or in some other worthy clerical association, the combined
prayers of which would support them spiritually.

In a letter to Father Taylor, Father Reginald Vignoles of
Dunkeld diocese stated that his efforts to get other priests to
join the small band of Priest-Adorers had failed, but he " had
hopes of gaining one over." He added that during annual retreats
there were " signs of great fervour . . . but priests living alone in
country missions with little to do are apt to become lazy and will
not get up early in the mornings and hence the difficulty of
perseverance."

Father Vignoles' suggested remedy for this lack of perseverance would be membership of the Apostolic Union (of Priests),
whereby each would gain from the strength of all and as a result
more souls would be sanctified. Since Father Taylor was himself
a member of the Apostolic Union, he entirely agreed with the
suggestion made by the sole member of the Priest-Adorers from
Wigtownshire.

---

* The late Mgr. A. Canon Hamilton.

Another colleague, Canon Archibald Douglas of Annan, wrote as follows in November 1904:

> " Dear Father Taylor,
>
> I am very much obliged to you for making known to me The Association of Priest-Adorers, and for inviting me to become a member. It will be a great pleasure for me to do so. It is strange that I never heard of it before. I shall be able, I hope, to get others of the clergy who do not know of it to join also. I am sure it is of immense importance for us to encourage one another in making prayer, and prayer before the Blessed Sacrament takes a considerable place in our work for souls. I think sometimes we make too much of the visitation of our people, as if that was almost the only way of getting at our sinners . . .
>
> Believe me,
>
> Very truly yours, in Christ,
>
> Archibald Douglas."

Canon Douglas was to remain a faithful member of the Association for eighteen years—the year 1906-07 excepted when he was trying out a vocation in the Redemptorist Order. With great humility he related that in the eleventh month of his noviciate, his superiors requested him politely to " gang ava." His complete resignation and submission to the judgment of his superiors in the Redemptorist Order are shown in the final words he addressed to Father Taylor.

> " I have been refused: it is the will of God and I am content. I was not able in the noviciate to get a clear hour weekly for private prayer before the Blessed Sacrament, but if you will reinstate me I shall now be able to make my hour."

From a series of letters written by Canon Douglas to Father Taylor, one, amusing in its contents, relates the adventures of the former while on pilgrimage to the shrine of the Curé d'Ars, in 1905. The particular relevance of this letter to our topic is made clear by the fact that the saintly pastor of Ars was one of the earliest members of the Association of Priest-Adorers; and also that he had foretold that the hour of Adoration of the most Blessed Sacrament practised by priest members of the Association would do much to sanctify their lives.

When Canon Douglas visited Ars on the eve of the Saint's feast day, he found the small town packed to capacity with pilgrims, among whom were three cardinals, seventeen bishops and hundreds of priests. Having previously " booked " the first Mass for midnight on the beatified's feast day, with equanimity Canon Douglas assumed his place at 6 p.m. at the head of the long line of priests waiting to celebrate Mass at the altar where the Curé d'Ars had daily offered up the Holy Sacrifice. At 11.55 p.m., while vesting for Mass, the Scottish priest was more than shocked to learn that priest number two in the queue had already moved on to the altar and was about to commence Mass. Priest number three had moved up to prime place and he, in turn, was followed by number four and so on down the line, each unwilling to yield place to a "foreigner," with only a very limited knowledge of French. The impasse was overcome and the "auld alliance" between Scotland and France restored with the arrival of the Curé d'Ars himself—the incumbent of 1905—who settled matters satisfactorily by arranging that Canon Douglas celebrate Mass at 12.30 a.m. The priest who had dispossessed him from first place graciously served his Mass and Canon Douglas served Mass for priest number three. "About 2 a.m.," adds Canon Douglas, "I returned to such sleep as one could get on the ground outside."

Tribulations such as these in no way deterred Professor Taylor, for in the following year, on his way to the shrine of Our Lady at Lourdes, he himself visited Ars and celebrated Mass at the altar where the saintly John Vianney had offered up the Holy Sacrifice with such fervour. As with St. John Vianney, Monsignor Taylor's inordinate love of Jesus in the Eucharist was clearly apparent to all his parishioners, and indeed to all with whom he came in contact during his priestly life. The apostolate of the Eucharist, which was to be the keystone on which his sacerdotal ministry was based, was not the result of a sudden upsurging of grace; rather was it a carefully planned co-operation with the will of the Giver of all Grace, a subjection of self-will which allowed the mind to become attuned to the promptings of the Holy Spirit. Of this he writes in "Mes Pensées," while he was a student at St. Sulpice.

"There is no surer way of bringing peace to the soul than a good half-hour before the Blessed Sacrament; and let it be as close as possible, for the nearer we are to Him, the more it seems our fervour increases. We must not let ourselves be rebutted by continual coldness and distractions at the beginning. We must wait patiently, quietly gathered within ourselves, our eyes fixed firmly on the little golden door and presently He will come to us.

Beg of Mary, whom He can never refuse, of our patron saint and guardian angel, who rejoice so to see us there, docile at the feet of Jesus, to open our hearts wide that they may contain all the love, all the blessings, all the fervour and holy inspiration that the Master never fails to lavish on the friends who are fond of visiting Him.

Then let us turn our whole attention to Himself; lay all books aside and pray to Him with the utmost simplicity of heart. Are we ignorant what to say? Let us ask ourselves what we would speak of to the friend nearest and dearest to our heart, were he standing beside us. Tell Him that we love Him; all lies in that little word—LOVE: it presupposes that we believe in Him; it is the proof of the firmest of hopes, for despair never comes to those that love; and it intensifies our horror for sin and our heartfelt sorrow for having been so miserable and ungrateful as to wound Him by our coldness, our ingratitude, nay our downright insult and offence to His infinite Majesty and Purity.

Perhaps above all it presupposes thanksgiving; it is love which makes us grateful, for there cannot be true gratitude unless blended with love. Nor can true love be reproached with a want of respect or a neglect of the adoration and homage so intimately due to the Divinity. Ah no! Our God is a God of Love and true love is tempered by each and all of the other virtues, so that St. Augustine did not mistake himself in saying, ' Ama et fac quid vis.'

If some religions are based upon Faith, even to the extent of resting justification upon them, how much loftier is ours, where love is the means, the end, everything . . ."

Nor was the young student satisfied with expressing his love and adoration of God in private; he wished his life to be Christ-like and to extend his charity to embrace his brethren.

" A Christian, to be what the word implies, should model his life upon that of Christ; he should strive so that every thought, word, or action should, as it were, be so deeply tinged and coloured with his love for, and imitation of His divine Master, that he might be regarded as His follower by all. We are the good odour of Christ; we should be like that aroma which fills the hungry with a longing for the food of which it is a simple emanation and pale reflection, and which whets the appetite for that whence it is derived. Accordingly, it is not sufficient that we confine our efforts to our own salvation and stand meanwhile coldly by, while those whom perhaps, God has indirectly committed to our charge, whether that charge be borne out by influence or example, hurry on their way to a miserable eternity. Indeed, love of those with whom we come in contact is perhaps the highest mark of our fealty to Jesus. ' By this shall the world know that you are my disciples, that ye love one another.' "

It was in the spirit of the sentiments expressed above that Professor Taylor tried to fulfil his priestly duties. His axiom for life was clear-cut: Love God and your neighbour. As a priest he saw it clearly as his duty, not only to love God to the utmost of his being, but also to lead all men ever closer to Christ; and

D

to bring about this union with Christ more effectively he could think of no better way than by intense endeavour, to increase in the hearts of all—priest and layman alike—a deep and intimate love of our Lord in the Blessed Sacrament. This was the driving force which occupied his every moment; this is the reason why, in addition to his many other preoccupations, for the greater part of a quarter of a century, he remained the energetic National Director of the Priests' Eucharistic League (formerly named Priest-Adorers), and as long as it was necessary, of the societies associated with it—the Priests' Communion League and the Eucharistic League for Lay People—as well as being for a time a very active promoter of the Apostolic Union of Priests.

During the first quarter of the century Father Taylor's correspondence must have been prodigious. When one recalls that telephones were then a rare commodity, and that for the most part the railway, for longer journeys, and the open-decked tramcar for shorter hops, in or around the towns, were the only reliable means of transport for the majority, one can well imagine that the services of the Royal Mail were frequently called upon. One must not forget Father Taylor's sturdy upright bicycle which did him yeoman service in urgent journeys between the College and neighbouring parishes, as he speeded along, coat tails flying behind him, with his box of lantern slides perched on the carrier bracket of his lofty two-wheeled mount. But letters were his chief and speediest means of contact with distant correspondents.

Regrettably, not many letters written prior to 1915 survive, but from those which do it may be surmised that Father Taylor's correspondents hailed from divers places in Europe, and from much further afield. Several letters make specific mention of the Eucharistic apostolate on which Father Taylor had embarked; to these reference will be made later. The text of one, written by his brother, Rev. Alexander Taylor, D.D., in June 1904, shortly before his return home, is given in full, not only because of the reference to the work of the Priest-Adorers and the Apostolic Union, both of which Professor Taylor had recommended to his younger brother, but because it reflects the affection and esteem —albeit the spirit of independence of the younger—in which the eldest of the family was held by Alexander, and indeed by his parents and his brothers.

Collegio Scozzese,
Roma, June 12, 1904.

" My dearest Brother in Xt,

At last I am going to answer your kind and beautiful letters. How strange it is to be quite free again, to come up to my room, and not have to rush at my books; to be able to go out and breathe the sweet air; to think that I can write now to the many friends, who during the past six months, have been so patient, and so constant, and to think that all this is not for to-day, nor to-morrow, but as long as I shall stay in Rome. Fratello mio, one must have come through it to realize it. I have come out of a long, long tunnel and the sun is shining, and the birds are singing, and the grass is green, and the skies purest azure; and this is mine again to think about it all and to take it all into my poor cramped lungs, and my head that has been stuffed like—what? I don't know—anything that is very stuffed. But to begin by answering your questions . . . In a letter dated March 3rd you say to me some very beautiful and touching things, expressing the hope that you will find in this poor piece of incompetence the friend and co-labourer your heart craves for; and you hope that differences of temperament will not drive us, each to go his own way. Now, it cannot be my fraternal affection that you doubt; you had *better not* do that or I should be down on you severely. There are quite a *number* of reasons why I should love my brother Thomas and under God, he is himself the best reason why I should do so.

I think what you want to know is—am I going to put myself into your hands? You have thought out a lot of medicines for me, especially of the preservative kind. Ah! Caromio, Caromio! Am I going to be a T.T.?—Statim?*

Am I going to join the Prêtres-Adorateurs? Am I to give up smoking? (I suppose). Am I going to eschew to the best of my power musical evenings and all the other ' works and pomps '? etc., etc.?

Now, listen to me, my dearest brother. I know full well, that all this comes right out of your great loving heart, and you just want to do me good. The way that you find best for *you, because* it is best for *you,* your good heart prompts you to indicate to me. But Caromio, beneath it all, there is something that hurts me and it is this. If I do not follow that particular way, I cannot be your dear friend and your collaborateur. Is it so? Or, if I did not follow in one item all these propositions, but just brought you home myself, with much love and gratitude in my heart, and the firm determination to do my duty, by God's grace, grounding myself on *other* means out of the myriad at my disposal—tell me, dear brother, would I be just as welcome to you?

Is being ' addicted to the weed "—moderately—incompatible with sharing your fraternal confidence? And to feel my hand beside yours at the plough, must I be a T.T., etc.?

Understand, dear Brother, that I am not even hinting that I do not intend to adopt your counsels, one or all. I am coming to that presently. The question is, are they the conditions on which I can

* T.T.—Total Abstinence Pledge; Statim—immediately.

hope to be your *friend* and you *mine?*—For if you think you need me, I need you a great deal more. Leave me my freedom, dear brother, and my individuality and I shall probably follow you all the way, but the impulse must come from within. I want your good advice, your earnest exhortations. They have done me much good, more than I know myself, but don't be sad and don't be displeased if sometimes I am Alick, and you are Thomas. Is not that as it should be, brother mine? . . ."

The long disputation of the younger brother, having much right in its favour, demonstrates clearly the difference in temperament between the two priests; Father Thomas invariably accepted spiritual direction without question if he was convinced within himself it was good for his soul. How the practice could be put into operation was but a detail which somehow or other would be fitted into his overburdened plan of living. Dr. Alexander, on the other hand, showed that he reserved to himself the right to refuse excessive demands, even though they were in themselves essentially good. Perhaps more than anything else, the letter demonstrates the feelings of a younger brother who hangs on to the shreds of independence, convinced at the same time that the advice is as he generously admits, for his own good.

In the event, having made his protest, shortly after his appointment to a curacy at St. Anthony's, Govan, Father Alexander did become a member of the Priest-Adorers; by that time, too, he had eschewed the wine-drinking habits acquired by those who spend so long in Rome. Like his elder brother, he did not take the Total Abstinence Pledge for life, for as he put it, " I cannot help feeling ridiculous drinking, say, the Bishop's health, or the prosperity of my beloved Alma Mater, in cold water; but apart from functions like these, I shall in effect, be T.T." On one point Dr. Taylor did not yield: he did not at that time give up his moderate smoking of cigarettes. What he might have done had he been spared is not known, but tragically, within eleven months of the time this letter was written, the brilliant young priest had died, after less than a week's illness. It was a great joy to him, on his death bed, that a large group of children whom he had assiduously trained for the reception of their First Holy Communion in the few weeks before his death, had offered the Holy Sacrament up on his behalf.

Rev. Doctor Alexander's death was a sad blow to the Taylor family. At twenty-nine years of age, and in his second year of the priesthood, he had almost completed his first year of mission work when his premature death took place on 29th May, 1905, at St. Anthony's, Govan, where he had gained the affection and

respect of all, not only for his boyish high spirits, but for his
personal sanctity. It is a measure of the esteem in which the two
Taylor brothers—Dr. Alexander, assistant curate at St. Anthony's,
Govan, and Father James Bede, one time teacher in the parish—
were held, that a friend of both, many years later donated to the
third brother, Monsignor Taylor, a beautiful life-size statue of
St. Anthony for the Grotto shrine at Carfin.

Mr. Taylor records the death of his second youngest son in
his personal diary and described how his eldest son, Father Tom,
had been in constant attendance on his dying brother for the last
forty-eight hours of his life. The only indication of how Professor
Taylor accepted his brother's death appears in a few letters from
friends, remarking on his spirit of resignation to God's will.
Father Chandlery, S.J., his former tutor at St. Aloysius' College,
in a letter of sympathy commends him on his spirit of prayer
and resignation on the death of a brother who was so close to
him in years—only four years separated them—and closer still
in the bonds of fraternal affection. The fact is indisputable, that
the Taylors were a close-knit family, although neither the father
nor Thomas was demonstrative, especially in letters. But this did
not conceal their deeper feelings. With regard to letters which
must have been received by Professor Taylor at this time, with
rare exceptions all must have been destroyed. Even his diary
makes no reference to his brother's death; it would seem almost
as if for that period, except to a very few, he closed his mind to
the death of his brother, and concentrated even more on his time-
consuming occupations. For the next five or six years he was
embroiled in the task of compiling a handbook on the Shrine of
Our Lady at Lourdes—*Lourdes and its Miracles;* he was also
engrossed in propagating devotion to Sister Thérèse Martin, the
Little Flower of Jesus; but then, as always, what was foremost in
his life was his love of the Eucharist, and to this apostolate he
continued to dedicate his life. A series of carefully preserved
sermons, noted with the names of the churches in which they were
preached, show that he was invited frequently to preach at Holy
Hours and Forty Hours Adoration of the Blessed Sacrament,
throughout the Archdiocese of Glasgow. By 1907, his correspondence with members of the Eucharistic Association was on
the increase, and his communications with Father Couet, S.S.S.,
Director General of the Prêtres Adorateurs at Brussels, were
frequent. The latter seemed well pleased with the zeal of the
Scottish Director and in his letters gave his approval to Professor
Taylor's plans for increasing Eucharistic devotion.

During 1907 and 1908 hopes for a spiritual revival were running high among the Catholic minority of Protestant Britain; Archbishop Bourne, now at the see of Westminster, by an explicit act of Faith had agreed to play host to the dignitaries of the Catholic world, during the nineteenth Eucharistic Congress, due to take place at Westminster, in September 1908. Long before this date, permission had been sought, and granted by the City's Metropolitan Police for a solemn procession of the Blessed Sacrament, in which all the prelates attending the Congress would take part. To avoid undue disturbance, the route planned was to lead through the quieter streets around Westminster Cathedral. By the summer of 1908 the plans were finalised even to the extent of securing permission to bedeck the route of the procession with flowers, a ship-load of which had been generously promised by the Catholics of France.

Professor Taylor, at St. Peter's College, Bearsden, was fully conversant with the plans made, and was aware that two noted Jesuit Fathers—Rev. Hubert Lucas and Rev. F. de Zuleta—had been invited to address the Congress on the implications of the Papal Decrees on the history of the Eucharist; and that others even more distinguished had been invited to speak on many aspects of the subject. With a temerity entirely in keeping with his character, and with the conviction that his action was justified, he wrote to Rev. Father Couet, S.S.S., Director General of the Prêtres Adorateurs at Brussels, proposing that, in addition to the two papers to be read by the Jesuit Fathers on the promulgation of the decrees on the Eucharist, a further paper should be read by some well-known English Priest-Adorer, with a view to making the work of the association better known, and by so doing foster in the hearts of priests an increased love of the Blessed Sacrament. Father Couet gave his approval to the proposed plan, and instructed Father Taylor to make the necessary arrangements. In effect, this was a tall order, for decisions had already been made on the papers to be read at the various meetings and the timetable for the halls available had reached saturation point.

Nothing daunted, Professor Taylor wrote immediately to the English Director, Rev. M. P. Hanlon, Wonersh Seminary, Guildford; the latter's reply reveals his interest:

12th May, 1908.

" My Dear Father Taylor,

    I have had a letter from Monsignor Bute in reply to the question I put to him at your suggestion, and so far the result is very satisfactory . . .

He put your suggestion about a paper by one of the Priest-Adorers—probably Canon Sheehan—before the Archbishop (Bourne), who was greatly pleased at the idea, and he told the Monsignor to write to Father Cologan—Secretary for that department of the Congress—to say that it was His Grace's wish that a paper should be read . . .

(Sgd.) M. P. Hanlon."

His Grace's wish was honoured and an additional hall was hired to allow Canon Sheehan's paper—and that of a few others —to have a hearing.

But as those who plan well know, man proposes and God disposes. In an article entitled, "From Doneraile," written in retrospect twelve years after the Congress and published in *Adoremus*—the official organ of the Eucharistic League—Father Taylor explains how he first came to know Canon Sheehan and why the latter declined Archbishop Bourne's invitation to address the Congress in 1908. The following is an excerpt from Father Taylor's article:

". . . It is a matter of keen regret to the writer (i.e. Father Taylor) that a second and still more interesting communication from Doneraile was inadvertently destroyed. This letter was the reply to a request, supported by Archbishop Bourne, that Canon Sheehan would deliver the paper on the work of the Priest-Adorers, at the Westminster Eucharistic Congress. In 1908, however, his health was already impaired and he sought to be excused, urging that the correspondent (Fr. Taylor) should replace him. In the issue, Monsignor Parkinson of Oscott College read the paper which inaugurated the revival of the Eucharistic League in Great Britain, and the writer dealt with the Priests' Communion League, then newly founded by the Fathers of the Blessed Sacrament for the spread of the principles of the *Tridentina Synodus*."

In 1904, Professor Taylor had read Canon Sheehan's book, *My New Curate*, in which the Priests' Eucharistic League had been commended. It was in reply to Father Taylor's request that the Canon should use his pen further on behalf of the Association that the following letter was addressed to Father Taylor:

Doneraile, Co. Cork.
June 2nd, 1904.

" Reverend dear Father,

I am deeply gratified to learn by your letter of this morning that you are interested in the Sodality of Priest-Adorers.

I have had the privilege of being a member for nearly fifteen years, and some five or six years ago I wrote a letter, in the *Irish*

Ecclesiastical Record, strongly urging the young priests of Ireland to take up this most sacred and most salutary devotion, on the grounds that it was the peculiar province of the Priesthood as the " *Custodes Domini,*" and on account of the enormous advantages that should necessarily accrue.

The idea was taken up at one or two subsequent Retreats but not warmly . . . But my failure has made me reluctant to put my name forward again; and I am quite convinced that a vigorous effort to push on this great Sacramental Union would come now with more effects from yourself.

I fear one of the causes of the apathy of our priests was the want of a little magazine in the English language, such as *Emmanuel* (the American organ of the Society). The French *Annales* are not popular.

From reason and my own experience, ranging now over fifteen years, I am convinced that there never has emanated from the Church of God, a more important movement than this of binding priests together around the great ' Central Sun of Christianity.' Its appropriateness, its utility, nay the very *justice of things,* should recommend it almost as an essential part of priestly life . . .

You will have done a great work if you succeed in propagating it amongst your priesthood and students. I am hopeful, too, of my own country when the time and the apostole shall come . . .

In conclusion, let me hope that you will persevere boldly in this most important work which you have undertaken. I pray God's blessing upon it.

Yours in Christ,

(Sgd.) P. A. Sheehan."

In a few words and with abnegation typical of him, Father Taylor, in the article quoted above, glosses over the difficulties which confronted him in 1908. Father Couet, Director General of the Eucharistic Association, had given him *carte blanche* to make whatever arrangements were necessary in the difficult circumstances. Among the eighty or so Priest-Adorers in Britain all had the sanctity, but which among them had the personality and the experience to read such an important paper? The time factor, also—the Congress was less than ten weeks distant—was an added difficulty. In the natural order, it was a moment for despair; in the supernatural order, it was a call for rash action in answer to divine prompting. Father Taylor wrote immediately to Monsignor Parkinson, Secretary of the Priests' Apostolic Union, with whom he had corresponded over a number of years. The Monsignor felt that he could not refuse the opportunity to promote increased Adoration of the Blessed Sacrament, but how could he advocate with sincerity and conviction on behalf of an association about which he knew so little? On July 19th, came the answer for which Father Taylor had been waiting and for which he had prayed so anxiously. Monsignor Parkinson's letter was as follows:

" My Dear Father,

I thank you most sincerely and heartily for the grace you have sent me, and which this day I have seized hold of. To-day I made my hour (of Adoration) for the first time, and recited the prayer of dedication with all the fervour of which I am capable . . .

I shall be going to Belgium at the end of August, and I will then pay a visit to the head house (of the Blessed Sacrament Fathers) at Brussels.

Believe me, my dear Father,

Yours devotedly in J.C.,

Henry Parkinson."

So much successfully achieved—an eminent prelate who was now a Priest-Adorer had agreed to read the paper at the Congress —Professor Taylor, with grateful heart, set out for Lourdes to take part in the jubilee solemnities at Our Lady's Shrine, and to seek her intercession for the plans which were already being formulated at Brussels, for a supporting address on the less well-known work of the " Priests' Communion League for the Promotion of Daily Communion " among the laity. His love for the Mother of Christ was well known; annually at Lourdes the little priest, in the harness of the *brancardier,* might be seen helping the ailing pilgrims who had come to seek solace at their Mother's shrine; at home, his reputation had been enhanced by his popular lantern-lectures on Lourdes. In addition to these interests, Professor Taylor's name was constantly making news in connection with the growing cult of " The Little Flower," whose cause he had sponsored at the request of her three sisters in the Carmelite convent at Lisieux. Finally—and perhaps it is a fact less well known now—in the wide field of apologetics, he was ever ready to wield his pen to confute arguments raised against the Church in the press or in literary reviews.

These extraneous assets—if one may use this phrase to describe activities not immediately directed towards the increase of devotion to the Eucharist—were claimed by Monsignor Taylor to be an important part of his priestly apostolate. Assuredly the choice of Professor Taylor for such an important task at the Eucharistic Congress must admit the premise that it was already recognised that he was at one with the vanguard of those whose constant endeavour was to implement the papal decrees; and he himself, by his pledge to The Priests Daily Communion League, which was to be the subject of his address, was fully committed to do this by every means available to him. From what platform could the views of the Leaguers be disseminated to greater advantage, than from that of the Congress at Westminster, where a multitude of priests would assemble to honour their Eucharistic King? Indeed, the first resolution passed at the mass meeting in the Albert Hall, in the presence of the Papal Legate to the Congress, His Eminence Cardinal Vincent Vannutelli, Bishop of Palestrina, expressed in essence the aims of the Apostolate on which Professor Taylor had been engaged since his ordination:

"This Nineteenth International Eucharistic Congress pledge all who assist at it to promote, by every means in their power, solid and earnest devotion to the Blessed Sacrament of the altar according to the mind and teaching of the Holy Catholic Church."*

It is fitting to add that at Caxton Hall, at the conclusion of the reading of the two papers by Rt. Rev. Monsignor H. Parkinson, D.D., and Rev. Thos. Taylor, on behalf of the many dignitaries and others present, Cardinal Logue, Archbishop of Armagh, said they had been privileged to listen to two very eloquent discourses on the subject of the Blessed Eucharist. He did not intend to offer any criticism for none was possible. The only thing he could do was to praise. The subjects had been treated with great earnestness, piety and lucidity.

The Right Rev. T. L. Heylen, C.R.P., President of the Permanent Committee of Eucharistic Congresses, confirmed the words of Cardinal Logue and went on " to pay a warm tribute to the work being done by the Priests' Eucharistic League, and said that all bishops and priests should follow the example set by them." In this respect His Lordship associated himself with the two authors whose papers had just been read.†

While concentrating in great detail on the role Professor Taylor played in the Congress at Westminster, it must be remembered that he was one of a body of speakers who addressed the sectional gatherings in several halls, between the 9th and 13th September; but it is also worthy of note that of all the many excellent papers read, the three dozen or so published in full—the paper by Father Taylor being one of these—are claimed in the *Report of Nineteenth Eucharistic Congress* to form the " more valuable contribution."

---

* 19th *Eucharistic Congress, Westminster,* 1908, Sands and Company, 1909, p. 544.
† ibid., pp. 274-5.

Soon after the last of the distinguished visitors had left England, His Grace Archbishop Bourne, organiser and guiding light of the Eucharistic Congress, received from His Holiness Pope Pius X a gracious letter of congratulations, from which we quote the first paragraph.

"The Eucharistic Congress held in your city, wherein as we have learned, not England only, but nearly the whole world, has witnessed and done honour to your piety, has brought to Us the consolation for which We looked, in measure equal even to Our desire. Indeed, the published accounts and still more clearly the welcome report of Our venerable Brother, Cardinal Vannutelli, Our Legate, have so described the Congress, that, while the first of its kind in England in order of time, it must be accounted as without rival throughout the Universal Church for its concourse of illustrious men, the weight of its deliberations, its display of faith and devotion to the Holy Eucharist, and the splendour of its religious ceremonies . . ."*

A reading of official and press reports of the Congress gives the impression that the congratulations from His Holiness were well merited. But the external splendour of the final procession, wondrous as it was, fell short of what it might well have been, if the plans of the Congress officials in co-operation with the Metropolitan Police had been permitted to operate. The public press (*The Times, Daily Telegraph, Daily News, Pall Mall Gazette, The Church Times,* etc.) gave full coverage to the lamentable cancellation of the Blessed Sacrament procession at the eleventh hour, when already all the necessary arrangements had been made for carrying the Blessed Sacrament in solemn procession through the side streets to Westminster Cathedral. A bigoted minority invoked an obsolete penal law and put pressure on Prime Minister Asquith who, according to the official report of the Congress, sent a private intimation " deprecating the procession to be held on Sunday." His Grace of Westminster, in reply, sent the following telegram to Mr. Asquith, who was at that time on holiday at Slaine Castle, Aberdeenshire.

"Having considered your communication, I have decided to abandon the ceremonial, of which you question the legality, provided you authorise me to state publicly that I do so at your request. You must recognise the extreme urgency and delicacy of the position in which you have placed me."

On Saturday morning a further reply was received from the Prime Minister, and on Saturday evening at the Men's Meeting

---

* 19th *Eucharistic Congress,* Sands & Co., 1909, pp. 610-611.

in the crowded Albert Hall, the Archbishop made the painful announcement " that at the eleventh hour the Prime Minister had intervened and prohibited the carrying of the Blessed Sacrament in the procession arranged for the following day."*

Professor Taylor was one of the audience in the Albert Hall when Archbishop Bourne made his momentous announcement. Just over fifteen years later, Father Taylor was compelled to make a similar announcement to his parishioners, at the eleventh hour, when the police informed him that a Corpus Christi procession, which was planned to walk through the streets of the village of Carfin, where he was by that time parish priest, was illegal. The details of this so-called " banned procession " and Cardinal Bourne's visit to the parish a few weeks after the incident, will be related in a later chapter when the history of the Carfin Grotto of Our Lady of Lourdes is being told.

From 1908 onwards, slowly and almost imperceptibly, the papal decrees on the Eucharist were implemented; in convents, where hitherto the rule had permitted Sisters to communicate only at specified times throughout the year, the change had brought a wealth of joy to those who had long hungered for the Daily Bread which nourishes the soul; in seminaries, too, there was a noticeable increase in those who frequented the Communion rails regularly and, what was even more encouraging, daily. Leo XIII and Pius X, supported enthusiastically by the Fathers of the Blessed Sacrament, had initiated a new era in the history of the Eucharist.

Zealous and devoted priests like Professor Taylor, members of religious orders, as well as a strong nucleus of lay people—all alike fired with the love of God—were able to discern the full implications of the papal decrees; and driven on by " a charity which knows no bounds," they sought to bring their brethren within the ambit of the Eucharist.

In theory, the Eucharistic Associations were suspended during the years of the First World War, when periodic reports and the *libelli*—essential conditions of membership—could not be transmitted to the Continent. On the cessation of hostilities in 1918, Father Taylor wrote immediately to the Director General, then in Paris, enquiring what action was to be taken with regard to the associations. Very soon, National Directors were restored and the Eucharistic Associations were set up once more on an official basis.

---

* All quotations used in text are taken from *Nineteenth Eucharistic Congress*, Sands & Co., 1909.

The story of their development in the post-war years is told by Father Taylor in *Adoremus,* the official organ of the Eucharistic League, which was launched and edited by him during its teething stages. The following is a summary of notes provided by the editor in Vol. 1, No. 3, March 1920:

" At a meeting of the Directors of the Eucharistic League held at Liverpool, in February 1919, it was proposed to seek permission from Cardinal Bourne to approach the Hierarchy to have the League properly established under Provincial Directors. To this project the bishops gave their blessing. At the same meeting it was decided also to publish an English magazine for the members, under the editorship of Father Taylor, Director for Scotland."

In the same issue, Father Taylor announced that " he must relinquish the post he had temporarily undertaken, and that Rev. M. P. Hanlon, Redhills, succeeds to the task."

The editor, Father Taylor, adds a few words of explanation for his resignation.

" Briefly, his mission is a scattered country parish of some, 3,500 souls, with but two priests to attend their spiritual wants. Secondly, some ten years ago (about 1910), his superiors entrusted to him the collection of funds for the " Holy Childhood Society for the rescue of heathen children "—a society so well known abroad and so little known in these lands. Thanks entirely to Soeur Thérèse of Lisieux, the empty coffers began to fill; but whereas it was easy to handle £300 of even three years ago, it is more difficult to deal with its present income of nearly £2,000 per annum."*

" Conscience spoke and a choice had to be made. The Holy Childhood won . . .

The burden of *Adoremus,* if burden so glorious an apostolate can be called, is transferred to other and willing shoulders. One happy consequence will be its more punctual appearance."

In the 1920, June issue of *Adoremus,* the new editor, Father Hanlon paid the following tribute to Father Taylor, the retiring editor:

" One cannot let the occasion of this number pass without some tribute of praise and gratitude to Father Taylor. In the midst of a very busy life, he gladly undertook the work of securing contributions and of seeing through the press the first numbers of *Adoremus.* Had it not been for his generous sacrifice of time and labour, the proposed work might have been delayed for many months. The high optimism that now prevails as to the future is due in fullest measure to Father Taylor's solid work. We trust that the leisure that he will now enjoy may give him opportunity for many articles for *Adoremus.*"

---

* The subscription was then one halfpenny per week and subscriptions from groups or individuals were of small amounts. Hence detailed accounts were involved.

This editorial note was written in 1920, at a moment when Father Taylor was about to embark on a new project—the building of the shrine in honour of Our Lady of Lourdes, at Carfin. This project, combined with parish work, literary activities, missionary and vocational interests, was destined to deprive him, for many years, not only of all leisure time, but to encroach on his hours of rest to such an extent that it became a by-word in the village that the light never went off in Father Taylor's bedroom.

A few years later, further pressure of work compelled Father Taylor to relinquish the direction of the Eucharistic Leagues in Scotland at a time when it was recognised that they were firmly established; notes in Father Taylor's writing affirm that priest membership in England* had gone up from eighty-four (prior to 1908) to nearly 700 in the early 'twenties. It may be assumed that there was a relative increase in Scottish membership.

The transfer to mission work at St. Francis Xavier's parish, Carfin, in 1915, was to introduce a new aspect and direction to Father Taylor's apostolic work. Henceforth he would be the spiritual guardian of souls entrusted directly to his care. For close on half-a-century, it was obvious to those who were his charge, that under God, Jesus Christ in the Blessed Sacrament of the altar was the lodestar of his sacerdotal life. Pilgrims to Our Lady's Grotto learned of his love for God's Mother; others who read his books were aware of his unique devotion to the Little Flower; but those for whom he, as spiritual father, was directly responsible, revered and respected him, not only because he was the priest in charge of their parish, but because the profound and personal love he himself had for Our Lord Jesus Christ in the Holy Sacrifice of the Mass, emanated from him into their lives and brought them closer to Almighty God.

---

* It is open to question whether the word *England* is to be taken literally, or whether the numbers quoted are for *Britain*. As Father Taylor was National Director for Scotland, it is possible (though unlikely) that the Scottish numbers are included.

Chapter VIII

PARISH PRIEST

There was a vast difference between the conditions prevailing in Britain in the first year of the twentieth century, when Father Taylor had commenced duty as lecturer in Sacred Scripture and Church History at St. Peter's College, and those of 1915 when he left the College to take charge of the little country mission at St. Francis Xavier's, Carfin. The rejoicing for Baden-Powell's relief of Mafeking heralded his arrival in College, and the rape of neutral Belgium marked his departure. The Boer War was to last for a further two years, until 1902, and although Britain was then alone in her " splendid isolation," the war was limited in scope to the continent of Africa, unlike that which threatened Europe in 1914. In 1900, the glorious reign of Victoria was slowly drawing to a close and the death of the aged sovereign, six months later, was mourned by the country. Mr. Taylor records that in Greenock " all works stopped, shops shut all day and services (were held) in all churches except R.C." It would seem that discontent over the rejection of Gladstone's Home Rule for Ireland Bill still rankled in the hearts of Irish Catholics in the Greenock area. From the same source we learn that neighbouring parishes had shorter memories, for on the eve of Victoria's funeral " Thomas went to a service in Gourock church." Throughout his life Father Taylor generously acknowledged the debt Scotland owed to the sons of St. Patrick and their valour in the struggle for the Faith; but never did he permit himself to be involved in political issues, especially in questions where loyalty to civic leaders was concerned. At times during ceremonial occasions at the Grotto he was inclined to forget that the Papal flag did not take precedence over the Union Jack; but invariably he saw to it that St. Andrew's flag, symbolic of Church and State dignity, should be hoisted and left to flutter gaily alongside the Papal yellow and gold.

During the major part of Professor Taylor's time in St. Peter's College, an uneasy peace prevailed in the country, punctuated by the threatening rumbles of war. The incident at Sarajevo in 1914 forced Britain to take up arms on behalf of Belgium against the growing might of the Kaiser's German forces. The call to arms for the Boer War was minimal in comparison with the frenzied patriotism shown by the young men who, in 1914, rushed to join the colours and fight alongside their compatriots in the muddy trenches, stretching across Belgium and south through France. In reverse, Belgian refugees, driven from their homes, sought refuge wherever they might find shelter. The first 1,000 arriving in Glasgow found themselves in the care of two chaplains from St. Peter's College: Father Claeys—himself a Belgian—and the forty-year-old Father Taylor. Ably assisted by the Belgian sisters from the recently founded convent of the Helpers of the Holy Souls at Langside, the homeless Belgians were placed as far as possible in family groups in the towns and villages of Clydeside. Apart from his official duties in the College, this was the last onerous task undertaken by Father Taylor before he left the College to take up duty elsewhere.

It is the lot, and for the most part the wish, of the majority of secular priests to follow their sacred calling in active parochial work. Of these, some, whose abilities and attainments suit them to the work, are drafted to administrative or specialised work in the diocese; others after a few years on active mission work, are transferred to seminaries throughout the country. A few choose to dedicate the remainder of their lives to this work. Father Taylor spent fifteen years in seminarian work, but towards the end of 1914 the call to pastoral work began to haunt him. The positive reason is not certain, though the condition of his health may have influenced his decision. He had a trying bout of influenza and a series of colds throughout the year, but in spite of those handicaps he had carried on with his welfare work among the Belgian refugees, his literary work and his many other commitments.

His father's diary records on the 1st January that Thomas conveyed " remarkable " news to his parents on that day. One can only surmise that the news was his intention to apply for a transfer to parochial work. This surmise is confirmed, for a month later, having just recovered from a further attack of influenza, Father Thomas visits his home and requests his father to type a letter to the Archbishop, applying for a parish. This letter, posted on the 22nd February, was acknowledged by the Bishop's secretary a week later. Mr. Taylor makes no further mention of his son's transfer from the College until it had become a *fait accompli* and we learn that on Friday, 9th July, " T.N. goes to St. Francis Xavier's, Carfin; Father Denis McBrearty (Carfin) goes to St. Aloysius', Springburn."

Mr. Taylor may be forgiven for his brevity at this time, for the health of his youngest son, Father James Bede, C.M., was giving serious cause for alarm. Since his ordination in May 1910, the latter had spent several spells in hospital in Ireland and now, in May 1915, he collapsed once more while preaching a mission in Newtownards. His superiors sent him to St. Mary's Vincentian House at Lanark to recuperate after his discharge from a Belfast hospital. It was a source of considerable joy to Father Thomas that his well-loved younger brother was sufficiently restored in health to be able to stay with him at the presbytery at Carfin during the first few weeks of convalescence. Added to this was the personal satisfaction Father Taylor enjoyed of having beside him one on whom he could rely and with whom he could discuss many of his problems.

It is the experience of the writer, and of others who over the years have helped Monsignor Taylor with his vast correspondence, that often the helper sat beside the priest while the latter himself did the writing. When dissatisfied with a particular paragraph or sentence construction in a work of importance, he would read it aloud and ask for comments. One might be fortunate enough to provide *le mot juste* which he sought, but this was rare, for Father Taylor's command of the English language invariably left his helpers struggling far behind. Apart from Professor Phillimore of Glasgow University, Sister Aimée, S.N.D., of Notre Dame Training College, and Dr. Patrick McGlynn, his closest friend for half a lifetime, there were very few whose advice he accepted in his literary work. In this connection, Dr. McGlynn, himself a classical scholar of high repute and the distinguished author of a two-volume lexicon of Terence's Latin vocabulary, recalls how on various occasions Monsignor Taylor consulted him late at night on some urgent literary work. With a smile, the Doctor remarked that he " had read proof " by telephone of articles going to press the next day. What the good and obliging Doctor did not know was that His Grace, Archbishop McDonald of Edinburgh, the third of the triumvirate of friends, had communicated on one occasion with Father Taylor, in an effort to curtail Dr. McGlynn's extra-curricular activities, at a time when the latter was seriously involved in the Scottish foundation of the Don Bosco Guild of Teachers, of which he was a founding member and first President. His Grace's letter is a masterpiece of dramatic irony, couched in most amicable terms. Doubtless Father Taylor saw the point—he was most considerate when there was a risk to health—but it is far from certain whether his friend, " the most Catholic layman in Scotland," as His Grace of Edinburgh described Dr. McGlynn, could be so easily shackled. Happily, Dr. McGlynn is still with us and would, if his health permitted, continue the scholarly work and the Church's activities to which he has dedicated his life.

The following is the letter sent by Archbishop McDonald to Canon Taylor:

St. Bennet's,
42 Greenhill Gardens,
Edinburgh, 10.
24th April, 1945.

" My dear Canon,

I hear serious reports of Pat McGlynn. Unless he radically takes himself in hand and does less, he will undoubtedly have a very serious breakdown, or worse. There is no need for him to do all the donkey work in regard to the Guild. If he does it, he will be left to do it and soon he will not be able to do that or anything else either. He ought to give it up entirely or let all the detail of organisation be carried out by other hands.

Mrs. McGlynn is *very* anxious about him and with good reason. May I suggest that you should write to him to this effect. I suggest writing and not 'phoning or paying a visit, because though it is more pleasant for both of you to 'phone and still more to visit, still this takes more out of him, and in particular visits are tiring because they will always drag out longer than intended, and every minute takes something out of him that he cannot afford to give.

I need scarcely say that no one knows that I am writing this, and no one suggested my writing, but I feel that unless we are very careful we shall have years of regret later for not having taken ordinary precautions now. When he is dead and gone, it will not be possible to 'phone or visit or ask advice, and unless these precautions are taken without delay, I really feel that this is what is going to happen, and regrets will have to take the place of remedies. It is madness for Pat not to go to bed early and to shut the 'phone off so that no one can get at him till he gets up again.

I put this up to you as his best friend. You will have no difficulty in verifying the facts for yourself, but I fear that I am not an alarmist in this matter. I only wish I was.

This note requires no reply. A little remembrance, please.

Very sincerely yours,

✠ A. J. McDonald.

Over forty years before this letter was written, Father Taylor had been asked by a Catholic historical society in Paris to contribute an article on some aspect of Scottish Catholicism. Finding himself unable to undertake the task at that time, he recommended that approach should be made by the society to Dom A. J. McDonald, a highly respected young Benedictine Father. The Benedictine was later to be elevated to the Hierarchy, and while Archbishop of St. Andrews and Edinburgh was to remain a friend and loyal supporter of Canon Taylor's Eucharistic and Marian Apostolate, until his death at Edinburgh on 22nd May, 1950.

But this belongs to the future, and in July 1915, Father Taylor's main concern was to establish himself in his new parish and to set about the pastoral work for which he, under his superiors, was primarily responsible. As the following letter of appointment received from the Right Rev. Monsignor Canon J. Ritchie, Vicar General of the Archdiocese of Glasgow, makes clear, Father Taylor must now make certain changes in his way of life:

> Archdiocese of Glasgow,
> 160 Renfrew Street,
> Glasgow.
>
> 30th June, 1915.

" Dear Father Taylor,

The Coadjutor-Archbishop tells me that he has seen you in connection with your promotion to the charge of a Mission. I write now the formal letter to intimate that you have been appointed to the charge of the Mission of Carfin—vacated by the appointment of Rev. D. McBrearty to the charge of Springburn Mission. You will kindly take up your new duties on Friday, 9th July. You would do well to call at an early date on Fr. McBrearty, who would give you every information.

I am sorry that the change just comes when your holiday is due; but you will be able to arrange for the usual holiday when your assistant, Father Murphy, shall have returned on the 23rd July. Of course, he has arranged for his supply.

I was to have spoken to you on two points:

1. The necessity for looking well to the finance of the Mission, attending to the collections, and knowing the value of a penny in expenditure.

2. The necessity of residence, as you will not have now, as at the College, the facilities of going about doing other work.

As His Grace has spoken to you on these subjects, there is no need for my labouring the points.

I am asked by the Archbishop to send you his kind, good wishes, in which I cordially join, that your work at Carfin will be in every way successful. I may add that you will find Carfin what they call ' a good Mission.'

> With kind regards,
>
> Yours sincerely,
>
> (Sgd.) John Ritchie, V.G.

The " good Mission " at Carfin where Father Taylor was sent as pastor in 1915 had already celebrated the golden jubilee of its foundation a few years earlier. It had been established as a Mass-centre in 1862, by the Rev. John McKay, priest-in-charge of St. Ignatius', Wishaw. In the following year a modest chapel-school was built, the details of which appear in the *Catholic Directory* of 1864:

> " Carfin—a commodious school-house has been built here within the past year. The Protestants of the neighbourhood sub-scribed generously towards it. Average attendance at Day-School, 160."

Father Taylor was to realise before he was many years at Carfin that he owed much to the magnanimity of Protestant sub-scribers. We are told in the St. Francis Xavier's centenary brochure of 1962 that the coal-masters and industrialists, " normally were anxious to improve the conditions of their employees," who were living in Carfin, Newarthill, New Stevens-ton and Cleekhimin, the villages which made up the parish. In 1865, the new parish was dedicated to St. Francis Xavier, the ardent Jesuit missionary of the Indies—a fitting choice for the eldest off-shoot of the parish of St. Ignatius at Wishaw.

The first resident priest to take charge at Carfin was the Rev. Thomas Moran, who in 1875 lived in a small " but and ben," a two-roomed apartment, scarcely bigger than the homes in the " miners' rows " where most of his parishioners lived. In the following year, the mission-station at Cleland, hitherto served from Wishaw, was added to Carfin. A personal whim on Father Moran's part led him to take up residence at Cleland, and from 1876 until 1890 Carfin appears in the *Catholic Directory* as a station served from Cleland.

Although Cleland was to see its new chapel-school completed and solemnly opened in 1877, the new church at St. Francis Xavier's, Carfin, which had become a necessity for the more populous area of the joint mission, followed within five years. The *Directory* relates that the opening service was performed on Sunday, 2nd July, 1882, by Archbishop Eyre of Glasgow, with the Rev. John Maguire (later Archbishop of Glasgow) acting as Master of Ceremonies.

Shortly after the opening of the new church at Carfin, Father Thomas Moran, doubtless weary of church building during the seven years he was pastor of the joint Carfin-Cleland mission, returned to Ireland, where he died in November 1921, parish priest of Newcastle and Fourmilewater, in the Diocese of Water-ford. Father John Hughes took charge of the mission when

Father Moran left and, like his predecessor, the energetic and friendly Father Hughes lived at the commodious presbytery already erected at Cleland. The administration of the double mission proved difficult, and in 1890 Carfin once again, after an interval of sixteen years, became an independent mission with its own resident priest, the Rev. Charles Aloysius Cunningham, a native of Glasgow, who had been ordained at the Scots College, Rome. During the six years Father Cunningham served at Carfin, a much needed new presbytery was built adjacent to the church; this presbytery was extended in the 'thirties, during Father Taylor's time, to accommodate the three curates who were then essential to the needs of the busy parish.

The next priest to take charge of the mission at Carfin was Father Thomas Smith, a native of Dumfries. His time there was short; after four years of suffering from a progressive paralysis in 1900, at the age of thirty-eight he died, a victim of the disease. His illness made an assistant priest necessary, and with the help of the energetic Father Michael Ahern, Father Smith was enabled to provide the parish with a handsome two-storey school, accommodating 400 children.

From all the evidence readily available at present—between the years 1862 when the parish was founded and 1963, the year following its centenary—it may be assumed that Monsignor Taylor and Father Thomas Smith were the only two priests to die working in the Carfin mission.

Father Smith's successor was Father Charles Webb, a native of Brighton, who had been ordained in Glasgow in 1889. If the failing health of the previous pastor made the presence of an assisting priest imperative, the needs of the increasing population made a similar demand in Father Webb's time. Father O'Dea, an ebullient young Irishman, was succeeded in turn by two curates of German birth, Father William Orr and Father Gisbert Hartman, all three serving under Father Webb.

It is possible that the interest roused in the parish for amateur dramatics and the other social activities organised by Father O'Dea, may have prompted Father Webb to build a larger parochial hall. His transfer to Cardowan in 1908 prevented him from furthering his plans, but before he left Carfin he had made an important purchase: he secured an acre of waste ground opposite the church; this land was to become the site of the Carfin Lourdes Grotto, erected by Father Taylor in 1922.

Rev. Denis McBrearty, Father Taylor's immediate predecessor, spent seven active and rewarding years at the Carfin mission before his promotion to a larger parish nearer the centre of the

Archdiocese. He had the joy of knowing that he was leaving to his friend and successor a loyal and united parish, comprising the scattered villages of Newarthill, New Stevenston, Jerviston and Cleekhimin—the extremities of the mission, which had for its heart and centre the parish church of St. Francis Xavier at Carfin.

A copy of a circular letter issued by Father McBrearty gives an indication of the financial condition of the parish in 1911. By way of explanation, it must be stated that during the fifty years since its foundation this small mining parish had built a chapel-school, a new parish church, a large primary school, an extensive two-storey presbytery, and in addition had added several extensions to the church buildings; these factors considered, the debt Father Taylor inherited from his predecessor was far from exorbitant.

APPEAL on BEHALF of

CARFIN SCHOOL BUILDING FUND

Dear Sir or Madam,

The Congregation of St. Francis Xavier's, Carfin, is making a special effort to raise £500 to defray the cost of a further addition to the School.

About two years ago, a large wing was built at the cost of £1,700. That addition was then considered sufficient for all requirements; but the increasing demands of the Education Department oblige us to provide still more accommodation.

The cost of the proposed enlargement is a cause of anxiety to a humble congregation already burdened with a heavy debt of £6,000; and they confidently look to their many friends to help them in their endeavour to give effect to the demands of the Education Department, without loading the Mission with an increase of debt.

A Sale of Work will take place at the end of the year. Donations and goods will be gratefully received.

(Sgd.) Denis McBrearty,

March, 1911.   Administrator of Mission.

Referring to this appeal, it should be explained that before the passing of the Education Bill in 1918, Catholics, bound by the tenets of conscience, were unable to send their children to the public schools provided by the Education Department for all Scottish children. Since the education of children to the age of fourteen was mandatory throughout Britain, it behoved the leaders of the Catholic Church to provide alternative arrangements to satisfy the demands of the State. At considerable sacrifice to themselves, this onerous task was undertaken by Catholic missions throughout Scotland. It was all the more burdensome as normal education rates were required from all ratepayers, whether or not they took advantage of the system offered by the State. For many years fairly generous grants had been allowed by the Department to the voluntary Catholic schools, but these grants carried with them the condition that the recipients maintain their buildings to an agreed standard; that necessary facilities should be provided for non-academic subjects, such as cookery and woodwork classes; and that at all times the education of the pupils should reach the standards prescribed by the Education Department for schools in Scotland. It is to the credit of Catholic teachers who, by national standards, were seriously underpaid, that the results achieved by their pupils were as good and sometimes better than those attained by pupils trained by their better paid counterparts in State schools. Over the last half-century since the Act was passed, the Catholic minority in Scotland has good reason to be grateful to the Church leaders who had the wisdom to entrust the educational future of Catholic children to the care of a Department which has generously fulfilled its obligation.

But as yet in 1915, Catholic missions were bearing the full burden of building and maintaining schools and providing salaries for their teachers. The priest-in-charge of the mission held the invidious post of Manager of the school and was directly responsible to the Hierarchy—the custodians of Catholic education—and the Education Department, the providers of the necessary grants.

Shortly before Father McBrearty was transferred, the damage from subsidence due to undermining became apparent in the school and church walls, and it soon became evident that drastic repairs would be required eventually.

All things considered—even the prospect of further deterioration in mission property—Father Taylor had every reason to look forward to his work among the humble people whom the Vicar General of the Archdiocese referred to as the " good Catholic colliers " of Carfin.

But how did the Irish mining community view its new pastor? A change of parish priest in country districts half-a-century ago was a momentous occasion; then, the priest was the heart of the parish, and from him emanated the energy which gave force to Catholic life among his parishioners. Rumour was rife and gossip inevitably made comparisons between the genial Father McBrearty who had left them and the scholarly, slightly withdrawn personality who had taken his place. Miners, who spent

more than half their working hours sweltering in the sunless
bowels of the earth, held their own assizes as they " cooried on
their hunkers " * at the gable-ends of long rows of monotonous
red-brick " but-and-bens ";† in the wash-houses which stood like
sentinel posts behind the houses, the women folk reversed or
confirmed the judgment of their " guid men " as they lathered
and swished at their corrugated wash-boards, with a keen ear
always alert to every crumb of added gossip.

These good people already knew, even before his arrival, that
Father Taylor was " a man of books." Had not the amiable
Father McBrearty, who had known the newcomer since childhood, informed them that their new parish priest had spent
fifteen years lecturing to future priests in the great College at
Bearsden? And had he not written books that had become
famous all over the world? That would account for his being so
small and slight and having trouble with his chest. But would a
college man like Father Taylor, they wondered, understand the
ways of the miners? He had better not try any of his high falutin'
college ways on them: they were simple country folk and they
were not interested in all this nonsense about a young French
nun who had died less than twenty years back and was not even
a saint. St. Patrick was good enough for them, and for their
fathers before them; what need of a French nun, just because
Father Taylor knew her sisters in a convent in France? But what
was more, they muttered, he was English—at least his father
was, although his mother was of Irish descent. But then, her
father though Irish, came from a Protestant family . . . So the
questions and rumours ran among the solid, Irish, Catholic community, who feared the Protestant religion as strongly as they
distrusted traditional Sassenach oppression. In an age of extreme
political and religious views, there was little room for ecumenical
fraternity in the hearts of many Christians in the Scotland of fifty
to a hundred years ago.

It is possible, and indeed probable, that Father Taylor felt
some degree of anxiety about his new duties. But more than
most he relied on the supernatural guidance in which he tenaciously put his trust. It was not a meaningless motto he had
adopted on his twenty-first birthday when, like St. Francis
Xavier, he offered his life " for Jesus and Souls." The Hand of
Providence seemed to guide his destiny, for now his immediate

---

* The traditional crouch, with knees-bent posture, adopted by miners who were obliged
to work in cramped positions under low-hanging roofs.
† Room and kitchen.

responsibility was the spiritual welfare of the two or three thousand souls residing in the parish, the example of whose titular saint had influenced him so strongly as a young man.

A parishioner, who as a youngster served many an early Mass for Father Taylor, treasures in his memory a vivid vignette of the forty-one year old parish priest a few days after his arrival at Carfin. The little lad was playing near his home at that part of the road to New Stevenston known locally as " The Bell." A voice disturbed him at his play and he looked up, startled, to see standing over him a strange priest. The little one's memory—still clear in maturer years—was that of a well-dressed man with a gentle voice. The memory of the words spoken have faded with the years, but the spirit of kindliness experienced at that first meeting has survived half-a-century.

Another, a lady who worked devotedly for many years for Monsignor Taylor, recalls another aspect of the new pastor. Her reminiscences are confirmed by others of the same and later generations. Her picture is of a small, slight priest as he mounted the pulpit to preach his sermon. With fascination she watched him as he blessed himself with great reverence—Bernadette's Sign of the Cross he often called it—and then having adjusted his spectacles, he gazed with penetration at his congregation. Next, while clasping the ledge of the pulpit with both hands, he proceeded in a sonorous voice to proclaim the Latin text for his sermon. To the little girl who watched and listened with awe, the dramatic exposition in English as he developed his theme held a strange fascination. Occasionally he read a relevant quotation from a heavy tome which rested on the pulpit ledge, but rarely if ever was he known to consult notes while preaching a sermon.

Others remember how, early and late in his career, he vociferated against the spiritual ailments of the parish; Mass-missing, late-coming, drink and gambling were castigated in turn as he drove his points home with a clenched fist on a long suffering pulpit. In build he was small of stature, but the strength of his voice was in inverse proportion to his size. Without an amplifier his words could be heard easily at the farthest end of a crowded church or hall.

The kaleidoscope of memory moves and other vignettes appear: a humble priest visiting a sick person, slightly ill at ease with the distraught man of the house, but completely at ease in comforting the ailing mother or placating the tiny children. An invariable injunction to the children was to go up to the chapel and " ask Jesus to make Mammy (or Daddy) better." Always he set great store on the prayers of young children.

It was Father Taylor's kindly manner with children, which more than anything else, gained him early esteem in the parish. He was drawn to them, not because of their natural attractions, but because of the innocence of their immaturity; he enjoyed their company, while they for the most part were at ease with him. A constant theme of his was that parents should be careful never to yield to a child, even at the tenderest age: love and affection at all times, but a weak yielding for the sake of peace, never. There was little he himself liked better than having his brother's children staying with him at the presbytery at Carfin, where they were capably looked after by Miss Currie, Father Taylor's efficient housekeeper. As a rule, when he visited his parents at Greenock, he himself restored the children to their homes after the short stay at Carfin.

The building of the Lourdes Institute in 1920 and the proposal to build a Lourdes Shrine in honour of Our Lady, inspired Father Taylor to invite his sole surviving brother Henry, known in the village as Harry, to move his home from Gourock to Carfin parish, in order to take on the post of general supervisor of church property at St. Francis Xavier's. Thus it was that Mr. and Mrs. Harry Taylor, with their family of three boys and a girl, took up residence about half-a-mile from the parochial church, in the neighbouring village of Newarthill. Of this family only two have survived—the two younger children: Thérèse (Mrs. D. Harvey) and Henry. Rev. Thomas F. Taylor died in 1956, and his brother James during the war years.

Rev. Mother Marie de Lourdes (formerly Winifred Delaney of Newarthill), now with the Ursulines in Australia, recalls how on a number of occasions when Father Taylor was visiting his own parents at Greenock, she and his niece Thérèse were invited to accompany him. These journeys stand out like milestones in Reverend Mother's childhood: clearly she remembers how Father Taylor looked after them; how he loaded them with sweets and the other " goodies " that children love. The kindliness of the elderly couple at Greenock also strikes a happy chord. Strict and upright they always were, but their home was a happy one where visitors were made welcome.

Monsignor Taylor's niece, exercising the privilege of kith and kin, adds further information: " Yes, we loved these visits to my grandparents' home. Uncle was most kind and generous to us, but," she added with a smile, " once we had arrived and our meal was over, generally he retired for several hours and had a snooze on the sofa. It was my grandparents who had all the trouble of looking after us." It may be taken for granted that the loving grandparents enjoyed the "trouble"; and who but the very young would grudge a busy priest a few hours' relaxation in his parental home?

Winifred Delaney's family emigrated to Australia about 1927 or 1928, and the letter following expresses the joy Father Taylor experienced a few years later when he learned that the daughter of one of the most loyal Catholic families of the parish had been called to dedicate her life to God's work in the Ursuline Order in Australia.

Tel.: Motherwell 208.   Carfin,
                                               Motherwell,
                                               Scotland.
                                               5-1-1932.

" My very dear child in Xt.,

It was with inexpressible joy that I received the good news. As your own Little Flower puts it: 'The dove has entered the ark.' Thanks be forever to God, to Our Lady, St. Winifrede and St. Thérèse, for that grace beyond price bestowed upon your soul. The gates have opened, and Winnie has passed into the Temple of the Lord to make ready her wedding dress against the day when the Bridegroom will come to seek his little bride. You will not realise the splendour of the gift Jesus has dowered you with, the exquisite beauty of this unfading 'rose,' till the glad hour of your everlasting Bridal—when the King of Kings will set His humble princess by His side. In that hour, how you will rejoice that you kept your heart a 'garden enclosed' for Him alone! Meantime labour hard to ensure that your heart be enriched with every virtue—with humility and royal charity most of all—so that your spiritual trousseau will delight the eyes of Jesus when, the days of preparation ended, He claims Sister Mary Winifred definitely as His spouse.

At the close of Benediction to-night I replaced the Blessed Sacrament in the angel-pyx you saw as a child, before it became God's dwelling—your mother's lovely gift to the Tabernacle. I remembered, as often before, the inscription carved there, the prayer that a blessing would rest on the 'flowers' your good parents have presented to God. The divine benediction, the favours of Heaven's Queen, the Roses of your 'Thérèse,' have descended like dew on their offspring. But the choicest rose, the most enviable favour, has been granted to her who will—I hope and pray—be ere long the royal consort of Christ the King. Through the Nativity and Passion Plays you helped to make him known and loved. This new Grace is an instalment of the great reward.

God bless you—dear little one! I know you must feel the long silence. But my heart is not silent. It is singing 'Alleluia.' And it has not been and will not be silent before God, even though the written word may linger. If you read the 'Notes of the

Grotto,'* you will know that Mary and her Little Flower keep
their wretched instrument busy. And you know that there are a
host of other spouses of the Lord in India, America and elsewhere,
who look for a letter. But I am slow with the pen, and delay
follows upon delay, so you must forgive.

I need not give you ' news '—I am sure your aunts keep those
at home posted with the doings at Carfin. Your father and mother
will let you know when ' roses ' fall on the Grotto, and will tell
you the story of its great days. I cannot end, however, without
begging of you to keep the work here more than ever in your
prayers. The Grotto is built on what the Immaculate asked of
Bernadette: on penance and prayer. Please secure for it in your
new home all the aid you can.

I had forgotten that copy of the *Autobiography,* and I take it
as an omen that St. Thérèse will watch over Winnie, and that the
new family of which Sr. M. Winifred is a happy member, will
keep the Grotto Crusade in their prayers. It would seem as if Mary
and her Saints wanted to use it for England, as well as for Scotland, so many are the pilgrims that come from the South. As for
the poor priest at the Grotto, I am confident you will not forget
his needs.

Once more, 10,000 blessings!

Affectionately in Xt.,

T. N. Taylor."

The unbounded interest Father Taylor had in the spiritual
welfare of the children led him to introduce his first innovation
in the parish. Hitherto at Carfin, as elsewhere, the little ones—
his own name for younger children—had not received Our
Blessed Lord in the Holy Eucharist until they were eight and
sometimes nine years of age. Within a few months of his appointment to the parish, with the help of the teachers in the school,
he set about preparing the first group for the early reception of
their First Holy Communion. This, for the children, was a solemn
occasion, and before long the practice became commonplace for
the First Communicants to dress in white.

To provide these dresses and suits must have entailed considerable sacrifice for the parents, but the solemn little procession of
white-clad five- and six-year-olds walking in twos from the
nearby school to the church, added dignity and solemnity to the
celebration of the Sacrament. On the Sunday following, and
indeed for several weeks thereafter, the First Communicants
enjoyed the privilege of being the first to approach the Altar
rails.

---

* These appeared in the Catholic press for many years and were the links between
emigrants and Carfin.

Nowadays, it is a growing and commendable practice for families to receive the Holy Eucharist along with the First Communicants. The writer is unable to vouch for the common practice in Carfin in the years immediately after the 1914-18 war, but certainly from the mid-twenties St. Francis Xavier's Church was choc-a-bloc with relations and friends on the Saturday of First Communion, and the majority of those received the Sacred Species after the little ones had left the Communion rails.

From his earliest years as a priest-member of the Eucharistic Leagues, Father Taylor had constantly preached frequent and daily Communion. Now, in charge of his own parish, he took steps to further the Eucharistic Crusade, first of all among the children. Theologians, and others who claim to know, suggest that habit is not a sound basis for receiving the Sacraments. If this be so, those of us who were encouraged by Father Taylor to form the good habit, while we were young, of receiving Our Lord in the Blessed Sacrament each time we attended Holy Mass— other conditions being observed also—have been receiving Our Lord's body in the Eucharist with a little less than a worthy intention. Rightly or wrongly, Father Taylor advised parents to encourage their children " to get into the habit of assisting at Holy Mass and of receiving Holy Communion frequently or daily if possible." His claim was that the children of to-day are the parents of to-morrow; and a tradition formed would be passed on. The Almighty, in His omniscience, may judge Monsignor Taylor's maxim and motives and the worthiness of those of his congregation who followed his advice; the fact remains that during Monsignor Taylor's pastorate Carfin parish was renowned for its Eucharistic tradition.

A spiritual renewal in a parish is not brought about by the natural gifts and accomplishments of the people; nor by the skilled oratory, the powers of persuasion and the dramatic appeals of its priests. These human aids have their purpose in life, and when used to advantage play an important part in propagating the word of God. But a Christian, lacking in depths of spirituality, vaunting a love of a God whom he does not himself love, is but an empty shell. The true strength of every Christian —layman and priest—lies in the fulness of his spiritual life, in the extent to which he conforms his will to the Divine plan, as it applies to him. This conformity of the soul with its Creator is achieved only by constant and sincere prayer.

It is almost impossible to consider any aspect of Monsignor Taylor's personality, without associating him instinctively with prayer. God's name came easily to his lips, and when he was

heard murmuring a kindly " God bless you, child," one sensed
the words were not a trite salutation on parting, but a prayer
sincerely uttered by a priest who had the listener's interest at
heart. When during a sermon he turned away from the congregation to face the Blessed Sacrament in the tabernacle on the
high altar, those who had the privilege of listening to him on such
occasions were left with no doubt that the spontaneous prayer
he uttered from the depths of his soul was far more compelling
in example than any well-planned sermon he might preach. In
the dark winter of his life, as his eyes began to dim, and the
reading of the Divine Office became impossible, he was not content to yield compliantly to the exigencies of advancing years.
He could no longer read nor write, but he could, and did,
increase his hours of prayer. When he was not occupied in the
presbytery or in the Grotto, one could always find the ageing
priest sitting in one of the front seats before the high altar in the
church. His prayer in these latter days was not one of meditation.
It was too easy for an old man to fall asleep in a quiet church.
Hence his favourite devotion was the Rosary, the most efficacious
prayer, he claimed, after the sacrifice of the Mass. Not for him
the five decades only; the full fifteen decades was the minimum
goal he set himself daily. A passer-by making a short visit to the
church might find himself invited to join in Monsignor's Rosary,
and if by chance he had time to spare, before he was aware of
what was happening, to his surprise he would find that he and
the good priest would have completed the whole Rosary. Even
during hours of Confession, from the seclusion of the small confessional at the back of the church, Monsignor's voice could be
heard droning out the Paters and Aves as he awaited the regular
penitents who preferred him as confessor. Arising from his
frequent visits to the church, the practice became habitual for a
band of elderly villagers to wend their way to the church, after
their evening meal, and there join Monsignor in the recitation of
the Rosary, after which they ended with the traditional prayers
and ejaculations so well known in the parish.

    There are examples in abundance which demonstrate Mon-
signor Taylor's propensity for prayer and how, whenever possible,
he induced others to join him. One delightful incident which
occurred a few years before Monsignor's death, clearly illustrates
this point. M.K., his loyal secretary at this time, discovered one
night after she had finished typing his letters, that she did not
have her mantilla with her for the short visit to the church which
she made nightly in Monsignor's company. The staff had gone
to bed, and Monsignor, a stickler for the rule that a woman's

head should be covered in church (even though it was after 11 p.m.), felt around the coat-rail for a suitable head-covering. Several hats were examined before he found what he was searching for—his own biretta which he offered to M.K. with the words, " Would you mind wearing this?" The good Lord must have chuckled at the unusual sight of the bare-headed Monsignor being guided into the church by his purple-tasselled biretta-adorned secretary. It is only right to add that Monsignor, too, saw humour in the situation.

In lighter vein too, though still on the subject of prayer, is our reference to the times Monsignor did yield to the exigencies of old age and fell asleep during the recitation of the Rosary. This occasionally happened at the Dominican Rosary Hour, which has been observed for many years in the parish from 8 to 9 p.m. on the eves of First Fridays. When the Rosary was being recited in church, Monsignor had introduced the custom of the congregation alternating with the priest in saying the first part of the Paters and Aves. An understanding congregation soon recognised the symptoms. If Monsignor gave the response to the Hail Mary and then went on to the next one without stopping, this was a warning sign that he was dropping off to sleep, with the result that the congregation as a rule finished the Rosary themselves. But more disconcerting was the time when, having finished the Rosary themselves, they paused for a bit before going on to the ejaculations which normally followed. The silence interrupted the Monsignor's sleep and without hesitation he resumed the Rosary exactly at the point where he had fallen asleep four or five minutes earlier. But these aberrations, slightly amusing when they occurred, were easily forgiven and forgotten; it is unlikely that any worshipper was deterred from coming to church just because a near ninety-year-old Monsignor, seated comfortably before the Lady Altar, unwittingly had a little cat-nap halfway through the service.

If the spiritual welfare of his congregation is the chief and most essential charge on a priest, the administration of the parish and the financial stability of its balance sheet is often the greatest source of worry. This was even more true over sixty years ago when Father Taylor first arrived at Carfin. On his first visit to his son's new parish, Mr. Taylor noted that the walls of the church and school showed ominous cracks; as subsidence from undermining progressed, deterioration advanced rapidly, and ultimately one wing of the school required to be sealed off completely. Father Taylor's immediate problem in 1916 was to make the school buildings sufficiently safe to comply with the exacting demands of the Scottish Education Board.

The cost of essential repairs had rocketed during the war years, at a time when the financial demands on school Managers (in effect the parish priest) were already high. How Father Taylor successfully managed St. Francis Xavier's parish school during the war years, in spite of the additional cost of repair due to subsidence, is a tribute to his astute judgment and to his understanding of his fellow men. To put it more simply: then, as on later occasions, he proved himself a clever beggar in a just cause.

Money was scarce, building materials were costly and tradesmen, fully engaged in the war effort, were not readily available. The money factor, which had proved a perpetual headache to most of Father Taylor's parish priest colleagues, was to him a problem also, but not one which he could not solve. He worked on the simple principle, that if a cause was worthy the Lord would provide the means, if sufficient effort was put into the project. What more worthy cause than keeping God's house in repair, and providing a place for the education of the children of the parish?

The cracks in the walls of the church were becoming a serious menace to worshippers, and if repairs were not done soon, the fate of the church might be the same as that of one wing of the school; this had to be sealed off completely for the safety of the children and staff. The Archbishop willingly granted permission to Father Taylor to take the necessary steps to realise sufficient funds to defray the heavy costs anticipated in the venture. Granted a free hand, he used his native wit and inherent business acumen to sum up the situation before tackling the problem. With Machiavellian cunning, he changed his usual form of signature; the well-known Thomas N. Taylor—or alternatively T. N. Taylor—blossomed into his full name, Thomas Nimmo Taylor, during the ensuing issue. His plan was to make a personal appeal to the coal masters and estate owners of the district, those men who were the employers of the workers from Carfin parish. Worthy priest though he was, he saw no reason why, for pragmatic purposes, he should not make full use of the name given to him in memory of his grandfather, Thomas Nimmo, scion of a staunch Protestant family from the north of Ireland. Fortuitously the coal master who owned the " Blackie " pit in the New Stevenston area of Father Taylor's parish, was also named Nimmo, though it must be added that the James Nimmo Coal Company was in no way responsible for the subsidence which caused damage to church property at Carfin; nevertheless, by its prompt and generous donation to the church restoration fund, the company set a fine example for others to follow. Mr. John Whiteside, an official of this company, became Father Taylor's staunch ally and friend; it was Mr. Whiteside who advised him on the procedure he was to adopt in launching his appeal for aid, not only to the coal masters and landlords of estates in Lanarkshire, but to others of note whose affluence would not be seriously diminished by a little philanthropy on their part. In the case of one coal company, which had not replied to Father Taylor's appeal, Mr. Whiteside himself wrote to the officials concerned and recommended Father Taylor's appeal as worthy of their support.

A series of letters show how Father Taylor acted on the advice of his mentor; initially, he wrote to the Colville family, owners of the Cleland estate, on which the Carfin mission was situated; thereafter, he made representations to the coal masters holding mineral rights in the area, intimating to them the extent of the damage and the estimated cost of repairs.

The response of the coal masters shows that these hard-headed business men were as philanthropic on this occasion as the *Catholic Directory* indicates their predecessors had been at the time of the building of the chapel-school in 1862 and the parish church in 1882. A draft-copy of Father Taylor's first letter to Mr. David Colville follows:

J. M. J. T.
St. Francis Xavier's,
Carfin,
By Motherwell.
15 - 6 - '16.

" Dear Mr. Colville,

I am not sure if you have heard of the mischief caused to our church and school by the working of the Black Band seam underneath these buildings. The damage is so considerable that a large portion of the new school wing has had to be abandoned, and the remainder has severely suffered.

At the moment of writing I am told further operations are in project which might easily bring about a collapse of the entire fabric. It would, therefore, be a very great relief to the Catholic population of the district, if these new operations which menace us, received your favourable consideration, so that the future safety of the buildings might be secured. I understand that this can be done without unduly interfering with royalties and dividends.

These buildings, sacred to us and costing over £18,000, have been erected by the pence of the six hundred families in this parish,

E

each and all of the working class. At present these poor people are adding to their burden a supreme effort to find money to repair the existing damage. £3,000 will hardly be sufficient for that purpose. The thought of further operations and the inevitable ruin that must result will, I fear, dishearten them completely.

I am well aware of your sympathy with the working class, and I trust you will be able to give us the assurance we desire, that no further mischief will be done. In return, you will have the grateful prayers of our seven hundred little ones at school, their parents, and

Yours very sincerely,

(Sgd.) Thomas Nimmo Taylor."

Mr. Colville's reply was prompt and encouraging:

Dalziel Steel and Iron Works,
Motherwell.

21st June, 1916.

" Rev. Sir,

CLELAND ESTATE

I have your letter of the 17th instant, and much regret to hear of the damage being done to your school and church. This is the first complaint I have had on the subject.

I have passed your letter on to Provost Wilson (Factor of Cleland Estate) . . . I hope that some arrangement can be arrived at to stop the destruction referred to.

Yours faithfully,

(Sgd.) D. Colville."

Having examined the damaged property, Provost Andrew Wilson, C. & M. E., wrote as follows:

Cleland Estate Office,
Newarthill.

11th July, 1916.

" Rev. and dear Sir,

It may be no disadvantage, but I am of opinion your estimate of the sum necessary to repair the school and chapel is very, very high.

It might be advisable for you to get an estimate from a plasterer or other tradesman—not a binding estimate, but simply an obligement.

If you care, I will get it done for you.

Yours faithfully,

(Sgd.) And. Wilson."

After further inspection of the site of the damaged church property, Mr. Wilson came to the following conclusion:

"The damage done to the buildings is occasioned by the collapse of an old working near the surface, due to the working of the Blackband Coal. The working of the Blackband seam would not have occasioned such damage.

The Virtuewell coal seam proposed to be worked is about fifty fathoms from the surface and is probably over thirty inches in thickness.

To protect your school and chapel, about two to three acres of coal would require to be left unworked, containing at least eight thousand and 280 tons (8,280)."

A draft of a letter written by Father Taylor to the landlord on the 28th July of the same year, shows how negotiations had developed in his favour:

St. Francis Xavier's,
Carfin.

28 - 7 - 1916.

" Dear Mr. Colville,

I have to thank you for your two letters and for the kindly interest and prompt action displayed in a matter which the Catholic workers of this district have so much at heart.

Mr. Wilson proposes to save our church and school by arranging to have sufficient coal left unworked. He suggested that our feu-duty should be raised from £13 to £20.

Taking it that such was your wish and judging the sum to be merely partial compensation, I approached the Archbishop of Glasgow. His Grace willingly consented to the proposal, and was, like myself, touched at your kindness, for Carfin was a considerable source of anxiety.

May we ask you to complete your good offices by arranging for the insertion of a clause, guaranteeing us from *all* further damage from underground workings? The members of the congregation will then have their minds at rest.

Mr. Wilson admitted that my estimate of £3,000 was correct, as far as the value of the buildings was concerned, but declared that they could be patched together for much less. I therefore called in two experts. They declared that the gable (of the school) must be taken down, and that £1,000 would cover the cost of patching. Adding to this the considerable expenses already incurred and allowing for the usual increase on estimates, I now think—and am delighted to know—that a sum of £1,500 will meet the necessary expenditure.

I know how busy you are, but it would give me great pleasure
to be allowed to thank you personally if it suited your convenience.

In the meantime accept the assurance of our very grateful
prayers.

> I remain,
> > Sincerely yours,
> > > (Sgd.) Thomas N. Taylor."

Further correspondence ensued between Father Taylor and the
factor of Cleland Estates, the most telling of these letters being
one written by Mr. Wilson on the 15th November, 1916:

" Rev. and Dear Sir,

Your letter of this date to hand, for which I thank you.

I do not think there can be any misunderstanding in regard to
the terms of my arrangement with you. The coal to be left unworked was the Virtuewell seam; you remember I went to the pit
and inspected the place of the new mine.

My arrangements with the trustees and the Mineral Tenants
were almost completed when your next letter was sent to Mr.
Colville wishing to have full protection. The matter since then
has been allowed to rest.

I am strongly of opinion that the completed arrangements with
regard to the Virtuewell seam should be given effect to.

I trust you may not be put to any further vexations, troubles
and expense by the coal workings.

> Reverend and Dear Sir,
> > I am,
> > > Yours faithfully,
> > > > (Sgd.) And. Wilson."

Further correspondence on this issue—if such existed—is no
longer available, but it may be assumed that by the terms of the
agreement the Virtuewell seam has never been worked. Within
a quarter of a century practically all coal-mines in the area had
closed down. To-day, more than half-a-century later, even the
" bings " and derelict pit shafts have disappeared, as have also
the squat miners' rows. Apart from a few privately built semi-
detached bungalows and tenements, the police station, the public
school, St. Francis Xavier's church and presbytery and the old
chapel-school, the Carfin which Father Taylor first saw in July
1915, bears little resemblance to the village as it is to-day.

As well as the suggested guarantees of future security from
undermining, the immediate satisfying results of Father Taylor's

appeal was the receipt of generous donations from Protestant coal-masters and industrialists to the Restoration Fund. Of the series of letters extant referring to this fund, one in particular received from Mr. Whiteside of Nimmo's Holytown Colliery is worth recording:

March, 1917.

" My dear Sir,

I have just received your welcome letter. Your news is good. You are doing fine. Just keep at it now.

You give me credit for something that I don't quite understand. Surely it is you yourself who have accomplished this work; and you tell me what you have done and how you have succeeded. I simply listen to the good news.

The United (Colliery Co.) have done fairly well by you in the circumstances, not being under any legal obligation. Still they were under a higher, namely a moral obligation, as they wrecked your buildings and reaped the reward.*

Mrs. D. Colville has done well and I think her gift (£50) is excellent. Had David himself lived a bit longer, you would have fared even better.†

Mr. D. J. Colville may yet make up for his mother's short-comings; let us hope so—we shall wait and see.§

I quite agree with your Committee in respect that you write Duncan J. Millan, M.P., as also Lady Hamilton Dalziel. I would trouble you a little further by asking you to write the following gentlemen:

Lord Newlands, Lord Lieutenant of the County, Mauldslie Castle, Carluke;

Robert King Stewart, Esq., Murdeston Castle;

Mr. McFarlane, Chairman, Auchinlea Coal Coy., Cleland.

Mr. McFarlane is very well to do, and being a member of your church, I would expect him to be quite willing to help you with this work.

Many thanks for your prayers and good wishes.

I remain, Dear Sir,

Yours very sincerely,

(Sgd.) John Whiteside."

Whether Father Taylor accepted Mr. Whiteside's advice and communicated with the people named, is not known. At any rate, the Restoration Fund reached the target that was set, thanks

---

* United Collieries donated £150.

† Mr. David Colville had died suddenly towards the end of 1916.

§ Mr. D. J. Colville, through his late father's Trustees at Dalziel Steel Works, donated £50 in May, 1917.

being due not only to the industrialists and coal-masters who responded generously to Father Taylor's appeal, but also to the less affluent people of all religious persuasions—small business men, people from the professions and a large body of workers who could afford to give little more than the widow's mite.

After half-a-century the name of another donor is revealed. Celtic Football Club donated £25 to the St. Francis Xavier Restoration Fund. Mr. William Maley requested that for " obvious reasons " the name of the Club should not be communicated to the press.

Captain Colville had advised Father Taylor not to undertake permanent repairs during the war years. Consequently, the gable-end of the school was temporarily shored up to prevent collapse on the adjoining hall. In 1918, the problem passed out of the latter's hands when the Education Board took over all Catholic schools; in 1937 the entire school fabric was razed to the ground and a modern one-storey building was built to accommodate the pupils of the village. Eight years earlier another school, combined primary and secondary, had been built in the New Stevenston region of the parish; this is now within the confines of the parish of St. John Bosco's, New Stevenston.

But what of the damage done to the church of St. Francis Xavier? Once more we find ourselves returning to Father Taylor's profound belief in the efficacy of prayer. The following is his own story, backed by the testimony of an older generation:

> " We decided," he recalls, " that the children, and as many of the adults as possible, would make a novena of Masses and Communions for the canonisation of the Little Flower. The novena was to be offered in thanksgiving to the Blessed Trinity for the singular blessings conferred on Sister Thérèse; and the petition to the Carmelite nun was that she would intercede with the Almighty for the preservation of the Church. If anyone could make the impossible happen," Father Taylor added naively, " she could. On the day the novena commenced," he continued, " a few of the men pasted large sheets of brown paper across the cracks on the walls of the church and thereafter we left the rest to Thérèse."

The story had a happy ending; the cracks which had been worsening rapidly prior to the novena did not widen any further and the paper held. A year or so later, when tradesmen arrived to carry out the decoration of the church, the paper patches had to be scraped off to allow the cracks to be filled.

A man of lesser faith than that of Father Taylor might have hesitated much longer before committing himself to the extensive repairs and renovations which were introduced in the church at the end of the war; but, undismayed by the near-wrecked condition of much of the adjoining school, and putting his trust in his heavenly benefactors, he proceeded to put the House of God in order.

By 1920, the greater part of the " temporary " repairs had been completed; and only now, fifty years later, is the structure of the church beginning to show the marked signs of old age.* In that year a refugee Belgian craftsman lined and panelled the high altar and two side altars of Our Lady and St. Joseph. A handsome statue of the Sacred Heart, subscribed for by the parishioners several years earlier in memory of Father Smith, a former parish priest, was placed on a suitable pedestal adjoining the high altar; flanking it on the other side, the statue of Saint Francis Xavier, the titular saint of the parish. The latter statue had been presented to Father Taylor for the church by a Mother Superior of the Helpers of the Holy Souls whom he had known for many years. Had the thought occurred during Monsignor's lifetime, the writer would now be in a position to explain why the Apostle of the Indies is depicted baptizing a child with features of the negroid race. For want of more definite information, one might assume that the sculptor wished to represent the Saint baptizing an African child from Mozambique, where he wintered at the outset of his missionary journey to India.

Other additions were made to the church; parquet floors were laid in the sanctuary and new Stations of the Cross were hung. Over the years since then, a galaxy of images calling to mind saints of popular appeal, have been added; but so far St. Patrick stands in a unique position near St. Joseph's altar, rivalled only on the right-hand aisle, by Father Taylor's special friend, St. Thérèse of the Child Jesus.

The preservation and administration of Church property has always been an important part of the duties of the priest in charge of a mission, but a worthy priest realises that temporal affairs must never absorb his attention to the exclusion of the spiritual care of his parishioners. A spiritual renewal and a fortifying of faith was Father Taylor's foremost aim for his flock. Hence a few months after his coming to Carfin, the Vincentian Fathers preached a fortnight's Mission to the congregation. As in many parishes in the west of Scotland, a triennial Mission was the common practice. In the ensuing year, a renewal Mission followed; this encouraged the staunch in their fervour and the

---

* As this book is going to press (April 1972), a new parish church is being built, adjacent to the Grotto. It is anticipated that the new church buildings will be completed in 1973.

backsliders to make amends. As Father Taylor became more experienced and the parishioners grew accustomed to his ways, frequent novenas were added to the list of religious services. The parish was encouraged to share in the liturgical festivals of the Church, and Easter and Christmas were highlighted as times of general Communion for the parish. The numbers receiving Holy Communion regularly, and even daily, increased tremendously during the early 'twenties, so that one saw many men approaching the altar rails, not just on " Men's Sunday " but on the " Women's Sunday " also. This was a break with the tradition that the men of the Sacred Heart Confraternity receive Holy Communion on the first Sunday of the month, the women on another Sunday, the Children of Mary on the third, and the young men on the fourth. Few were those, especially among the men, who had received more regularly than once a month, in many parts of Scotland before the First World War.

The Eucharistic tradition in Carfin has often been commented on by those who visited the parish—priests preaching missions or on pilgrimage to the Grotto. One Irish visitor who spent a week at Carfin during the summer of 1926 was astounded at the crowds who thronged the aisles, not only on Sundays but also on Saturdays and weekdays; up the left-hand aisle to the Communion rails and down the right, and heaven help anyone who broke the rule. No matter who the celebrant was at Mass, Father Taylor was always there to help distribute Holy Communion. As a young curate, he wrote that nothing in life gave him greater joy that celebrating a " Communion Mass." For this reason he was rarely the celebrant at last Mass on Sunday, during which traditionally the congregation was not allowed to communicate.

On one occasion at Carfin, Monsignor Taylor was forbidden by the celebrant, a religious superior, to assist with the distribution of Communion to a crowded church. The celebrant in this case was Archbishop McDonald of Edinburgh, who had been visiting the Grotto the previous day. Father Taylor prevailed on His Grace to remain overnight at Carfin and say nine o'clock Saturday morning Mass. Judge the surprise of the congregation—over three-quarters of them children—when they saw on the altar, not Father Taylor nor Father Murphy, but a strange priest who, without any assistance from the Carfin priests, distributed Holy Communion himself to the vast crowds who approached the altar rails. The numbers were not unusual, for when not attending school many children in the parish were daily communicants.

Commenting in 1929, on attendance at daily Mass, Father Taylor wrote:

> "Four hundred children attended Mass daily—or almost daily —throughout the holidays (of summer 1928). The children and their parents were urgently invited to improve, if possible, that record. At nine o'clock Mass on Monday (1st July 1929), the little church of St. Francis Xavier was stormed by an army of 540 school children. It was a treat to hear them say aloud the custo- mary Mass prayers. May Our Lady and the Little Flower obtain for them the grace to finish the holidays as they have begun. Their attendance is one of the Grotto miracles, as many of these children come from a considerable distance."

In the following week, Father Taylor gave thanks to Our Lady and St. Thérèse for a torrent of grace which brought a record number of 600 children who attended holy Mass during that week. But parents were not to be out-done, for in the following year (1930), at the close of the renewal of a Mission in the parish, we learn that "never before in the parish had Communions equalled that of the closing Sunday."

The year 1931 shows the children still faithful to daily Mass. One Wednesday in July when heads were counted, "570 were present and nearly all received Holy Communion."

A picture of an astounding General Communion, at an Easter Sunday Mass, is still very clear in the writer's memory. Father Taylor was celebrating Mass in a church packed to full capacity. On such occasions, when it was anticipated that most of the congregation would communicate, an extra large ciborium, con- taining sufficient hosts for the vast numbers, was placed on the corporal. By some mishap this was not done, and when Father Murphy arrived on the altar to help distribute Communion, he discovered on the corporal only the smaller sacred vessel, con- taining consecrated hosts sufficient for about one third of the congregation. The two priests were faced with the meticulous task of dividing the consecrated species into fragments for close on six hundred communicants. Time and again the worried priests were compelled to return to the altar for a further division of the Bread.

Elsewhere will be told the story of what Canon Taylor gleefully called the "Miracle of the Loaves and Fishes." He may not have known that his parishioners had already copyrighted that title for the Easter morn on which he had made his big blunder during Holy Mass.

Increased attendance at daily Mass and more frequent recep- tion of daily Communion, although the most important, was not the only noticeable result of the growing love of our Divine Lord in the Eucharist, apparent among the parishioners of St. Francis Xavier's. Since the late 'nineties, by slow degrees, the festival of Corpus Christi was being solemnised publicly in parochial churches throughout Scotland. In 1895, St. Mary's, Dundee, startled the Presbyterian city when 600 members of sodalities, in addition to a general congregation, accompanied by Bishop Smith carrying the Blessed Sacrament, walked in solemn procession from the church along the public streets of the city. Two years later, the feast of Corpus Christi was similarly solemnised at St. Mary's, Abercromby Street, Glasgow. An aged parishioner of Burnbank who died several years ago, recalled that he was an altar boy during the first outdoor Corpus Christi procession held at St. Cuthbert's, Burnbank, Lanarkshire, in June 1895. Several parishes followed in the footsteps of the pioneers, but it was not until 1916 that Carfin was to add solemnity to the celebration of the feast of the Body of Christ.

In 1916 and 1917 the processions were small and without claims to grandeur. A simple altar was erected behind the presbytery and the Blessed Sacrament was carried in procession from the church, through the school grounds to this altar; here, Benediction was given before the procession returned to the church. To the great disappointment of the congregation at Carfin, in 1918, His Grace the Archbishop of Glasgow refused permission for the procession to walk along the main street of the village, even though a number of parishes in the Archdiocese had enjoyed this privilege since the turn of the century. Nothing daunted, Father Taylor and his flock elaborated their annual preparations for the solemnisation of the festival within the church grounds. Three years later, in 1921, ecclesiastical and civic authorities granted permission for a solemn Corpus Christi procession through the village streets. His Lordship Bishop Grey Graham carried the Blessed Sacrament on this occasion; the procession was repeated in the next two years, the ceremonial and pageantry becoming more ambitious and spectacular each year. Knowledge of elaborate Continental processions, acquired in his student days at St. Sulpice and in more recent visits to France and Belgium, inspired Father Taylor to model the Corpus Christi processions at Carfin on that of the Holy Blood processions at Bruges. In this he was encouraged by his close friend, the Belgian-born Monsignor Claeys, a former colleague on the teaching staff of St. Peter's, Bearsden.

A correspondent in the *Motherwell Times* gives a vivid account of the 1923 Corpus Christi procession at Carfin and the environment in which it was held. Several extracts from the article follow: *

" Last Sunday all roads led to Carfin . . . There are some 1,600 Roman Catholics in the village, which is a portion of the parish of St. Francis Xavier's, embracing Carfin, Newarthill and New Stevenston, and Sunday was their red letter day . . .

. . . On Sunday last (3rd June 1923), the three morning Masses were crowded with worshippers. Then the finishing touches were put to the decorations. Already the entire route had been transformed into an avenue of greenery. Trees and branches lined it from the little church to Carfin Cross and then from Carfin Street and Merry Street to either entrance of the Glenburn grounds (on the road to New Stevenston). Everywhere fresh foliage hid brick and mortar from view . . .

At half-past four, the beautifully dressed children filed out from the school and were followed by the Boys' Guild, the men of the parish, and members of the various societies in their regalia. Next came what was really the procession proper of the Blessed Sacrament—altar boys in scarlet, sweet children in white, strewing petals from their flower baskets, pages in their striking attire of red, white and gold, marshals with their great sashes, attendants with lanterns or palms, boys waving censers, and finally the priest carrying the Host . . . under a richly-embroidered silken canopy . . .

. . . The women followed, numbering at least 2,000. The younger ones wore flowing veils. Among the girls, two groups were remarkable. The first was twelve maidens, white dressed and white veiled, who carried sheaves of wheat, and in their midst a pretty child bore a bunch of grapes on a salver—the wheat and grapes being symbolical of the bread and wine used at the Last Supper and in the Catholic Mass. Another group with red veils bound by gold ribbon, carried the emblems of the Passion of Christ—cross, thorns, nails, etc.—symbolism again, since Catholics believe the Mass to be a renewal of the Sacrifice of Calvary.

From school and playground and Grotto, the processionists marched to the grounds of the presbytery, where from a huge permanent altar behind the church, Benediction with the Host was given in the open-air to the vast crowds. Thereafter the pilgrims wended their way through the densely-lined streets, alternately singing Eucharistic hymns, or reciting the Paters and Aves of the Rosary. It was a most orderly procession that passed along, with its beautiful background of green, overhead the coloured streamers, and every here and there altars, mottoes, flowers and lights. The reverence shown was indeed striking; Catholics dropped on their

---

* *Motherwell Times*, 8/6/1923.

knees as the priest passed on with his sacred Burden . . . Others looked on reverently, touched doubtless by such a display of faith in post-war days, when there is so much lack of interest in the things that are unseen . . ."

In June of the following year (1924), permission having been granted by the County Council for the annual public religious procession, Father Taylor and his parishioners bent all their endeavours towards making the solemnization of the festival worthy of the Christ King who would be borne through the streets of their village. But the procession was not to take place; almost on the eleventh hour, when arrangements were well-nigh complete, the Superintendent of Police informed Father Taylor that the proposed procession was illegal, in proof of which he produced a typewritten copy of Section 26 of the " Catholic Emancipation Act " (1829), the terms of which made it illegal for Roman Catholic clerics to walk in public in their robes of office.

In the absence of Archbishop Mackintosh, Monsignor Ritchie, Vicar General of the Archdiocese, advised Father Taylor to transfer the ceremonial procession to the private grounds adjacent to the Carfin Grotto, across the road from the church. Hurriedly, the parishioners prepared a field and erected a wooden altar in preparation for the forthcoming ceremony.

This was the first occasion when Benediction of the Blessed Sacrament was given in the Grotto; thereafter it became traditional for the feast of Corpus Christi to be annually observed there with spectacular solemnity and splendour. Through no design on his own part, Father Taylor was compelled to honour Mary's Son in the shrine built in her honour. The motto of Our Lady's Shrine at Lourdes—" Per Mariam ad Jesum "—was reversed. Unwittingly, the unsought publicity over the so-called " banned " procession, planned to honour Our Lord Jesus Christ, brought ever-increasing numbers of worshippers to Our Lady's Grotto Shrine at Carfin.

Although the Corpus Christi procession remained primarily a parochial activity, from 1924 it was absorbed in the story of the Grotto and will be referred to elsewhere in this book, as will also the passing of the Catholic Relief Bill (1926), which was a direct result of proceedings initiated in the House of Commons by Captain Francis N. Blundell,* Member of Parliament for the

---

* Francis Nicholas Blundell (1880-1936), M.P., 1922-29, Chamberlain of the Sword and Cape to H.H. Pope Pius X, Benedict XV and Pius XI.

Ormskirk Division of Lancashire, at the urgent request of Father Taylor.

. . . .

The years between the two world wars were for Father Taylor perhaps the busiest years of a fully occupied life. Judged on apparent results, one might be tempted to say, the most fruitful years. He himself would not have agreed, for he has been known to remark more than once that it is worth a lifetime of penance to lead even one soul back to God. The Good Sheep, he claimed, could fend for themselves, but the Lost Sheep must be sought out and returned to the Fold. This is one reason why St. Francis Xavier's Church, during Monsignor Taylor's pastorate, has been known as one where the penitent had always the opportunity of making his peace with God, in the tribunal of Confession. The fact is borne out in the bulletin appearing in the *Catholic Parish Magazine* as early as 1918:

" Parish Clergy	Rev. Thos. N. Taylor (1897), Rev. John J. Murphy (1914).
Sundays - -	Masses, 7.45, 9.30 (for children) and 11.30 (with sermon).
Weekdays -	Masses, 7.15 and 8. If there is only one Mass, Holy Communion will be given at 7.30 and Mass at 8.
Devotions -	Wednesday at 7.30.
First Fridays -	Holy Communion at 5 a.m. Masses 7 and 8.
Confessions -	Every morning during Masses. Every Friday 6.30 to 8 p.m. (except First Friday). Every Saturday from 6 to 9 p.m. On eves of Feasts from 6.30 to 8 p.m. At any time on application to chapel house."

The number of services was augmented when occasion demanded. On Wednesday evenings, two Benedictions became normal practice from the early 'twenties: the first at 6 p.m., a short service; the second at 7.30 p.m. was much longer and was popularly referred to as " Little Flower Devotions." People travelled from neighbouring parishes and from Glasgow to be present at this service and listen to extracts from the *Annals of St. Thérèse.* After the Rosary had been said, and Benediction given, there was, as a rule, an exodus of Carfin people from the church before the reading of the " Roses " of St. Thérèse began. Carfin people had already heard the story of most of the favours at one or other of the services in the Grotto; the visitors from a distance had not. Tuesday evenings were always reserved for the weekly Eucharistic Hour; this was additional to the "Holy Hour" preached on the first Sunday of the month. Monday seemed to be the night when most societies met, probably because it was the only evening of the week when there were no services in the church.

Another practice which developed naturally over the years was the recitation of the Fifteen Decades of the Rosary prior to the first Mass on weekday mornings; to the Rosary was added the Stations of the Cross at five o'clock on mornings during Lent. How often did Monsignor speak of the faithful little band who accompanied him from Station to Station at five o'clock on chilly spring mornings? Nor were these worshippers always adults: more than one priest, who as a youngster made the Stations of the Cross with his parish priest before serving at the six o'clock Mass, is now fulfilling his vocation as a diocesan priest, or as a priest member of a Religious Order.

One might think that the parishioners of St. Francis Xavier's had a surfeit of religious services. For some, yes; but from the vast majority there was no complaint. Each was attracted to the spiritual exercise of his choice, whether it be monthly nocturnal adoration between 11 p.m. and 2 a.m. on Thursday evenings, Holy Hour of Adoration on Tuesday evenings, or the Dominican Rosary at 9 p.m. on the eve of First Fridays; all had their adherents. But taking precedence over every service, and casting a fortifying mantle over the parish, was the regular attendance at the Sacrifice of the Holy Mass.

One might well ask how Monsignor Taylor was able to cope with the more than full programme he set himself, for it must be recalled that the building and administration of the Grotto of Our Lady and St. Thérèse was in itself a mammoth task; in addition, there were his other preoccupations—his literary work and his Foreign Missions apostolate. Alone he could not have done it, a fact he himself frankly admitted. He was blessed, before the Second World War, in having very able senior curates. Father John Murphy, who had come to Carfin in 1914, the year prior to Father Taylor's arrival, was an efficient and lovable young curate who supported his parish priest in every aspect of his work. Rarely was Monsignor Taylor absent from his parish, but when this did occur, Father Murphy proved a very able deputy. Indeed in his own right he distinguished himself in certain aspects of parish work which complemented the high ideals of his parish priest. With his artistic flair for the dramatic he was enabled to grasp Father Taylor's overall plan for the early Corpus Christi processions, and work out the satisfying details. As a young priest at St. Patrick's, Dumbarton, Father Taylor had attempted to produce a stage play, but his effort did not meet with great success. His dream was to revive the medieval mystery plays, and it was along these lines that Father Murphy found his bent. Under his guidance the Passion and Nativity plays produced in Carfin gained national fame. Not only did the players fill the halls of neighbouring parishes, but on several occasions the Carfin Passion Play was shown to a packed audience in the Alhambra Theatre and other large halls in Glasgow. Father Murphy was the practical man who trained the artists to a high degree of perfection: Father Taylor was the visionary who created the spectacular religious atmosphere and saw to it that the talents of individual artists were not allowed to interfere with the aesthetic grandeur of the religious spectacle. To further this aim, artists were not named on programmes, and audiences were asked to refrain from applause at the end of scenes of outstanding merit.

The highest testimony to Monsignor Taylor's work as a parish priest was that Father Murphy, who had spent seventeen years of his priestly life as assistant curate at Carfin, worked on the same principles as Father Taylor had done, when administering his own parish at Whiterigg, particularly in his successful drive to increase attendance at daily Mass and the reception of Holy Communion.

Of other curates who assisted Canon Taylor prior to 1939, the one who was most widely known and best-loved, and who remained longest at Carfin, was Rev. William Smith, R.I.P. He is best remembered for his brusque though kindly manner and his direct approach. Afflicted though he was by an asthmatic cough, the handicap did not curtail his activities in the parish. It was said that Canon Taylor feared Father Smith's ready tongue. Certain it was that Father Smith did not hesitate to warn his superior when for various reasons he thought him in the wrong. One example of this was when a number of people gathered in the Grotto between 9 o'clock and 10 on a cold, blustery December night in the mid 'fifties. The traditional evening procession through the village in honour of the Immaculate Conception of Our Lady had just finished; the little altars in the windows had been removed and the last candle extinguished. In a floodlit Grotto the processionists assembled in the Rosary Square to sing a final hymn. That at least had been the intention before Monsignor had forgotten the lateness of the hour, the coldness of the night, the discomfort of the people and his own advancing years. A strident voice was heard interrupting Monsignor's flow of words: " It's getting late, Canon, and these

people want to get home." A hurried " Goodnight and God bless
you all," from the by-no-means abashed Monsignor and the
worshippers were rushing helter-skelter from the Grotto to avoid
the heavy shower which came down in torrents ten minutes later.

Father Smith's interest in the work at Carfin brought him back
to the parish after a spell as army chaplain in the Middle East.
Letters from overseas friends of Carfin report on Father Smith's
work from the time he left Carfin during the war until he arrived
at his final station in the Holy Land. His progressive journey,
they wrote, was marked by the setting up of a praesidium of the
Legion of Mary wherever he was stationed. His return to Carfin
showed a man of failing health; even a short spell in a country
parish did little to help and eventually, having resigned from
active parochial work, he succumbed in 1961 to the asthma from
which he had suffered a living martyrdom for many years.

Other curates have assisted at Carfin, some for short periods,
others for longer, but none remained as long as the two named
above.

When the Diocese of Motherwell (comprising the County of
Lanark) was erected as a Suffragan See of the Province of
Glasgow in 1948, transfer and promotion of priests became more
frequent. Since that time, a number of able young curates have
assisted at Carfin. All were zealous workers and each co-operated
in Monsignor Taylor's exhaustive—and exhausting—projects.
Not all of them agreed with their parish priest all of the time; but
they worked industriously and conscientiously for the spiritual
welfare of the parish and Monsignor Taylor was the first to admit
this, even though his views were not always theirs.

Perhaps of all the assistant priests who served under Monsignor
Taylor the two who had the most difficult time were Fathers
Peter Murphy (R.I.P.) and James Comerford, each successively
senior curate in the years prior to Monsignor's death. The late
Father Murphy, quiet but dependable, proved himself an invalu-
able aid to Monsignor Taylor for several years. His personal
devotion to the Mother of God gained him Monsignor Taylor's
high regard as he pursued his exacting duties in parish and
Grotto Shrine.

Father Comerford, who succeeded Father Murphy as senior
curate and who perhaps loved the traditions of Carfin parish as
much if not more than any other curate who worked there, was
appointed Administrator of St. Francis Xavier's in 1958. His was
an onerous service. On his young shoulders fell the arduous
burden of running a busy parish, of administering the Grotto
Shrine and of caring for an ailing parish priest. It is to his credit

that in spite of many handicaps he succeeded in fulfilling the responsible task entrusted to him by his superiors.

It has been alleged by some and repeated by many, that Monsignor Taylor was not—in the true sense of the word—a "parish" priest. His interests were so manifold, it is claimed, that his parishioners did not always receive the attention and care the faithful in other parishes enjoyed. The statement is arbitrary and its interpretation depends on the views held by prelate, priest and parishioner as to what are the duties of a priest in charge of a parochial mission. It is difficult to be objective on an issue in which one is already convinced the statement is wrong, but an attempt will be made to explain the grounds of denial.

If the first duty of a priest in charge of a mission is to strengthen and safeguard the spiritual welfare of his flock, it is unlikely that anyone will find Monsignor Taylor wanting on this count. Enough has been said already on his untiring zeal to increase in all the desire for stronger and deeper spiritual life based on the Holy Mass and the frequent reception of the Sacraments. Further, more than in other parishes, devotional services to honour Our Blessed Lord in the Eucharist, His Mother and the Saints, were provided frequently and regularly for those who wished to take advantage of them. Nor can Monsignor Taylor be charged with failing in his duty as priest by neglecting to show in his personal example the high standard of sanctity to which all might attain. Much criticism of Monsignor had been made, but even those who liked him least, when put to it, admit his holiness. A few years ago the writer was advised to write to Canon Thomas McLaughlin, now living in retirement, to ask for information and comment on Monsignor's life. Since it was known that Canon McLaughlin was National Secretary to the Association of the Propagation of the Faith at the time Monsignor Taylor was President, hopefully she invited Canon McLaughlin to be "Devil's Advocate" and comment on any human failings which he had noticed while working in close association with Monsignor. The following was his reply:

Corsee Cottage,
Banchory, 25/X/66.

"My dear Miss McGhee,

I knew Monsignor Taylor for over forty years and stayed with him often.

He was a very saintly man and a marvel in work and holy living—as near a Saint as any priest I've ever known. So I could not be his 'Devil's Advocate.'

I am sure you will write a worthy pamphlet on him, for the
future to know him . . .

Yours very sincerely,

(Sgnd.) Tom. McLaughlin."

Countless others, from all walks of life, have repeated the same
theme, in slightly different words, but brevity restricts us to one
or two remarks from a former curate who must remain anonymous. This high-spirited young priest, with whom Monsignor
had often crossed swords, agreed that " Monsignor Taylor was
a very saintly man—but saints are hard to live with." A slightly
different slant is given by the same priest in the next comment:
" He had Pope John's saintliness but not his sense of humour."

Nor can Monsignor be charged with failure in fulfilling the
administrative side of his parochial duties. He inherited a debt of
almost £6,000 when he came to the parish, and at his death all
church property at St. Francis Xavier's Mission was completely
free of debt, while a healthy sum of over £30,000 had been loaned
to the Diocesan Fund. In the interim he had built an extension
to the church and presbytery, erected two parish halls, and constructed the Grotto Shrine of Our Lady of Lourdes and St.
Thérèse of the Child Jesus, the like of which, it has been claimed,
has no parallel in the British Isles, nor perhaps even in the world.

In which ways, then, did Monsignor Taylor fail as parish priest
if not as the guardian and guide of his people, nor as the custodian of their temple, nor in the example of good living he set
them by his own personal sanctity? The reasons must be sought
elsewhere than under these guiding lines, and their justification
confirmed or denied.

It has been alleged that Monsignor was more interested in the
pilgrims to the Grotto than he was in his parishioners. Those
from his parish who had the misfortune to be in trouble or
genuinely ill would not agree that Monsignor neglected them.
It is true that he could not always himself bring the last rites
to the sick or dying; this was the duty of the curate in a particular
district; but he did try to visit the chronic sick periodically,
especially those who were elderly. Curates complained that some
sick people in their districts made it obvious that they preferred
to have Canon Taylor visit them. Very sensibly he allowed the
curates to look after their own districts, especially when it was
a case of administering the Sacraments; but if the patient was in
distress, and it was obvious he required an experienced counsellor, Monsignor made an effort to visit him, even though the

visit could only be fitted in at ten o'clock at night. It is undoubtedly true, as many have complained, that he gave much of his time to pilgrims to the Grotto, more especially to those who were ill or those who had spiritual problems or temporal difficulties. His afternoons in fine weather were spent in the Grotto and he was at the beck and call of all who sought his help. It would be untrue to say that he ignored people from his own mission who needed his help, while specifically he offered solace to visitors. There was ample opportunity for everyone to speak to him after any service in the morning or in the evening or at any time during the day, but the difficulty did exist that if anyone wished to consult Monsignor Taylor in the evening, he would find himself one of many in a queue, and even when his turn did come, the interview was liable to be interrupted by an urgent telephone call, or the arrival of an important visitor.

The objection was also made by a few that unless a man was a volunteer worker in the Grotto, the Canon had little time for him; nor, it was claimed, did he favour the young ladies of the parish who were not members of the Legion of Mary. The objection with regard to able-bodied men, without family commitments, who did not volunteer their help in one or other of the many tasks involved in the building of the Grotto, has some degree of truth in the claim; the construction of the Grotto was primarily a parish project, undertaken with the aim of bringing honour to Our Lady. Many from within—and outwith—the parish gave generously of their time and labour over the years; the interest of some flagged at times, but in an emergency these could be relied on to offer a helping hand, whether it was parish or Grotto work; the remaining minority were the lookers-on who praised or blamed as the mood moved them. Such are found in every parish—the people who refuse to co-operate in the full life of the parish. Others should act as pass-keepers, they claimed; as marshals in the Grotto, on " big " days; as Guards of Honour to the Blessed Sacrament carried in procession. Always, others should do it, never they themselves. The spectator from the sidelines who hurls blame at the sweating players is popular, neither with the players nor the officials of a team; nor were the non-working critics in the parish of St. Francis Xavier, popular with priest or parishioner. A like comparison might be drawn from all walks of life.

The contention that those who were not Legionaries of Mary were beyond the pale in Monsignor's estimation, certainly does not apply in the case of the writer, as the following story will show.

The Legion of Mary was well established at Carfin in 1938, the year in which the incident took place. One morning after Mass she was invited into the sacristy by Monsignor Taylor. Rather reluctantly she entered, for she had suspected what was coming. After a few tentative remarks, he asked her if she had thought of joining the Legion. She was, and still is, well aware of the wonderful work those dedicated people have done for the Church, but with some temerity she told the Canon that she did not think she was suited to that type of work. (She has always found it easy to find excuses when she was unwilling to do extra work.) However, she did promise she would consider the matter again. A month passed during which time Monsignor Taylor did not revert to the subject and consequently she was compelled to open the discussion herself and tell him that her answer was still " No."

His reply was most unexpected and better than she had dared hope for, since she knew well how dear to his old heart the Legion of Mary was. " Your decision disappoints me, child, but at least," he added with a smile, " you have come back to tell me. Others don't even trouble to do so."

Becoming more confident, she went on to say, " Now, Father, if you had suggested that I should apply for membership in the Tertiaries of St. Francis, I might take you up on your suggestion." He looked at her quickly in a manner so typical of him. " Perhaps you're right, child. After all, the Tertiaries are an Order; the Legion of Mary is not."

On one point not directly related to the above it must be conceded that the parishioners—or more accurately the societies and sodalities of the parish—did have a legitimate grievance against their parish priest. Father Taylor was actively interested in these and whenever possible he allowed himself the privilege of acting as chaplain. During the winter this was usually possible without too great a strain on society or chaplain. How different was the position during spring and summer months! On innumerable occasions committee members waited for the arrival of their chaplain, each time vowing that this would be the last time they would wait. Then he would arrive, smiling benignly, as if time had no significance. And indeed, for Father Taylor, time often stood still when he was engrossed in the troubled story of an unfortunate who required consolation and guidance.

" It were much better," was the lament from long-suffering Tertiaries, Legionaries and Knights of St. Columba, " if he were to resign as chaplain and appoint one of the curates to take on the responsibility in his place." This he was unwilling to do,

especially in the case of the Tertiaries, for he himself had been
a professed member since his College days at St. Sulpice. However, he did compromise and for many years the monthly meeting
of the Third Order of St. Francis took place on a week night
instead of on a Sunday afternoon during the busy seasons at the
Grotto, when there was neither a hall free in which to hold the
meeting, nor a priest available to give Benediction; the curates,
too, were fully occupied in the ceremonial processions taking
place in the Grotto.

On this count the parish societies had a grievance against their
parish priest, but in the long run some at least gained; for not
only did they eventually have their own meeting and Benediction
on a week-night, but also, they were able to take part in the
Sunday afternoon Rosary, procession and Benediction. What a
pity that many of us lost whatever merit we gained from the extra
penance, by lamenting long and loud at the inconvenience we
had suffered!

It is an uncommon family that does not periodically experience
a squabble. The wise father rides the storm and retains the affection of his children in the measure in which he exercises his
authority for their good. The parish is the family writ large: its
spiritual life and moral fibre, its solidarity and loyalty to the
Church, its Christian spirit and sense of charity is influenced
greatly by the pastor who is in charge. Each human being has
natural and spiritual characteristics, particular and peculiar to
himself; for good or ill these characteristics colour his personality
and his way of life. The priest, who has the responsibility of a
parish, uses his own special gifts and qualities in the manner best
suited to his own nature and to the mission which is his charge.
This is his prime duty and responsibility; but there is a wider and
equally compelling duty, that is imposed on him by his membership of Christ's Church and which is binding on all Christians,
priest and lay person alike; namely, to help all Christians to be
true followers of Christ. A page from " Mes Pensées " has some
bearing on this and may explain in some measure why Monsignor
Taylor became engrossed in conversation with casual visitors,
and why most of his parishioners were willing to overlook the
inconvenience of being kept waiting by their dilatory parish
priest:

> " By what methods can a priest influence his flock and mould
> them into a resemblance of that ideal which he has formed of a
> good Christian, a true follower of Jesus Christ? *Not only his flock,*
> *but every person entering into the sphere of his action,* no matter
> how far removed from all formal and spiritual intercourse, ought

to carry away with him something of his love and zeal: something of that saintly influence that the saints have always exercised on those with whom they came in contact: a something which will make them better than they were before, a love for what is good and holy, and a hatred of all that is evil. It is principally by our private conversation that we produce upon them this spiritual influence and assist them in mounting a step higher in the ladder or perfection, or withdraw them, were it only a little way, from the paths of vice . . ."

Almost the last word is spoken, but the question still hangs fire. Was Monsignor Taylor the PARISH Priest of St. Francis Xavier's in the most literal sense of the term? Those who claim that he was not—and the plaintiffs seem to be from outside the parish and a few of these are priests—must draw the conclusion for themselves. Did Monsignor Taylor work as hard for the spiritual and moral well-being of St. Francis Xavier's parish as the average conscientious parish priest is expected to do? Or did he neglect his own flock while healing the spiritual ailments of others from outside? If the former, his parishioners have little reason for complaint, and outsiders have less; if the latter, those from the parish who have suffered from Monsignor's neglect have some reason to lament; but in true Christian spirit, while remembering that he may not have reached the degree of perfection to which he aspired all his life, they will continue to pray for his eternal rest, as he so ardently hoped all of us would do.

CHAPTER IX

VOCATION AND FOREIGN MISSION CRUSADE

The year 1920 was an important landmark in the history of the parish of St. Francis Xavier, its people and its priests. In the hubbub of the erection of the first Lourdes Institute, and the proposal to build a Grotto Shrine in honour of Our Lady of Lourdes, two important events in the spiritual growth of every parish, have been submerged by more spectacular events which attracted the public eye at that time. The first was the ordination to the priesthood of Rev. James McQuade, C.SS.R., and this was followed by the profession in the Little Sisters of the Poor, of Sister Lucille de Marie (Rose Garvie). These two young people were the very first of a long line of parishioners who were destined to dedicate their lives to God's work. Although fourteen years were to pass before another young man would be ordained priest (Rev. Thomas Taylor, son of Henry Taylor, Monsignor Taylor's brother), in that interval a steady stream of Religious left the parish to enter convents and priories in Britain and overseas. The parish Centenary Brochure of 1962 shows that religious vocations have increased greatly since 1920; and in the few years following Monsignor's death, two more boys, who knew well the regular penance of rising early to serve Monsignor's 6 a.m. Mass, have been ordained priests, while others are serving their novitiate in Religious Orders. Nor have the young women of the parish been outdone in generosity: four of their number, all children at the local schools while Monsignor Taylor was still active, have been professed in different convents throughout Britain since his death.

The following list of priests, brothers and nuns who were natives of St. Francis Xavier's parish, appeared in the Centenary Brochure of 1962: *

PRIESTS
ORDAINED

Rev. James McQuade, c.ss.r.	- 1920	Died 1931.
Rev. Thomas Taylor - -	- 1934	Died 1956.
Rev. Michael B. Maher - -	- 1939	Died 1970.

---

* A number of the priests and religious are now at addresses other than those given here.

Very Rev. Patrick Donnelly, w.f.   1941   Superior, White Fathers' House of Studies, London.

Very Rev. Thomas Swanzey,
  s.d.b., ph.d. - - - - -   1941   Rector, House of Philosophy, Tewkesbury.
Rev. J. P. Rae, b.a. (Oxon.) -   -   1944   Died 1959.
Rev. Thomas Garvie   -   -   -   1945   U.S.A.
Rev. Hugh McGurk -   -   -   -   1945   St. Catherine's, Harthill.
Rev. Thomas McGurk, m.a.
  (Cantab.)   -   -   -   -   -   1945   St. Mary's College, Blairs.
Rev. Gerald Maher, m.a. (Cantab.)   1945   St. Mary's College, Blairs.
Rev. Duncan Kane -   -   -   -   1946   St. Flannan's, Kirkintilloch.
Rev. John F. Breslin, s.t.l.   -   -   1953   Secretary to Bishop Scanlan (and now to Bishop Thomson).
Rev. Lawrence Connelly -   -   -   1954   Died 1964.
Rev. P. J. Markey, s.s.s. -   -   -   1955   U.S.A.
Rev. John C. Brady -   -   -   -   1956   St. Joseph's, Blantyre.
Rev. Patrick Lynch -   -   -   -   1956   St. Mary's College, Blairs.
Rev. J. A. Donnelly, o.carm.   -   1957   The Friary, Aylesford.
Rev. J. J. Kelly, o.carm. -   -   -   1959   St. Mary's Carmelite College, Aberystwyth.

BROTHERS

John Brady (R.I.P.)   -   -   1920   Bro. Denis, o.f.m.
Cornelius Boyle   -   -   -   1926   Bro. Cuthbert, o.f.m. Bucks., England.
Francis McGuire -   -   -   1956   Bro. Joseph Martin, c.s.sp. Bromley, England.
James McGuire (ord. 1968) -   1958   Bro. Paul, o.c.r. Louth, Ireland.

NUNS

Rose Garvie -   -   -   -   1920   Sr. Lucille de Marie, Little Srs. of the Poor, Cadiz, Spain.
Catherine McGunnigal   -   1922   Sr. F. Raphael, Poor Clares, Darlington, England.
Mary Mitchell -   -   -   -   1923   Sr. Margaret, Srs. of Mercy, London.

Jane Cavanagh   -   -   -   1926   Sr. M. Margaret,
                                        Poor Clares, Darlington,
                                        England.

Agnes Damarodos -   -   -   1930   Sr. M. Aloysius,
                                        Srs. of Mercy, Edinburgh.

Annie Smith   -   -   -   -   1932   Sr. M. of St. Casimir,
                                        Helpers of the Holy Souls,
                                        Portsmouth, England.

Margaret Mitchell -   -   -   1933   Sr. Mary Philippa,
                                        Faithful Companions of Jesus,
                                        Preston.

Ellen Cavanagh   -   -   -   1935   Sister Veronica,
                                        Srs. of Divine Providence,
                                        Brittany, France.

Winifred Delaney -   -   -   1939   Sr. M. de Lourdes,
                                        Ursulines, Armidale, Australia.

Mary Mitchell -   -   -   -   1939   Sister Mary,
                                        Faithful Companions of Jesus,
                                        Kent, England.

Margaret McQuade   -   -   1939   Sr. Marie Thérèse,
                                        Srs. of St. Joseph of Newark,
                                        Rearsby, England.

Margaret Cullen   -   -   -   1939   Sister Vianney,
                                        Srs. of St. Joseph of Newark,
                                        Nottingham, England.

Margaret McShane   -   -   1940   Sr. M. Dolores,
                                        Good Shepherd, Bangalore,
                                        India.

Mary O'Reilly -   -   -   -   1940   Sr. M. Chatilda,
                                        Dominicanesses, U.S.A.

Norah McGowan (R.I.P.) -   1943   Sr. M. of St. Aelred,
                                        Good Shepherd, Liverpool,
                                        England.

Delia Glackin -   -   -   -   1943   Sr. M. Julie of the Assumption,
                                        N.D. de Namur, Forest Row,
                                        Sussex, England.

Letitia McGurk   -   -   -   1948   Sr. Catherine,
                                        Srs. of Charity, Dundee.

Mary Garvie -   -   -   -   1948   Sr. Lucille,
                                        Little Srs. of the Poor, U.S.A.

Matilda Kearney   -   -   -   1949   Sr. M. Alphonsus Liguori,
                                        Good Shepherd, Bellary, India.

Mary Quinn   -   -   -   -   1950   Sr. M. Mercedes,
                                        Srs. of St. Joseph of Newark,
                                        Cleethorpe, England.

Mary McGlynn   -   -   -   1958   Sr. M. McGlynn,
                                        Daughters of Mary, Help of
                                        Christians, Hastings, England.

Rosemary Reilly -   -   - 1959   Sr. M. Bernard,
                                   Srs. of St. Joseph of Newark,
                                   Grimsby, England.
Catherine McGuire -   - 1961   Sr. Catherine,
                                   Franciscan Sisters, Dundalk,
                                   Ireland.

To this list may be added the name of Helen Quinn, which was inadvertently omitted from the official list. She was professed Sister Helen of Jesus in the Carmelite Order in 1950, and is at present in the Carmelite Convent at Ware. Others, too, have been omitted unwittingly from the record, simply because the compilers had no official means of tracing them. Monsignor Taylor's health was failing badly at that time and consideration and charity seemed to make unessential enquiries about his spiritual sons and daughters inadvisable. However, an examination of old correspondence brought to light the fact that from one family alone, who emigrated from the parish, three young women, a daughter and two nieces, have been professed nuns in convents in New Zealand. Priests and nuns are usually reticent about discussing the origin of their own vocation, but Sister Mary Bertelle (now in New Zealand), the eldest of the three Religious who have been " the product of that hallowed little spot so far away," has been prevailed on to tell us a little of her early life at Carfin. She recalls that Carfin was a little mining village when she lived there as a child. Her letter, written in December 1966, continues:

"I knew Monsignor Taylor (R.I.P.) well; in fact, this saintly, dear old man laid the first seed of my Religious vocation many years ago in Carfin when I was still a schoolgirl. We were a family of fourteen, seven boys and seven girls—and our family, the Devon family—had belonged to Carfin parish for many years ... I was born at New Stevenston in Carfin parish, was baptised, received my first Holy Communion and was confirmed there ... as well as receiving ninety-five per cent of my Primary education in the local school at Carfin ... When I was in Standard V we left Carfin parish for Mossend, and not long afterwards we sailed for New Zealand ... The late Monsignor was indeed a very saintly soul and dearly loved the Little Flower. While speaking to me one day, he handed me a copy of the Autobiography of St. Thérèse to read ... The life of this beautiful soul impressed me so deeply ... and urged me to reach for something that I felt then was beyond my reach, as I had never even met a nun, nor had I any hope of ever doing so ... I was two years in New Zealand when Monsignor Taylor's words were realised. 'You will be a nun,' he had told me, 'but you will have to pray hard and ask Little Thérèse to help you through.' God and the Little Flower," she concluded, " got me there."

Sister's last meeting with " the dear old saint was at a ' Limelight Lecture ' which was being held to defray expenses in the building of the Grotto, which was in his mind at that time." (This meeting probably took place in 1921.) Two nieces followed Sister Mary Bertelle's example in due course: Mother Judith joined the Congregation of Brigidines and Sister M. Martin joined the same Order as her aunt at St. Joseph's Convent at Wanganui. One of Sister Bertelle's treasured souvenirs is " a little card that is hard to decipher, written by Monsignor Taylor himself " a few years before his death. Many people wrote to him in the last years, and these letters were answered, at his dictation, by his secretary, but few may claim to have received a communication written by his own hand.

But Sister Bertelle's story is only one from many of a kind. Over a dozen different congregations of nuns have at at least one girl from Carfin parish in their community; even to hazard a guess at the number of young women outwith the parish who have been guided in their choice of vocation by Monsignor Taylor would be an impossible task. He seemed to have an unerring instinct in directing young people—men and women—towards the Order best suited to them. This point is illustrated in a letter received from Rev. Thomas Daly, S.D.B., Salesian College, Farnborough:

3 . 9 . '66.

" The work of Monsignor Taylor for the Missions was unending. After God and His Holy Mother, he was the means of many young Scots going to the Foreign Missions in India and China."

Here Father Daly refers by name to a number of Sisters who have joined the Order of the Good Shepherd in India and to which reference will be made later. He continues as follows:

" My life-long friend, Father Francis McDonald, M.B., who was a doctor in Glasgow and to whom A. J. Cronin, the novelist, dedicated his book, *The Keys of the Kingdom,* on the advice of Monsignor Taylor joined the Columban Fathers, almost in the first year of the foundation of this Irish Mission Society, and spent over twenty years in China."*

When we Salesians began our work for poor boys at Aberdour (Scotland), he helped us with many generous donations. He did the same for another House at Blaisdin Hall, Gloucester, which was started by my brother . . .

---

* On request, Father Daly supplied additional information about Father McDonald: " He joined the Columban Fathers in 1920, and was ordained at Saint Columban's College, Dalgan Park, Galway, 22nd December, 1924. He left for China the following September. He is still alive in one of the Houses of the Society in Australia. It would not be prudent to write to him as he is ill . . . I am sure he would not mind being mentioned in Monsignor Taylor's biography. I will take the blame if necessary."— 10 . 9 . '66.

His devotion to the Blessed Sacrament was the centre of his life and nothing pleased him more than to see the children, especially during holidays, attending Holy Mass and receiving Holy Communion.

He was a great soul and I am sure he is now enjoying his well-earned rest in heaven with those saints he loved on earth . . .

Wishing you every success in the work you have undertaken . . .

Yours sincerely in Jesus Christ,

(Sgd.) Father Thomas Daly, S.D.B."

How much easier it would have been to write an account of Monsignor's life if it could be said that he confined his vocational interests to the two dozen or more religious houses and seminaries where the young people from St. Francis Xavier's had gone to prepare for their dedicated work in the service of God. How simple it would be to write a brief note on the Carmelite Order, the spiritual power-house on which he constantly relied and to which he had directed three young people from his own parish; or on the Helpers of the Holy Souls, friends of Monsignor's since long before he came to Carfin and right up to the time of his death; or indeed on any one of the religious orders throughout Britain and more distant parts of the world, wherever the sons and daughters of Carfin are to be found. But nothing connected with the study of Monsignor's life is simple and direct, apart from his abiding love of God and all God's creatures. To him, as a Christian and a Catholic priest, the mandate was straightforward and direct; he was empowered by every means at his command to spread the " Good News " among the people of God. To those of lesser faith, the path he followed in furthering his Missions and Vocations Crusade seems a devious and complex one, abounding with difficulties; to Father Taylor it was but a sacred duty which he could no more evade than he could the other aspects of his sacerdotal obligations.

The record of known vocations from St. Francis Xavier's parish between the years 1920 and 1960 is relatively high for a small country parish: a total of more than eighteen priests and thirty religious within forty years suggests a healthy spirituality among the parishioners and their priests. No one would wish to deny that a share of the credit must go to parents and to zealous curates as well as to the vocations-conscious parish priest. But over and above the number of those who chose the religious life from within the parish itself, there are those from outwith the parish whose contact with Monsignor Taylor influenced them towards the life of a religious. Certainly the Grotto of Our Lady and St. Thérèse attracted to Carfin people of active faith, whose souls were already prepared and ready for the Master's call. The word of spiritual guidance from an experienced counsellor of souls brought these to the point of decision; several letters—there may have been many more—bear testimony to the fact that a seeming chance remark uttered by Father Taylor brought about a favourable condition in the soul, which eventually led to a religious vocation. It is not correct, however, to state, as so many have done, that Monsignor's active interest in the encouragement of religious vocation among the young was a feature of his life since 1922 only, when the Grotto Shrine was opened in the parish and contact with pilgrims provided the opportunity to meet young people already amenable to the workings of grace in their souls. Old correspondence shows that shortly after the turn of the century, he was directing young people in their religious vocation, not only to communities at home, but very soon to missionary work in Africa, and not many years later, to India and China. How Father Taylor came to have contact with so many religious houses may never be known, but it is clear from a series of letters received by him that he was in communication with the Sisters of the Blessed Virgin Mary at St. Mary's The Bar Convent, York, as early as 1901. Rev. Mother Superior, Inst. B.V.M., has graciously provided the information that Father Taylor sent Miss Sarah McErlean as a postulant to St. Mary's Convent in 1911, and it is possible that he may have directed another girl to the community some time later, although the evidence is not conclusive in the second case.

Father Taylor's close association with the York Convent—one of the earliest foundations in England—may be due to the fact that his own mother had been educated at Loreto Convent, Letterkenny, one of the houses of the Irish branch of the Institute.*

At any rate, we find that Rev. Mother Mary Cecilia of the Sacred Heart wrote to Father Taylor in May 1901, to thank him for two lectures he gave to the children of St. Mary's Convent, York. Shortly after this, he made the acquaintance of Mother M. Loyola of St. Mary's, and a series of letters—over fifty in number—show how Father Taylor helped Mother Loyola in her spiritual life as well as in her literary work. This good nun was a saintly soul, whose sanctity shows through her letters, even when she is discussing the religious text-books which Father Taylor loaned to her for reference in her writings. Added to her heavy duties as a

---

* Institute of B.V.M. (Eng. Prov.) was founded by a Yorkshire woman, Mary Ward, in 1609. The Irish branch of the Institute was founded in 1822 by Frances Ball (a native of Dublin), who had been trained for this purpose at the Bar Convent in York.

teaching nun was the additional task of writing religious text-books for schools, a number of which were subsequently translated into French for use in French schools. Father Taylor proved of considerable help in this work for he was in a position to advise her on the suitability of specific books, as well as loaning to her many books from his extensive personal library. In a recent letter, Rev. Mother Superior recalls the close connection which had always existed between Carfin and The Bar Convent, York, and how highly, over the years, the Sisters of St. Mary's had always esteemed Monsignor Taylor of Carfin.

Nearer home, and at a more recent date, the monastery of the Poor Clare Colettines was opened at Blantyre in 1952. But that year does not mark the beginning of Father Taylor's association with the Congregation; the links of friendship had been forged forty years earlier and already, in the 'twenties, two girls from the village had joined Poor Clare communities elsewhere in Britain. It may indeed have been because of the high regard in which he had always held the Poor Clares that many years ago, in a moment of tactless impetuosity, Father Taylor permitted himself to comment publicly on the action taken by certain members of the Community in Edinburgh.

It seems that a number of Sisters had become involved in a civil dispute with the Archbishop of Edinburgh, a dispute which had no direct bearing on Father Taylor at Carfin, except that he was an intimate friend of His Grace as well as being acquainted with most of the Sisters concerned in the issue. Rightly or wrongly—the one who writes this does not know the ins and outs of the case—Father Taylor supported Archbishop McDonald in the dispute while the action was *sub judice*. Public comments made by Father Taylor were reported to his superior, the Archbishop of Glasgow; as a result, Father Taylor unreservedly withdrew his injudicious statement.

What was not revealed at the time was, that in spite of his public indiscretion, the parish priest at Carfin was the one who was asked to make discreet enquiries to ensure that the Sisters concerned in the dispute would not be unprovided for should they decide to be laicised as a result of the civil action. Father Taylor may have been, on occasion, tactless and impetuous, and indeed influenced by the indiscreet advice of friends, but as far as the writer knows this was the only time he was required to offer a public apology for his indiscretion. The experience gained taught a lesson which stood him in good stead in ensuing years, when he contributed weekly to the Catholic press, in the widely read column featuring Carfin Grotto news.

The account reproduced below, which was graciously provided by Reverend Mother Abbess, Poor Clare Monastery, Blantyre, is of particular interest in that it provides information revealing entirely different aspects of Monsignor Taylor's character, information which would not have been available but for Reverend Mother's kindness:

" MONSIGNOR TAYLOR AND THE POOR CLARES

15th March, 1966.

When on December 1, 1963, word reached us that dear Monsignor Taylor had passed to his reward, our hearts were sore indeed. We felt we had lost a very dear friend and saintly priest. His interest in us was so genuine and his appreciation of our life so deep we treasured every second of his visits to our Convent, which nearly always coincided with August 12th—feast of St. Clare—and October 4th—feast of St. Francis. Christmas and Easter, too, saw him on his rounds of the convents, among which Blantyre was a foremost place, for he made no secret of his affection for us.

But his interest in our Order goes much further back still. Actually, it began in 1912, when Sister Maria who founded the Poor Clare convent in Cork, Ireland, and from which the Poor Clares in Blantyre was later to be founded, was a young nun in the Poor Clares, Tournai, Belgium. Being a foreigner, she longed for an English-speaking priest in whom to confide. Her Director, the saintly Father Willie Doyle, S.J., who was later killed in action in World War One, recommended Father Taylor, who was at that time in Belgium. Needless to say, Father Taylor was only too happy to oblige, and when later, in 1952, he met Mother Columba, the Foundress of the Poor Clares, Blantyre, one of his first enquiries was for the little Sister from Cork who entered in Tournai. After forty years, he still remembered the incident!

Later, Sr. Maria was questioned as to her impressions of Father Taylor at that period. ' He was a saintly priest,' she said, ' but oh, so thin and frail! I thought he would soon follow his young priest brother to the grave.' How heartily Monsignor laughed when he heard that!

In June 1952, Mother Columba and a Sister companion, who were making preparations for the Blantyre foundation, had an interview with Bishop Douglas, then Bishop of Motherwell. Before leaving, he asked if they had seen Carfin. ' No,' they replied. ' Oh,' said the Bishop, ' you can't be in Scotland and not see Carfin!'

Next day a telephone call came to Elmwood Franciscan Convent, Bothwell, where the Sisters were receiving hospitality. Monsignor Taylor was sending over a car to bring the two Poor Clares to Carfin! How he got his information they did not know, but they were happy to accept his kind invitation. A delightful afternoon followed, during which Monsignor was completely at their disposal. He was thrilled to learn they knew all about his English translation of the Autobiography of the Little Flower—and from that day a deep friendship was formed, which not even death could break. As the Sisters were leaving, Monsignor presented them with 2lbs. of tea, and with a twinkle in his eye, he remarked, ' Irish tea, too!'—becoming by this action one of their first benefactors in Scotland.

October 1952 saw the five pioneer Poor Clares in Blantyre. But oh, what a disappointment awaited them! Instead of a house, more or less ready for occupation, walls shorn of their plaster met their gaze. Dry rot had been discovered in several rooms! This had to be dealt with first, all other work being held up in the meantime. So back to Glasgow they went again, this time to their kind friends, The Bon Secours, who shared their distress to the full!

Winter set in, work was still prolonged, and their kind friend at Carfin thought a visit to the Grotto would revive drooping spirits. They accepted, and arrived just as Benediction was about to be given in the church. Monsignor asked if they would like to attend, and of course they agreed they would. So in they quietly slipped, never dreaming what was to follow. It was a special Benediction for the school-children, given by Father Smith. As soon as the Poor Clares were in their places, Monsignor took over himself. He explained to the children who the nuns were, why they had come to Scotland; told them of their disappointment at not finding the house ready, and ended by saying, ' They have no home! Ask the Child Jesus to give them a home!'

At this point all the little heads turned round to get a look at the nuns. And were they not embarrassed! But there was nothing they could do about it. Indeed, his intentions were so excellent, they had not the heart to scold him afterwards.

April 4th, 1953, saw the Poor Clares installed in their new home. Only a few hours had passed when the door-bell rang, and there stood dear Monsignor Taylor to welcome them to Blantyre. Over and over again, this exquisite thoughtfulness on the part of the Monsignor had been a source of great joy to the nuns. When on August 12th, 1953, they celebrated the seventh centenary of the death of St. Clare, it was he who gave the Solemn Benediction, ending with the *Te Deum*—and as he afterwards said—making a hash of it in his excitement. To the Poor Clares his contagious enthusiasm more than made up for a few unfamiliar notes.

As the months slipped by, Monsignor's interest was extended to the garden. It needed a Grotto, he thought, where the Sisters could walk in procession. Since they could not come to Carfin, why not bring Carfin into the garden? No sooner said than done. All arrangements were made: his own three workers, Mr.

CARDINAL BOURNE PREACHING IN THE GROTTO, SUNDAY, 20TH JULY, 1924.

St. Francis Assisi Shrine is Blessed by Very Rev. Fr. Stanislaus, 22nd September, 1929.

Brennan, Mr. Carr and Mr. Curran, were scheduled for nine o'clock next morning. Orders were duly given, and work began at breakneck speed. Monsignor told the Sisters he would return later to instal Our Lady. They were aghast! ' Finish the job in one day? Impossible!'

Smiling to himself, he left the convent. He knew his men! The work would be finished—of that he was quite sure—and he revelled in advance in the Sisters' delight. By mid-day he was back again to inspect the men's progress. Excellent! Even he was amazed at their work. All would be ready by evening, and Our Lady would be in her niche. Where the statue was to come from, the Sisters did not know, but judging by the knowing looks exchanged between the Monsignor and his men, they did. As the evening Angelus rang out, work had ceased on the new Grotto. All was in readiness for Monsignor's return.

Soon the gate swung open, and there stood the Monsignor with a large statue of Our Lady in his arms.* The men were by his side in a flash, the Community was called out, a procession was formed, and Our Lady—still carried by the Monsignor—was officially placed in the empty niche. How lovely she looked with the evening sun streaming in on her! Only then did the Sisters realise what an exquisite statue it was—full four feet high, a crown on the head and stars at the feet. Later, they learned it had occupied a place of honour in Monsignor's own study. His joy knew no bounds that evening! The Rosary was recited first, then hymn followed hymn. Finally, " Our Lady of Fatima " crowned a perfect day, and Monsignor and Co. returned to Carfin, leaving a very happy community behind in Blantyre.

His interest was not confined to the garden Grotto only. One day a Sister complained of the ravages wrought in the garden by a pigeon. He was very sympathetic, but when Sister suggested shooting the pigeon he was aghast. What would St. Francis think of such conduct?—he who so loved all feathered creatures! But the sight of her lovely heads of cabbage almost ruined by Brother Pigeon had hardened Sister's heart and all she could promise was to be kind to Brother Pigeon, provided he was kind to her cabbage. With that Monsignor had to be satisfied. When he next visited the convent, he enquired how the pigeon was behaving. ' Dreadful,' replied the Sister. ' He has even brought his wife now!' Suppressed laughter was her only sympathy this time, and so she added, ' And believe me, Monsignor, if I had a gun, you would have pigeon pie for supper long before this.'

How he enjoyed that! Shortly before his death, he said to a friend of the Community, ' I never got the pigeon pie after all.'

---

* Monsignor Taylor was in his eighty-first year at that time.

He had a delightful sense of humour and, when relaxed, would chatter away to his heart's content. He loved a good story and had an endless supply of his own.

There are many other beautiful traits in dear Monsignor's character, all deserving special mention. We have confined ourselves to those few, knowing well, other pens will be eager to add their quota of praise and esteem for a truly great priest."

Monsignor may not have got his fingers on Sister's pigeon pie, but certain it is that he had his finger in many another pie associated with the Community. After his death in 1963, Monsignor's secretary, "M.K.," offered to help the Poor Clares with their secretarial work. This offer was gladly accepted, for the Sisters had known her for some years, and had realised how much Monsignor had relied upon her help. One of the junior typists had on various occasions visited the Poor Clares, with work which "M.K." had undertaken to do for them. These visits to the Convent roused in the young girl an interest in the contemplative life of the Poor Clares, and eventually she sought permission to become a postulant at the Blantyre Priory, where she is now, looking forward to her profession next year. Is it but a coincidence that the young lady who had given so many hours of loyal service to Monsignor's work should be the instrument by means of which his friends at the Blantyre Convent should receive the latest recruit to their Order? If coincidence it is, may the same be said of what follows? The school where the young postulant had received her secondary education had in its nine years of existence seen four or five boys leave to try out their vocation in seminaries or with religious orders, but it was a matter for concern that not one of the girls had been equally generous. It is certain that prayers were offered up for the intention of vocations among the girls, and one member of the staff at least had asked Monsignor Taylor to take a benign interest in this matter. Some months later, the news reached the school that a former pupil had applied for admission to the Poor Clares. This news came as a great surprise, for no one on the staff had suspected the former pupil concerned of having thoughts of a religious vocation; but they did not know either that the girl had as her immediate superior in the office where she worked, one who had been Monsignor Taylor's confidential secretary for years. Nor was anyone aware either, until the young girl herself revealed the story recently, that the first time the thought of a religious vocation occurred to her was when, as a twelve-year-old, she listened to her form-mistress reading extracts from the

Autobiography of Saint Thérèse, the book which had been translated into English by Father Taylor sixty years earlier, at the
time when he was engrossed in furthering the cause set up for
the beatification of the French Carmelite nun. But St. Thérèse
relinquished her prior claim on a possible postulant to her own
order; instead, she led the girl slowly but certainly to the convent
of her namesake, Sister Marie Thérèse, Rev. Mother Abbess of
the Poor Clare Monastery, at Blantyre—a convent where Monsignor Taylor was always a welcome friend.

In the final reckoning, Almighty God in His Providence is the
arbiter of all human action; He uses divers agents and instruments for infusing His grace in receptive souls. Might it be
assumed that Monsignor Taylor, aligned with St. Thérèse, his
powerful advocate in heaven, played a decisive role in realising
God's plan in the soul of the young Poor Clare nun? Or must
the circumstances just related be attributed solely to chance or
coincidence?

It is easy to believe that Monsignor Taylor's interest in religious vocations is still going on, now that he is nearer to the
Source of all vocations. Father Byrne, Director of Vocations with
the Holy Ghost Fathers, believes this to be so, and at present he
is collecting information on this aspect of Monsignor's apostolate.

It seems a far stretch from contemplative nuns of strict observance to a Society of priests whose object is the conversion of
infidels in pagan lands. Monsignor Taylor had no difficulty in
bridging the gap between them. Both claimed him as a special
friend, while he held each of them in high esteem; all the more
so, since the Xaverian Missionary Fathers, like the Poor Clares,
were comparative newcomers to Lanarkshire, each having been
introduced shortly after the founding of the Diocese of Motherwell. At what stage Monsignor first interested himself in the St.
Francis Xavier Mission Society is not clearly known; but we
know that Monsignor himself had accepted Xavier's motto, " For
Jesus and Souls," as his own on 16th December, 1894. In the
course of the following year, the Society was founded at Parma,
Italy, but it was not until 1952 that the Xaverian Fathers introduced houses of training in Scotland. In view of the ardour and
zeal which Monsignor showed throughout his life for the apostolate of the Missions in distant lands, the remarks noted in his

diary on December 16th, 1894, and on December 17th, 1895, seem significant:

> December, 1894: " May God grant me grace of a holy life spent for His glory and for souls. Xavier's motto: ' Jésus et les âmes.' "
>
> December, 1895: " Oh, my God, make me a good, holy priest; make me persevere above all; . . . Father Many settled that my vocation lay in Scotland. *Fiat voluntas Tua.*"

The last entry, " Fiat voluntas tua," seems to suggest that the decision made by the Spiritual Director was not the one the seminarian himself had chosen; a " Deo gratias " might have been his prayer had Father Many's decision coincided with his own. In the circumstances—knowing of the student's admiration for the Apostle of the Indies—it may be safely assumed that the future parish priest of Carfin watched with interest the growth of the young Society, which was founded in 1895, to carry on among infidels the work commenced by St. Francis Xavier several centuries earlier. What Father Noara, S.X., former rector of the Xaverian Juniorate at Coatbridge, says about the welcome extended by Canon Taylor to the Xaverian Fathers when they first arrived in Scotland, will not come as a surprise to those who knew of Monsignor Taylor's missionary zeal; nor will Father Noara's vivid letter, written from his Mission in Sierra Leone, fail to rouse happy memories of the dear old Monsignor, who time and again emptied his pockets of the last half-penny in his ardent efforts to help priests and nuns in the Foreign Missions.

Catholic Mission—Tele.
Via Magburoka,
Sierra Leone, W. Africa.
7th October, 1966.

" Dear Miss McGhee,

Thank you for your letter and I am so grateful to you for having undertaken such a good and necessary work as to collect data on our great friend and saint—Monsignor Thomas Canon Taylor.

I am a bit busy, really, as I am trying to finish my new church and at the same time to do my work of looking after the schools and catechumens; but how could I refuse to say something at least of the many good things that Canon Taylor has done, and given to me for the last five years that I have been at Coatbridge.

I came to know Canon Taylor when I first went to Scotland in September, 1958. We, the Xaverians, were strangers in the country, getting introduced into the English language and English manners of life for the future Mission of Sierra Leone, which then was still a British Colony and Protectorate.

Canon Taylor extended his warm open friendship to us all, not only as priests, but especially as missionaries—people exclusively devoted to the Foreign Missions. And because of that and for the edification of his people, whom he wanted all missionary minded, on December 3rd (the feast of St. Francis Xavier), the Xaverians had to go to Carfin, for so many years for the annual renewal of their religious vows of poverty, chastity and obedience.

But only on my return to Scotland after six years of missionary work in Sierra Leone, had I the chance to become intimate with the lovable old Canon Taylor. Because of this friendship I would go to see him quite often, and he would complain earnestly if I let too long a spell of time elapse without seeing him. I would ask his prayers for our incipient Missionary Seminary at Coatbridge. I had a faith in Canon Taylor's prayers; his works and sufferings, his study, his talks, everything was completely dedicated to God, for the Foreign Missions, through Mary and the Little Flower.

And what about his money? His money again, all his money was Foreign Mission property. I loved to see Canon among his many Carfin children during the Sunday Mass. When not saying Mass, he was directing the prayers, and the expression 'Black Babies' would recur several times and the Our Father and Hail Mary's would go freely for their conversion—something natural, something Canon Taylor had taught the children to take for granted. At the end of the Mass, Canon would stand at the end of the benches, near the exit for the children, and there, holding an old basket, he would collect the pennies for the Black Babies; all the children knew the procedure very well; as they were leaving the benches, one by one, each dropping a penny into the big basket, they would bend their heads for Canon's blessing; 'God bless you,' he would say, and with the big hand would press their little heads down, and they emerged smiling, with total satisfaction for that fatherly affection.

He had a very original way of begging for the Foreign Missions; the originality of the plan lay in its simplicity. Persuasive simplicity.

He would hold both hands of a young visitor to the Grotto, often the first time of seeing him. 'Do you smoke?' he would ask.

'Yes, Canon.'

'And how many a day?'

'Some thirty or forty cigarettes, Canon.'

Quickly he would work it out in his mind and tell him: 'See how many in a month; see how much money in a year you are giving to Mr. Wills! Now, listen to me. For the sake of Saint Joseph, for the love of the Little Flower, cut it down, or better still, stop it altogether and give me the money for the Foreign Missions.'

Some of those visitors would, at the beginning, object to adopting such drastic measures and plead with the Canon that he would make it just a gradual thing for them; but, generally, he was not to make any concession; he was adamant. Without mentioning the name of the person concerned, he would give them a classical example of someone who, confident in the help of St. Teresa, from being a heavy smoker became suddenly and easily a complete abstainer. And as a result, the Canon explained for my understanding, the monthly dues for Mr. Wills were now transferred through Canon Taylor to the Foreign Missions.

My visits to him were always protracted ones, because he wanted to know the progress of our Missions and the individual missionaries that he knew. He wanted stories, stories from the Missions; he was never too tired to listen to them; he was like a child then, listening to something that surely interested him; he was at the same time trying to fix these stories in his memory so as to be able to retell them to his parishioners.

One knew that the visit was coming to an end, when he started his search in the drawers of the desk or in his pockets: 'So . . . I want to give £20 to Bishop Azzolini in Sierra Leone and £15 to my friend Father Fochesti in Japan.' By then he had cleared most of his pockets (of course only he knew the number and location of these pockets), and he had put several heaps of pound notes on his desk.

'Count them all now, and see if the £35 for my friends are there . . . Of course I must put something there for our Seminary in Coatbridge! Let me search again!'

This time it was the secret pockets; possibly money he had received for 'special intentions.' 'Here is other £22 for your Seminary. But now that not a penny is left in my pockets, and to-morrow is the end of the week, where shall I get the money to pay Tommy and the other men in the Grotto . . . ? Alright . . . Let Teresa of the Child Jesus and St. Joseph see to that.'

Several times I had Canon Taylor open our Garden Fete at the Seminary grounds, sure that he would attract more people than any show or film star; and so it was. At the end of his opening speech he would pull, still from his big pockets, a white bag full of silver coins.

'See,' he would say, showing the bag to the crowd, 'see what I have been able to save for Father here.' And with the feeling of creating a surprise, he would ask, 'Guess now, how much money is in the bag . . . ! There is at least as much as one of your grocery stores can give. There is £30 inside this bag, and I give it for the work, Father, here, is doing for the Foreign Missions. This is also to show how you people have to go and spend in this Garden Fete, because this money you are spending is money for the Foreign Missions and is money spent in the best way, as it is for the best cause.'

Everybody admired the Faith of this man of God, his tremendous Faith and continuous sense of prayer; his enthusiasm and zeal for the things of God; for the souls of the poor pagans; and for all that led to the increase of God's glory and the welfare of His children.

I have a lot of things to say about my great, deceased friend, Monsignor Thomas Canon Taylor, but I have a lot of things to do now, among them to finish my first church built in Sierra Leone, to be opened by Bishop Chalui on the feast of the Immaculate Conception, but I can promise you, Miss McGhee, for the affection that I treasure for the late Canon, I'll do so as soon as circumstances will allow me.

May God bless your work,

Yours in Domino,

(Sgd.) Fr. P. Noara, S.X."

The Helpers of the Holy Souls Convent at Newmains also has reason to recall Monsignor Taylor's fatherly interest. As we shall see elsewhere in this book, Monsignor's association with the Helpers goes back to the foundation of the Langside House in 1912, and perhaps even beyond that date, but in spite of valiant efforts made by the present Community, little relevant information can be obtained from the few aged Sisters surviving the time of Rev. Mother St. Edith, the founding Mother Superior. Evidence does exist of the connection between Langside and Carfin after the opening of the Grotto, and of the pilgrimages organised for the Union of Catholic Mothers by Mother Juliet, H.H.S., at Langside, during the 'twenties and 'thirties. More recent in memory is the opening of the Newmains House of the Helpers of the Holy Souls, and it was here that Rev. Mother Mary Joseph, H.H.S., gleaned some comments from a few of the Sisters who had known Monsignor Taylor for a number of years. One nun writes:

" All I had heard about Carfin prejudiced me against it to the extent that I refused to go when a first opportunity was offered me to visit the Grotto. But I eventually went with a group of people from Glasgow, and my views were completely changed at once. I became as enthusiastic of the Shrine as I had been opposed to it before.

There was an amazing atmosphere of the supernatural in this spot, attributed not only to Our Lady of Lourdes, St. Bernadette and the Little Flower, but also to Monsignor Taylor himself. He was the heart of life at Carfin. Some, better qualified to do so than I am, will certainly speak of his daily occupations, among which prayer held a prominent place; he had the gift to make others pray too; he knew how to make them fall on their knees.

All the Saints in Heaven were his friends, and he gave the impression that he was actually in their company; but among them none was dearer to him than the Saint of Lisieux, whose precious relic he always carried with him. With it he performed many wonderful cures, not only to bodies, but to souls. Most of these were the secret of the favoured ones who received them, but in spite of this fact, very long would be the list of the known facts which took place during the many years when Monsignor Taylor was the parish priest of St. Francis Xavier's.

For me, personally, Carfin remains in my memory as a spot blessed by God, a spot which God chose as a special meeting-place, between Himself and those of His creatures in need of graces; a spot where Heaven seemed nearer and where prayer could not fail to be heard; a place where the Mercy of God was shown to the eyes of all, indeed where sight was restored to many a blind soul.

I would like to say more, much more, but time is short. I conclude by an earnest wish that the *Annales de Lisieux* will dedicate to him another number, as I did find that the article written on him last year was far too short for what could be said on his devotion to St. Thérèse Martin."

Other Sisters from Newmains remarked on Monsignor Taylor's amazing vitality and how, even at an advanced age, he wandered through the Grotto grounds exposed to the rigours of a Carfin winter, without the protection of extra clothing. Time, they said, did not count when a soul needed help; his labour was a work of joy. The Sisters add that from time to time Monsignor very generously gave donations to them for their Missions. When Sisters returned from Foreign Missions, they made a point of visiting him to report on their work in the Mission fields.

Other religious orders in Lanarkshire, as well as the Xaverians and the Helpers of the Holy Souls benefited from his enthusiasm and missionary zeal. Missionary Fathers are a moving population; to-day at home and to-morrow in the jungles of Africa. Superiors of houses are usually men of experience and of years: many have died, and those surviving who knew Monsignor Taylor have moved to other houses throughout the country and are not easily accessible: it is thus with the Fathers of the Holy Ghost and equally true of those orders who concentrate on parochial work and the spiritual needs of the diocese—the Capuchins at Greyfriars, Uddingston; and the Vincentians at St. Mary's, Lanark. The Jesuit Fathers at Craighead and Glasgow fall into a slightly different category: Monsignor Taylor was an illustrious former pupil, and they watched his progress with benign interest.* For many years he chose his confessor from their ranks, Father Montgomery, S.J., being the one who ministered to his spiritual needs during the final years.

Neither the boundaries of a parish, nor the frontiers of a diocese or country, ever proved a restraining influence on Monsignor Taylor's spiritual and beneficent activities. The whole world was his field of activity and no call for help went unheeded; if he could not send the temporal help, direly and constantly needed by the mission fields, Monsignor could and did help spiritually; and when he prayed for a special intention so also did his parishioners at Carfin, as did too the Congregations of religious who were united with him and his intentions by the strong bonds of prayer.

From the large number of religious communities scattered outwith and within Britain, and with which Monsignor was associated in the twentieth century, perhaps no religious house, either for men or for women, in its entirety commanded his love and esteem as did those houses of the Congregation of the Good Shepherd attached to the Provincial House at Bangalore in India. Even before ordination, Monsignor was already acquainted with the Good Shepherd Sisters, and certainly before he came to St. Francis Xavier's parish at Carfin, he had been responsible for directing two girls to the mission fields in India. Since that time, as shown by the following record provided by Sister Mary Emmanuel, R.G.S., one-time teacher at St. Francis Xavier's school, Carfin, and perhaps one of Monsignor's most loyal friends, a steady stream of girls have offered their young lives to their Master for service with the Good Shepherd Congregation in India.

Name, Parish, etc.	*Contact with Mgr. Taylor*
1. Sister Mary of the Heart of Mary (R.I.P. 1932), Margaret Brannan, Glasgow (parish unknown). Arrived India 2/8/1908.	Direct contact, Good Shepherd Convent, Dalbeth.
2. Sister Mary St. Veronica, Margaret Ingram, Buckie, Scotland. Arrived India 22/9/1914.	Direct contact; lived with aunt who was housekeeper, St. Peter's, Bearsden.
3. Sister Mary St. Angela (R.I.P. 1959), Margaret Moore, Rathfriland, Ireland. Arrived India 5/1/1917.	Direct contact. Pupil teacher in Good Shepherd Convent, Dalbeth.

* Rev. J. Tracy, S.J., took considerable trouble in his search for information on Mgr. Taylor's academic progress while a pupil at the College. Mr. James Taylor's personal diary supplemented the information provided by Father Tracy.

Name, Parish, etc.	Contact with Mgr. Taylor
4. Sister Mary Emmanuel, Rose A. Allen, St. Ignatius', Wishaw. Arrived India 12/4/1919.	Direct contact. Staff of St. Francis Xavier's School, Carfin.
5. Sister Mary St. Raphael, Margaret Gormley, St. Mary's, Hamilton. Arrived India 13/8/1921.	Indirect contact through Mgr. Taylor's friend, Fr. Conway, Hamilton.
6. Sister Mary St. Felicitas, Rose Steele, Holy Family, Mossend. Arrived India 23/12/1923.	Direct contact.
7. Sister Mary St. Bernadette, Jane Kane, St. Mary's, Hamilton. Arrived India 23/12/1923.	Direct contact.
8. Sister Mary St. Andrew, Catherine Corns, St. Anne's, Cadzow. Arrived India 13/12/1924.	Direct contact.
9. Sister Mary St. Thomas, Margaret Carroll, St. Mary's, Larkhall. Arrived India 13/12/1924.	Direct contact.
10. Sister Mary of St. Margaret Mary, Margaret McCall, St. Mary's, Hamilton. Arrived India 17/9/1925.	Direct contact.
11. Sister Mary of the Rosary, Possilpark, Glasgow. Arrived India 10/9/1927.	Direct contact through the Grotto and mutual friends.
12. Sister Mary Rose Virginie, Bridget Grimes, St. Ignatius, Wishaw. Arrived India 10/9/1927.	Direct contact.
13. Sister Mary of the Passion, Helen McKenna, Our Lady of Good Aid, Motherwell. Arrived India 3/12/1932.	Direct contact.
14. Sister Mary of Our Lady of Mount Carmel, Mary Downey, St. John the Baptist, Uddingston. Arrived India 3/12/1932.	Indirect contact.
15. Sister Mary St. James, Mary Kilpatrick, Our Lady of Good Aid, Motherwell. Arrived India 14/4/1939.	Indirect—worked with Monsignor on Holy Childhood. Father friend of Monsignor.
16. Sister Mary of Good Counsel, Clemma Kilpatrick, Our Lady of Good Aid, Motherwell. Arrived India 26/6/1945.	Indirect. Father friend of Monsignor.

Name, Parish, etc.	*Contact with Mgr. Taylor*
17. Sister Mary Dolores, Margaret McShane, St. Francis Xavier's, Carfin. Arrived India 26/10/1945.	Direct contact. Parishioner.
18. Sister Mary St. Alphonsus, Matilda Kearney, St. Francis Xavier's, Carfin. Arrived India 6/11/1946.	Direct contact. Parishioner.
19. Sister Mary St. Catherine Labouré, Agnes McKeown, St. Augustine's, Coatbridge. Arrived India 26/8/1958.	Indirect—but knew Monsignor through Grotto.

But this list does not name all the girls Monsignor directed to the Good Shepherd Congregation. Other two girls were sent to the Mother House at Angers to serve their novitiate prior to sailing to India, but war, with its dire consequences, affected the lives of aliens in France. The health of these two young girls was undermined by the rigours of internment, and as a result one, a girl from the parish, was sent home because of ill-health; after the war she sought admission to the Convent of the Daughters of Mary, Help of Christians, at Hastings, where she is now a professed nun. Her friend in exile, Sister Mary of St. Theresa, R.G.S., although not a parishioner of St. Francis Xavier's, Carfin, was the daughter of James Roche, one of Monsignor Taylor's most reliable volunteer workers in the Grotto. During 1941, Sister Mary of St. Theresa fell ill at Angers, and having made her final vows as a Religious of the Good Shepherd, she succumbed to her illness without ever having gone to India, where she had longed with all the ardent enthusiasm of her young heart to go. The Centenary list records that still another girl from the parish, Sister Mary of St. Aelred (Norah McGowan), entered the ranks of the Good Shepherd at Liverpool, where after twenty-five years of dutiful service as a Religious, she died several years ago.

Correspondence refers to others, too—Religious of the Good Shepherd—whom he had counselled in the years before he had come to Carfin.

A card, dated July 1913 and signed by Sister Mary of St. Ignatius, R.G.S., East Finchley, relates that Father Taylor's " two Dumbarton postulants are going on very nicely and hope to be clothed in August."

A letter, undated and obviously quite old, refers to Father Taylor's association with the Good Shepherd Convent at Dalbeth in the years before the First World War.

Staplehurst,
Kent.

" Dear Rev. Father,

As it is forty years on Our Lady's Birthday since I left home, I beg you to remember me in your prayers and Holy Mass on that great day . . .

I found St. Thérèse a good friend to me, and I often read your last letter of 1914 . . . I have happy memories of going up to Bearsden to see you and then going on to Dalbeth . . .

From your grateful child in Our Lord,

(Sgd.) Sr. Mary of St. Odelia, R.G.S."

Another letter, this time from the Good Shepherd Convent at Ford, Liverpool, also makes reference to Dalbeth:

21/2/39.

" Very Rev. and dear Father,

It was a very special pleasure to have the good wishes for my Jubilee from such a *very* old friend as you are. I am sure you remember as I do, the old days at Dalbeth and the familiar faces of Sister Mary of the Immaculate Heart and Sister M. of St. Francis Assisi. May they rest in peace! These were very happy days, simple days; times have changed greatly since then.

Thank you very much, Father, for your good wishes and above all for the remembrance in the novena of Masses.

I am most grateful . . .

(Sgd.) Sr. M. of St. Ignatius, R.G.S."

From Colinton, Edinburgh, come further memories, but not through correspondence. Sister Mary Francis, R.G.S.,* shortly before her death, recalled her friendship with Monsignor Taylor, a friendship which stretched further back than she would dare to admit. She, and Sister Mary Antony who died a number of years earlier, had known Father Taylor well and had revered him for his priestly sanctity. On one occasion, about twelve to fifteen years before the interview with the present writer took place, when Sister Mary Francis, already well on in years, was ill, word was sent to Monsignor Taylor at Carfin. He himself was confined to bed with a heavy cold at the time, but nothing daunted, he insisted on hiring a taxi and travelling the thirty miles to Edinburgh to visit and bless his ailing friend. It was a fine tribute to Monsignor's memory that Sister Mary Francis left the seclusion of her own room to speak with one whose only claim to such a

---

* Sr. Mary Francis was a witness at the exhumation of the remains of Margaret Sinclair, Servant of God.

privilege was that she too could claim a small measure of Monsignor's friendship.

Esteemed and loved as were these life-long friends from the early days at Dalbeth, perhaps no community of nuns anywhere in the world commanded the special and personal friendship and love Monsignor Taylor had for the " colony " of Scottish Sisters attached to the Provincial House of the Good Shepherd Congregation at Bangalore. These " Indian Scotties " as they call themselves were very specially his spiritual daughters and were (and are) fulfilling their vocations in India either directly, or indirectly, because of Monsignor Taylor's aspirations to recruit harvesters for the vineyards where the labourers were all too few.

Of the three girls he sent to Bangalore before the outbreak of World War I, only Sister Mary of Saint Veronica (Margaret— " Daisy "—Ingram) remains; her two friends from Dalbeth days have already joined their Master in the True Fold. The senior member of the " Colony " from Lanarkshire, Sister Mary Emmanuel, last year celebrated the golden jubilee of her profession as a Religious of the Good Shepherd at the Provincial House, and it seems appropriate that the written account so lovingly composed by her in memory of her dear spiritual Father should be included here. She was one of Monsignor's closest confidants and when Monsignor wrote to her, he knew that all the plans and hopes that he confided in her would have the support and backing of the entire Community of Sisters and children in all the convents under the care of the Provincial House of the Good Shepherd at Bangalore:

Sister Emmanuel wrote as follows:

23rd Oct. 1965.

" Mgr. Taylor's connection with the Good Shepherd Convent in India is a long tale which started in 1908 with the first recruit he sent out from Scotland. It is a tale of fatherly guidance, prayer and kindness; one that has been a spur and uplift, a support and encouragement down the hot, dusty and exile years for a batch of Scots whom he always referred to as ' mes chères filles.' In all, twenty Sisters of the different convents of the Good Shepherd in India have known and loved him, and in most cases he gave direction to their vocations. I have always felt that my *missionary* vocation came from his enthusiasm, although it is only fair to say that he never suggested it, for at that time both he and I expected that I would enter a teaching order at home. It was during the war years of the First World War that I came into contact with his endeavours for the Holy Childhood Society, and gradually my vocation became orientated to the East where he had already sent three Sisters, two of whom preceded him to heaven and the third is still in ' battle array.'

I left Britain in the first vessel available for civilians after the Armistice of 1918. It was early March 1919, and the Mediterranean was still dangerous going, due to sunken vessels in the region of Port Said, and floating mines. Through the years since, Sisters have followed in twos and threes—each departure being a triumph for his missionary heart. In some cases he financed the journey himself. He once told me that, as a young professor in St. Peter's Seminary at Bearsden, he had asked his Archbishop to allow him to volunteer for the foreign missions. I can still see his characteristic smile—half-laugh, half-smile—as he narrated the result: ' Go on with your work here; that is your mission.' He said that he had then settled with Our Lord that he was a foreign missionary, and would work on the Missions through the Sisters he had directed to India, his mission-field.

At this time one of the sorrows of his apostolate was the lack of vocations among the poor of his own parish of Carfin. The future proved the efficacy of his prayers for this intention. How joyfully he wrote later of the priests and nuns from Carfin who left home to join Religious Orders.

Already, with his courageous parishioners, he was at work on the Grotto—the first Grotto of 1922, before it was extended, and before he had planned the wide horizons for the venture even then forming in his fertile brain. Already he envisaged it as a rendezvous of worship and prayer, a social focus for the Church in Scotland and beyond. It was in 1937 that he wrote jubilantly that his ' little Margaret ' (Sr. M. Dolores McShane) had been netted for God; and that two years later she was followed by Matilda Kearney (Sr. M. of St. Alphonsus). He was always very proud of the two Carfin parishioners who reached India after the terrible experiences of the Second World War.

Monsignor's correspondence with Bangalore covers a period of fifty-five years, and with me personally forty-four years. It has been his delight down the years to send a collective letter which went the rounds of our convents, which are really hundreds of miles distant. None have survived the perusal. Very often he sent sums of money which were to be divided among his Sisters, so that each would have some special desire fulfilled. These fractional sums gave great joy, and some ' canny ' Scots had spent the amount many times over in anticipated purchases before the deal was accomplished. The money went in such multifarious ' riches ' as bath-tubs, water cauldrons, kettles, rice bowls and bright flowered material for frocks.

Under his inspiration and presidency, came into being the wonderful ' Friends of Bangalore ': the group earned our prayerful gratitude for its heroic kindness to the Good Shepherd nuns in

India—money gifts marking the silver jubilees and hailing the temporary homecoming of Sisters, gifts that gave inspiration and appreciation for the generous sacrifice behind them.

Monsignor's letters were usually reports of the wonderful enthusiasm of Scotland in its mounting achievement for the Propagation of the Faith and the Holy Childhood Society, and the growing proportions and popularity of the Grotto, as shrine succeeded shrine in artistic statuary, and its infancy took shape in a wild dream come true; also of the dark days of opposition and cold-shouldering, though he was always ready to see the silver lining of God's plan. Visits of prelates of the Church were to him the seal of God's approval. The culmination of his joy was reached in the visit of Cardinal Tien in 1962. He had written of this impending visit, and it was a proud, happy, ageing, little Monsignor who reported to me that the distinguished visitor had come, and in sheer triumph he confided also that the Cardinal had said that he came to visit *his friend,* Monsignor Taylor—they both had missionary hearts.*

Here is a postcard from Rome, sent by him in 1950—the sole survivor except for pictures with his greeting and signature; he always signed ' *Father* Taylor ' in writing to his ' daughters ' in India. It put him in the right relationship. This postcard was followed by another a few days later, from Rome, describing an audience with the Pope. This audience seemed to have meant much to him. I remember his words well. ' To-day I had the intense happiness of seeing—in the words of St. Catherine—" the sweet Christ." The Holy Father pressed my head between his hands, what joy!' Visits to Lourdes always brought us well packed-in postcards, testifying to his intimacy with his Queen, and especially in the joy of his Golden Jubilee Mass there. We never felt forgotten. He was ever ready to share his joys with us.

Of course one cannot think of Monsignor Taylor apart from his ' little friend ' or ' her,' as he familiarly referred to St. Thérèse of Lisieux. Annually, he wrote from Lisieux when he went there for his retreat, sending little souvenirs for all from ' votre petite soeur.' He spoke of settling things with her as one would speak with the assurance of the co-operation of one's own sister.

I do not know whether or not he inaugurated the Blessed Sacrament procession at Carfin, but in 1916 he directed one inside the school grounds. It was looked forward to with great enthusiasm and fervent preparation. The weather had been wet, very wet for weeks, and normally one could have little hope for a change. It was so unpromising that even his most ardent supporters had abandoned hope, but no one dared voice this to him. He was sure of his tactics. He had ' settled it with *her.'* The

---

* Cardinal Tien died within two years from when the letter was written.

morning of the great day was dry, but gray and threatening, yet
Monsignor set everyone bustling, assuring them that the sun was
just behind the clouds—some wiseacres, taking care to be well
beyond his earshot, questioned 'How far behind?' About mid-
day, like a flare, the sun shot into view and enthusiasm became
infectious, and the wiseacres came in for more than their share of
teasing. The evening was beautiful and the procession a great
success. When all was over and everyone was congratulating
himself and everyone else on the marvellous weather, Monsignor,
who was transported with joy, said, 'Yes, yes, but next year I
shall settle with *her* for *two* days; it is too rushed to have everything prepared in one day.' He had no misgivings as to the
answer.

He was immersed in the joy of the canonisation of St. Thérèse
—seeming almost to lose his identity in the triumph. It was the
end of a long labour of love; he had introduced the cult of the
Little Flower to the English-speaking public, and despite the
adverse criticism of some, he never wavered. Quite late in his
declining years he, with failing eyesight, took up the task of
translating from photostat copies, the passages in the original
Autobiography written by the Saint and deleted by Mother Agnes.
It was his intention to revise his translation of the Autobiography
and insert the deleted parts. I think God did not give him this
satisfaction.

Monsignor had given me a precious relic of St. Thérèse which
had been given to him by Pauline (Mother Agnes). A French
missionary, later Bishop of Mysore, begged the Superior of our
convent to lend him this relic for a year as he was trying to open
a new Mission centre in an area outstandingly pagan, where
the Hindus were not very approachable. He set up a shrine of the
Little Flower there in 1928 where the Catholics could come for
prayer and instruction. The result was a phenomenal appeal to
the non-Christians and in a year's time a small Mass centre was
built, and soon a church dedicated to St. Thérèse was opened and
a shrine to the Saint built. The relic is on perpetual loan. This
church of St. Thérèse is at Robertsonpet (called after the donor
of a space of waste land). It now has 3,824 Christians and serves
two outlying Mass centres at Chinsarahalli and Susaipalya in
Mysore State.

The highlight of a holiday back to Europe for the Superior and
Sisters of our convents in India was a visit to the Grotto and to
Monsignor Taylor. It was a permission always given by Mother
General in France as a *sine qua non* of a holiday in Scotland, and
it was the one most enjoyed. These visits added many devotees
to his list. I had that happiness in 1956. How he insisted on a
cold, blustery wet day, to do the honours of the Grotto himself—
even to insisting that Emmanuel (Sr. Mary Emmanuel) and he
should sing a joint Christmas carol to King Emmanuel in the

Bethlehem cave (it was August). I do not take any pride in the harmony, but he was delighted. I was in admiration of the magnitude and beauty of the statuary. His artistic taste was reliable.

In 1958, when darkness was closing in upon Monsignor, he wrote with a very shaky, groping hand, a word of greeting on the back of twenty pictures for the Sisters in India. We each have this souvenir of a wonderful Father whose prayers must have tided us over many hard days. What difficulty the task must have been can be guessed by the almost indecipherable writing. He wrote little after that himself, but a kind hand took down his dictated letters. In 1962, he autographed the Centenary booklet for us. In the letter accompanying it, written by a friend, he said : ' In my Masses and Rosaries, my Indian " Scotties " are warmly remembered. I send a God's blessing across the ocean.' He sent us with a chuckle which we almost heard here, the wonderful epithalamium* of Dr. P. McGlynn that we might share the joy.

After that it was a record of breaking-down which we knew was the slow dawn of his eternal country. His memory is a cherished light in the hearts of his Indian Scotties.

(Sgd.) Sr. M. Emmanuel, R.G.S."

Nuns travel lightly and store not the treasures of this earth. All the more welcome then is a little card yellowed with age, and some letters which have survived, a few of them for more than half-a-century, since they were written in November 1914. Sister Mary of St. Veronica, the longest serving " Indian Scottie " now at the convent of the Good Shepherd at Bellary, and to whom the letters were sent by Father Taylor, has with great kindness granted permission to have the letters reproduced here in Monsignor Taylor's memory.

4 - XI - '14.

" Dear Sister Margaret,

It was a relief to learn that you reached Bangalore and that the ' dove ' is safe ' in the clefts of the rock.'

Ah! 'Let Thy Face shine upon me, and Thy Voice sound in mine ear—for Thy Face it is fair, and Thy Voice it is sweet.' You are already all His, dear child, and His for all the days that are to come. ' Who shall separate us from the love of Christ?' Who indeed?

St. Agnes was not so old as you are, when she gave herself to her Lord; Thérèse was but fourteen when she asked that favour of Pope Leo. How many other young hearts have surrendered themselves fully to the one Heart that is worth loving, the one Heart that can repay.

---

* Dr. McGlynn composed poems in honour of Monsignor's birthdays, and for other special occasions.

God is an abyss. Do not climb painfully down the precipice. Cast yourself headlong! Trust in Him even as Thérèse trusted. 'As you trust in Him,' she writes, 'so shall you receive: such is His unbounded mercy.'

Remember that prayer is the key to His Treasury, and use it, not a dozen but a thousand times daily. Go into the chapel of your heart: there is a Real Presence there—not of Jesus alone, but of Father, Son and Holy Ghost: worship there frequently— say a *Deo Gratias*, a *Domine non sum digna*, a *Veni Domine Jesu* and a *Gloria Patri*. Beg of him for a great, a very great love of Holy Rule, in other words, of His Will: for a love of His Mother and Saints; for a passionate love of Himself—a love that will never cool.

May the Holy Child grant you a happy Christmas, and may He make it very bright for the dear ones at home. I shall not forget you at the altar *that* day.

In J., M., J. and Th.,

T. N. T."

At Christmastide, 1920, Father Taylor wrote as follows to Sr. M. of St. Veronica:

St. Francis Xavier's,
Carfin,
Motherwell.
21 - 12 - '20.

" My dear child in Jesus Christ,

Christmas will be over, but its graces and aroma last far beyond the lovely feast. You tell me the Divine Lover is feeding you with dry food and that the St. John's days are over. But did you go in quest of Him up the sides of Thabor or up the hill of Calvary? Do you wish to spend your days with St. John gazing enraptured on that Face of ecstatic beauty, or with St. John wondering at the adorable Countenance from which all human beauty had totally disappeared, the Face of the Leper upon Golgotha? Do you wish to journey Homewards in comfort and ease, whereas the Master warned all who seek His company that they must shoulder the daily burden of the galling Cross and so bear Him company to the end? Did He say that the easy-going will enter the Kingdom, or that it suffereth violence and the violent will carry it away?

Say *Deo gratias* one hundred times in thanks for this precious cross, the pledge of His high love for His unworthy bride. Now more than ever you must cling fast to Him—you must trust Him —you must be loyal and true to His least little laws.

Remember that you may merit more in one day of desolation than in a month of ecstasy. Think of Soeur Thérèse and her dark

tunnel. In one minute Jesus can do the work of a hundred years.
What beyond doubt most hurts Him—in one sense more even
than grievous sin—is want of confidence. Never dare to doubt
His love, His swiftness to pardon, His divine patience. 'Jesus
loves most, not those to whom He gives much, but those of whom
He asks much.' He is asking now from His Queen, and will repay
a thousand-fold. Be brave, staunch and generous!

Continue to pray for me as I do for the four little shepherdesses
of Bangalore.*

In haste,

Affectionately yours in Christ,

T. N. Taylor."

When the last war ended, hopes ran high among the
" Indian Scotties " that their spiritual Father would travel to
India to visit them. Tentative enquiries were made about book-
ings and sailings, but the plan came to naught. Money was
without doubt an obstacle, for Monsignor rarely had much in
reserve—all spare cash went to charity. What required more
serious consideration was the time element. A visit to India
would entail an extended tour of the sub-continent, for the
" Indian Scotties " were well scattered, and the decision to be
absent from his own parish and from the Grotto was not one to
be made lightly, even if the approval of his superiors was granted.
Much to the disappointment of all the religious communities in
India, another of Monsignor's pipe dreams was never realised.

It goes without saying that the majority of priests and nuns
doing Mission work will have a strong devotion to the Little
Flower, the patroness of the Missions. It may be stated further
that from Monsignor Taylor's friends, St. Thérèse has every
right to claim a special affection. This was certainly so, in the
opinion of one solitary " Sassenach " Sister at Bangalore, who
found herself resisting the traditional overtures from north of the
Border. She had tried hard to rouse in her own heart the affection the " Indian Scotties " had for the Little Flower, but the
spark semed to be lacking. Christian charity she had in plenty
and when the Scottish Sisters asked her to mount pictures of
St. Thérèse for private devotion in their cells, she had no hesitation in doing so, especially as she was gifted in this type of
artistic work. After Monsignor Taylor's death in 1963, obituary
cards bearing Monsignor's photograph were sent to Bangalore
for distribution among his friends. Poor Sister found herself

---

* The four shepherdesses were the first four of the " Indian Scotties " at Bangalore.
Of these four, only Sr. M. St. Veronica and Sr. M. Emmanuel are alive to-day,
April, 1972.

starting once more to mount pictures, this time of Monsignor Taylor himself. At this stage she felt she could no longer resist the attack from north of the Border, and forthwith she decided to accept the dictum, " If you can't beat them, join them." Now she, too, treasures two little pictures, one of St. Thérèse and one of Monsignor Taylor.

Referring to the strong affection Monsignor Taylor had for the Good Shepherd Sisters of Bangalore Province, Mother Provincial, addressing the " Friends of Bangalore " assembled to meet her at Bishopton, spoke in generous terms of Monsignor's work on their behalf. She ended her address in words like these, " Pray to him that he will continue in Heaven to exercise his influence on behalf of the Good Shepherd Congregation in India, and that he will send girls from Scotland who will be worthy successors to those who have gone before them." This indeed was a splendid tribute from an Irish Mother Provincial, not only to Monsignor Taylor, but to the good Sisters who labour under her in the vineyard of the Lord.

To conclude the story of the " Indian Scotties," perhaps Sr. M. Emmanuel, the one whom Monsignor Taylor referred to as " my girl," will forgive the liberty of printing the following extract from a letter written by her on August 20th, 1919. It should give her joy to know that her " dear Father " had kept her letter for all those years until his death :

Convent of the Good Shepherd,
Bangalore.
August 20th, 1919.

" My dear Father,

You ought really to treasure this letter as it is the last will and testament of Sister Rose.

This last-named hopes to finish her existence on the morning of September 14th, when the Bishop has promised to give her ' remains ' the holy habit of religion. His Lordship has granted the dispensation of avoiding another long month of weary waiting; so at the end of the 5th month she hopes to be clothed.

When Sister X, who begins life on that day, writes, she will describe the sentiments of the deceased Sister Rose.

I have visions of a *De Profundis* at Carfin. Please do not, but echo instead an *Alleluia*.

Respectfully yours, my dear Father,
The ' growing-feeble ' Sister Rose."

While giving the funeral panegyric on the death of a clerical friend in 1923, Father Taylor used these words, " The secret of

successs at home and abroad is the missionary spirit." Humility
kept him from knowing how appropriate these words were to
his own life. Without his stepping a foot on the soil of Mission
lands, before his death in 1963, Monsignor Taylor's name was
known thoughout the Mission lands of Africa and Xavier's
India, and even further afield in distant China, as well as in the
South Pacific Islands.

In 1911, Father Fraser, a Scots-Canadian priest, one of the two
English-speaking priests then on the Chinese Mission, visited St.
Peter's College with the intention of recruiting volunteers from
among the students for service on Missions in the Far East.
Father Fraser's description of the dire need in China for English-
speaking priests fired the enthusiasm of a number of students
and staff. As one might expect, Father Taylor was in the vanguard of enthusiasts. One of the students, Andrew McArdle,
transferred to Maynooth College in Ireland, and after ordination
went to the Mission of Hu-Chow in China. In the Sept.-Oct. 1920
issue of *The Annals of the Society of the Holy Childhood,* Father
Taylor, its editor, writes, " The zeal of St. Stephen consumes his
children by the Clydeside. £20 comes from old friends in St.
Saviour's, Govan (from A.P.F. Circles), and again from the
Academy lads at Townhead, Glasgow, where—as elsewhere—
the Marists keep the missionary flag flying. Who, I wonder, will
be next to follow their old pupil, Father McArdle, out to
China?"

The question was answered within a year or two when Father
James Conway, curate at St. Mary's, Hamilton, and close friend
of Father Taylor, sailed to China to join Father McArdle there.
Even before this, we read in the *Catholic Parish Magazine* (Aug.
1918), that the conscience of Scotland was beginning to react
slowly to the urgent needs of Missions in the East: The " Father
McArdle Farthing Fund," if not snowballing, was growing per-
ceptibly. In August 1918, the total already acknowledged,
198,375 farthings, was increased by 11,468. One generous donor,
" S.J.H.", contributed 3,024 of this latter sum; Father Taylor of
Carfin, 740; Father Murphy of Carfin, 240; the latter's mother,
480; and St. Laurence's Boys' School, Greenock, 1,000 (per Mr.
McCurdy, successor to Mr. James Taylor, ex-Headmaster). The
amount contributed to the China Fund in 1918—about £13—
seems shamefully low, but it would have been lower still if Father
Taylor and his friends had not raised it by more than 25 per cent
of the total.

There is a dearth of written evidence of Father Taylor's personal and private financial help to Foreign Mission countries in

the years between the wars; this was the time when he was heavily engrossed in furthering the love of our Blessed Mother in Scotland, through devotion to her at the Lourdes Shrine at Carfin. This, too, was the time when devotees of St. Thérèse clamoured for his attention. Perhaps this, also, was the time when his hand went most generously to his capacious pockets to help the missionary priests and nuns who thronged to Carfin to seek the help of their Blessed Mother and of the Patroness of the Missions, in the titular parish of the patron of all Missions, the Jesuit pioneer of the East, St. Francis Xavier. Personal gifts elicit immediate gratitude, but not always a written receipt: nor was Monsignor Taylor actively interested in keeping a record of his disbursements in the causes of charity. For these and other reasons, written records are not easily available to the writer of these lines. However, memories in the village of Carfin are long and easily recall the constant flow of petitions soaring to Heaven from parishioners and pilgrims on behalf of our hard pressed missionary workers overseas. Prayers for China, as well as Russia, were constantly on Monsignor's lips. For over forty years the heathen children were prayed for during the thanksgiving prayers after Communion; when the Communist Party began to spread its tentacles, there was added the ejaculation, " Saviour of the World, save Russia."

Although much of the work done by Monsignor Taylor in a private capacity to help missionary work in the Far East has gone unrecorded, evidence does exist of the continual help he gave to the late Thomas Cardinal Tien, S.V.D., former Archbishop of Peking. In 1965, the near-blind and ailing Cardinal, through his personal secretary, Rev. Bartley F. Schmitz, S.V.D., wrote as follows:

Archdiocese of Taipei,
Office of the Cardinal,
1—188-1 Hoping E. Road,
Taipei, Taiwan.

Oct. 20th, 1965.

" Dear Miss McGhee,

His Eminence told me that his relationship with Canon Taylor dates back to the year in which he became Archbishop of Peking (April 1946). Monsignor Taylor sent him regular annual donations going as high as £600. He missed one year, and wrote that he could not find His Eminence's address and, therefore, sent his donation elsewhere.

His Eminence was very pleased to be able to visit Canon Taylor in Carfin in 1962 and, if I may add a personal note, I was impressed by the great amount of work accomplished in building the Shrine of St. Thérèse.

Assuring you of my prayers and the blessing of His Eminence on your work.

I am,

Sincerely yours in Christ,

(Sgd.) (Rev.) Bartley F. Schmitz, S.V.D.,

Secretary to Cardinal Tien.

In further letters written to the writer on January and February 1966, Father Schmitz provides this information:

" His Eminence . . . took possession of his See in 1947, but if I remember correctly, by 1949 he was already expelled from Peking . . .

I asked His Eminence personally whether he actually received a true relic of the Holy Cross from the Canon when we visited Carfin in 1962. His Eminence assured me that he did receive the relic, and only this relic of the true Cross, no other.*

His Eminence also stated that the relic is now in Holy Family Church, 50 Hisn Sheng S. Rd., 2nd Section, Taipei, which is in charge of the Canadian Jesuits.

Assuring you once more of our interest and asking prayers for our many intentions.

I remain, very sincerely yours,

(Sgd.) Bartley Schmitz, S.V.D.,

(Secy.)

A letter written by Cardinal Tien in January 1959, shows how His Eminence appreciated Monsignor's help to the Chinese Mission over the years.

Very Rev. Canon T. Taylor,
St. Francis Xavier's,
Motherwell, Carfin.

" Dear Friend,

I am taking the opportunity presented by Father O'Toole's return to England to send you a small token of my deep appreciation for all your kindness of the past years. Under separate cover you will receive a coloured reproduction of ' Our Lady of China,' by Mr. Lee Hung-nien, and a Chinese embroidery on silk.

---

* The Press at the time reported that His Eminence Cardinal Tien had received several relics from Monsignor Taylor.

Perhaps you would be interested in a further description of the painting by Lee Hung-nien, who was a student at our S.V.D. Catholic University of Peking. Our Blessed Mother is represented in the garb of a priestess of the T'ang Dynasty, who began to rule about the year 618 A.D. This is especially evidenced in the stole which she wears. Mr. Lee is particularly noted for his excellent representations of veils . . . when you see the picture you will understand why.

In her arms, Our Lady is carrying the Infant Christ, who is wearing a red jacket and rabbit-fur slippers—both symbolic of royalty in China. Our Lady is standing on clouds which shape themselves remotely into dragon tails, which is another indication of royalty. Two doves are pictured about Our Blessed Mother's head; the one holding the red rose of suffering, the other the white lily of purity—thereby very beautifully epitomising the lives of Jesus and Mary. It is also interesting to note that Mr. Lee painted most of the Madonna while yet a pagan. In fact, Christian Art was the cause of his conversion to the Catholic Faith.

Forgive me for going into such length over such a small trifle; but I thought you may be interested in knowing these facts. About the silk embroidery, I can say little since it came to me quite by accident.

Except for my eyes, my health is very good. I pray for you frequently and beg a remembrance in your prayers for myself and the persecuted of China.

Yours very sincerely,

(Sgd.) ✠ Th. Card. Tien, S.V.D.

Until his death, " Our Lady of China " hung in Monsignor's bedroom, and although deeply appreciative of Cardinal Tien's kind thought in sending it to him, it is doubtful if it was other than in his mind's eye that he could picture the delicate workmanship of the Chinese artist who had painted the Madonna.

Cardinal Tien's visit to his friend at Carfin was a tribute to Monsignor's assistance to the Chinese Mission for over a quarter of a century. The visit, on Monsignor Taylor's request, was kept informal but nevertheless a sizable number of people turned out to see the old friends greet each other, both prelates almost blind and Cardinal Tien partially paralysed in the right arm. It is not often such a striking compliment is paid to a humble priest in a small country parish.

Reference has already been made to Monsignor Taylor's association with the Xaverian Fathers in Coatbridge, and Father Noara alludes to Monsignor's gifts to Father Fochesato, S.X. Father Fochesato was one of the group of Xaverian Fathers who came from Glasgow to Biggar to try to set up a seminary there. The difficulties were insurmountable and the Bishop of Mother- well granted permission to transfer the foundation to the more populous area of Coatbridge. Father Fochesato left Scotland in 1956 for Japan, and from that time he, in Kobe and elsewhere in Japan, was the instrument through which Monsignor Taylor's missionary spirit found active expression in furthering the ideals of St. Francis Xavier in Japan. A file of letters from him indi- cates Monsignor Taylor's spiritual and financial help for his missionary friend; the latter in return had no qualms in seeking help, even for such a large sum as £5,000. With the strong faith in God on which the missionary can only place his hopes, Father Fochesato writes from Hyuga-shi in Nov. 1958:

"If this amount will not be collected, then we shall have to tone down our ambitions, but this would be very sad indeed. I know that such an amount of money cannot be had from one person. Then maybe the best way would be to interest a large number of people, and I have been wondering whether my good friend, Canon T. N. Taylor, with a full load of T.N.T. could not blast an advertisement for this pressing need in favour of the beloved of Our Lord, the little children of this land . . ."

Whether the kindergarten and the other hopes ever became reality is not known, but everyone knew that Mgr. Taylor could not refuse a missionary Father or Sister anything that was in his power to give, although in this case, it seems more than unlikely that such a huge sum could be provided.

The first letter received by Mgr. Taylor from his Xaverian friend is amusing in content. Monsignor had from some time previous to 1955 been in contact with the French Carmelites in Japan, and he asked Father Fochesato to call and see them. Of this visit Father writes:

"This morning I had the pleasure of visiting the Carmel at Osaka. The Father who accompanied me there told the Sisters in Japanese that I had come from Scotland—then England; but all this meant little to them. Then I whispered to the Father that I had seen 'Carfin' before coming to Japan, and immediately I heard several nuns whispering with evident excitement. 'Carfin! . . . Carfin!' And then one of them started to explain in French. In French I answered that Canon Taylor had said he would be pleased if I would come here to visit them. They told me that there were twenty-four nuns altogether, nineteen Japanese and five French. The Reverend Mother Superior, newly appointed at the time, was Japanese . . . One of the French nuns told me that she herself had come over from Lisieux only three years ago and that she had seen you there before leaving.

They sounded so thrilled and happy that I could have stayed there much longer. I told them to pray for you and for your sight, whereupon the Reverend Mother remarked, ' Now, I can understand why he does not answer my letters.' "

Poor Reverend Mother! Little did she know that there were hundreds of devoted friends from all over the world, who rarely received—nor did they expect to receive—answers to their letters. Reverend Mother and her good Sisters continued to write to Mgr. Taylor, but what was much more important, at Father Fochesato's request, they continued to pray constantly for his intentions.

In 1963, the good Carmelite nuns had the tragic sorrow of losing their two friends: Father Fochesato, S.X., died on 16th August, 1963; and Monsignor Taylor three and a half months later, on the 1st December.

One is conscious that the surface only of Monsignor Taylor's activities in the mission fields has been touched. Where evidence has been supplied by Monsignor's friends it is given; or where a series of letters, written by someone who is now dead, exists, the writer has borrowed *ad lib* for quotation purposes. In this connection it is to be regretted that only a few letters from the late illustrious Mother Mary Kevin, O.S.F.—" Mama Kevina " —of Uganda, remain among Monsignor Taylor's correspondence, and these are of a confidential nature, letters exchanged by trusted friends.

However, from one letter we may quote what Mother Kevin had to say of her last visit to Carfin:

> Horline Hall,
> York.
>
> 5th April, 1955.
>
> " Dear Rev. Monsignor,
>
> Thank you very much for the lovely day at Carfin—may God reward you for all your kindness to us. It's always a very real spiritual uplift, to me, meeting you.
>
> Begging your blessing,
>
> Yours ever gratefully in Xto,
>
> M. Kevin."

The coincidence of the dates—the feast day of St. Francis Xavier—on which the young Sister M. Kevin left London on December 3rd, 1902, to begin her missionary life in Uganda, and the day of her burial in Uganda, December 3rd, 1957, alone might have suggested that the most suitable priest to preach the panegyric at her Requiem Mass, celebrated at Paisley, was the well-known parish priest of St. Francis Xavier's, Carfin. The choice was all the more suitable as Monsignor Taylor had known of and admired Mother Kevin's work for close on forty years and on many occasions had spoken publicly of her great missionary zeal.

Very Reverend Mother Mary Alcantara, O.S.F., Superior General of the Franciscan Missionary Sisters for Africa, wrote from Kampala to thank Canon Taylor " for that wonderful panegyric " he had preached at Paisley. Everyone, she said, had been deeply touched by the loving tributes he had paid to their dear Mother. Her hope was that when the time came for her to return to Paisley, she would have the opportunity to have a long talk with Canon Taylor on Mother Kevin's African people. Meantime she promised the one return which was in her power, and that was " a special place in the prayers of the African Little Sisters, and that is worth having."

Over the years and across the continents, the kaleidoscope of Monsignor Taylor's mission-minded life emerged from correspondence in a constantly regular though confused pattern. The harvest of his labours was gleaned from almost every field of the missionary world: in the 'forties and 'fifties Father de Witte, C.S.Sp., claimed and received spiritual and material aid for the Uganda Missions from his great-hearted little friend in " bonnie Scotland "; Archbishop Leon Nigris of the Propaganda Fide at Rome, himself beggared in the cause of charity, beseeched—nay demanded—help in the name of Christ's love for the hard-pressed contemplative Sisters of Carmel in the East. The changing picture is suffused and there emerges three father figures: Bishop Azzalini, S.X., of Sierra Leone, a well-kent figure on his visits to the West of Scotland; Archbishop Hurley, appealing desperately, but this time not in vain, for the children of Durban; and His Grace of Pretoria, expressing heartfelt gratitude for a generous and wholly unexpected donation from Monsignor Taylor, sent through St. Paul's Convent, Lelly, to the little convent of native Sisters of St. Brigid. Again the kaleidoscope changes and figures appear from Saigon and war-torn Vietnam, from Shillong and distant Taipei, from persecuted Mexican priests and lay missionaries in Borneo—shadowy figures unsure of an answer to their appeal, but sincere in their gratitude and prayers for the one from far-off Scotland who always, if at all possible, helped in a little way to lighten their immediate burden.

This financial help which Monsignor Taylor sent to the Foreign Missions came from his own personal resources; royalties from his books, money bequeathed to him for charitable purposes, or given to him by the many people whom he met and who entrusted him with their own personal donation towards his favourite charity. There were also the donations towards the Missions " for the fags I did not smoke." Regularly a few pounds arrived from the few who as a voluntary penance had promised to give up smoking for life. Monsignor disturbed the complaisance of heavy smokers when he produced the little unsigned slip inscribed as above and explained that this was three or four extra pounds he would be able to send to China or Japan. Taking it broadly, he was intolerant of those who found it difficult to stop smoking. His secretary at one time, having listened to a long harangue against the amount of money going up in smoke, somewhat shamefacedly was compelled to admit, " But, Father, I—I—smoke." Taken aback but momentarily, he looked up quickly from the A.P.F. Missions appeal on which he was working and gave the unexpected and undeserved rejoinder, " Child, you already do quite a lot for charity." The writer wonders what Monsignor would have said if she had replied, " All right then, Father, I'll turn the ' No smoking' sign in this room inwards. I feel like a smoke at this minute." She was not as brave as his curates were; they walked into the call-rooms, turned the notice to the wall and lit their cigarettes. One Irish curate said, " There was a rumpus the first time, but the Canon let us be after that."

It will be little comfort to those who tried the " No Fags—For the Missions " campaign—and failed—that the idea did not originate in the mind of the non-smoking President of the A.P.F., but in the fertile brain of his friend, Dr. Patrick McGlynn. In order to encourage a third friend to give up the heavy smoking which was endangering his health, Dr. McGlynn volunteered to abstain from smoking during a pilgrimage to Lourdes, the money saved to be sent to the Foreign Missions. The Doctor kept his word then, and at Mgr. Taylor's suggestion he did not resume the habit, the result being that the Missions have been the gainers now for more than thirty years.

One further source of help for Missionary Fathers in dire need was the surplus stipends for Masses requested for the intentions of donors. Perhaps Monsignor Taylor was in such a position that there were in his Mass diary fewer days when he was free to accept Mass stipends than there were in that of most secular priests. He had a very wide circle of friends, most of them advancing in years. Voluntarily, he made the practice of offering up Holy Mass for their feast days, jubilee anniversaries and birthdays. All these intentions left him but few free days for which he could accept stipends, and mostly these were reserved for the urgent " intentions " of his parishioners. The constant flow of pilgrims to the Grotto brought additional requests for Masses, and letters arrived daily containing offerings and requests. Monsignor Taylor had little choice in discharging his obligation to have Holy Mass offered up for these intentions except to send the offerings to the Mission fields or to sparsely populated parishes in the Highlands of Scotland and Wales where priests, desperately short of money for their multifarious charitable activities among the poor and destitute, welcomed the chance of discharging Monsignor's obligations.

About this duty he was most meticulous. Immediately the request came, it was noted, not always in orderly fashion in one of his diaries, but invariably on a scrap of paper which went into his " Mass pocket." Once a week—that was the rule, at least when the writer of these lines worked with him nearly twenty years ago—he took stock; every little scrap of paper was examined carefully and arrangements made where the Mass intentions should go—a few to lonely priests in outlying parishes; some to religious orders and seminaries in the home missions; but the bulk, when the intentions were not urgent or immediate, were sent to Foreign Missions where priests were short of " intentions." Although the requests for Masses arriving by letter (which normally contained postal orders) were always attended to, not always were the letters acknowledged. This usually caused some worry, for invariably a few weeks later, further letters would arrive enquiring if the money had arrived safely. A quick search through a bulging " In tray " would unearth a letter marked, " Mass arranged," but bearing no further remarks, a sure indication that it had not been acknowledged. While examining Monsignor's correspondence for this biography, only two letters of many hundreds were discovered which were not marked " Mass arranged." Everyone who ever sent a stipend to Monsignor Taylor with the request that a Mass be offered for a particular intention, will be comforted to know that even these two Masses, referred to above, have also been celebrated, although the writer well knows that Monsignor Taylor erred on the right side by having many additional Masses offered up against human lapse or carelessness on his own part.

A story he once told the writer on an evening when he was marking up his Mass diary and arranging surplus " intentions " for the Missions, stands clear in memory. Monsignor was arranging for an unusually high number of Masses with religious orders at home and abroad. Although surprised at the number, the listener did not question it, but the explanation was soon provided. Without letting fall any clue which might lead her to guess of whom he was speaking, he related that in a certain parish which might have been anywhere in Europe, some years prior to the conversation, a certain priest had died. It seems he had been recognised as a good, industrious and zealous worker in all his ways. The priest appointed to his place, a friend of his, had the excellent habit which many priests—Monsignor himself being one of these—have, of slipping into the church for his night prayers. One night when kneeling quietly in front of the sanctuary, the priest had the vague impression that a shadowy figure had moved across in front of the high altar. Putting the experience down to his imagination, he continued with his prayers. The next night the same thing happened, but he was convinced this time that he recognised the vague silhouette of his deceased friend. When it happened a third time, and when this time he was positive that the shadowy figure was really that of the dead priest, he sought advice from his superiors. He was told to ask the " spirit "—for such it must have been—in the name of God who he was, and what he wanted. According to Monsignor Taylor, the figure confirmed that he was Father X, and that during his life he had neglected celebrating Masses which he had promised for certain intentions. Until his obligations were fulfilled, his soul would not be at rest.

On that evening the writer sat beside Monsignor Taylor, while he arranged for a number of Masses to be celebrated by certain religious orders, as early as possible, " for a very special intention." Need she add, that as she walked home after eleven o'clock, her Irish heritage of belief in the supernatural, made her see the ghosts of dead relatives rise up from every darkened gable-end.

So far, little reference has been made to one of the most important aspects of any Foreign Mission Crusade: the three Pontifical Mission Aid societies, known in Britain as the Association for the Propagation of the Faith, the Society of St. Peter Apostle for Native Clergy, and the Society of the Holy Childhood. These three Mission aids for many years have had their headquarters at Rome and under the control of the Congregation for the Propagation of the Faith, a commission having jurisdiction over missionary countries. The National President of these societies in Scotland since 1955 has been a member of the Hierarchy. Prior to that year, Monsignor Taylor, in succession to

his great friend, Rev. Dr. Mullin, had presided over the societies
from 1946 until 1955, when he resigned in favour of His Lordship Bishop Walsh. But the Pontifical societies, as now established in this country, bear little resemblance to the isolated little
" circles " of the A.P.F. and of the Holy Childhood which were
in existence over half-a-century ago.

CHAPTER X

HOLY CHILDHOOD AND A.P.F.

The account of missionary activities undertaken by Monsignor Taylor, and described in the preceding pages, were the result of personal ideals deeply embedded in his nature. Although directed by his superiors at St. Sulpice to follow his vocation in Scotland, and again while he was on the staff of St. Peter's College (as stated by Sister Mary Emmanuel, R.G.S., and others who were in a position to know), he nevertheless considered himself a missionary priest. His first and obvious duty was to his flock at home: this he did to the utmost of his ability. If his thoughts and methods seemed intransigent to some of his colleagues and even to his superiors, their opposition did not deter him; at times he was laughed at and joked about—mention of his name could raise a story at many clerical tables—but those who mocked had little real knowledge of the depth and sincerity of his missionary spirit. As President of the Pontifical societies for Mission aids in Scotland, he invited Scottish Catholics—his own parishioners had already heard the plea many times—to " give until it hurt," not just the penny or shilling they could afford; he exhorted them to give the shilling, the pound they could not afford. This, he claimed, was the contribution that had most value in the sight of God.

An examination of many letters of acknowledgment from Foreign Missions shows how much he himself gave; Monsignor's bank account might reveal how frequently he " was in the red " with his bank balance. At his death, his trustees found it difficult to discharge the few little bequests of appreciation which he wished those who nursed him so devotedly during his last illness, to receive. With more selfish ambitions he might have died a rich man—his books were best sellers at home and in the United States, and ran into many editions—but his money, his heart and his prayers were for those " who know not Christ." It cannot be wondered at then, if in addition to his own private and personal crusade on behalf of missionary countries, he also played an active part in encouraging in others a zeal for the Pontifical societies which were the Church's chief mission aids to the non-Christian countries of the world.

ARCHBISHOP McDONALD OF ST. ANDREWS AND EDINBURGH, FATHER TAYLOR AND DR. PATRICK McGLYNN, WITH GROTTO WORKERS, JULY, 1931.

STANDING: 2nd left, Harry Taylor; 3rd left, Dr. McGlynn; Extreme right, Cormac McGhee (Author's father)
KNEELING: 2nd left, Patrick McShane (Author's uncle); Extreme right: H. Devlin (Grotto Foreman).
CENTRE BACK: H. Donnelly (Grotto Gardener)

GOANESE SAILORS ON PILGRIMAGE TO OUR LADY'S SHRINE IN THE LATE 'THIRTIES.

In more recent years these societies, the Association of the Propagation of the Faith, the Society of the Apostle Peter for Native Clergy and the Society of the Holy Childhood, have been established on a firm official footing under the Congregation for the Propagation of the Faith, at Rome. Annually, each contributing country sends its National President to the permanent Commission at the Palazzo di Propaganda Fide, Rome. From 1948 until 1955, when he retired, Monsignor Taylor was National President for Scotland. But these seven years, during which he held high office in the Pontifical societies and which put him constantly in the limelight, were but the culmination of years of pioneer work when he, and a few zealots like Monsignor Mullin, Monsignor McGettigan, Monsignor Ritchie, and earlier still, and perhaps the greatest of them all, Dean Tracy of Barrhead —prepared the harsh ground so that Scotland might become a country which contributed to, rather than one which received financial help from the Mission Aid Societies. But if in the mid-century, Monsignor Taylor's name was constantly associated with the A.P.F., in the early decades of the century, the Society of the Holy Childhood was his chief preoccupation. Whether or not he himself coined the name by which the Society was known to children all over Scotland—" Black Baby " Society —he certainly made it well known.

The Holy Childhood Society (like the A.P.F.) was founded in France in 1843, and introduced into England almost immediately by its founder, Monsignor Forben Jansen, Bishop of Nancy. A little information on Bishop Jansen and the early development of the Society in Britain is provided by Father Taylor in the *Annals of the Holy Childhood,* of which he was editor during the formative years in Scotland, from 1912 until 1920, after which he retired from the editorial chair in favour of his friend and fellow-worker for the Missions, Rev. H. F. Hall, Cathedral Choir School, London, who had in that year been appointed General Treasurer for England. Father Taylor had been Scottish Director since about 1909 or 1910, and he continued to hold this official post for many years.

Twice denied his own wish to work overseas on the Mission fields, his personal disappointment did not embitter him. His sympathies lay with the active workers in the vineyard. Of Bishop Jansen, the founder of the Holy Childhood Society, Father Taylor wrote:

" He was only too well aware of the awful massacre of innocent babes in the Far East, and conceived the idea of making the

Catholic children of Europe save the souls of their less fortunate
little brothers and sisters of heathen lands."

Referring to what an Associate member of the Holy Childhood
contributes, Father Taylor continues:

" Two things—the alms of prayer and the alms of money. The
more important is the first, consisting of a daily *Hail Mary,*
together with the ejaculation, " Holy Virgin Mary, pray for us
and the poor heathen children." The second, alms, takes the form
of a halfpenny contributed once in the month. Older folks, and
the young folks likewise, may give more."

The startling fact is then revealed by Father Taylor:

" In many districts it is possible for the missionary to purchase
a child for half-a-crown or less, and that amount may be subscribed by such as can afford it."

It is hard to believe that trafficking in human life had lowered
the value of a little child to half-a-crown, and indeed much less.
This explains the rather unfortunate expression, " Buy a ' Black
Baby ' for half-a-crown." Cardinal Tien, himself a pagan converted to Christianity, sensitive about the expression, suggested
instead that " Half-a-crown to raise a child for Christ " might be
more appropriate than the materialistic earlier one.

It has been suggested that Father Taylor exaggerated the condition then prevailing in heathen lands. On the contrary his
evidence came directly from Missionary Fathers serving in the
East. Father Fraser, Scottish-Canadian Missioner, wrote from
China in 1919:

" Dear Father Taylor,
           . . . I began work this morning on a foundling asylum
here in Taichowfu. As soon as it is built, it will be crowded with
infants abandoned by their parents. The other day a school-
master from my own parish visited me. He desired to know if I
wanted any babies because many were being drowned. Every
family, said my visitor, is guilty of infanticide. When a number
of baby girls have been born, and one after another has been
drowned, eventually the father takes the last unfortunate to the
mountains at night, and burns her alive. He thinks that by so
doing baby girls will not show their faces again in his family.
This happens in every village in my parish, and there are 1,325
villages in the parish . . ."

The explanation for the massacre of little girls is given by Mgr. Faveau, Vicar Apostolic of Chekiang, in a letter he wrote to Father Taylor:

"In China," Mgr. Faveau writes, "where there is a constant struggle for existence, the parents abandon their female children. Since they earn no money, they are looked upon as a burden to the family. These abandoned children are found by the Sisters, who care for them in the orphanages, baptise them and educate them.

While on a visitation recently, I have several times seen the dead bodies of children lying on the banks of canals and being devoured by dogs. These poor creatures might have been saved for a few coppers—these children are dying in thousands because we have not the means to support them."

A final letter from one whom he knew and who had taught in his own school at Carfin before leaving to join the Good Shepherd Convent at Bangalore, India, is that which Sister M. Emmanuel (Rose Allen, Wishaw) wrote in 1919:

"Rice is three times its normal price just now, and Mother Prioress has to turn away hundreds of children-in-arms from the convent door. Their fate? To die of hunger or to be abandoned by their parents."

It was to help save the lives of these helpless little infants abandoned by parents whose pagan culture had little respect for human life in the East and in Africa, that the Holy Childhood was formed in the middle of the nineteenth century.

During the half-century or so from its foundation, the development of the Society in the British Isles was spasmodic, never at any time earth-shattering in its success. And yet it grew, though imperceptibly, spreading across to missionary Ireland where its tendrils gained a firm grip and flourished vigorously, and to Scotland, where it clung tenaciously but very precariously for most of the time until 1910. In 1909, Mr. Edwin de Lisle, General Director of the Society in Britain, sadly reports in the *Annals*:

"It will be observed with regret that there is again a falling off in the English subscriptions, while in Scotland they have almost ceased to come at all."

In effect, the total subscribed by Scotland was six pounds, five of which were donated by one Scottish school, that of the Sisters of Charity, Dumfries.

Happier times were on the way. From an article entitled "Looking Backwards," written by Father Taylor in the *Annals* of 1920, we learn that in 1910 he had "the pleasure of announcing that Scotland had begun to do its bit for the little folk of China and the African jungle," and the contribution for that year was £50. Within the next ten years Scottish contributions rose (in spite of the war), and in 1920 the £5 of 1909 had become £1,700.

In parenthesis, the writer wishes to say that, very deliberately, she has attempted up to this point, to keep the name of St. Thérèse out of Monsignor's life story—an almost impossible task, for " SHE " was part of his life. However, as he himself helped to raise Thérèse to the Councils of the Elect, this aspect of his life will be dealt with elsewhere and full rein will be given to the impact she had on his life. But, try as she might, the writer was unable to explain the sudden success of the Holy Childhood in Scotland, and indeed elsewhere, without attributing to Directors, extraordinary powers which in their humility they would have laughed to scorn. Having said this, to explain a deliberate omission, " Revenons à nos moutons " and hear what Father Taylor had to say about the sudden rise in contributions to the Society which had been set up specially for the flocks of little children who could claim neither shepherd nor fold:

> "In 1909, we gave the Holy Child a present of five pounds. Next year we gave Him fifty. That lover of children—black or white—the 'Little Flower of Jesus,' had come to the rescue, and under her patronage the income rose until in the March of this present year (1920) the five pounds became £1,700 . . .
>
> In 1911, the Vice-Postulator of the Cause of Beatification of Sister Thérèse, 'The Little Flower of Jesus,' replaced Mgr. Demimaid as Director-General of the Society of the Holy Childhood. The new Director, Mgr. de Teil, well aware of the influence of Soeur Thérèse, had her portrait hung in his office, and besought her to take charge of the gigantic family—somewhere over a million orphans and pupils—entrusted to his care . . ."

A further detail is supplied in the analysis of contributions of the year 1919. In that year, the Archdiocese of Glasgow contributed over £1,300, and of this sum St. Francis Xavier's School, Carfin, contributed £160, with Notre Dame High School following with £101. While giving due credit to Father Taylor for his splendid efforts in setting the Holy Childhood Society on a healthy footing in Scotland, one cannot help giving an extra special pat on the back to the children of St. Francis Xavier's,

their teachers, and the parish priest, Rev. D. McBrearty, all of
whom as a combined team, in 1915, a few months before Father
Taylor came to Carfin, contributed £8 to the Society. In that
year the students of Notre Dame High School topped the list for
Scotland; St. Francis Xavier's contribution, low as it may seem,
was more than double that of each of the four other Lanarkshire
schools which had sent money to the Director.*

Monsignor Ritchie seemed to know what he was talking about
when he praised the " good Catholic colliers " of Carfin. Since
1915 they have proved over and over again how missionary-
minded they are. Anyone who might be interested may care to
check the *Annals of the Holy Childhood,* and there is little doubt
that the result of the search would put St. Francis Xavier's
school very high on the lists for generous contributions.

About 1920, Father Campling, later Bishop Campling, of
Uganda, visited Carfin and stayed with Father Taylor for a
month—this because of Father Taylor's successful work in
connection with the Mission Aids societies. It may also be worth
mentioning as one of the many little coincidences which keep
cropping up with regard to Monsignor's life and works, that the
organiser of the Holy Childhood Society in the Lanarkshire
region for a long number of years was Miss Margaret Steele,
R.I.P., formerly a teacher in one of the schools in Monsignor's
parish; she was followed in office by her friend, Miss Mary Carr,
a colleague from the same school; the present organiser of the
Society in the Diocese, Miss Mary T. McGurk, does not now
reside in the parish, but she was at one time a parishioner when
New Stevenston was part of the parish of St. Francis Xavier.

Of interest also, to the readers, might be the fact that the
membership card for the Holy Childhood Society from about
the year 1915 was one planned by Father Taylor, in consultation
with the Director-General, Mgr. de Teil. This card featured His
Holiness Pope Pius X, and underneath the Pontiff's picture was
a message to children, reproduced from his own handwriting.

After the end of the First World War, plans were afoot to
co-ordinate the Mission Aid societies under a permanent commission at Rome. The letter reproduced below, conceivably,

---

* These four schools were St. Mary's, Lanark; Holy Family, Mossend; St. Bride's,
Bothwell; and St. Cuthbert's, Burnbank.

might have had some bearing on this, although it is but a surmise on the writer's part:

> Archbishop's House,
> Westminster.
>
> October 21st, 1919.

"Dear Father Taylor,

I have just returned from France after a most pleasant and consoling visit to Lisieux. I was also able to have several conversations with Monsignor de Teil about the Holy Childhood and I have no doubt I shall be able to arrange something later on.

> May God bless you always,
> Your devoted servant in Christ,
> (Sgd.) F. Card. Bourne."

From the detailed account given in the last pages, one would imagine, in the earlier years, that Father Taylor gave little or no care to the other societies which provided spiritual and financial help to the missionary countries. St. Peter's College Magazine of June 1912 proves the contrary. An article written by Father Taylor gives an account of a visit to the College of Father Francis Ross, a newly appointed Director of the British branch of the Association for the Propagation of the Faith. The working of the A.P.F. was discussed fully by Father Ross during his visit, and in his article Father Taylor gives a detailed explanation of Father Ross's talk. The "circles" of the A.P.F. were recommended: only ten members were required for these, and a start might be made by two or three. For this purpose, collecting cards and certificates might be had from Father Ross, or from Canon Ritchie (Diocesan Treasurer of the A.P.F.), or from the writer. The writer, of course, was Father Taylor, and it would seem that he was either secretary or promoter of the A.P.F. for the Archdiocese in 1912. At any rate he was not long in Carfin before he had set up a number of "circles" of the A.P.F. in his own parish, under Mrs. Hugh Kearney, a hard-working lady president who had overall charge.

Apart from the above, the writer regrets that she can say little else about Monsignor Taylor's early connection with the A.P.F. In later years, the whole parish, the whole country knew plenty. Most parish priests will be aware of the mumblings among some of their faithful when the latter are asked to put an extra penny in the collection plate—the changed circumstances of our time provide envelopes and increase the demand by a shilling or so. The faithful of Carfin, too, grumbled and mumbled about extra increases in the normal dues, designated for the support of their church and their pastor. But the A.P.F.! That was a different matter. This voluntary association made the heaviest demands on their pockets, and yet the members gave without hesitation. Always towards the end of the financial year, Monsignor worked out the Association's balance sheet in the parish. For a number of years after the Second World War the parish target was £1,000, and towards the end of the financial year all were told how much the parish was short of its target. A few weeks to go, and £100 short! Somehow or other the money turned up, and even more at times than what was hoped for.

Rumour was current that Monsignor Taylor himself always made up the deficit. He certainly helped when he had the money available—to him there was no better way of spending it than in giving to the Missions—but the people of the parish excelled themselves in generosity. The writer remembers one particular year when the parish, in spite of valiant efforts, was short of £40 from meeting the required target. On that occasion, two elderly people, individually, made private visits to the Canon and each presented him with £20. It was all they had in this world and they did not grudge it. By sheer coincidence, they lived next door to each other and neither was aware who helped to clear the second half of the £40. Canon Taylor and those two people are dead now, but a scribbled note left among Monsignor's papers reveals the names of the two generous donors. One was a dear old lady, well known for her charity, the other was an old age pensioner and one-time collier, for whom £20 must have meant almost a lifetime's savings.

The point of the above story is to show that Monsignor Taylor had his parish behind him in all his projects. What has been said of these two elderly people might well be said of many in the parish. Their priest led and they followed. Other parishes were known to organise bazaars, garden fêtes and sundry functions to help defray parish expenses; Carfin organised similar functions in order to give a generous subscription to the Association for the Propagation of the Faith. If it is true that Monsignor Taylor was a missionary priest, it is equally true that under his leadership the people of St. Francis Xavier's parish became the most mission-minded in Scotland. Priest and people were in

complete accord with the words spoken by the great Cardinal
Manning and quoted frequently by Mgr. Taylor:

> "It is quite true that we have need of men and of means at
> home, and it is because we have need of men and means at home,
> and of more men and of more means by a great deal than we yet
> possess, that I am convinced we ought to send both men and
> means abroad."

These words of the eminent Cardinal express Monsignor
Taylor's ideals, and the ideals of those parishioners who supported him so loyally in his missionary apostolate.

Chapter XI

MARIAN DEVOTION

Love of Our Lady comes almost as naturally to a child from a good Catholic family as the air he breathes in, or the food he reaches for without effort or training. One might say further that this devotion to the Mother of Our Saviour was even more true, close on a century ago, when the child was the offspring of an Irish mother. The reason for this is not hard to seek: the Penal Laws against Catholics had deprived the persecuted Irish of the Divine Food in the Holy Mass, but no one could take away from them the muttered *Aves* which were raised up in every house and hovel where the name of God was reverenced and honoured. The " Maidin Mhuire,"* which came easily to Irish lips was the Irish mother's symbol of her close proximity to " the things that are unseen." The " Mhuire! Mhuire!" of a distressed Irish person is a prayer of pleading, which has become part of the Irish heritage. In joy or sorrow the Mother of God is near, and a child reared in such an atmosphere inherits this familiarity with his Blessed Mother, which makes the love he bears her an unconscious act of devotion, a devotion inherited from a long line of ancestors, whose devotion to Our Lady was an integral part of their lives.

What was obvious and expected in dutiful devotion to the Blessed Virgin Mary, on Mrs. Taylor's part, was not lacking in her husband either. Comparisons are invidious and often fail to make their point, but, basing assessment on written evidence and the few chance remarks let fall by Monsignor Taylor and related by his friends, the writer of these lines dares to opine that if one is to be chosen, Monsignor Taylor's English father was if anything even more steadfast, in Christian devotion, than was his Irish mother. And yet it was with his mother that in his memory he associated the family Rosary, with all its " trimmin's." His recollection of the boys gathered around their earthly mother in the evening act of devotion to their heavenly Mother, gives the pattern of life in the paternal home at Greenock.

The practice of a private daily Rosary seems to have been habitual to Monsignor Taylor from childhood onwards except

---

* Virgin Mary.

for a short spell during his student days at St. Sulpice, but as his diary records, the practice was resumed when the pressure of study lessened.

A letter sent to Father Taylor in 1901 by Mr. John M. M. Charleson, formerly a Presbyterian minister, but at that time a member of the Catholic Church, is of particular interest for several reasons, but chiefly because it is apposite to the devotion of the Rosary. Mr. Charleson writes:

> 22 Skirving Street,
> Shawlands,
> Glasgow.
> 26th December, 1901.

" My dear Father Taylor,

I had little heart for writing, when I was in a sense going through a " *Vallem Umbrosam Tenebrosam,*" yet reproving myself all the time for my disquietude. For Faith had not gone from me, but was pointing to the Eternal Goodness and Truth; and behind and around the shadow, and within my heart the Divine Light, with a certain mild constancy, flowed in its infinite calm flood. It is very wonderful. And through all, I am unable to express to the good Lord my thankfulness for undeserved benefits.

What a height of saintliness you pray that I may ascend to, ' that one's crosses and very pain may be an intoxicating bliss.' May that pure prayer recoil upon your own soul! . . .

I had not understood that you were to give me so careful and beautiful a form of Rosary devotion, as you have now done. From Sunday first, then, I shall offer up the fifteenth decade for your intention of ' Perseverance.' The fifteenth does seem more apt than the fourteenth. Why do you ask such as me if I would object to others being included, in this holy circle of angelic prayer? Whomsoever you admit, with glad obedience, I also. The more the stronger as you well say . . .

On Sunday morning, Bishop Maguire is to confirm me. Soon now, it seems, I shall be in the beloved city. Pray that I may have the grace of true vocation, and that my surrender of self may be absolute, whole and entire, wanting nothing to make it more complete.

> Humbly and sincerely,
> Yours in Jesus and Mary,
> (Sgd.) John M. M. Charleson."

Soon after the above was written, Mr. Charleson was admitted to the Scots College, Rome, where he was ordained priest in 1904. As priest in charge of Holy Cross, Croy, Father Charleson was well known for the honour he gave to Our Lord in the Holy

Eucharist, by the elaborate ceremonial of the Corpus Christi processions which were held annually in the streets of the parish.

In a letter Monsignor received from Mother Loyola of St. Mary's Convent, York, in 1903, reference is made to some form of the Rosary, which seems clear to her although vague to those who do not understand the context:

"Thank you for the Rosary condensed, which is rich and fragrant like some sweet essence. I like it; is it yours? I like also what you say about *Voluntas Dei*. Do you like Father Faber's hymn to it? I do not know St. Rose of Lima's Litany of the Perfections of God, but I like the grand Hymns of Praise found in the Prayers of St. Gertrude."

It is clear that there existed a deep affinity of soul between the mature Mistress of Novices at St. Mary's Convent, York, and the thirty-year-old Professor of Holy Scripture at St. Peter's, Bearsden. Nor did he suffer the embarrassment of the young— he was only twenty-seven when he offered counsel to the middle-aged Mr. Charleson; age mattered not in the line of spiritual duty. The position, however, was reversed in 1905, when after the death of Father Alexander (Monsignor's younger brother), Mother Loyola took on the task of administering a few words of spiritual admonishment to the broken-hearted elder brother:

"I hope you won't mind a thought that came to my mind as I read your letter—though it is a bit of presumption to say such a thing to a priest. Well, as I looked down the letter, I thought— Alick's name all the way; his heart is sore, sore through and through. He has made the sacrifice generously; he has given back to God what was His; he has been glad in the highest part of the soul that this dear brother should go to the Father. But to rise to the supernatural must be a strain on nature; there must be a physical reaction after the acceptance of such a cross. He must know this; he would not allow anyone he was directing to call irresponsiveness of soul, weary with effort to hold fast to God's will, by the horrible name of ' lukewarmness.' Why does he not comfort himself as he would feel bound to comfort another, by assigning this effect to its true cause? But the physician cannot heal himself. Only the great Physician can come in, pouring into the tired soul oil and wine.

This I have been asking Him to do. Please do not be vexed with me for telling you my thought.

I do feel such compassion when a cross has the super-added weight of a sense of His absence—He who is needed now more than ever to fill the empty place in the heart.

I did not know Alick was so young. There must be something singularly attractive to God in the soul of a young priest, when, in spite of the labourers being few, and this one eager to work, He can call it thus early to Himself.

I feel very privileged to have shared with him the merit of your Holy Sacrifice on St. Ignatius' day (Mother Loyola's feast day), and I thank you very much for that wish, the best that the Feast brought me: May St. Ignatius obtain for you the grace to do all things, absolutely all things, ' ad majorem Dei gloriam.' "

Even while mourning for his brother's death, Monsignor Taylor could remember his friend's feast day! Busy as he invariably was, he always found time to remember little mementoes which gave pleasure to his friends.

The propagation of Rosary devotion was a lifelong crusade, but truth demands that it should be made known that Monsignor Taylor earned for himself some criticism for the manner in which he propagated the Rosary crusade.

The late Very Reverend Malachy Lynch, O.Carm., in the year before his death, in his own inimitable fashion expressed a view shared by some:

Whitefriars,
Faversham.

2nd December, 1966.

" I once gave a Mission in Carfin and I can vividly remember Canon Taylor walking up and down the aisle saying the Rosary while I said Mass. I was not used to that practice, and I thought that it was a grand old Scottish custom, but I found that the congregation disliked it just as much as I did, but were naturally hesitant about doing anything about it . . .

Also I could not understand why there was a church and school on one side of the street, and the great Grotto on the other side. Why he didn't build a new church in such perfect surroundings I could not understand.

He was very generous to me and I was glad of my stay with him. I am sorry to say that that was the only occasion on which I met him . . ."

Had Father Lynch himself been less hesitant than he claims the congregation was, he might have received an answer to both questions. The answer to the second is easily given: Father Taylor did not have the permission of his ecclesiastical superiors to build a church. The answer to the first is not so easy, for obviously there must have been an underlying reason before Father Taylor would allow any devotion to the Saints to interfere with the solemn Sacrifice of the Mass. But Father Lynch was not alone in complaining about being distracted by the public recitation of the Rosary during Mass. The practice went back over many years, possibly to the time in the early 'twenties when the numbers attending daily Mass increased greatly. These were the days when the congregation at Mass were passive participants; few in the parish could read or understand Latin; equally few were those who possessed a missal and who followed the Mass intelligently; a number, especially among the women, used a prayer book—a communal, well-thumbed " Key of Heaven " or " Treasury of the Sacred Heart "; others again used their Rosary beads for private devotions during Mass. Father Taylor's real concern was for those who knelt through Mass without using either prayer book or Rosary beads, quite oblivious of the Sacrifice that was being enacted on the altar. It was in order that the latter might gain some advantage from spending half-an-hour in church, that Father Taylor introduced the Rosary during Mass. It might be added that in addition to the Rosary, specified prayers were said in " preparation," immediately before Holy Communion and in thanksgiving immediately afterwards.

With the coming of the " Dialogue " Mass and Mass in the vernacular, there was no longer any necessity to recite the Rosary in order to keep people occupied during Mass. Moreover, a greater number of people owned missals in the 'fifties and 'sixties than in the years between the wars. Even if the practice of reciting the Rosary publicly during Mass had not been forbidden eventually by Mother Church, in all probability it would have died a natural death, at Carfin, for the changing ritual of the Mass introduced a more active participation by the faithful and thus it was no longer necessary to introduce additional prayers to keep the less attentive occupied. Monsignor Taylor, who was in the forward ranks of priests who gave English translations of Latin services (at marriage ceremonies, funeral obsequies, etc.) would be, also, one of the first to welcome any changes which would enable worshippers to participate actively or orally in the supreme Sacrifice of the altar.

But devotion to the Rosary in honour of our Blessed Mother was only one feature of Monsignor Taylor's apostolate to give her honour. Old students from College days recall his devotion to Our Lady of Lourdes and the popularity of his " lantern lectures " on Lourdes. Mother Loyola, too, makes mention of them in one of her letters and in so doing unwittingly makes quite a boob.

At the beginning of February 1905, he had written to her, mentioning the success of his lectures and had asked her to remember him in her prayers on the 11th February. Her reply must have raised a " Tut! tut!" from Father Taylor.

" I have been trying to think," she wrote, " what special feast of yours February 11th is. There is a feeling as if you had told me and that I ought to know. Anyway, I wish you a very happy one and a renewal of the graces the day itself brought you years ago. Is it the anniversary of your ordination, I wonder?"

Mother Loyola may be forgiven for not knowing that the 11th February was the anniversary of the first appearance of Our Lady to the child Bernadette in 1858. Father Taylor would be one of the few from Britain who visited the shrine at Lourdes regularly; in 1905 neither national nor diocesan pilgrimages had been inaugurated, although three years later, in 1908, a jubilee pilgrimage was to leave the shores of Britain for the momentous jubilee celebrations at Lourdes.

But St. Mary's Convent at York, the oldest foundation of nuns in England and one dedicated particularly to the Blessed Virgin, was not prepared to stay long ignorant of exact details of Our Lady's appearances at Lourdes; and so at the earliest opportunity it was arranged that Father Taylor should travel down to the convent at York and give a lantern lecture to a group of children assembled from all the schools in that city. Mother M. Cecilia of the Sacred Heart, in her letter of thanks to Father Taylor, expresses the views of the audience on that occasion:

" They have shown the greatest appreciation of both lectures and say that you, yourself, did them good because you were so earnest.

It is so kind of you to join in our novena to our Lady of Lourdes. I feel greater confidence now, because I do not think she could refuse you, when you are so devoted to her.

Thanks again for the leaflets and for all your goodness to us . . .

(Sgd.) M. Cecilia, S.H.

The above letter is short but important because it confirms several marked qualities in Father Taylor's character: his earnestness; his ability to instil in others the faith which he himself had in his own prayers; and lastly, the thorough manner in which he propagated devotion to our Lady of Lourdes by following up his lecture with the distribution of leaflets.

The Rosary, lantern lectures on Lourdes, his own annual visits to the Shrine, do not give the entire picture: Father Taylor was nothing if not thorough in every spiritual crusade on which he was engaged. In major projects he was a perfectionist and no-where was his zeal more marked than in his apostolate to make Our Lady more honoured in Scotland.

Father Taylor attended the jubilee celebrations at Lourdes in 1908, but not just as an ordinary pilgrim; the lectures he gave on his return and his later writings make it clear that he did more than fulfil the spiritual exercises at the Shrine. The *Milngavie Herald* of the 27th November, 1908, gives a comprehensive account of a lecture on " Lourdes and Its Miracles," given by the Reverend Professor Taylor of St. Peter's College, to a large audience in the Burgh Hall, Milngavie. His sincerity, it was reported, in describing the " Miraculés " he had met during the jubilee solemnities of Sunday, August 23rd, held his audience spell-bound. Madam Wuiplier (née Marie Lebranchu), better known as " La Grevotte " of Zola's novel on Lourdes, was one of these, and she was able to provide Father Taylor with fitting evidence that the wonderful cure she received through Our Lady's mediation on the 17th August, 1892, was final and com-plete, in spite of Zola's vile efforts to explain her cure as a temporary amelioration only, followed by a complete relapse. Zola went even further to cover this falsehood; Father Taylor relates in his book, *Lourdes and Its Miracles,* that Zola even essayed bribery to make the " miraculée " leave France. " But Marie did not leave France," Father Taylor continues, " and whereas Zola is no more, there was none more lively at the jubilee procession of August 23, 1908, than ' La Grevotte.' "

Father Taylor's crusade was already bearing fruit among the Catholics of Scotland, and during ensuing years members of his own family and a number of his friends were won over to the cause of Our Lady of Lourdes, by his persistent propaganda on her behalf. His younger brother, Father Alexander, had visited Lourdes in 1900, Father James Bede some years later, and in 1912 Father Taylor's parents with a number of friends accom-panied him on the third Scottish National Pilgrimage to Our Lady's Shrine in France. Of this pilgrimage Mr. Taylor notes in his diary:

> " Although Father Taylor was living with us, his whole time was taken up with the invalids, their housing and the baths. He was a Director of *brancardiers,* with about forty assistants. Only occasionally did we get speaking to him, but we were very pleased he was so useful. D.G. "

An unsolicited testimonial to Father Taylor's knowledge of Lourdes and his influence with the authorities there, is provided in a letter sent to him by the late Monsignor Hugh Provost Kelly of St. Patrick's, Dumbarton:

6th June, 1913.

"Dear Father Taylor,

You will be pleased to hear that our Pilgrimage Party is practically formed. We are now over fifty. The journey and stay in Lourdes are both arranged for, and all that remains is to make things right with Father Superior.

May I ask you to use your great influence with him to get us all the privileges possible.

The fire is burning here, and I want to keep it burning with God's help. It is quite clear to me that it is we who are wanting in Faith and not the people.

If you could come and see me some day next week, we could talk the whole thing over.

Am I to keep places for your Whiteinch friends? A Miss Mealy has written to me asking to be allowed to join. What shall I say?

I remain,

Sincerely yours,

Hugh Kelly."

Mgr. Kelly seems to have been the organising secretary of this pilgrimage, but Father Taylor seems to have had the last word in its direction.

It is not clear when the thought occurred to Father Taylor that a simple guide book, written in English, would encourage people to visit the Shrine. Although a letter written by Dr. Boissarie, Director of the Medical Bureau at Lourdes, seems to suggest that in the year 1906 Father Taylor was already interested in the complex question of the " miraculés " of Lourdes, yet it was not until 1911 that *Lourdes and Its Miracles, a guide to Mary's Shrine*, was published by the Orphans' Press, Rochdale. A second edition, revised and enlarged, was published by the *Universe*, Effingham House, London, in 1919. The approbations published at the time speak louder than any words the writer of these lines may express. The Bishop of Tarbes and Lourdes wrote as follows:

"Reverend and dear Professor,

I am greatly touched and edified by the obvious devotion shown in your work, as well as by your words: 'ad majorem Mariae gloriam "—for the propagation of the cult of Our Lady of Lourdes.

By your work you also promote the glory of Our Lord Jesus Christ: for the honour given to Our Blessed Lady has for its final aim and goal her Divine Son, the Redeemer and Saviour of Mankind: " Through Mary to Jesus."

Your countrymen have always been remarked on at Lourdes for their deep and sincere faith, which is always kept under control even when they are faced with the most touching experiences. They seem to be calm, although their voices tremble with emotion while singing their hymn, " Faith of Our Fathers."

This faith held by their ancestors will triumph at the blessed Grotto at Lourdes, and it will make the pilgrims from your country the apostles of your people. If your book, *Lourdes and Its Miracles,* contributes to this great good, I do not doubt that this will be your greatest reward. It is above all else the only reward worth having, the only one you yourself pray for.

May we hope to see you soon at Lourdes, Reverend and dear Professor! Pray for the one who sends you his affectionate blessing, in the name of Our Lady of Lourdes.

(Sgd.) Francis Xavier Bishop of Tarbes,
7th February, 1911."

The Right Rev. Bishop Grey Graham, Bishop Auxiliary, Edinburgh. (From the *Ave Maria* of July 8, 1911):

" Many an English-speaking visitor to Lourdes has felt the want of a good guide-book, in his own language, to help him to see and to understand all the wonderful things at the great shrine of our Blessed Lady . . . Up to the present, no such handy and practical book had been available. Now, however, Professor Taylor . . . has supplied the much-felt want in his *Lourdes and Its Miracles* . . . The author is a recognised authority on the subject, having spent many years in studying and visiting the marvellous Grotto . . .

Nearly every page of Father Taylor's little book is illustrated by photographs of the more interesting events and functions connected with the shrine. We feel sure that a guide-book so excellent, inexpensive and serviceable, will do much to spread devotion to Our Lady of Lourdes . . . and we wish it a wide circulation in all English-speaking countries.

✠ H.G.G."

President of the Medical Bureau of the Grotto of Lourdes (Dr. George Cox, M.R.C.P.):

" The want of a clear, concise statement of what has been occurring at Lourdes for the last fifty-two years has been felt for a considerable time by English-speaking pilgrims. The few works on the subject that exist in the English language, although highly interesting and valuable in themselves, are more useful to readers at home than to visitors who come here for a short pilgrimage, and whose time is fully taken up by their daily devotions and exercises . . .

. . . The present little volume meets the requirements (of the latter) in a manner that ought to satisfy most pilgrims coming to the hallowed Grotto of Massabieille . . .

I wish the little volume all the success it so well deserves . . .

(Sgd.) George Cox, M.R.C.P.,
Bureau des Constatationes Medicales,
Lourdes, October, 1910.

A few footnotes provided by Father Taylor by way of explanation, in *Lourdes and Its Miracles,* may indicate the amount of research he undertook in the preparation of his book. Of Dr. Baissarie, the Director of the Medical Bureau since 1892, Father Taylor says:

"The writer wishes to record here his gratitude for the many kindnesses of Mary's chevalier, who was much interested in these pages. He counselled that stress should be laid on the proved miracles of Lourdes, as being God's argument in these days against infidelity. *Requiescat!*"

Jeanne Abadie, the lad who accompanied Bernadette and her sister Toinette in their search for fire-wood on the banks of the river Gave, was the last surviving member of the trio. Father Taylor "had the privilege of questioning this last survivor of that memorable day on the subject of the apparitions." He also met Bernadette's youngest brother at "Maison de Bernadette," next to the mill which the Bishop had bought for her father.

One further name is of interest. Referring to the Medical Bureau in 1908, Father Taylor writes:

"Here at the Medical Bureau Mgr. Hugh Benson—and the privileged writer of these lines—spent much of the stirring times of the Golden Jubilee celebrations. The Monsignor's vivid souvenirs are enshrined in a volume of the 'Catholic Library' entitled *Lourdes,* and again in his novel, *The Dawn of All!*"

A plain postcard with a scrawled inscription records Monsignor Benson's appreciation of Father Taylor's help in these momentous days.

The years slip in and in 1914 Father Taylor was back again in Lourdes for the silver jubilee of the Eucharistic Congress. If anyone should believe that devotion to Mary would ever rival the honour due to her Eucharistic Son, in Father Taylor's heart, his exuberant words of July 1914, give the lie to the belief:

"The year 1914 saw the great climax of the Lourdes celebrations, when the silver jubilee of the Eucharistic Congress was held in what is at once the City of Mary and the City of the Eucharist . . . Never had Lourdes seen the like. The splendours of the Congress outrivalled the great Jubilee of 1908, and it lasted from July 21 to July 26, Cardinal Granito di Belmonte acting as Papal Legate. It took three hours for the Procession of the Blessed Sacrament to travel from the Grotto to an Altar prepared above Rosaire."

Within a week hostilities broke out and pilgrimages were discontinued for the duration of the war, but in spite of difficulties Father Taylor returned to France in 1915. Absence from the Shrine during the war years must have given him time for thought, for very soon after his arrival at Carfin a small statue of Our Lady of Lourdes was erected in the presbytery grounds; but this was only a signpost to greater things. If Father Taylor's other achievements fade into the oblivion of time and all else is forgotten, surely the chronicles of the Catholic Church in Scotland will be enriched by the mention of the one who was mostly responsible for bringing Our Lady out of the shadows of obscurity, into which she had been thrust over three and a half centuries ago.

The culmination of Monsignor Taylor's crusade to honour our Blessed Mother was the building of the Marian shrine, known locally—and internationally—as the Carfin Grotto; or as the press put it in the exciting years when the Grotto made front page news, the " Scottish Lourdes." It was not the first shrine built in honour of Our Lady of Lourdes outside France. The Belgians early expressed their love for Our Lady under this title and were rewarded in 1875 by the canonically-established miracle of the curing of Pierre de Rudder's badly damaged leg, at the Grotto shrine built at Oostacker near Ghent.

Father Taylor tells us in *Lourdes and Its Miracles* that it was not only in Belgium and France that shrines had been built, but that they were to be found in the Vatican Gardens, at Vilnour in India, at Santiago in Chile, in Constantinople, and indeed " wherever missionary priests and nuns have trodden, there also the Fair Virgin of Lourdes is known." What Father Taylor has not said is that as a gift to his friends on Foreign Missions, he himself has on several instances provided the statue for the Mission Shrine. It would therefore be more than surprising if Father Taylor's own mission were to lag behind in the fervour it showed to Mary Immaculate.

It might well be asked how the Grotto at Carfin began? Many accounts of the history of the shrine have been published in the

press, in booklets, in periodicals, all over the world; but in substance they add nothing further to what Monsignor Taylor
himself said, in 1958, in one of his last articles, written for *Claves
Regni*, the magazine of St. Peter's College, Cardross—the College
at which he had served as a member of the staff for the first
fifteen years of this century.

> " The best-loved Marian shrines," Monsignor wrote, " have
> owed their beginnings to some visible act of divine intervention;
> we all are familiar with Lourdes, with Fatima, and there are many
> others. This was not so at Carfin; the Grotto there was not the
> result of any apparition; it was the expression of fervent devotion
> to Our Lady of Lourdes. In July, 1920, a group from Carfin took
> part in the Scottish National Pilgrimage to Lourdes. They returned
> home full of enthusiasm and it was decided to erect a small grotto,
> together with a parochial hall, on a piece of waste ground, about
> an acre in size, across the way from the parish church. Permission
> was obtained from the ecclesiastical authorities and on 19th
> September, Sunday of the Dolours of Mary, the first sod was
> turned and the site duly blessed. Next day the work began."

Old-timers confirm these facts, but add that it was Father
Taylor's own fervent devotion to Our Lady of Lourdes that
inspired them with enthusiasm to erect a small grotto in honour
of Our Lady. With a fine appropriateness for detail, he invited
one of the older miners of the village, a worthy by the name of
Andy O'Donnell, to cut the first sod, while Miss Thomasina
Garvie, daughter of one of the pilgrims who had been to Lourdes,
had the privilege of holding the banner of Our Lady on that
auspicious 19th September, 1920.

Monsignor Taylor continues:

> " The Catholic miner possessed the combination of qualities
> required for such a task: patience, endurance, faith profound; he
> lacked only the leisure. However, the time proved extraordinarily
> propitious; for a strike of almost a year's duration afforded him
> the long hours necessary to realise his dream. Winter passed.
> Summer came again and the autumn and the making of the grotto
> embankment proceeded. The enclosure was levelled and the banks
> began to take shape.
>
> It was difficult and arduous work, and as winter came again
> the place became a quagmire and the volunteers dropped off, one
> by one, till one alone remained. Matters looked so unpromising
> that an urgent appeal was made to the Little Flower of Jesus.*
>
> A relic of the Saint was inserted at the spot which the workers
> should reach; and on the following Monday they returned. In

---

* Father Taylor's extraordinary devotion to St. Thérèse is explained in next chapter.

a few months the work was completed. High up on the embankment they had prepared, set with shrubs and flowers, they placed a beautiful statue of Our Lady; below they placed the figure of Bernadette, and on the wall in front, a little piece of rock from the niche at Lourdes was inserted. To complete the picture, an artificial streamlet was laid on from the main water supply, at the request of those who had visited Lourdes. All was now ready. On Sunday, 1st October, 1922, the Grotto was dedicated to Mary Immaculate. Over two thousand people attended the ceremony, among them an organised group of Lourdes pilgrims and a number of non-Catholics. The clergy in attendance included the writer (Father Taylor), with Father J. J. Murphy (then Assistant Curate at Carfin); Father J. Conway, formerly of Che-Kiang, China and St. Modan's Cove; Monsignor T. J. Doyle, Dean Brown and Father Petrauskas. (All have since gone to their eternal reward)."

One cannot but remark on Father Taylor's absolute trust in the powers of intercession of Blessed Thérèse. She, the " Little Queen," as her father used to call her, had loved the Queen of Heaven while on earth; she would not fail to help others to love and honour their heavenly Mother, now that she had joined her in heaven.

None of those who began the Grotto envisaged anything beyond a little local sanctuary. The first volunteers who set to work wheeling sods from the foundations of the new hall to form the Grotto they had decided to erect, did not suspect that they were laying the foundations of the first National Marian Shrine. To quote Father Taylor again:

" At the most they hoped that it would be a joy to their fellow Catholics in the neighbourhood and in a small way a lantern to light to their Mother's arms those outside the fold of the Church."

In *The Carfin Grotto,* Canon Taylor describes the scene that confronts the eye of the pilgrim as he enters the Grotto and follows the traditional processional route through the grounds. Since the layout has not been much changed since 1958, when the article was first published, his own words will be reproduced here with suitable comments wherever necessary.

"Passing between the castellated turrets of warm multi-coloured stone which flank the ' ever-open door,' the pilgrim enters into a vast square, capable of holding twenty thousand people and covered with crushed red whinstone. To the left is the Shrine of Our Lady of Lourdes; the statue is set high up on an embankment, in a lovely setting of rocks and plants, with the figure of Bernadette kneeling at her feet. On the right is the shrine of St. Thérèse, the Little Flower of Jesus, the Saint, standing on a rockery of Westmoreland limestone, in a bed of roses, symbolic

of the graces her hands let fall from heaven. And high up on
the south end of the hillside towers Miriam Chapel—from
which Benediction of the Blessed Sacrament is given and where
the Holy Sacrifice of the Mass is offered on solemn occasions—
sheltered against the vagaries of the weather by its great panels
of glass. It is a wonderful scene, almost defying description.

Further along the main avenue which leads from the Square
rises the imposing altar of Christ the King. He is seated on a
marble throne, reminiscent of the Chair of St. Peter. (The shrine
of Christ the King, Father Taylor tells us, was donated by the
Rt. Rev. Mgr. James Canon Mullin, late of St. Peter's Partick, a
great friend and benefactor of the Grotto.) Some distance to the
left, set in a beautiful shrubbery of heather and shaded by tall
trees, is St. Margaret of Scotland, bearing the Holy Rood in one
hand, with the other feeding her beloved orphans; . . . and on
the opposite side, Ireland's St. Patrick looks down on a huge
Mass Rock, the gift of an Irish Protestant landowner of Rath-
friland. (This gift was arranged through the good offices of an
Irish priest who was familiar with the Grotto.)

The main avenue then swings round in a wide arc, enclosing as
it proceeds a huge sunken area, transformed into the garden of
the Holy House, with its wonderful sanctuary of St. Joseph. Our
Lady's Spouse is installed opposite the great archway which gives
entrance to the garden; seven foot high niches in the curve of the
retaining wall display to advantage seven artistic bas-reliefs of
Our Lady's Dolours; immediately underneath, is placed Michael
Angelo's famous Pieta, Our Lady of Pity, with her dead Son in
her lap. (This statue has been recently moved to the arched
enclosure where formerly the large processional statue of Our
Lady Health of the Sick had been housed.) At the other end of
the garden stands a striking reproduction of the Holy House of
Nazareth, with its three caves and its exquisite statues—an exact
replica of the dwelling place of the Holy Family, faithfully con-
forming to the plans provided by the Bishop of Loreto. The whole
sanctuary is a sermon in marble and stone."

To the House of Dupon, at Bruges, goes the credit for the
design of the Holy House and the execution of the unusual
figures of the Holy Family. M. Gerard Dupon, who died recently
(November 1970), has been responsible for many of the major
treasures of the Grotto; in particular, the statuary and the
beautifully coloured star window in the Bethlehem Cave, the
huge and unique Grotto Monstrance and the Blessed Sacrament
canopy, as well as many of the major reliquaries in the Chapel
of All Saints.

But, excellent as these masterpieces are, their beauty would be
lost if the background in which they were set did not provide a

pleasing harmony. To do this was the task of the Grotto volunteers. The overall result was achieved by team-work; the idea materialised in Monsignor's Taylor's fertile mind; the blueprint of the plan was executed by M. Dupon; and the Grotto workers did the rest. Of all the undertakings in the whole Grotto, Monsignor Taylor has said that the erection of the House of Nazareth was the most intricate, because of the series of cupola roofs, each on a different level. One worker summed it up succinctly with, " A tricky bit job that! "

The next part of Monsignor's description deals with what the pilgrim sees on the return journey, along the processional route:

" Entering the lower avenue, there rises the New Mount Fatima, with the familiar group, Mary of the Immaculate Heart, ' Our Lady of Fatima,' and her little favourites, Lucy, Francis and Jacinta. Leaving Mount Fatima, the pilgrim turns to find himself confronted by a massive Calvary with its more than life-size bronzed figures. From a lofty wooden cross the Crucified Christ gazes compassionately down on Our Lady of Dolours, St. John and St. Mary Magdalen. The whole effect of the group is enhanced by the blood-red flowers, the immense boulders, and the weeping trees. In a few moments the visitor arrives at a picturesque lake, dedicated to Our Lady; its glory is made complete by the fascinating statue, specially designed for Carfin, ' Our Lady Star of the Sea.' The young mother, her veil and tresses tossing in the breeze, stands on the foam-capped waves, holding her babe aloft to welcome all who come to visit her Grotto. Smiling down from the summit of the tiny islet, she dominates the whole landscape."

Prior to 1954, the present Mount Fatima was the site of the statues of St. Joseph, St. Anne, with her child Mary, and St. Joachim. To allow for the additional space required for the Fatima group of statues, that of St. Joseph was installed in the sunken garden and a new shrine was erected for the Holy Child, St. Anne and St. Joachim, on the avenue beyond that of St. Margaret. It is said—the writer cannot vouch for its veracity—that when St. Joseph's statue was moved, one of the workers asked, " Canon, what's going to happen to the old couple now that their son-in-law has gone?"

The casuistry of the reply has a semblance of Monsignor's quiet wit. " They are going to stay with their grandson. They may be happier with him."

Monsignor continues:

" Beyond the lake rises Mount Assisi. There, St. Anthony with the Holy Child surmounts a delightful rock garden, while below, at the foot of the garden, St. Francis, seated on a boulder, preaches to his beloved birds. Away to his left, a small Chapel of Our Lady of the Angels, in imitation of his Portiuncula, has been excavated. On his right, also in true Franciscan tradition, lies an incomparable Bethlehem Cave. Here the rock-like walls, the singular charm of the figures, the soft light and the angels of the star window, all combine to portray a scene which deeply stirs the heart of even the most casual visitor . . . On the opposite side of the adjacent square there stand three life-like groups. In the centre is St. Pius X, with two young first communicants; on his left is St. John Bosco, apostle of youth, with two of his spiritual children (one of whom is now St. Dominic Savio), on his right St. John Baptist de la Salle, patron of all teachers, with one of his little pupils."

Other shrines were mentioned in *The Carfin Grotto;* the marble plaques of the Seven Sacraments, originally placed on Mount Assisi but later reset in the wall below the Miriam Chapel; the unusual bas-relief Rosary shrine of Our Lady, with St. Dominic and St. Catherine of Siena, donated to the Grotto by a relation of Bishop Patrice Flynn, friend of Monsignor Taylor since St. Sulpice College days; the statue of Philomena— now sadly out of fashion—and her devotee, the Curé d'Ars, both mounted near the slopes of Mount Assisi, a perpetual reminder of the generosity of two pilgrims from Glasgow, a mother and daughter, who gave their life savings to enrich their heavenly Mother's sanctuary at Carfin; the last to be mentioned, but far from being the least important, is the massive Flemish sculptured wooden statue of Our Lady Health of the Sick, the gift of a local school-teacher. Formerly this statue rested on its own plinth in an alcove arch, fronted by huge glass wheeling doors, near the entrance to the lower Grotto. Time and exposure to the inclement weather corroded the fine iron framework of the plate-glass door and regrettably, this handsome gift of a notable Highland family had to be disposed of as no longer serving a useful purpose.

On the request of a friend, the following story provided by the late Monsieur Dupon is included here. How could a writer refuse the wish of one who, on more than one occasion, sat through the long night watches correcting the typescript of this biography?

Some time after the massive wooden statue of Our Lady Health of the Sick had been installed in the Lower Grotto, Father Taylor noticed that several defects were appearing in the fabric of the statue. A rather peremptory letter signed only " M.W—," by one of Father Taylor's secretaries, brought the sculptor, Monsieur Dupon, post haste to Carfin to interview " Father "

M.W—, who had sent the letter of complaint. It must be added by way of explanation that the Taylor-Dupon association—later to become a closely knit partnership—was then only in its infancy, and as yet Monsieur Dupon and Monsignor Taylor did not fully understand each other. Judge, then, Monsieur Dupon's discomfiture when he discovered that Father Taylor's secretary was not one of the curates, but Miss W—, a teacher in the local school. Monsieur Dupon insisted that the statue should be returned to Belgium for repair, and once there, he refused to allow its return to Carfin until a suitable enclosure was erected to protect the statue of the Madonna from the vagaries of the Scottish weather. Father Taylor gave immediate instructions to Monsieur Dupon to have a massive glass door made to fit a prepared alcove. The work completed, the artist found he was unable to find a company willing to ensure the transport to Scotland of the huge plate-glass iron-fitted door; and that there would be further delay due to sectioning the door into smaller segments.

Father Taylor's reaction was immediate: " Have faith," he wrote. " We will insure the door in the Company of Heaven."

The story ends happily. The door arrived safely and was soon fitted in the prepared alcove, after which Monsieur Dupon arranged the transport of the processional statue, which is known at Carfin as " Our Lady, Health of the Sick."

The giant-size statue was transferred in the last few years to the shrine which was at one time known as the Holy Souls shrine. Here for a number of years, on the 2nd November, Holy Mass was celebrated for the repose of the souls of deceased relatives. After Mass it was the custom for those of the congregation who were free to do so, to travel to St. Patrick's cemetery at New Stevenston, where a public service was held for the Holy Souls. At solemn processions on Assumption Sundays the massive statue of Our Lady Health of the Sick was carried by teams of twelve stalwart men around the processional route, an honour often allocated to members of visiting pilgrimages.

Finally, mention must be made of the original plaster statue of Maria Goretti, fashioned by Monsieur Dupon; this statue, which once stood in the Upper Grotto, has now been removed to the parish church for protection against inclement weather.

Before continuing with a short history of the Grotto, in the article from which our extensive quotations have been taken, Monsignor Taylor writes a short paragraph on the extent of the

Grotto grounds and the environment in which the pilgrim would find himself any fine summer eve in the early 'fifties:

" The Grotto, covering some seven acres of ground, is beautifully laid out; the rock gardens and rare blossoms of every kind, the spacious green lawns and the crushed red whinstone covering the many avenues that wind through the Grotto, are a delight to the eye, and the statuary of the domain is of a very high order, traditional and devotional, hewn in the main from Carrara marble. Make a visit there any summer's evening and you can see upwards of a hundred people walking around the Grotto, some silently saying their prayers, some in groups moving around the shrines; some from home, some from other lands; not all of them our own colour and often not of our own faith—all of them drawn by the beauty of the place and the spiritual peace which it affords. From May until October, on each Sunday and on special days, the pilgrims will come in thousands from all parts of Scotland and beyond its borders; and by the time summer is over upwards of a quarter of a million people will have made the pilgrimage to Carfin and joined in the processions, the rosaries and the singing of the Lourdes anthem, to give honour to Our Lady, her Son and His Saints."

Wednesday evening was always a popular day for visitors, for Canon Taylor was invariably at home then. On this day, too, there were several services in the church, as well as the veneration of the relic of St. Thérèse, after Benediction had been given. Another attraction on Wednesday evenings was that roses might be blessed specially in honour of the Little Flower of Jesus. Monsignor Taylor had been granted the faculty, by the Carmelite Order, to perform this office. Bank holidays and other public holidays, also, brought a steady stream of visitors, some to visit the shrine, but others to meet Monsignor Taylor himself, who in his own right was much sought after by those who were in trouble of any kind, spiritual or temporal.

Before returning to the story of the early development of the Grotto, it is well to note a few important changes made by the present Administrator, the Rev. George Mullen, priest-in-charge of the parish of St. Francis Xavier. As already mentioned, when the statue of Our Lady Health of the Sick was installed in the Upper Grotto, Father Mullen arranged for the Pieta, formerly erected on a site in the sunken garden, to be placed immediately in front of an imposing cross in the alcove, which originally housed the Flemish processional Madonna. Also, in the centre of the large square stretching between Mount Assisi and Pius X altar, a marble image of Our Lady of the Poor—a copy of the original statue erected at Banneux, in Belgium—has now been set up permanently on the spot where it had been lodged temporarily by Monsignor Taylor, a few years before his death. Several additions have been made to the shrines and statuary of the Grotto: the first, a group of three statues, symbolic of the fourteenth Station of the Cross—the dead Christ and Mary His Sorrowing Mother, with Mary of Magdala standing near. These three figures are placed in a glass-fronted alcove, directly under the Miriam Chapel of the Blessed Sacrament: Clearly the words of the Holy Mass are re-echoed in this scene; " Christ has died. Christ has risen . . ."

On the far boundary of the Lower Grotto, a new set of Stations of the Cross, subscribed for by individual donors, has been erected recently, on Father Mullen's instruction. These brick-built Stations replace the set of wooden crosses which earlier lined the same avenue, and which had to be removed during Monsignor Taylor's lifetime because damp had caused the wood to decay.

The most striking addition to the Grotto in recent years, however, is the imposing heroic-size statue of St. Andrew, patron saint of Scotland. Raised on a mound at the farthest extent of the Grotto domain, and overlooking the sunken garden, it may be seen from almost every point in the Grotto. Monsignor Taylor's dream at one time was to have an altar erected at this point so that Benediction of the Blessed Sacrament might be given for the third time on Corpus Christi Sundays, at the outer limits of the Grotto.*

This dream was not realised, nor was that expressed in a letter to M. Dupon, the Flemish artist to whom Canon Taylor was so heavily indebted for generous and willing help over a quarter of a century. " Before I go," Monsignor Taylor wrote to his friend, in 1953, " I would like to see, in the Grotto, shrines to St. Peter and St. Paul, St. John and St. Jude."

In 1946, his hopes for St. Jude seemed promising, for a small legacy had been bequeathed to him for this specific purpose. The aftermath of the war brought soaring prices and the sum of money made available was not sufficient to defray the expenses of a marble statue; hence it is more than likely that the legacy joined the accumulation of money set aside in the Grotto general fund. It was this fund, upwards of £1,500, which covered the expenses of the Fatima Shrine, the last of the greater shrines installed in the Grotto by Monsignor Taylor. Another effort

---

* In recent months a small Blessed Sacrament altar has been erected immediately below the Madonna shrine.

which came to naught was his attempt to find a further donor for the shrine in honour of Blessed John Ogilvie, the Scottish martyr. An artist had been commissioned to undertake this work, but a long period of illness followed by the sculptor's death, had left the work in the initial stages of production only, and so, this project, too, had to be abandoned for the want of further donors. Monsignor Taylor's veneration of the Scottish Jesuit martyr was well known, and when he was free to do so, he led a group of his parishioners in the "Ogilvie Walk" which took place annually from Glasgow Cross, where Father Ogilvie had been martyred, along High Street to his burial place somewhere near the pre-Reformation Cathedral. In view of the increasing devotion to Blessed John, it was in keeping with Monsignor Taylor's character that in church and Grotto, constantly, he urged Scottish Catholics to pray for the canonisation of the Scottish martyr priest. " Scots people do not pray sufficiently," he said, " or they would have their own Scottish saint before now."

Although matters religious and spiritual were all of interest to Father Taylor, our present theme is of the Grotto and its early development. The Archbishop's advice had been to keep the shrine a very modest one, and this indeed was Father Taylor's original intention, for the mass unemployment of the early 'twenties was as obvious to the cleric as it was to the layman. Indeed, it was because of the great numbers who were out of work that Father Taylor was enabled to call on sufficient men to undertake the back-breaking work involved in clearing and preparing the site for the Grotto. How generously the volunteers responded is shown by the result.

The first statues installed in the Grotto, those of Our Lady of Lourdes and Blessed Bernadette, were provided by Mr. Patrick Nugent, a generous-hearted bookmaker in the village; not only did he provide the required money, but he gave of his time and labour. Day after day, he and his band of workers volunteered their services for the arduous work then in progress at the Grotto site. It was well that one family in the village was in a position to donate the money for the first statues, for valiant hearts, brawny muscles and empty pockets are generally unable to clear heavy bills. Conditions were to improve in subsequent years, for donors were forthcoming not only from the parish, but also from all over the country, as well as from overseas.

Although there was considerable excitement locally, the forthcoming official opening of the shrine received little mention in the Catholic press. In July 1922, the *Observer* reported that " the people of Carfin parish are engaged in conducting electricity, light and water to Our Lady's Grotto."

The same paper reports on 22nd September, 1922:

"The Grotto has been closed until such time as the dedication ceremony takes place. The date fixed may be postponed a little owing to the trouble in Italy, whence the statue comes."

The opening ceremony on Rosary Sunday received more ample coverage:

"The Grotto of Our Lady of Lourdes was formally opened on Sunday, October 1st, 1922, by Rev. Father Taylor. The following priests were present: Rev. Fathers Taylor, Brown, Murphy, Doyle, Petrouski, Conway and O'Brien. The various Parochial Societies took part in the Procession. A short service was held in the church by Father Taylor. Many people could not gain access to the crowded Grotto. A pleasing feature was the remarkable number of non-Catholics who attended the ceremony. Another service was held in the grounds at night. The Grotto is considered as a landmark for the Catholics of Lanarkshire. There were present, Catholics from Greenock, Gourock, Falkirk, Port-Glasgow, Shotts and Wishaw."

During the winter months of 1922, little mention, if any, is made by the press of Grotto activities, although it is reported that Father Andrew McArdle, home from the China mission, preached a charity sermon in the newly opened Lourdes Institute at Carfin. As a result, the Chinese Mission Fund was enriched by £65.

The threat of inclement weather did not deter Father Taylor in 1923, nor in any year thereafter, until his health failed him, from resuming services in the Grotto early in February. The Sunday nearest to February 11th, recognised as Lourdes Sunday, was to become, traditionally, the opening season in the Grotto, and Rosary Sunday was the last of the great processions of the year. After the feast of Christ the King was declared a major feast in the calendar of the Church, the Grotto season was extended until the 26th October when a goodly number of processionists generally turned out to give homage to their heavenly King. It would be misleading, however, to suggest that there was ever a " close " season in the Grotto, for at any time of the year, whenever a group of people arrived at the Shrine, Father Taylor was more than willing to lead them in prayer, even though the five decades might understandably be reduced to one decade and a few ejaculations, when the snow lay heavy on the ground. Such consideration was not normally accorded to the more sturdy of his own people; hail, rain or snow, on the 8th

December a long procession of people wended their way round the village, in the chill of the winter, publicly reciting the fifteen decades of the Rosary, and always, whatever the condition of the weather, the service ended with a few prayers in front of Our Lady's statue in the Grotto. Another practice, and one still observed at Carfin, is the lovely one of visiting the Bethlehem Cave in the Grotto after midnight Mass in the church on Christmas morn. For these solemn occasions a beautifully made *bambino,* the gift of the Sisters who have charge of the birthplace of St. Thérèse, at Alençon, was used. After midnight Mass in the church, the *bambino* was taken from the crib there and borne in procession to the Cave of Bethlehem in the Grotto. Although they were always careful not to let him know, it was a source of amusement to the little altar-boys to see their parish priest stepping out briskly at the head of a carol-singing procession, carefully carrying his precious burden in outstretched arms.

But none of this was in the minds of the people of Carfin when they read the account of the first procession in the Grotto on Lourdes Sunday, 1923 : *Observer,* February 17, 1923 :

" *Carfin.* Very Rev. Canon Mullin, of Maryhill, preached in Our Lady of Lourdes' Grotto on Sunday to an immense audience, it being the feast of Our Blessed Lady."

A month later, Our Lady's Grotto is found worthy of a three and a half lines' mention only, in the press, while a Passion Play presented by the Carfin Players in the Lourdes Institute is boosted to a paragraph of twelve lines. It must be added as an extenuating circumstance that this production had already proved so popular that it was booked up for the Town Hall, Hamilton, and for larger halls in the city of Glasgow; further, the proceeds were for Father McArdle's China Fund, a project guaranteed in advance to win popular support in Carfin.

A careful scrutiny of all the newspapers of the time might produce further information, but, judged on the files of newspaper clippings which Canon Taylor kept, the Carfin Grotto did not make front page news to any great extent before May 1923. The space covered in the file by cuttings during the first eight months of the Grotto's existence, is one and a half pages; during the two months, June and July, immediately after the Beatification of the Little Flower of Jesus, thirty pages are covered with clippings, and these come only from leading newspapers. Those of us who are familiar with Monsignor Taylor's confidence in the powers of intercession exercised in heaven by St. Thérèse, will require no further explanation for the complete change of attitude adopted by the press after the beginning of June 1923, other than that suggested in notes which he entered in the file of press cuttings for that month, and which are given below:

"In April, Father Taylor went to Lisieux and to Rome for Beatification of St. Thérèse—Lisieux again. Received promise of prayer for Carfin. Returned May. Installed small statue of St. Thérèse."

A further note was added:

"Carfin to Lisieux, 13th July."

Two visits to Lisieux within three months require explanation, even though the first visit was to join the official Lisieux group travelling to Rome for the Beatification ceremony; and the second when he broke his journey while on the way to join the Scottish group of pilgrims at Lourdes. Monsignor explains the second visit as follows in *The Carfin Grotto*:

"As early as 1923, a statue of the Little Flower had been given a place of honour in the Grotto. This led to a storm of protest in certain quarters. However, her three sisters in the Carmel of Lisieux silenced the criticism most effectively. 'The child who had loved Mary so passionately,' they declared, 'would certainly not rob Our Lady of her glory . . . Keep her statue in the Grotto. We shall ask Thérèse to draw souls to Carfin, and so prove how she loves Our Lady.' "

An account has already been given of the tremendous crowds which attended the Corpus Christi procession in June of 1923, but reference was not made then to the installation, two months earlier, of the statue of Blessed Thérèse in the Grotto, the reason being that the procession in honour of the Eucharistic King was primarily a parochial affair—these processions had been taking place annually through the streets of the village for several years before the Grotto was opened, and before the Little Flower was beatified. If the numbers attending the solemn procession in honour of the most Blessed Sacrament increased, because of the added attraction of a Marian Shrine and a newly installed statue of Blessed Thérèse, notwithstanding the fact that the ceremonial Corpus Christi procession was held outwith the Grotto grounds, it would seem that the object for which the shrine of Our Lady—and of the Little Flower—had been erected, was justified. The Queen of Heaven and the "Little Queen" were to be the magnets which would draw more and more people to the throne of the Eucharistic King.

The answer was immediate, and to quote Father Taylor again, "Within three months, over a quarter of a million had wended their way to the Scottish shrine of Our Lady of Lourdes." One would not expect *The Glasgow Herald,* a reputable Glasgow newspaper, to be hoodwinked by emotional, religious hysteria, and so the view expressed in its columns on the 25th June, 1923, is worth quoting:

> " Thousands of people from all parts of Scotland, and not a few from over the Border are making the village of Carfin a centre of pilgrimage."

The word " pilgrimage " had been used for the first time by the press to describe a visit made to the Grotto and church at Carfin, by a group of over a hundred pupils from Notre Dame High School, Glasgow, on Saturday morning, 16th June. Their devotional exercises commenced with Mass and Holy Communion in the church, after which they visited the Grotto of Our Lady where the Rosary was recited and the Lourdes hymn sung—all this before they broke their fast. At mid-day they assembled in the church for Benediction of the Blessed Sacrament, followed by another visit to the Grotto, before they set out on the return journey to Glasgow. In the nature of things, it seems fitting that an Order dedicated to Our Lady should have the honour of being the first pilgrims to make the visit to Our Lady's shrine in real penitential fashion. The practice was repeated by the students of Notre Dame school and college for many years, a practice which must have had the complete approval of the highly esteemed and scholarly Sister Aimée, N.D., of Dowanhill, who had been the critic whose opinion, on his literary work Monsignor Taylor had valued most of all. Not only were the " N.D.'s " first in the field in giving " official " honour to Our Lady at Carfin, they were also generous in material help. The Order was among the first of these from outside the parish to offer material help: as well as providing the original small " Notre Dame Altar," which had to be demolished when the Miriam Chapel of the Blessed Sacrament was erected in the enlarged Grotto; regularly, the Order also provided innumerable plants, shrubs and supplies of turf, from the gardens of its Houses in England.

It is almost impossible in these days of indifference to imagine the stupendous fervour of the pilgrims to Carfin in the pre-war years. Sensationalism and emotionalism there was in plenty—the press made the most of their stories—but behind it all there was a profound outpouring of faith, as if the sluice gates had been opened and hitherto dammed up wells had been released. Until then, Catholics in the West of Scotland had professed their faith with a certain amount of reserve, especially their veneration of the Blessed Virgin. But now, when thousands flocked to Carfin to honour her publicly, onlookers of other denominations were compelled to give the changed circumstances serious thought. The national press on the whole commented favourably on the crowds of pilgrims who came to pray at Carfin and a number featured leading articles from time to time during the ensuing years; but not all could see eye to eye with the views held by Catholics, and dissenting opinions were expressed by a number of individuals, especially in the form of " Letters to the Editor," but at no time did Father Taylor allow himself to be lured into acrimonious statements in any newspaper, even though at times he must have been sorely tempted to do so, when the fair name of Mary was insulted and held up for ridicule.

A cross-section of the views published by several papers is reproduced below in order to throw into relief the opinion held by the majority at that time:

Evening Dispatch, Monday, 2nd July, 1923.

THE SCOTTISH LOURDES
By Our Special Correspondent.

" To stand in the main street of Carfin, the little mining village near Motherwell, and watch the people streaming into the Grotto, which has come to be known as the Scottish Lourdes, is an experience not readily to be forgotten. There are many inclined to scoff at matters of this kind and to argue that this pilgrimage is merely a transitory and spasmodic awakening of religious sentiment, and that when it has shed the glamour of novelty the movement will, like other revivals which have taken place in various parts of the country, gradually lose its interest and in a short time be dead.

That remains to be seen, but those who visit the grotto with open minds cannot fail to be moved and touched by what they will see there, and they will come away—no matter what their denomination may be—marvelling at the faith and sincerity shown by the thousands of pilgrims who pass through the shrine in the course of an afternoon.

It is difficult to estimate the size of a crowd of this character, but it is no exaggeration to state that during yesterday afternoon several thousands of pilgrims came to Carfin and worshipped in the grotto. Parties of varying numbers travelled from all parts of the midlands of Scotland, and all manner of conveyances were pressed into service to transport them to the shrine. Between 2.30 and 3.15, the writer counted twenty-one large charabancs arriving in the village; and, in addition, there were many private motors, traps, motor cycles, and combinations, while large numbers also came on ordinary cycles.

In no conditions could Carfin ever look attractive or inviting, and the bright sunshine only accentuated its drabness and unprepossessing appearance, but from about two o'clock the long straight main street was one continual bustle and movement. Inside the grotto, hundreds were either kneeling in prayer or standing in hushed silence, but the road outside provided a striking contrast. There was a steady hum of traffic, and the blare and hoot of motor horns seemed strangely incongruous in such surroundings . . .

These are changed days for Carfin, and the enterprising people of the village are not permitting the opportunities presented by the influx of visitors to be lost. One establishment has erected a marquée behind its premises, and in this meals are provided, while in numerous private dwellings, arrangements have also been made to supply the material needs of the pilgrims.

The grotto is never closed, and from early morning until late at night it is scarcely ever devoid of worshippers. Immediately after morning Mass had been said in the Roman Catholic Church yesterday, almost all the congregation went across the street to the shrine and spent a short time there in devotion.

It was especially touching to see a large party of little boys and girls—some mere toddlers—kneeling in front of the statue of Our Lady of Lourdes; several of the children were so tiny that after saying their prayers they had to be lifted up in order to kiss the stone brought from under the spot at the French shrine where the apparition is said to have appeared to the child Bernadette.

Although the largest contingents did not arrive until the afternoon, a number of pilgrims visited the shrine in the morning. One lady, who suffered from lameness, was accompanied by her husband. The latter told the writer that they belonged to Edinburgh, and had come to Carfin for the benefit of his wife. She thought nothing could cure her but a miracle, yet she had sufficient faith to believe that her visit and intercession would do her good.

Two particularly pathetic cases were those of an old man, who was so weak and infirm that he almost had to be carried from his car to the grotto, and the other, little more than a youth, could only totter along on crutches, trailing his feet behind him. Such incidents are common, and they must make people thankful that they are straight of limb and sound of health.

In a chat with the writer, the priest in charge, Father Taylor, remarked that what struck him most about the pilgrims was the content and pleasure which a visit to the grotto seemed to bring to those who were invalids. They might not be cured, but they all went away much happier than when they came. For that reason alone he was satisfied that they were doing good work.

As an instance, he cited the case of two Protestants, a mother and daughter, who had come to the shrine from Kilmarnock. The mother was paralysed and had to be pushed in a chair, while the daughter had a palsied arm. By mistake they went to Wishaw station, and the daughter had to push the chair for three miles to the grotto. 'Handicapped as she is,' he said, 'I do not know how she managed to do it, but the visit certainly cheered mother and daughter up immensely. They were both devout members of the Protestant Church, yet they seemed to benefit.'

As the day wore on, a steady tide of pilgrims flowed in and out of the grotto . . . many were kneeling on the ground with Rosaries in their hands, while skirting the banks of the grotto was a long queue, standing six and eight deep, waiting their turn to drink from the well and kiss the Lourdes' stone. Many carried bottles, and these were filled with water from the pool. This would later be administered to friends who were unable to make the journey."

The writer of the article next made brief mention of a Petition Box which stood near to the statue of Our Lady. Here the pilgrim placed his petition to Our Lady. After a time the written petitions were removed and burned unread. This custom was based on one practised at Our Lady's shrine at Lourdes. Since the last war this practice has been discontinued at Carfin; Monsignor Taylor felt it was no longer necessary since the intentions of pilgrims to the Grotto were remembered daily at every service held, both in the parish church and at the Grotto shrine.

The lengthy article in the *Evening Dispatch* ends as follows:

" Having completed their devotions, the majority of the pilgrims crossed the road to the Roman Catholic Church, and during the afternoon the pews were crowded with figures kneeling in silent prayer . . .

The opening of the grotto has undoubtedly acted as an inspiration to many Roman Catholics, particularly in the district, and about the middle of this month a party from Carfin is leaving for Lisieux, in Normandy, in order to be present at the celebration of the Feast of Our Lady of Mount Carmel."

The visit to Lisieux referred to above is, of course, the occasion when Father Taylor discussed with the sisters of St. Thérèse the advisability of retaining in the Grotto shrine of Our Lady of Lourdes at Carfin, the statue of their recently beatified sister, the Little Flower of Jesus.

Another article, this time published in the *Universe* and copied by other papers, gives the story of the growth of the Grotto during the first year of its existence.

Although the article is subscribed, "From a correspondent," Father Taylor's notes reveal that the writer was Father W. Cooksey, S.J., Craighead, Bothwell.

Universe, 5th October, 1923.

SCOTTISH LOURDES

" As one who has been familiar with Carfin Grotto since its inception, kindly let me give as briefly as possible the material facts.

The village, a drab and uninviting hilltop in the Scottish coal-field on the L.M.S. Glasgow and Edinburgh line, is united in the Faith, and in its esteem and affection for its parish priest. Hence it is not remarkable that it cherishes a deep devotion to Our Lady of Lourdes and to the Blessed Little Flower of Jesus. It is also noted for its generosity to the Society of the Holy Childhood.

During the coal strikes which followed the War, the miners united—under the foremanship of the local bookmaker—in laying out the field opposite the priest's house and church, and in pre-paring the foundations for a village institute and parish hall; this was duly built and dedicated, on completion, to Our Lady of Lourdes, whilst still surrounded by debris from the foundations, and the paths of mud, worthy of the Ypres Salient. Whilst laying out this waste into lawns and gardens, it was decided to erect a grotto of Our Lady of Lourdes on the irregular ground west of the hall, and for this purpose life-size marble statues of Our Lady of Lourdes and of the Ven. Bernadette were ordered at Carrara. Whilst the excavations were being made and the rock-gardens erected, changes were made in the plan. Outside opinion being asked, it was considered that of the multitude of Catholics in Clydesdale, many would probably visit Carfin on feast days and would require greater accommodation; the arena was accordingly designed to accommodate 2,000 people, and the statue placed in a niche facing the setting sun.

At the same time, the analogy of Oostaker in Belgium, and its artificial water supply, was urged as a precedent, and the assistant priest of Carfin (Fr. J. Murphy) crossed to Belgium and examined Oostaker and all its works; and in consequence an artificial spring was included in the design.

In the autumn of 1922, exactly one year ago this week, the shrine was dedicated and a small fragment of Our Lady's Rock at Lourdes enshrined, in the presence of a few of the neighbouring clergy.

Gradually the idea of a pilgrimage to Carfin spread amongst the devout of the neighbourhood, until Spring wrought its annual change and the beauty of the setting of the Shrine unfolded itself. But it was not until the Beatification of the Blessed Thérèse was drawing near that its fame reached the ears of the secular press.

Simultaneously with the Beatification and erection of a very small and modest shrine in her honour on the north side of the arena, the unsought publicity in the whole press of Great Britain brought thousands every Sunday, and hundreds every week-day, until it is jocularly said that every charabanc in Scotland can find its way to Carfin unattended.

The greatest number present has been seventy thousand, and the most striking cures have been claimed by Protestants.

The storms of the Scottish autumn and the snow on the bens have reduced the attendance; the frequent outdoor services will soon be discontinued as winter is upon us, but the grotto will remain open and pilgrims will still continue to come.

As for the conclusions to be drawn, it can only be said with truth that, as at Lourdes and Holywell, the material cures are as a drop in the ocean as compared with the beneficial spiritual effects produced. On Sunday, the 23rd inst., I witnessed the arena and the church in turn twice thronged by an orderly, reverent and deeply devout mass of pilgrims, who were marshalled by efficient and recollected stewards in the church and grotto and by two policemen only in the streets.

There was an entire absence of fuss and excitement, and the only evidence of emotion was the intense pity the sick and the afflicted evoked. Even the commercial intruders in the village street have been suppressed or made unobtrusive and quiet.

The well-springs of Grace are secret, and we cannot distinguish cause and effect. There is a special movement of Grace at work in Scotland as there is elsewhere, and it cannot be said with certainty whether Carfin is truly a cause or an effect. One is inclined to the opinion that Carfin is a subsidiary broadcasting station for Our Lady of the Immaculate Conception relaying from Lourdes. But the receptivity of Clydesdale was there before, and that receptivity has found its sympathetic vibration in Carfin, and in the personality which conceived and carried out the Carfin Shrine, a retired professor of theology who is thoroughly enjoying himself; but I cannot reveal in pen and ink the secret of his enjoyment, which can only be fully shared by pilgrims."

While granting that the number " seventy thousand," quoted in the article reproduced above, was variously used by a number of newspapers, the writer of these lines would like to suggest that reporters were unable to give even an approximation of the numbers present in the Grotto. Top estimates of pilgrims present in the village on the busiest days in 1923 vary from thirty thousand to seventy thousand. One thing is beyond dispute, and that is that the crowds were so great that the Grotto precincts could not accommodate them. One priest who accompanied a group of his parishioners on pilgrimage to the shrine, reported that it took them three hours moving slowly in a queue to reach the drinking well near the statue of Our Lady. The writer's own memory of these days was that the village of Carfin was a seething mass of people on special feast-days, while on ordinary Sundays the Grotto seemed to be full to capacity at all the services. Later years were to see even greater numbers, but by that time the Grotto grounds had been extended and the vast numbers could be accommodated with greater ease.

The foregoing articles, taken from the secular and Catholic press, make no direct mention of the alleged improvement in health and even of cures, claimed by a number of people during the months of June and July of the year 1923. If advertisement were required to make the shrine at Carfin known, it was provided by the national press towards the end of June. Spiritual favours were known to have been granted; but the return of a " prodigal son " does not make front page headlines in the press, and indeed is rarely mentioned publicly. Temporal favours in answer to prayer are evident to the eye of the onlooker, and are accorded a much greater accolade, usually being deemed greater proof of the power of the Almighty than the healing of a diseased soul. Hence, almost overnight, Carfin made front page news because of the " Faith Cures " which were alleged to have taken place after the water from the shrine of Our Lady of Lourdes had been applied to the sufferer. The following account is one of the first to catch the public imagination:

Sunday Post, 24th June, 1923.

FAITH CURE AT CARFIN
OLD WOMAN THROWS ASIDE CRUTCH

Exclusive to the *Sunday Post*

Glasgow, Saturday night.

" The drab little mining village of Carfin, situated about two miles from the Craigneuk district of Wishaw, has become the Lourdes of Scotland.

During the last two or three days, between four and five hundred people, drawn from all parts of Lanarkshire and beyond, are daily visiting the Grotto erected there in connection with St. Xavier's R.C.

There has been at least one remarkable case of faith-healing associated with the waters—that of Mrs. Holmes, an old woman of seventy-six, residing at 57e Watson's Land, Whifflet, who, after ten years' suffering as a chronic invalid, has abandoned her crutch, astonishing all her friends by her astounding cure.

I have seen and spoken to Mrs. Holmes, and I can vouch for her renewed vitality, which she attributes solely to the beneficent healing influence of the water at Carfin Grotto.

Mrs. Holmes told me that, hearing from some friends of faith cures at Carfin, she resolved to journey thither by motor, accompanied by some friends.

After taking part in a ritual service conducted by the Rev. Father Taylor, Carfin, the waters of the Grotto were administered to her. She returned home believing that she was healed. Next morning she rose from bed feeling better than she had done for years. So well, indeed, was she that she discarded her crutch and found herself able to walk without even having to lean on the chairs, as hitherto.

Her improved condition had been maintained all week, and on Sunday following her cure she returned to the Grotto accompanied by friends who carried the now discarded crutch rolled up in paper.

The party's appearance among the worshippers at the Grotto caused no little surprise, and, on her story becoming known, there was general thanksgiving and congratulations . . .

Mrs. Holmes' condition continues to show unabated improvement, indicating that the cure promises to be of a permanent nature. When I saw her at her home, at Whifflet, the old lady said she had to thank God for restoring her to her normal health and strength.

'I have not known,' she continued, 'what it meant to have a night's sleep for the last ten years. Often so agonising has been the pain that I have prayed to be taken out of my misery . . .'

'It was not until that morning following my visit to Carfin that I was able even to put on my stockings or lace my shoes. My sciatica, rheumatism, and hip-joint disease commenced about ten years ago, every day getting worse. My doctor could do nothing further to help me, as my condition had become chronic, and it was only at the suggestion of friends that I volunteered to visit the Grotto at Carfin.'

The old woman's story is well known to her neighbours, who all testify to her remarkable recovery."

For a few weeks the crutch, which had been used by the old lady and given by her to Father Taylor, might be seen near the shrine. The *Observer* reported in the following week that "Father Taylor possesses a Protestant doctor's certificate which clearly states the afflictions under which Mrs. Holmes laboured prior to going to Carfin."

Undoubtedly, the publicity which the press gave to Mrs. Holmes' claim to a definite improvement in her condition was responsible for the claim being noised abroad that Carfin Grotto water had beneficial powers. Continuously and persistently Father Taylor, and other priests, also, reiterated that the power did not lie in the water—it was ordinary drinking water laid on by the County Council—but in the faith and prayer of the suppliant. The Catholic *Observer* elaborated this point in its columns on the 7th July:

> "It seems as if Scotland—indeed all Britain—has awakened to the fact that all is ' not of the earth, earthy.' To judge by the crowds visiting the Carfin Grotto, the materialism of the past few years is ready to yield to a renewed and widespread belief in God and the supernatural.
>
> As we stated in our issue of last week, the water of the Grotto is ordinary water. It does not come from Lourdes, though some Lourdes water was used when the Grotto was first opened. There seems, therefore, to be no definite reason why the waters should be curative—if they are curative. No special claim has been made so far on this point, although everything bears out the testimony of grateful sufferers that the waters do possess a particular efficacy. Priests and other well-informed and pious persons are inclined at present to favour the view that faith and prayer play the greatest part in the cure. In spite of everything, however, the fact remains that it was only after drinking of the waters of the Carfin Grotto that any of these cures have been effected."

The wiseacres who forecast a nine days' wonder were proved wrong, for during many years to come, crowds continued to flock to Carfin. As for the press, reporters were indefatigable in their search for copy regarding each alleged cure. To scan the newspapers of those stirring months of summer, 1923, is to be confronted with what a cynic called an epidemic of cures. In increasing numbers, the press reported, that pilgrims to the Grotto claimed either an improvement in general health or a cure from some malady from which they had been suffering. These claims were made by pilgrims who came from different parts of the country: Carfin, Whifflet, Uddingston, Burnbank, Greenock, Edinburgh, to mention but a few. The accounts varied: the cure of a child suffering from tuberculosis; partial sight restored to a blind child; the cure of persistent skin disease where the parents had been warned not to use water on the child's skin; badly ulcerated limbs which had not responded to medication over a period of about ten years; deafness, and many other maladies.

He would be a presumptuous person who would dare to say that all these claims were false. This would presume a denial of the efficacy of prayer and of one of the Church's most consoling dogmas—the Communion of Saints—and the intercessory powers of the Saints in heaven. It is possible that newspaper reporters, in their zeal for a story, exaggerated in some cases, for if each one of the cases reported was absolutely genuine, the newly-founded Grotto at Carfin could claim about two or three dozen rather striking temporal favours in the first year of its existence. The writer's objection is not to genuine claims of prayers having been answered and temporal favours—and indubitably, spiritual ones—being accorded; her objection lies in the manner in which the press reported what was supposed to have happened. Extraordinary powers were attributed to the water which flowed into the Grotto, while very rarely was reference made to the anguished prayer of the suppliant, who in faith and humility had, often with great difficulty, travelled to Carfin to seek help at Our Lady's Shrine.

The evidence for the alleged cures referred to above has been gleaned from the newspapers of that summer of 1923, but more convincing is the evidence supplied by those who lived through that era and were old enough to understand that their village was playing a special role in the Divine Plan. These ageing citizens, many of whom had helped to build the Grotto, were aware that things were happening which they could not explain; they are quite convinced that many spiritual and temporal favours were granted in answer to prayers offered up to Our Lady of Lourdes, at her shrine at Carfin. The writer of these lines, then having youth on her side, during these exciting first years of the Grotto, cannot recall exact details. Her memory is of tremendous crowds; of long lines of strange monsters called charabancs; of countless people moving slowly towards the spot where they were to venerate the little fragment of the rock on which the Blessed Virgin had stood when she appeared to Bernadette; and of the sick and paralysed being helped along, in their invalid chairs, to the well where the Grotto marshals, with their official white armlets, were kept fully occupied supplying the pilgrims with cupfuls of the water. But, most vividly of all, she remembers Father Taylor; he always seemed to be here, there and everywhere at the same time, at the beck and call of all who sought his help.

Had Father Taylor deliberately planned to institute a propaganda machine to restore in the hearts of the faithful of this country, the devotion to the Mother of God, so long neglected, he could not have been more successful in his efforts than he was. The unsought publicity of the press of Britain brought multitudes to Carfin, some to satisfy their curiosity, the majority to pray.

Although many people in Scotland accepted what was going on at Carfin without troubling too much about the effects the resurgence of Marian devotion in Scotland might have, it was clear that not all approved of this increase of devotion to the " Virgin Mary." The views of a few dissenters were reported in the *Glasgow Herald* in the week following Assumption Sunday, a day on which it was estimated by some Carfin had seen its biggest crowds of the year.

Rev. T. B. Stewart Thomson, while preaching in Dalziel Parish Church, Motherwell, is reported as follows:

" Motherwell's ancient superstition of centuries ago had broken out again, and he was told, incredible though it might seem, that even Protestants were repairing thither (to Carfin) and carrying away vessels of the miraculous water. It possessed no medicinal qualities, but because it had been blessed by a priest and bubbled out, beside a statuette, it was supposed to render the service of all devoted doctors and nurses unnecessary . . .

He knew that Roman Catholics of the district had been warned that it was not the water that cures, but their faith. Doubtless the more intelligent and spiritual believed and understood this; but then, why go to the Grotto at all? Why not exercise faith at home? A fortnight ago as he (the preacher) passed by, he saw hundreds of men, women and children reciting the Rosary as they knelt down on the ground. Doubtless there had been cures at Carfin. Faith, as had been seen, was a great healing power, but our faith needed no grottoes. Those thousands of pilgrims around the statuette of the Virgin were strangely like the cripple at Betheseda. They were so intent on the externals and accessories of their hoped-for cure that they did not see Jesus in their midst."

And what did the humble priest who was at the centre of speculation have to say about what was alleged to be taking place? He cautiously refrained from communicating with the press, although he himself was convinced that favours, spiritual and temporal, had been granted as a result of intercession at Our Lady's Grotto at Carfin. Unceasingly he warned pilgrims that the water at the Grotto in substance was no more beneficial than ordinary drinking water; supernatural favours could come only as a result of Faith, Prayer and Penance. Eventually, a few of the more thoughtful journalists were beginning to look beyond the much quoted " application of waters," to what Father Taylor had to say to the sincere pilgrims who thronged the Grotto. In August of 1923 he is reported as having " laid emphasis on the duty of bearing the Cross." A few newspapers gave more explicit details. "Father Taylor advocated," they wrote, "the repeating of the Rosary for fifteen days, although it was not necessary to attend the Grotto to do this, unless they lived in the vicinity."

The genuine pilgrim had already known this; for close on twenty years Father Taylor had been preaching the message which Mary Immaculate had given to Bernadette, at Lourdes, seventy years earlier. His thrice repeated call, " Penance! Penance! Penance!" could be heard, not only in the Grotto precincts, but in the street outside. A few years later, when the amplifying system had been installed, his message carried throughout the village. Even during the first year since the erection of the shrine, the practice of visiting the Grotto and reciting the Rosary, for fifteen consecutive days, became the recognised form of Marian devotion at Carfin. Almost from the outset, a public " Quinzaine "—the recitation of the Rosary in honour of Our Lady of Lourdes—was observed at Carfin to run concurrently with the " Quinzaine " at Lourdes; this devotion ends on the 4th March, the date of the third apparition of Our Lady.

Speaking of the " Quinzaine," Father Taylor had this to say:

> " On 18th February begins what is known at Lourdes as the great ' Quinzaine,' or period of fifteen days. It will be remembered that Our Lady, at her third visit, asked Bernadette to come each day for fifteen days to the Grotto, doubtless in memory of the fifteen mysteries of the Rosary. It was during that period that, without revealing her identity, she gave the child her messages, and disclosed to her the spring of healing water. The ' Quinzaine ' which ends on Monday, March 4, will be duly observed at Carfin, and during its course the intentions of the Grotto pilgrims will be prayed for. Neither will the dead be forgotten."

In the " Carfin Grotto Notes "—a special feature of the *Glasgow Observer* from 1927 — Father Taylor reported in March 1929:

> " All week the Communion rails have been thronged with children and adults making the ' Quinzaine ' in honour of the fifteen visits of Bernadette. During the Masses, the Rosary and the Raccolta prayer were recited for the intention of the pilgrims, and after the second Mass all present proceeded to the Grotto, where Father Taylor recited the Litany and the invocations on behalf of the Grotto's countless friends. In spite of the intense cold, there was a sufficient number present on Sunday to hold the

three o'clock service and have Benediction of the Blessed Sacrament. All week there has been a steady stream of pilgrims from the neighourhood making with Blessed Bernadette their visit to the Grotto not merely for temporal favours but with the hope that their Mother will say to them, as to the shepherdess of Lourdes, ' I shall make you happy in the next world.' "

Almost from the opening of the Grotto there was a marked improvement in the moral tone of the village, a fact verified by several national newspapers at the time. What the *Sunday Mail* reported in July 1923, differs little from what other newspapers presented to their readers from time to time, in slightly different form:

"I happened to drive through Carfin on Tuesday evening and was surprised at the number of strange motor cars that were there with sightseers on a weekday. I was told that the bulk of the pilgrims were shop assistants from Glasgow who were utilising their half-holiday to visit the now famous Grotto and see things for themselves. During the course of the conversation with a native, who is not Roman Catholic and who has no more belief in the curative effect of the County Council water inside the Grotto than he has from his own supply from the same source, I learned that the moral tone of the whole village has certainly been uplifted by Father Taylor, the originator of the Grotto idea. Formerly many young men banded themselves into groups for Sunday card gambling and their language while engaged in the game was more forcible than polite. Now, these same young men are seen engaged in prayer at the Grotto on Sundays, or in helpful attendance on strangers and fellow worshippers at the shrine. That speaks volumes for the ministry of Father Taylor . . ."

As the first year of the Grotto's existence neared its close, the number of pilgrims increased rather than decreased. An unusual sight in Scotland was the first torchlight procession held in the Grotto in honour of Our Lady's birthday on 8th September. More striking still was the scene that greeted the eyes of the " guid folk " of Motherwell when they saw puffing into their local railway station, two special trains conveying over 1,000 pilgrims from Dundee, and from other places on the route south. When the travellers and the invalids had disembarked from the trains, all lined up in processional order before starting out on the two and a half mile walk to Carfin. At the head of the procession were four cripples, in bath chairs, and these were wheeled all the way up the steep inclines from Motherwell to Carfin, other sick pilgrims being conveyed by motor coach. As the worshippers made their way slowly along, they were joined by others who had arrived by ordinary trains, and all, in true devotional spirit, joined in the recitation of the Rosary and in the singing of hymns until they reached the Shrine. Having spent several hours at Carfin, where they took part in the customary devotional services of the Grotto, in the evening the visitors set out, again in processional order, on the two mile walk to the railway station at Motherwell, where they boarded the special trains for Dundee. The spirit of prayer and penance displayed by the visitors greatly impressed all those who witnessed the procession as it made its way, in orderly fashion, through the streets of Motherwell, to and from Carfin. On that autumn bank holiday could be seen, not spectators or seekers after sensation, but people intent on doing penance and on giving greater honour to God through devotion to Our Blessed Lady, the Mother of Our Lord.

The precedent set up by the people of Dundee in the autumn of 1923 was to continue for many a year and was to be repeated by many another city, town and village, until the outbreak of the Second World War made travel impossible. From the outset, Edinburgh, Dalkeith, Aberdeen, Fife, as well as Glasgow and Lanarkshire parishes, came on regular pilgrimage, but to the neighbouring parish of St. Mary's, Cleland, goes the honour of being the first to come, on foot, to the Grotto in parochial pilgrimage. This practice was followed by other parishes in the neighbourhood, in particular by St. Patrick's, Shieldmuir, the latter walking along the uphill back road, led by their priests, past the area known as Ravenscraig—now the site of Colville's strip mill.

Many may have considered that after the novelty of the first few months, the fervour of the faithful would be considerably diminished. This was not Father Taylor's view. Even before the end of the year, plans were being made to extend the Grotto, in order to accommodate the large influx of people who, he estimated, would continue to visit the Shrine. Also, the small Lourdes Institute, built three years earlier, proved completely inadequate to provide suitable amenities for the multitudes who flocked to Carfin. Father Taylor could foresee that if the Carfin Mission did not cater for the needs of the pilgrims who travelled from long distances, businessmen from outside would grasp the opportunity of setting up catering establishments, as well as repositories for pious objects, and souvenirs of Carfin.

At this time, his chief confidants and advisers in the Arch-diocese were the Belgian-born Monsignor Claeys, who proved of inestimable worth in helping with the plans for the extension of the Grotto; Monsignor Mullin, D.D., a friend of many years' standing, whose love for Our Lady of Lourdes almost equalled that of Father Taylor himself; and Canon Doyle, who as pastor of the neighbouring parish of St.Mary's, Cleland, was with his curate Father O'Brien, always willing to help the Carfin priests during the busy summer months at the Grotto. It used to be said of the jovial Father Doyle that he had a hand in everything at Carfin except the collections. To a greater extent still, Cleland's lovable young assistant curate, Father O'Brien, gave of his utmost in the service of Our Lady at the Grotto Shrine. Nor did the valiant men of St. Mary's, Cleland, lag behind on the path set by their priests; when a final reckoning is made in the heavenly balance sheet, the records will surely show that in the exhaustive plan of building a worthy shrine in honour of Our Lady of Lourdes at Carfin, the men of Cleland did not fail the patroness of their native parish of St. Mary. Volunteers came from all the neighbouring parishes, Shieldmuir, Motherwell, Mossend, Chapelhall, Coatbridge and Baillieston, but by far the greater numbers were supplied by Cleland. It was not unusual during the 'twenties to find a squad of upwards of a hundred " Cleland men " working throughout the day, and often well into the night, by the light of their carbide miner's lamp, on some task that had to be finished urgently. It was indeed a far cry from the time, many decades ago, when the rival factions—the " Leitrim boys " of Cleland and the " Donegal boys " of Carfin—used to fight it out over disputes which arose between squads of " navvies," while they were constructing the main railway lines between Glasgow and Edinburgh.

It may be assumed that it was with some misgiving that His Grace Archbishop Donald Mackintosh, appointed to the See of Glasgow in 1922, considered Father Taylor's request in 1923 for approval of extensive building plans for the Grotto and the Lourdes Institute. His Grace had visited the Shrine for the first time on the evening of August 15, 1923, shortly after the dispersal of an Italian group, six hundred strong, who had attracted the attention of the villagers, as they walked in procession from Holytown station to the Grotto, singing their beautiful Italian hymns in honour of the Madonna. Archbishop Mackintosh did not witness this pilgrimage; nor did he arrive in time that afternoon to see the touching scene of the crippled soldiers from St. David's Home, Edinburgh, being wheeled from Holytown station a mile away, exciting the curiosity of the onlookers as they recited the Rosary aloud. The Archbishop's visit was a private one, in honour of Our Lady, on the feast of her Assumption into Heaven.

A letter dated September 7th, 1923, shows that His Grace had been favourably impressed by his visit to Carfin Grotto. Among other things, he granted permission to Father Taylor to give Benediction of the Blessed Sacrament " on any day in the church if the pilgrims were sufficiently numerous," but " as to giving it in the Grotto or on the lawn—that had better be postponed, at least, for the moment." Because of the latter proviso, on many Sundays in 1923 and early 1924, after the processions in the Grotto were over, Benediction had to be repeated in the church four or five times to satisfy the spiritual needs of the numerous pilgrims. After the controversial procession on Corpus Christi Sunday, 1924, Benediction of the Most Blessed Sacrament was given frequently in the Grotto.

Archbishop Mackintosh's letter ends thus:

". . . As to the question of extension—say very clearly what you consider the needs in that direction are; find out from Captain Colville and the others, what terms they are willing to make and send your statement to 160 Renfrew Street, to be dealt with by the Finance Board and then to come to me. Please don't be niggardly in your proposals.

Also, if ever a *temporal* cure or improvement is reported, have the case examined in the best and fullest way possible and keep records. As you say, the call of the Shrine is wonderful in itself, and I think that itself calls for an act of thanksgiving to Our Lady and to the Little Flower. May it please Our Lord to glorify more and more His Holy Mother and His Beloved Saint.

Yours v. sincerely,

(Sgd.) ✠ D. Mackintosh."

On Sunday, January 6, 1924, His Grace paid a second visit to the Grotto, this time with the express purpose of discussing the plan for enlarging the Grotto. Conservative and orthodox though he had been in his manner so far, he was now convinced that it was imperative, to quote Father Taylor's words, " to widen the slates and lengthen the cords." A fortnight later, Monday, 21st January, St. Agnes' day, the gigantic task began.

To allow for immediate expansion, a field about five acres in extent, lying south and west of the original acre on which the first Institute and Grotto had been built, was taken over, and when the pioneer pilgrims of the year arrived for the feast day of Our Lady of Lourdes, 11th February, 1924, they found the work on the Grotto already far advanced. About three hundred volunteers from Carfin, Cleland and neighbouring parishes gave of their time and labour. So that the work might continue into the night, electric lights were strung along the working area and different squads of men worked on continuously.

The original niche with the statue of the Madonna was left unchanged, although a pulpit of rockery stones was raised above the niche to serve as a plateau for Benediction of the Blessed Sacrament, the cost of this first altar being defrayed by a poor girl in thanksgiving for a favour of health granted through the intercession of the Little Flower. The embankments round the niche and along the rim of the Grotto were widened, heightened and lengthened, and triple paths laid, so that fully a thousand processionists could be accommodated. On " big " days, these paths were lined with pilgrims in regalia, Children of Mary, Boy Scouts, Girl Guides, Tertiaries of St. Francis in their habits, or other pilgrims in regalia symbolic of their order or society, the whole providing a pleasing and colourful effect to the eyes of the pilgrims in the arena below. Some time later, a generous donor provided an unexpected gift of finest Lancashire sea-turf to cover the lowest bank of the arena. Behind the niche—commonly referred to as Massabieille—fifteen sapling lime trees, to symbolise the mysteries of the Rosary, were planted. These lime trees proved a veritable god-send to the writer of these lines while she was engaged on research on the story of the Grotto from 1924 onwards. Among Monsignor Taylor's possessions after his death were hundreds of copies of press photographs, the majority of them undated. By relating the height of the growing trees to that of the Lourdes Institute in the background of the photographs, an approximate date could be gauged for some. For anyone with unlimited time and patience, the task of putting these photographs in chronological sequence should prove a rewarding remedial exercise.

When permission was granted for the extension of the Grotto, it was accorded, too, for the enlarging of the Institute. Father Taylor ensured that the second Lourdes Institute—built on the site of the first one—was furnished with every convenience for gatherings, plays, and refreshments for the pilgrims. The cost for this building amounted to £6,000, most of which, Father Taylor assured His Grace of Glasgow, would eventually be reimbursed from the small profit made from the catering service, provided mostly by the Legionaries of Mary during the ensuing years, and from the ambitious productions of the village dramatic club, which were lauded throughout the West of Scotland.

Other innovations, for which permission was accorded in early 1924, were for an addition to the presbytery, to accommodate the clergy on the great pilgrimage days, and for a small repository to be built to supply pilgrims with souvenirs and other pious objects. About this time, too, Father Taylor conceived the plan of having a new votive church erected on Maryknowe—the new name given to the hill behind the Grotto. The distinguished Edinburgh architect, Mr. Reginald Fairlie, A.R.S.A., drew up a plan for the church, which was designed to hold six thousand inside and twenty-five thousand in the cloistered court in front. Archbishop Mackintosh gave his approval to the plan, with the proviso that all existing debt should first disappear before further steps were taken. With this thought in mind, negotiations were set on foot, and completed at Pentecost, 1925, to secure the forty acres dividing Maryknowe from Chapelknowe, at a cost of £5,000. Father Taylor's dream was that one day in the future the church would acquire an additional forty acres which would include Chapelknowe itself, the site, it has been claimed, of an ancient sanctuary. Enquiries instituted by him then elicited the information that this land was available if the requisite funds were forthcoming.

One wonders what might have been the result had Monsignor Taylor's dream been realised. The whole area which he envisaged—about ninety acres—would have been bounded completely around on all sides by highways and railway tracks, enclosing a modern sanctuary and the ruins of a medieval one; a fitting place indeed for the home of the religious order which he hoped one day would take up the reins when he had gone to his heavenly reward.

In the event, the Second World War came and all thoughts of building were put to one side. In 1930, the entire debt on all church property at Carfin—parish, Lourdes Institute and Grotto —amounted only to £15,000, a negligible sum if the wish of the people in the West of Scotland had been to see Monsignor Taylor's dream realised. The outbreak of war, in 1939, upset the regular flow of pilgrims to Carfin, and for over a decade thereafter, put an end to all unessential building plans. By this time Carfin Mission was cleared of debt and the surplus money accumulated was absorbed by a loan to the Archdiocese of Glasgow and later to the newly-erected Diocese of Motherwell. At the time of Monsignor Taylor's death in 1963, Carfin parish —Church and Grotto—was entirely free of debt and had a credit balance of over thirty thousand pounds on loan to the Diocesan building funds. Now, nine years later, in the golden jubilee year of the Grotto's foundation, Father G. Mullen, present parish priest of St. Francis Xavier's parish, knows the joy of seeing his own hopes—and those of his predecessor—being realised: a new church is being erected in the precincts of the Grotto.

Easter Monday, April 14, 1924, was chosen for the reopening of the enlarged Carfin Grotto, and the numbers present, among them a group of French students from Edinburgh University, led by their lecturer, Monsieur Louis Olive, augured well for that year. The visitors found the renovated Shrine already showing signs of its forthcoming charm. Masses of spring flowers on the embankments provided a colourful display, successfully conceal- ing the new look of the sloping banks. In less than three months the volunteers had achieved a small miracle; but the work was by no means ended. Their aim was to beautify the shrine in anticipation of the crowds which would flock to Carfin for the annual Corpus Christi procession through the village streets. This procession had become a county event, and as in the previous year when it was computed that about 40,000 crowded the village, many of them visiting the Grotto Shrine after the proces- sion, it was believed that in 1924 the newly enlarged Shrine would again attract considerable numbers.

As in former years, the village streets were adorned and the villagers, Catholics and non-Catholics, were looking forward to the devout pageant in 1924, when towards the end of the week prior to Corpus Christi Sunday, the thunderbolt fell. Canon Taylor relates what took place in the *Carfin Grotto,* and in other booklets written by him:

" Going to a sick-call, the writer (Father Taylor) met the police superintendent on his way to warn him that the proposed proces- sion was illegal. In the absence of Archbishop Mackintosh, the Vicar-General, Mgr. Ritchie, decided that it would be prudent to confine the procession to the Grotto grounds. An adjacent field was hurriedly laid out, and the workers set up on Maryknowe (on the far side of the Grotto), a simple wooden altar of white and gold. For the first time, the Eucharistic King blessed His subjects from Massabieille and from Maryknowe, more than 30,000 flocking to do Him homage.

Bigotry had won. It was not known then who compelled the police to resurrect the obsolete Act of 1829, but little did the ' common informer ' (these were the words used during a debate in the House of Commons) foresee how he was to advertise the Grotto and pave the way for the repeal of practically the last of the Penal Laws. The counter-attack began the same Sunday evening. Through a Knight of St. Columba, a communication was sent to the late Captain F. N. Blundell, Grand Knight of the Ormskirk Council in Lancashire. The Member of Parliament for the North-West Division of Lanarkshire, in which lies Carfin, as

well as other Labour members, were informed of what had taken
place, with the result that early in August, 1924, the Catholic
Relief Bill was introduced in the House of Commons.

The fall of the Labour Party delayed the matter, but on 10th
March, 1926, it was reintroduced by Mr. Dennis Herbert, non-
Catholic Member for Watford, and seconded by Captain Blundell.
There was strenuous opposition. The final struggle lasted five full
hours, but when the late Mr. T. P. O'Connor moved the closure,
the third reading was passed without a division. There was little
difficulty in the Upper House, and on December 15, Octave Day of
the Immaculate Conception, the Catholic Relief Bill received the
Royal Assent."

Canon Taylor omits to say in the above account that Mr.
Adamson, Secretary for Scotland, publicly in the House of
Commons, commended him for his tact and discretion throughout the affair. Many false charges were made against him in
connection with his administration of the Grotto, some of
which were reported in a few papers. Even the slanderous accu-
sations that pilgrims to the Grotto paid for the water they
procured from the shrine, failed to rouse him to a public reply.
It was not necessary to do so. The daily and weekly press conducted their own investigations and found all the charges made
against Father Taylor completely lacking in substance. Not only
did Catholics gain equality with other citizens in the passing of
the Catholic Relief Bill, but because of it Monsignor Taylor's
name gained added stature and dignity, thanks to the fair repre-
sentation of the national press and the sense of justice of our
Members of Parliament.

A last word in defence of the citizens of the Burgh of Motherwell. On his own admission, the ranting anti-Irish, anti-Catholic
Parliamentary representative for Motherwell was the one who
instigated the proceedings whereby the police were compelled to
invoke the obsolete Penal Law against the processionists at
Carfin. The extravagant statements made against Father Taylor,
the abusive threats the member for Motherwell uttered in the
House of Commons against those members who intended voting
for the repeal of the Penal Law, sounded the rumblings of his
own death knell as Motherwell's representative. At the next
General Election, the Rev. James Barr, the scion of loyal
Covenanting forebears, was returned with an outstanding
majority as the burgh's representative in the House of Commons.
The eminent divine's impassioned and forthright speech, perhaps
the most eloquent given on behalf of repeal throughout the
passage of the Bill, in a great measure counteracted the effects

of the insult offered to the Eucharistic Presence by the unwise measures taken by Motherwell's member, Mr. Hugh Ferguson, M.P., the man mostly responsible for the invoking of the obsolete Penal Law. When Mr. Dennis Herbert was being presented with a slight token of esteem by his Catholic friends, for whom he, a member of the Church of England, had done such valiant work, jokingly he remarked that the gift should have been made to Mr. Ferguson, who instigated the measures at Carfin whereby a Corpus Christi procession through the streets of the village was " banned "; and as a result of which Father Taylor took steps to ensure that the question of the Penal Law, which made this possible, should be brought before the judgment of Parliament. After Father Taylor himself, much of the credit for the repeal of the Penal Law must go to the Knights of St. Columba and their friends, who recruited support on all sides of the House and who made it possible for the last great disability suffered by Roman Catholics to be removed from the Statute Book.

Just as in 1923, when the story of the beneficial effects of the water at the Shrine made Carfin the focal point of newspaper interest, once more the press of the country took up the cudgels on behalf of Father Taylor and the village. It is unlikely that the publicity given to the happenings at Carfin could have passed unnoted by Cardinal Bourne at Westminster. His interest was a direct and personal one, not only because he was the prime dignitary of the Church in Britain, but for several other reasons. His Eminence had known Father Taylor since 1897 when he had offered the newly ordained Greenock priest a post in one of the colleges in his diocese; and it was through Father Taylor that Cardinal Bourne came to know of the Little Flower of Jesus, and had made the acquaintance of her four surviving sisters in religion. The measure of the Cardinal's esteem was that he wrote the preface to Father Taylor's translation of the saint's life and accorded an indulgence to all those who with proper dispositions read the book. Also it was at the wish of Archbishop Bourne that the address on the practical applications of the Eucharistic decrees, suggested by Father Taylor (then Scottish Director of the Eucharistic Leagues), took place at the Eucharistic Congress at Westminster; but above all, Cardinal Bourne was especially interested in the situation confronting Father Taylor when the obsolete Act of 1829 was invoked against him, and the latter was compelled to cancel his arrangements for a public procession in the village streets. Sixteen years earlier, Archbishop Bourne was faced with similar circumstances on a more elaborate scale. In September 1908, the Westminster Eucharistic Congress was nearing its successful end: the final addresses had been read; the mammoth rallies of the men and children had been held; arrangements for the culminating act of worship, a procession of the Blessed Sacrament, through the side streets leading to the cathedral, were well on hand; even the flowers to decorate the streets—a shipload gifted by France—had been prepared. On the eleventh hour, Archbishop Bourne, at the express wishes of Prime Minister Asquith, was compelled to cancel the glorious procession due to take place the following day. It is little wonder that the exalted prelate, whose dignified action was commended in 1908, should keep close watch on the actions of his friend, the little priest at Carfin, who was now undergoing a similar experience to that of his own in 1908.

The Cardinal's interest was soon apparent. One month after the incident at Carfin, Cardinal Bourne paid a visit to the village. " The occasion was unique," said an evening paper, " even for Carfin, as it was the first time a Prince of the Church had visited this quarter of Lanarkshire; indeed, several decades had passed since one had been in Scotland." According to all sections of the press, the multitudes present to honour the Cardinal must have numbered close on 50,000. The day was a gala day for the village. Once more the volunteers rushed to Father Taylor's assistance and prepared the village and shrine for their august visitor. Public processions of the Blessed Sacrament, with clerics in ceremonial dress, had been prohibited at Carfin. But no law could prevent His Eminence, informally dressed, from driving in an open hansom cab—provided by Mr. Thomas Garvie, a senior parishioner of Carfin parish—through the streets of the village, after the solemn service in the Grotto.

The *Glasgow Herald* and other journals reported the Cardinal's address as follows:

"His Eminence congratulated Scotland, the Glasgow Archdiocese and the parish of Carfin, on the spirit of devotion to Almighty God which was being shown by the people. It was a magnificent sight to see so many thousands gathered in the Grotto at devotional exercises . . .

If they asked how God had chosen that particular place in which to have His praises rendered, he would be unable to answer. It was a secret of Almighty God. But it was God's doing and it was His choice. No one could tell why Our Lord had chosen Palestine for his country, and the humble House of Nazareth for His Home. Why had He chosen to be born in a humble stable? Why had He chosen an almost unknown town in the Pyrenees in which to reveal His will to a peasant girl and inspire honour towards His Immaculate Mother. God had been pleased to set up this place, acting like a magnet, bringing thousands of persons to honour Himself and that Blessed Mother on whom He had deigned to bestow His numerous gifts. His first miracle was wrought at the request of His Mother. From that day, again and again, they had instances of miracles and of many special graces obtained at her request.

God's Church did not shut her eyes to facts. She investigated them, looked at them clearly, but never set them aside. Once ascertained, she faced them and accepted them in her heart. And she recognised the fact of the immense throng there that day.

He had been told that the Grotto had been made sacred by some signal instances of Divine favours. It rested with the competent ecclesiastical authorities to pass judgment on that point. But the fact that those present represented hundreds of thousands who had come, and who would come in the future, to the Grotto, was a fact they all had to recognise. God had chosen their district for devotion, and purposed that they might have an opportunity to be responsive and sanctify their souls . . .

People came to the Grotto in humble supplication to Mary for the needs and desires of themselves and their friends. Carfin was the gathering place of faithful hearts. It was inspired by the Little Flower of Jesus, one raised up in these latter years to show us the way to honour and trust in God . . ."

The Cardinal continued his address by sketching the life of Blessed Thérèse and the devotion of her " Little Way " to heaven, a devotion which was entirely practicable for everyone of the many thousands he addressed.

After Benediction of the Blessed Sacrament, given by the Right Rev. Mgr. Kelly of Dumbarton, in the presence of the Cardinal and thirty priests, the service at the Grotto Shrine ended. In the evening, after his drive through the village, His Eminence left for the Eucharistic Congress at Amsterdam, where he made reference to Carfin.

The Cardinal was delighted with his visit to Carfin; Father Taylor was pleased with the honour paid to his Mission by the Cardinal's visit; and the huge multitudes who were present were deeply appreciative of the unique privilege which had been theirs in being present at the Grotto on this momentous occasion. But soon a little tidal wave burst and Father Taylor became aware that he was at the centre of a whirling vortex. The following correspondence between Archbishop Mackintosh, at Rome, and Father Taylor explains itself:

Collegio Scozzese,
Roma.
30th July, 1924.

" My dear Father Taylor,

I understand that, on the occasion of a function recently held at Carfin, certain public pronouncements were made with regard to the nature of what is taking place in connection with the Grotto there. I quote the following from the *Universe* of July 25th, as typical of what other newspapers report, viz.: 'He (the speaker) could not tell them why Carfin had been chosen to be such a centre of devotion, but it was God's doing and it was His choice.'

As you are well aware, the diocesan authority in Glasgow—in dealing with Carfin—has, from the beginning, drawn a clear distinction between the marvels alleged to be taking place and the fact that multitudes throng to the shrine—inspired apparently with genuine faith and devotion; and, with reference to both these elements of the situation at Carfin, the attitude of the diocesan authority has been that implied by the formula, ' Non constare de supernaturalitate,' viz.: that there is no proof of the existence of anything supernatural in the situation.

The fact, therefore, that a positive and public pronouncement has been made with regard to the nature of the attraction which draws multitudes to Carfin and the fact that the said pronouncement is out of keeping with the attitude of the competent ecclesiastical authority, call for an explanation. Whatever explanation there may be to give—you will kindly give to the Vicariate at 160 Renfrew Street.

It must be kept clearly before the public that with regard to the shrine at Carfin and with regard to the situation existing in connection with it, the attitude of the competent authority has been and continues to be that implied by the words, ' Non constare de supernaturalitate.' This attitude is shaped on the traditional attitude of the Catholic Church in similar situations, and it should be the norm according to which the public attitude of the Faithful ought to be shaped. If the time ever comes for setting up another norm, it must be remembered that—under the Holy See—the only authority competent to pronounce upon the advent of that time and upon the norm to be set up is the diocesan authority.

Wishing you every grace and blessing,
I am,
Yours faithfully in Dmno.,
(Sgd.) ✠ Donald Mackintosh,
Archbishop of Glasgow."

The Archbishop of Glasgow was piqued, and it was incumbent on Father Taylor to provide an adequate explanation of the part he himself had played in the affair. The following is a copy of the letter he sent to His Grace, the tone of which suggests that he personally did not consider that Cardinal Bourne had done or said anything that would offend the competent diocesan authority:

St. Francis Xavier's,
Carfin.

25/8/24.

" May it please Your Grace,
    The first intimation of Cardinal Bourne's visit to the Grotto came to me from Your Grace through Father Doyle. The news was pleasant as I have known His Eminence for twenty-seven years, and one of his kindnesses was the sponsoring of the volume *Sister Thérèse of Lisieux*. But it was doubly pleasant, coming as it did from yourself. Father Doyle can tell you of our mutual delight.

My next step was to consult Your Grace as to the reception of my distinguished visitor, and you replied graciously that I was to welcome him as befitted a Cardinal. This I was delighted to do, thinking it to be for the good of religion, and for the honour of Our Lady and Blessed Thérèse. His Eminence kindly consented to prolong his stay in Edinburgh from Friday to Sunday so that our working people might be better suited.

Following the telegram of acceptance, there came an urgent letter from the Cardinal's secretary asking in the most insistent manner if my ecclesiastical superiors were in cordial sympathy with the visit. I had already stated that you had sent me the message of his coming. This assurance notwithstanding there was an emphatic enquiry as to whether a public visit had Your Grace's fullest approval.

My third step was to obtain from Mgr. Ritchie (Vicar General) permission to have His Eminence give Benediction in the Grotto and address the assembled crowd. The folk of Lanarkshire had never seen a Prince of Holy Church and I thought a short address would stir their faith. The Monsignor granted me cordially the permission sought. To make doubly sure, I asked if I might inform His Eminence that the programme had the fullest approval of the Archbishop of Glasgow, and I received in answer an emphatic affirmative. The Cardinal — from Oban — accepted the programme, and there was no further allusion to the matter.

I may add here that I also consulted the Vicar General as to whom I should invite to meet and honour the guest. He approved of an invitation to the entire Chapter. Owing to the smallness of the presbytery, invitations were confined to the Monsignori,

Canons, Father Doyle and Father Stevens. A number of other priests attended the ceremony of their own accord.

With regard to the pronouncement Your Grace refers to, I can only say I was not consulted in the matter, and that I am certain—in view of the letter already spoken of—that His Eminence had no thought of anticipating the decision of the competent authority. Everyone considered that his allusion to the alleged favours was tactfully made.

As to the crowds—I have already assured Your Grace that I did not invite them. I suggested one pilgrimage—that of the Italians: the others came and still come spontaneously . . .

Secondly, Your Grace, besides giving me an assurance on one of your visits that I was doing God's work, you wrote to me that you considered those great crowds to be so wonderful as to require an act of thanksgiving to the Madonna and her Little Flower. These perhaps were private judgments upon the situation at Carfin, but they gave me great heartening amid the opposition the work had to face. Had you bidden me close the Grotto, it would have been immediately done and much toil and enormous expense would have been saved to all concerned.

Instead of this you graciously approved of several matters which made me feel no doubt but that in your mind the Grotto was God's work. Through Lady Ann Kerr and her daughter, the Cardinal was made aware of your approval of those schemes— schemes which seem to presuppose a public admission that ' Carfin was God's choice '—not the choice of the writer of these lines. ' Elegit Deus contemptibilia mundi ': of this I am well aware. These schemes included the plan of a new pilgrims' shelter, an addition to the presbytery for priest pilgrims, the gigantic task of the extension of the Grotto—the latter trumpeted by wireless over Great Britain, not by my connivance—and the purchase of adjacent grounds and property. Moreover, there was the plan of the proposed Votive Church in honour of Our Lady and the Little Flower. Frankly, I thought it one of her ' roses ' that Your Grace should even have considered its possibility.

This plan, which he was assured by the Kerrs in London and Edinburgh had Your Grace's approval, His Eminence wished to examine, and he asked Mr. Fairlie (the Architect) to show it to him in Edinburgh. Since, however, the plan lay in Carfin, Mr. Fairlie came through to explain it to the Cardinal, who was most keenly interested. Knowing what he did of your public actions— if not pronouncements—in connection with the Grotto, it seems to me as though the Cardinal thought he was merely echoing Your Grace's sentiments when he addressed the vast multitude that day. The very weather was a ' rose '—for though we were literally ringed all round with rain, Carfin did not receive a single drop, and the sunshine in the Grotto was almost tropical—such as had not been seen for years.

Your Grace promised to come to us on April 14th. Sickness deprived the pilgrims of that pleasure. Would you come to us on September 7th, eve of Our Lady's Birthday, or if that be too near, then on the 'dies natalis' of Blessed Thérèse—September 30th? That would be a red letter day in the annals of the Grotto!

Need I say that Your Grace's wishes as regards the Grotto are commands which shall always be most loyally observed? Asking anew your blessing on the pilgrims and on the devoted workers.

I am, etc."

The unbiased opinion of one who knew not only Monsignor Taylor, but also Archbishop Mackintosh and his Vicar General, is worthy of consideration here. His comments follow:

" Father Taylor's letter shows that, despite the misunderstanding occasioned by newspaper reports, he took for granted that his explanation would be accepted and then, ignoring the misunderstanding, he goes on to speak of arrangements for an expected visit of Archbishop Mackintosh to the parish. A garbled account of this incident circulated and created the impression that Father Taylor was *persona non grata* to the diocesan authorities. This was not the case, even though Father Taylor himself sometimes imagined he was out of favour. Archbishop Donald Mackintosh, his Vicar General, Monsignor John Ritchie, and the assistant Vicar General, Monsignor William Daly, all had profound respect for Father Taylor's zeal, self-sacrifice and dedication to the cause of religion. One who knew all three would go so far as to say that they had a large measure of affection for 'Tommy Taylor.' Their esteem and affection, however, were not uncritical and, as responsible men in charge of an archdiocese of over half-a-million Catholics, many of whom at that time were suffering from the effects of the industrial depression, they could not in conscience give T.N.T. (Father Taylor's dynamic initials) a free hand in spending money, even though he was completely convinced that it was all for the glory of God. T.N.T. for his part was very sensitive and a refusal to approve of one of his pet schemes could hurt him deeply.

Monsignor William Daly, the assistant Vicar General of Glasgow Archdiocese, who had been a contemporary of Father Taylor at Issy and St. Sulpice, used to tell an amusing story, which illustrates the friendly understanding of each other's character, which existed between these men: it illustrates also the curious craftiness with which T.N.T. sometimes promoted his schemes and also the familiar way in which he involved the Little Flower in his unusual methods of attaining his ends.

Archbishop Donald Mackintosh had spent practically all of his career as rector of the Scots College in Rome before he came to Glasgow as Archbishop. He was an excellent administrator, but always remained a somewhat shy academic, and was never at his best in direct dealings with people, on which occasions he could be awkward and ill at ease. On one occasion in the 1920s, accompanied by his assistant Vicar General, Monsignor Daly, the Archbishop came to Carfin for the administration of the Sacrament of Confirmation. It was taken for granted by the two men that Father Taylor would take advantage of the visit of the Archbishop to secure some new scheme, and the Archbishop, recognising that he was no match for T.N.T. and would probably be unable to turn down some very earnest request, arranged with Monsignor Daly that they would both stick close together so that T.N.T. would not be able to catch the Archbishop alone. They arrived at the chapel-house and were installed in the parish priest's study, where they vested for the ceremony in the church. They stuck fast together, congratulating themselves on achieving this in spite of some obvious attempts on the part of Father Taylor to separate them. Then suddenly, as they waited for the ceremony to begin, T.N.T. came in looking his usual earnest self and said solemnly to Monsignor Daly: 'Someone downstairs wants to speak to you.'

The latter was taken aback by such an unexpected caller: he and the Archbishop jumped to the conclusion that some dissatisfied parishioner wanted to complain about T.N.T. The Archbishop nodded to the Vicar General that he had better go and attend to the matter. Father Taylor led the Vicar General downstairs by a circuitous route and ushered him into a room. The puzzled priest found the room quite empty and turned to Father Taylor for an explanation. The latter pointed to the inevitable statue of St. Thérèse of Lisieux and said with great emphasis: 'SHE wants to speak to you!' and, closing the door smartly, he disappeared.

When the Vicar General had recovered from his surprise and managed to make his way back to the upstairs study, Father Taylor had had a short, uninterrupted, private conversation with the Archbishop which was all he required."

Throughout the summer and autumn of 1924, pilgrimages continued to visit the shrine, the more outstanding being those organised by the Tertiaries of Aberdeen in September; the first rally at Carfin of the Catholic Young Men's Society, which culminated in an enthusiastic gathering in the newly built Institute in November; and three weeks later, the concluding procession of the year 1924, an army of pupils of the Marist Brothers from St. Mungo's Academy and other Glasgow schools.

The success of the first torchlight procession in 1923, suggested the idea of a more adequate lighting for the Grotto. The erection of standard lamps for this purpose was one of the immediate tasks on which the volunteers were engaged, once the embankments had been completed and the wall round the Holy Souls Altar—blessed by Cardinal Bourne—had been extended.

Exciting as the events of 1924 were for Father Taylor, the task before him in the summer of 1925 was one of personal love and devotion—the erection of a shrine in honour of the Blessed Thérèse of the Child Jesus, who was to be canonised on Sunday, 17th May, 1925. After the thrilling ceremony of canonisation by Pius XI, Father Taylor hastened back to Carfin for the inauguration of her shrine on the hastily prepared Little Flower Terrace, facing Our Lady's shrine at Massabieille. The statue, he tells us, had been obtained through the Carmel of Lisieux and its cost had been defrayed by general subscription, the intention being to allow even the poorest to offer his meagre pittance to the " World's darling," as the new saint was called by His Holiness.

Within the next few months Father Taylor was to welcome pioneer pilgrimages from Ireland and from England, as well as the first annual rally of Lithuanians and of Glasgow Tertiaries. Both Lithuanians and Tertiaries have gathered in the Grotto every year since, except for the war years.

It was on Assumption Sunday, 1925, that the first English train—carrying pilgrims from Carlisle and Lancaster, led by the Vicar General of the latter diocese—steamed in at the little platform at the goods station one hundred yards from the Grotto Shrine. Two years later, on February 11, 1927, the Grotto Halt was officially opened and easy conveyance was provided for pilgrims from all over Scotland and the South. Within three years from 1926, according to official estimate, 70,000 pilgrims had used the Halt. To provide even approximate numbers for those who came by motor car, cycle or on foot, would be utterly impossible. One can only accept the evidence of spectators and the reports of the press that many thousands attended the Grotto services during the summer months.

Father Taylor's initial plans did not envisage more than a modest shrine in honour of Our Lady of Lourdes. The beatification and canonisation of St. Thérèse introduced her to the Madonna's shrine; vaguely, Father Taylor hoped that at some future date a small shrine in honour of the Holy Child might be executed. The Sisters and students of Notre Dame had already provided a small altar with a beautiful crucifix, but Father Taylor's plans as yet had not gone beyond the limits of these first shrines.

The floodlit shrine of St. Thérèse built on a little pyramid of slag and rock proved a great attraction, and it became increasingly obvious that indeed the Grotto of Our Lady and St. Thérèse was a national devotional centre. Especially for pilgrims who came from distant parts, there was little in the village to occupy their attention between devotional services in the afternoon and evening processions. The Institute catered for their bodily comforts, but numbers were so great on many Sundays that only those who had ordered meals in advance could be provided for. It was Monsignor Claeys' wide vision which pictured a Grotto, with shrines to saints of popular devotion, erected along the processional route, throughout the extended Grotto. Hence it was with considerable joy that Father Taylor learned that a parishioner—one of the few in the village to own his own modest business—wished to donate a small statue of the Holy Child Jesus. Hastily the volunteers set to work and on an embankment backing the shrine of Saint Thérèse, an altar was built to enshrine the new statue. On 17th September, 1926, the *Universe* reported forthcoming events in the Grotto as follows:

CARFIN GROTTO—SHRINE OF OUR LADY AND THE
LITTLE FLOWER

FOURTH ANNIVERSARY: SUNDAY, OCTOBER 3RD, 1926

TRIPLE SOLEMNISATION OF THE FEASTS OF OUR LADY OF THE
ROSARY, ST. FRANCIS OF ASSISI AND ST. THERESE
at 3.30 p.m.

Solemn Procession and Blessing of the Roses of St. Thérèse,
Blessing of the HOLY CHILD CHAPEL and ST. MARY'S LAKE.
At 6.30 p.m., Torchlight Procession and Illumination of
the grounds.

The notice went on to say that special trains would run from Glasgow to Motherwell and Holytown, this in addition to the normal service of motor 'buses to and from the Grotto.

The daughter of the donor of the statue of the Holy Child clearly recalls that October Sunday, when as a tiny child, surrounded by teeming masses of pilgrims, she unveiled the statue her father had donated. In contrast to this joyful scene was a more sorrowful one which took place about this time: sadly, a small white coffin bearing the last earthly remains of the young girl who, on the 1st October, 1922, had unveiled the statue of the Madonna, was carried into the Grotto by her family, among whom was her father who had gifted the first two statues to the Grotto—those of Our Lady and Blessed Bernadette.

In the ensuing years, the Grotto began to take on the shape it has at present. Others from outside the parish soon followed the example set by the Sisters of Notre Dame, who had gifted the Holy Souls altar. An elderly lady provided the marble statue of St. Joseph, because she wished to see him " at the top of the ladder " as she made her final journey into eternity. The shrine was unveiled in March 1927.

On May Day of the same year, 10,000 blue-mantled Children of Mary were present to see the blessing of the statue of St. Anne with the child Mary; twelve months later, St. Joachim was to arrive; St. Anne was the gift of the Catholics of Quebec, St. Joachim of a Scottish convert settled in Montreal.

> " It is interesting to relate," wrote Father Taylor in *The Carfin Grotto,* " that the final two dollars for the statue of St. Joachim came from the purse of a generous-hearted Orangeman."

The erection of the mound on which the trio of saints— Joseph, Anne, Joachim—stood, was child-play to the formerly inexperienced Grotto volunteers. But more exacting were the demands made on a gang of over one hundred men—mostly bricklayers from Cleland—who during May and June, 1927, completed the onerous task of the excavation of Our Lady's Lake. An islet, surmounted by an entirely original statue of the Stella Maris—this outstanding masterpiece was the gift of an anonymous cleric—rises from a shamrock-shaped lake, the three sections of which are dedicated to the sons of St. Patrick who did the work; Margaret Sinclair, who came as a pilgrim to the Grotto shortly after it was opened; and Blessed John Ogilvie, the Scottish Jesuit who was martyred at Glasgow Cross at 4 p.m. on February 28, 1615. It was in details like the above that Father Taylor excelled.

He had a strong devotion to the Edinburgh working girl whose cause was already under consideration, so soon after death. And so it should not come as a surprise to hear that among his welter of correspondence Father Taylor kept a little package of letters and souvenirs relating to the young Edinburgh girl, whose life with the Poor Clare Colettines was cut off so soon by her death at the Marillac Sanatorium, Warley, in 1925. In addition to a number of secondary relics, authenticated by the Vice-postulators of Margaret Sinclair's cause (the late Canon T. Doyle, St. Saviour's, Govan, and the one who succeeded him in office, the late Monsignor John McQuillan, D.D., formerly St. Meddan's, Troon), there is a short letter written by Margaret herself to her friend, Mrs. Campbell, shortly before she set out for London, presumably to enter the novitiate of the Poor Clares, as Sister Mary Francis of the Five Wounds. A fortnight earlier, on 4th July, during a fortnight's retreat with the Sisters of Charity, at

Smyllum, Lanark, Margaret visited Carfin Grotto, where she spent two hours. A postcard sent from the shrine that day, addressed to Mrs. J. Sinclair, 277 Cowgate, Edinburgh, has been preserved in Monsignor Taylor's files, although the pencilled inscription has almost faded now. The message reads as follows:

July, 1923.

" D. Nellie,

This is the place I was at to-day and had a drink (at the well). The people are here in crowds although it is a wet day.

Sincerely yours,

Margaret."

Also carefully preserved are other mementoes: a few snippets of Margaret's hair, cut off shortly after her death by one of those who nursed her, during her last illness; and a Handmaid of the Blessed Sacrament medal given by Mrs. Sinclair to Father Taylor. Both these relics are now in the possession of two Carfin ladies, who received them as gifts from Monsignor, in acknowledgment of the generous service they had given to the parish and Grotto over many years.

A fortnight after the Star of the Sea—Our Lady of Carfin, as the statue was familiarly known—was blessed, one of the most striking shrines of the Grotto was dedicated. The austere beauty of the Calvary attracts many. Originally, the cross was formed of the trunk of a tall larch, gifted by a Protestant industrialist; damp and decay attacked the wood and eventually the tree had to be replaced by another, less striking perhaps, since the wood of the latter is planed and processed. Around the immense bronze Figure on the Cross are arranged the statues of Our Lady of Dolours, St. John and St. Mary Magdalen. The knoll of Calvary has increased in size over the years: the weeping trees, now fully grown in the forty years since they were planted, overflow on to the massive boulders nearby, giving the whole an air of dignity and tranquillity. The statuary was made in France and was blessed on Carmel Sunday by Father Stanislaus, O.F.M., Guardian of St. Francis', Glasgow. The message of the Crucified Christ, " Behold thy Mother," is also the message of the Grotto.

On January 2nd, 1928, was blessed the majestic figure of the Christ King. Father Taylor, referring to the devotion to Christ the King, stated in his booklet on the Grotto, in 1937, that it (the devotion) had been " inaugurated, one might say, by Pius XI, and had received during the Civil War, a tremendous impetus through the dying exclamation of thousands of Spain's martyred priests and nuns: ' Viva Cristo Rey!' "

It is at night, when the floodlights illumine the imposing mass of the white marble Christ King seated on the throne, resting on an altar-table, that the statue is most majestic, its commanding position dominating the entire landscape.

Ten months were to pass before another shrine was added to the Grotto, but there was no respite for the workers; lawns and avenues were laid; plants were set and the sites of shrines improved. The Grotto grounds were laid with paths along the main processional routes, down past Calvary and back to the Grotto, but so far the area in the lower Grotto in the far corner, below the shrine of St. Thérèse, was a morass of thicket and bog. To clear it was a task fit to dishearten the most valiant, but not so the loyal volunteers of Mary's Shrine. Led by their ingenious and hard-working overseer, the late Mr. Hugh Devlin, they toiled on, and before the autumn of the ensuing year, a dual stairway on either side of the Shrine of St. Thérèse led from the Upper to the Lower Grotto, which was now laid out with ashed avenues and grassy lawns.

What of the busy little priest who was the inspiration and mentor of the whole design? News of the Grotto had blazoned his name throughout the British Isles; French, Italian, American, Canadian and Australian journals, as well as the *Osservatore Romano* itself, carried stories of the Shrine at Carfin, as well as pictures of the multitudes who came there on pilgrimage. As the translator of the autobiography of St. Thérèse and witness at the tribunal of her Beatification, Father Taylor's name was already a household word among Catholics of the Western world. When, therefore, he visited the Eucharistic Congress at Chicago in the spring of 1926, and continued south through the States on a lecture tour on Our Lady and the Little Flower of Jesus, he was welcomed as a friend wherever he went. His own account of devotion to Saint Thérèse in the United States will be referred to in the next chapter, but passing reference is made here to his visit to the White House. He had been prevailed upon—not without misgivings on his own part—to present to President Coolidge a specially bound copy of his own translation of the Saint's autobiography. Senator Cameron, of Arizona, who had made all the arrangements, by some unforeseen circumstance, neglected to procure a necessary letter of introduction from the British Embassy. Father Taylor, Father Noonan, and Senator Cameron arrived at the White House at the appointed time, only to find that Father Taylor was refused permission to enter without the Embassy's letter of introduction. While the President waited, Father Taylor was bundled off, post-haste, in a cab to procure the required document. Most graciously President Coolidge delayed his next appointment for close on half-an-hour in order to meet the priest from Scotland who was the author of one of the best-selling religious books of that time. His parishioners at home were not to learn of this incident until an emigrant from Carfin sent home a press cutting with the caption, " Scottish priest who kept the President waiting." It would seem that Father Taylor reserved the same measures for those of lowly and high estate—at some time or other, all had to wait his time and convenience. The story is told that the tables were turned on him—inadvertently—on one occasion when he was the preacher at the Rosary Hour, at the Dominican Convent of the Holy Rosary, Glasgow. He was admitted to the parlour, where a certain Sister had been detailed to take him to a private room left at his disposal. Time passed and no one came for him; subsequently, the impatient Monsignor poked his head out of the parlour to find out what was happening. It seems the Sister concerned was in the Chapel singing Vespers, expecting to be notified when Monsignor arrived. All ended well and Monsignor could joke that he had received a dose of his own medicine from a very apologetic Dominican nun.

Not only did the Grotto Halt facilitate the arrival of pilgrims at Carfin—over twenty pilgrim-packed trains arriving for the great processions on Grotto feast days were not uncommon—but the railway company's display boards in every station advertised the Grotto's time-table for the season. Without any effort on Father Taylor's part, the railway company and the national press advertised the shrine at Carfin, and through purely material means, increasing numbers were brought to Jesus through Mary.

Lancaster and Carlisle sent the first large pilgrimages from England in 1925, although smaller groups had come North before that year. In turn came Manchester, Bolton, Tyneside, Liverpool, Chorley, Preston, Seaham (Co. Durham), Fylde, Wigan, Newcastle, Middlesbrough, Sunderland, led by their priests. The fervour of the English Catholics was so strong that in one summer (1930) Preston sent four pilgrimages on different Sundays. Before the war years, the practice had become common for some of the English pilgrimage trains to move north during the night, so that many of the pilgrims could fast overnight and so commence the pilgrimage with Mass and Communion immediately after arrival at Carfin. One of the smaller halls was put at their disposal (between the various services) throughout the day. After, or before the torchlight procession, according to the hour of darkness, Father Taylor would assemble the visitors in

I

the concert hall of the Lourdes Institute, where a performance of one of the religious plays from the extensive repertoire of the village dramatic club would be given; or alternatively, a lantern lecture on some religious topic would be given by Father Taylor himself.

Whether a drama production—these were reputedly of an exceptionally high standard—or a lantern lecture with comment by Father Taylor, calling on his own wide experiences, and making full use of his near photographic memory, the visitors always enjoyed the final hour's relaxation, following on their arduous day's devotional services. The weariness of the English travellers after a second night's travelling did not deter their hardy spirit, for time and again they, or their friends, returned north on annual pilgrimage. Father Taylor's efforts to restore the Mother of God to a place of honour in Scotland bore abundant fruit, if the devotion demonstrated by pilgrims who came regularly to the Grotto was a gauge of their love.

As a student in Paris, Father Taylor wrote that every lawful means available should be used to bring the faithful nearer to God. He was well aware of the pageantry so common on the Continent during Church festivals. It was Monsignor Claeys' idea that the Corpus Christi procession should be modelled on the solemn procession of the Precious Blood, annually held at Bruges. The picturesque figures, clad in medieval dress, the symbolism, the beautiful canopy and banners, all helped to raise the mind from the mundane. So too, on the feast of the Assumption, the beautifully clad Madonna, with her accompanying attendants, followed by fifteen maidens in three groups of five, symbolic of the Holy Rosary, attracted many who came to look and remained to pray.

Of all the Grotto festivals, the anniversary pageant on Rosary Sunday became the most resplendent and picturesque of the Grotto processions. Speaking of this, Father Taylor relates:

"All the riches of the Grotto treasury are brought forth and borne in triumph—the processional Cross, the exquisitely worked monstrance and canopy, the Belgian wrought reliquaries with their precious relics, the standards and regalia—all these, and much more, adding to the magnificence of the spectacle. The roses, however, the beautiful striking ceremony of their benediction, and the prolonged veneration of her relic, connect the Grotto anniversary closely with St. Thérèse whose feast falls at that time."

The Grotto continued to provide copy for journalists experiencing an arid spell in sensational news. The Editor of the

Edinburgh *Evening Dispatch* paid a back-handed compliment to the devotees of Our Lady, St. Thérèse and St. Francis on the occasion of the mile-long torchlight procession on the 30th September, 1928; Father Taylor repeated the comment as a paean of praise in his booklet, *The Carfin Grotto*, published in 1938:

"While Scottish Presbyterians were at church yesterday, they probably did not know that one of the most remarkable scenes in the religious history of their country was being enacted in a Lanarkshire mining village. It was only an anniversary of St. Francis and St. Thérèse. What was significant was the assemblage of 30,000 or 40,000 devotees in such a remote spot for such a purpose.

In the short space of six years this obscure village has become one of the strongholds of the Roman Catholic Church in Scotland, one of the most active sources of propaganda; and a spectacular festival such as that of yesterday shows the masterly skill with which that Church can stir the emotions and hold the allegiance of the people."

Monsignor Taylor, personally, rarely received a bad press; his sincerity and sanctity, his simple, direct faith, was recognised by all, Protestant and Catholic alike. What was not recognised by journalists of the Protestant press was that Monsignor, in God's design, may have been the instrument by which the "obscure village had become one of the strongholds of the Roman Catholic Church in Scotland." If any one of them had taken the trouble to listen to Father Taylor as he led his people in the Lourdes prayers, for the sick and the sinner, he might have realised that Father Taylor's faith in the Almighty was a living thing, which he could no more refrain from imparting to others than he could to stop breathing. It was by a definite, positive effort of will that he succeeded in transmitting his own convictions to others; if emotion was roused in the process, it came as a result of an act of faith; emotion was not the cause which produced the effect.

The statue of St. Anthony arrived in the Grotto in 1928 almost against Father Taylor's wishes. A humble donor from Govan persisted in her request that her life savings, £100, would be spent on a statue of the Saint of Padua. Twice her request was refused—there was no suitable site available and Father Taylor felt that other saints had prior claim—but on the third time her wish was granted. A rocky mound was built in the middle of the swamp in the distant corner of the Lower Grotto and the shrine of St. Anthony was erected, in honour of Father Taylor's two priest brothers, each of whom had served, one as priest, the other

as teacher, in St. Anthony's Parish, Govan. Not to be outdone
by his distinguished son, the founder of the order, St. Francis
of Assisi himself, did not long delay in making his way into the
Grotto. Once again the Grotto volunteers came in force and
Mount Assisi was begun. Gradually, a huge knoll was built up,
supported by strong retaining walls. Three years later, one of
the most beautiful corners of the Grotto was complete, with the
statue of St. Anthony and the Holy Child at the summit, looking
down into a delightful rockery garden, where was placed an
original statue of St. Francis preaching to the birds, a gift of the
Tertiaries of St. Francis. On the left of the Mount was erected
the Bethlehem Cave, on the right the Chapel of the Angels, or
Portiuncula, the former and the latter both closely associated
with the Poverello of Assisi. A long row of poplars, a gift to
Father Taylor from a Perthshire priest, now flanks the Mount
at the rear and sides. Monsignor Taylor claimed he could never
visit Mount Assisi without praying for the Dupon family, four of
whom had been actively engaged in creating the masterpieces of
sculpture in that corner of the Grotto.

Although the main precincts of the Grotto took on their final
outlines with the completion of Mount Assisi in 1932—with the
exception of the sunken garden, an addition necessitated by the
outstanding pilgrimages of Holy Year 1934—mounds and niches
were still available for further shrines. In 1929, a statue of the
Virgin Martyr, formerly honoured as St. Philomena, had been
added, and although the statue still remains, modern evidence is
not conclusive as to the identification of the young martyr known
under that name. Suffice to say, whether the name is or is not
Philomena, the humble factory girl who donated six years' savings
to honour a girl martyr of the early Church, will receive her own
supernatural reward for the spirit in which the gift was made.
No less generous was the girl's mother who donated the statue
of St. John Vianney, and a number of reliquaries in the ensuing
years.

One of the most memorable ceremonies in the whole history of
the Grotto was that which took place on August 24th, 1930. At
long last the Irish volunteer workers, who were mostly responsible for the building of the Grotto, were to take part in the
inauguration ceremony of Ireland's patron saint. In the presence
of what seemed to be every exile who had left the shores of
Ireland, the statue of St. Patrick was unveiled by Mr. Joseph
Devlin, M.P., from Belfast, a pilgrim and friend of the Grotto
since its inception. Mgr. Kelly, priest in charge of St. Patrick's
parish, Dumbarton, where the young, inexperienced, but very

enthusiastic Father Taylor had served the first three years of his sacerdotal ministry, blessed the statue of the Saint. Now, thirty-three years later, the one who was perhaps the best-known priest in the whole English-speaking world, was still the humble Father Taylor, priest in charge of a small country parish, with a population of between three and four thousand, but with a congregation that stretched into many millions over the years.

Someone once said, " When Irishmen decide to honour their God, they do it in style." The building of the Grotto is striking evidence of this; the unveiling of St. Patrick's statue is another striking example; but if numbers and fervour is a legitimate sign of the worship of God and loyalty to the Church, the pilgrimage of the Ancient Order of Hibernians in October 1934, the nineteenth centenary year of the death of Christ, holds the palm. The ecclesiastical ban on the order in Scotland had been removed in 1933 and the pilgrimage was one of thanksgiving to Our Lady, Mother of Ireland, and of reparation to her Divine Son, in this the centenary year of His death. Two years later, the order returned again to offer up an urgent appeal to Heaven for the beleaguered Catholics of Spain. In 1934, Father Taylor welcomed no fewer than twenty fully-packed train loads of members of the order; two years later, in 1936, the numbers were almost as high.

It was these mammoth pilgrimages which made the further extension of the processional route necessary. Four abreast was normal processional order, but when over 50,000 were processing through the Grotto, the pilgrims marched eight or ten abreast, and even then the hosts of pilgrims at the beginning of the procession were delayed for some time to allow the rear of the procession to leave the Upper Grotto. Naturally, such numbers could not all assemble in the Grotto proper. Hence, in more recent years, since the war, the large area—once the car park—behind the Lourdes Institute became the assembly area from which the procession started. The procession over, the pilgrims assembled in the Upper Grotto, in the wide expanse lying between the Shrines of Our Lady and St. Thérèse, and along the embankments flanking Massabieille; those who could not be accommodated in the Upper Grotto lined the avenues past the Christ the King Shrine and down to the Stella Maris Lake.

Formerly, on Ascension Thursday, school children from the West of Scotland gathered annually for a mass rally in the Grotto. On these occasions the facilities of the Grotto were stretched to their fullest extent and all available space was necessary to accommodate them. Since Monsignor Taylor's death, this annual rally, which was started in the first instance in the late 'twenties by Monsignor Mullin and the children from St. Augustine's parish, Coatbridge, and later sponsored by the Don Bosco Guild of Teachers, has now been discontinued. It is to be regretted that a half-day annually is not made available to schools in the Diocese of Motherwell, for a visit to one of the foremost Marian shrines in Britain, all the more so since permission may be granted for time off school for a variety of social and cultural activities.

With the extension of the Grotto, Father Taylor soon realised that a powerful amplifying system would be necessary to carry the voice of the preacher to the farthest extent of the processional route. In this respect he was a pioneer in Catholic circles in Britain. He commissioned the firm which had provided the amplifying system for the canonisation of St. Thérèse, in St. Peter's Basilica, to install a serviceable one in the Grotto. The result was a tremendous success. Villagers who were unable to attend the service in the Grotto could listen to the preacher in their own homes, and if they so wished could share in one or more of the Rosaries which were recited during the service. Occasionally a visiting priest, leading the Rosary, was at a loss when he found himself with a Rosary completed, the prescribed hymns sung, and the procession not yet arrived back in the Grotto. Not so Father Taylor; he was never caught at a disadvantage. Without book or notes, he could keep a congregation occupied for hours; prayer followed prayer; the Litany of Loreto or Memorare; the Divine Praises or the Angelus, and these interspersed by many hymns. It was a strange anomaly which could happen only in the Grotto: Canon Taylor started the hymns—in his declining years not always in tune—and the poor choir, isolated in the choir room, often had to join in as well as it could. The translation of the Lourdes Hymn which was used at Carfin, with its many verses, always held pride of place at the Grotto services, the resounding *Aves* being heard at the outer boundaries of the village. This translation, which remained popular in Scotland for over half a century, was preferred to the one made by the well-known poetess, Alice Meynell, in the early decades of this century, and of which Father Taylor wrote:

" Her translation was sublime, but not sufficiently direct for popular use."

So the two masters of their respective crafts—Professor Phillimore of the English language, Father Taylor of Marian devotion—undertook to complete their own masterpiece; the result was the *Ave Maria*, sung and loved for many years by Scots pilgrims to Lourdes and Carfin.

While the idea of a suitable votive church was still his ideal in 1934, the size of the processions made a further extension of the Grotto an immediate and extremely difficult necessity. How it was achieved is told in *The Carfin Grotto, the First Fifteen Years*:

"The deep downward slope of the ground (at the far extremity of the Grotto) had rendered this extension extremely difficult. Nevertheless, retaining walls were begun, thirty-five feet high at the extreme end and nearly four feet broad at the base. The undermined church and the presbytery at Cadzow, seven miles distant, were purchased for £25, and a benefactor carried the stone to Maryknowe. The former St. Francis Xavier's school at Carfin, also undermined, was bought next, and the same friend, with the aid of volunteers, transported its abundant building materials to the Grotto."

Elsewhere Father Taylor relates that for the latter task his men were allowed only one month to demolish the complete two-storey building, remove the stones and transport them by every available conveyance across the road and through the Grotto to the far end. In addition to the several lorries, provided gratis, every barrow and truck in the neighbourhood of Carfin was commissioned to have the site of the new school cleared within the given time. Only in the service of God could so much work be accomplished in such a short time, the fact being remembered that many of the volunteers had already done a normal day's employment before starting on Grotto work. It must be stated, too, that a few of the men engaged in building the massive wall, were not convinced that the foundation laid was embedded sufficiently for the height of the wall. But faith, it seems, can build walls as well as move mountains, and over thirty years later, the wall still stands, though the men of faith, and those of little faith, have gone to their reward.

The Little Flower avenue, leading from the Upper Grotto, and the Star of the Sea avenue from the Lower, were extended into the valley that leads to Chapelknowe; and ultimately these avenues circled round and met at the outer rim of what is now the sunken garden. At one end of the garden was built what was one of the most complicated of all the tasks undertaken by the Grotto volunteers—the domed replica of the " Santa Casa," or Holy House, originally at Nazareth, now at Loreto. The southern wall of the garden is adorned with seven bas-reliefs of Our Lady's Dolours, each seven feet high. A number of niches and alcoves were left in the interior wall, presumably for additional shrines, one of which Monsignor hoped would be in honour of Blessed John Ogilvie. As previously mentioned, a giant size statue of St. Andrew has, within the last few years, been erected on a thirty-foot wide buttress of the wall, standing thirty-five feet above the field below. This site, Father Taylor had dreamed, would form the pedestal of a magnificent altar, with a lofty cupola, whence Holy Mass would be visible to a myriad of pilgrims in the surrounding valley.

Like that of the votive church, this hope, too, was not to be fulfilled. In his heart he cherished the thought that some day Scotland would be honoured by a Eucharistic Congress: in his own way he was planning for that day. The booklet in which he expounded his plan was published in 1938, but in the following year the Second World War upset the plans of all. Four years later, Archbishop Mackintosh of Glasgow died, after several years of failing health. One is pleased to note that in his wisdom His Grace eventually saw it fitting, in 1937, to raise to the Cathedral Chapter, the little country parish priest, whose grandiose hopes for the Church in Scotland were in direct contrast to his humility as a priest of God.

At the parochial presentation to the newly appointed Canon, several of the senior priests present, as reported in the press at the time, commented that the dignity conferred on Canon Taylor had been long delayed, a sentiment which was endorsed by all his parishioners, and expressed by well-wishers in letters which arrived at Carfin from distant places. It was on this occasion, it has been alleged, that the post-office at Motherwell had to engage additional telegraph assistants to cope with the heavy load of greetings telegrams which came to Carfin.

Canon Taylor himself said that he claimed no reward for the work to which he had devoted his life. The compliment was to Our Lady, whose servant he was. On the eve of his tonsure he had dedicated his life, first of all to the service of His divine Master, Our Lord Jesus Christ; and secondly, by making the promise of " True Devotion," recommended by that great lover of Our Lady, St. Grignon de Montfort, his every action was entrusted to her hands, that she, guided by the wisdom of the Holy Spirit, might place them lovingly before her divine Son.

On Easter Sunday, 1934, Don Bosco of Turin was canonised. By a difficult-to-understand supernatural alchemy, " The Giant Saint," as Pius XI named him, insinuated his way in the following year, to one of the most prominent shrines in the Lower Grotto. Monsignor Taylor endeavours to explain—not too successfully—how this came about, in an article which was published in the *Catholic Herald,* April 20, 1935, the week following the unveiling and blessing of the statue of the Saint, by the Salesian Provincial, Rev. Father Tozzi, who himself had formerly known the new Saint.

The article reproduced here in its entirety gives an indication of Father Taylor's erudition. Week after week, until 1939, Carfin Grotto notes appeared in the Catholic press; invariably, for a number of years, they were prefixed by a little-known gem of English verse in honour of God or His Saints; next came information or topical news of the current Church festival; finally reference was made to Grotto news—the progress of new shrines, favours acknowledged and donations received, with a remembrance of ailing or deceased Grotto benefactors. These articles were eagerly sought by friends of the Grotto in Europe and America, as well as in Australia and the far-flung Mission fields, wherever Father Taylor's name was known and revered. The following is an extract similar to others of a kind appearing in the Catholic press:

" There was a man sent from God whose name was John."

" These words were first spoken of that doughty champion of God's law, John the Baptist, by the gentle evangelist, St. John.

Three hundred and fifty years ago at Lepanto, Don John of Austria, with a hundred sail, routed three hundred and thirty of the Turkish galleys. Thirty alone escaped. Fifteen thousand Christian galley slaves were set free, and thirty thousand prisoners taken. In Constantinople, the capital of the Moslems, consternation reigned. Well merited, indeed, was the new title, ' Help of Christians,' accorded in thanksgiving by Saint Pius V to the Maiden who is ' terrible as an army set in battle array.'

A century passed and a Turkish army, one hundred thousand strong, had encircled Vienna, the sole hope of Europe. The Pope and the emperor summoned another John, the King of Poland, John Sobieski, to save Christianity and civilisation. With a swiftness bordering on the miraculous, Sobieski, and his twenty thousand soldiers, swooped down on the foe. He spent the night praying in a little chapel on the lofty hill that overlooks Vienna.

During some digging operations that night on the hill, a paper was discovered on which were written these words, and only these words: ' There was a man sent from God whose name was John.' The incident was accepted as a message from on High. It flashed through the camp, redoubling the confidence of the soldiers. The disaster which before sunset had overtaken the magnificent and elated battalions of the Sultan is as unique in the annals of history as is the slaughter at Lepanto.

John Sobieski sent his famous message to the Roman Pontiff:
'Veni, vidi, Deus vicit: I came, I saw, God conquered.' Once
more the Rosary had done its work; once more the Help of
Christians had proved herself the Saviour of Christendom.

On the last day of January, 1888, there died in Turin one of
whom it could also be truly said: '*There was a Man sent from
God.*' Thousands who had passed under his influence, and
hundreds of thousands besides, knew that John Bosco, who had
come from God, had on that 31st January returned to His Bosom.
They felt that the proclamation of his sanctity was but a matter
of time.

In his career of long days and short nights, he had well won
the names of Patron of Youth, Pioneer of the Catholic Press,
Trainer of Teachers, Father of Missionaries and Hunter of Souls.
He had earned the title that one day Pius XI was to give him—
'a gigantic Saint.' In a famous vision he saw the missionary world
dotted with Salesian outposts from coast to coast. One of his chief
mottoes was assuredly: 'Serve the Lord in joy.'

Joy was to him the needle that drew after it the golden thread
of the love of God.

His life was spent putting joy into human hearts, and most of
all into the hearts of boys.

Nine years and nine months later to a day, the soul of a French
child returned to God. Known in her little world as Marie
Thérèse, she was called in the cloister Sister Thérèse of the Child
Jesus. Her life was as unlike that of the apostle of Turin as it is
possible to conceive. Yet the spirit is the same, and the points of
resemblance are many.

It would seem as if these two—who not long ago appeared
together at the bedside of a dying nun in France and healed her—
are destined to play an overwhelming part in the rescue of Christendom from the modern infidels. They are both saints of joy—
both child-like and lovers of children. Both wielded the pen—the
manuscript of Soeur Thérèse promises to be as enduring as *The
Imitation of Christ*. Both hungered after the souls of the heathen
and lamented the terrifying wastage of the Precious Blood.

If the daughter of Carmel died in utter obscurity, she had foretold that her glory, like her labours, would be posthumous, that
after her death all the world would love her—and the Pope has
christened her, 'Darling of the Whole World'—that in Heaven
she would work for Christ and the Church, ' until the last soul
had entered Paradise.'

Thus, too, spoke the dying Don Bosco. Tremendous as was the
success of his Festive Oratories and other Institutions, and great
as were the fruits of his missionary sons, he announced that much
more wonderful were the triumphs he would accomplish from
the heights of Heaven. Since he left his children for his abundant

reward, the fruits of his labours have multiplied a hundredfold, and gradually the world-wide chain of citadels of the Faith, which he saw in his vision, is being built up in the defence of the Church.

On Easter Sunday of 1934, Saint John Bosco was canonised. On the anniversary day, April 1, his statue was set up in the Grotto. Last Sunday it was unveiled. How it all happened it will be difficult to explain.

There are no Salesians in Scotland. Though the Provincial, Father Tozzi, paid a visit to the Grotto some years ago, the writer did not see him. Other shrines had been proposed for erection. An offering had actually been made of the statue of Saint Vincent, father of the Sisters of Charity and of the Society of St. Vincent de Paul. There was also the promise of a statue of Blessed John Ogilvie, martyred at Glasgow, Scotland's first Beatus since the days of Margaret, Scotland's Pearl.

How, then, did the newest saint in the Calendar, in these parts an unknown Italian, find his way to Carfin? It is perhaps as mysterious as is the choice made of him as patron by the Guild of Catholic Teachers, instead of the great Aquinas—the first proposal of its two thousand members.

Besides there was no donor of the statue. Subscriptions came in slowly and in small amounts. They are not even yet complete.

The position of the shrine is equally mysterious. When the statue of the Holy Child was removed from its elaborate sanctuary in the Lower Grotto to its new home at the end of Our Lady's Crescent, it was decided that the old one should become the shrine of Our Lady Queen of Apostles. It was to be adorned with statues or bas-reliefs of Saints Peter and Paul, Xavier and Thérèse, Peter Claver and Gabriel Perboyre.

For over a year the planning went on; special designs were sent from Belgium and from Italy. The purpose was to speed up the work of the Propagation of the Faith, the Holy Childhood and other missionary activities. Were not the missions dear to Our Lady of Carfin, to the Saint of Lisieux, and to her great friend, the Father in Rome? Meantime a place in the extension had been laid out for Don Bosco. Outcrops of limestone rock were formed. A tiny garden surrounded it. About a hundred pilgrims could view it from the roadway overhead.

Evidently all this did not suit Don Bosco. One fine day the missionary shrine receded into the distance. Within a month a vastly more imposing one on the same spot, quite rivalling that of Francis and Thérèse, sprang into being. At the head of a triple flight of stairs above the ruins of the mosaic sanctuary, he now stands, Saint Dominic Savio on one side and the celebrated Salesian missionary, Cardinal Cagliero, as a boy, on the other.

As at Massabieille, the embankment has been laid out with paths and stairways to be lined by pilgrims. The pilgrims were to

be boys, and on Sunday the boys were Scouts—a background
such as the Saint himself would have dearly loved. But at his feet,
between Mount Assisi and Our Lady of Carfin on her lake, it
would be quite possible to gather twenty thousand youths instead
of the two thousand who greeted the Saint last Sunday. Was that
why this man whose name was John and who was sent from God
chose the Carfin Grotto to be—what Father Tozzi publicly
declared it to be on Sunday—his national shrine?

Space allows only brief mention of the pilgrimage made by
Canon Taylor (and his friend, Dr. McGlynn, founding President
of the Don Bosco Guild of Teachers) to the shrine of the Saint,
at Turin. The published account of the journey reveals that the
pilgrims received, while there, two first-class relics of the Saint,
one for the Chapel of Relics at Carfin and the other for the Don
Bosco Guild. Because of Don Bosco's great interest in the welfare of youth, Canon Taylor honoured him as one of the premier
saints in the Grotto Shrine. His devotion was well rewarded, for
in a letter to a friend he remarked that on one occasion the
Saint's intercession saved him from being involved in prolonged
legislation in defence of his integrity.

On the day the statue of " the giant Saint " was unveiled, a
remarkable treasure, perhaps the most outstanding of the
Grotto's masterpieces, was carried in procession for the first
time: this was the unique Missionary Monstrance, the story of
which belongs to the history of the Chapel of Relics. The spring
of 1935 was notable, too, in Carfin for the three days of uninterrupted Eucharistic Adoration which marked the end of the
extended Holy Year. Canon Taylor had been accorded the
privilege of associating the Shrine of Our Lady at Carfin with
the Shrine of the Immaculate at Lourdes, in a union of sacramental adoration from 3 p.m. on a Thursday in April to 4 p.m.
on the Sunday following. Canon Taylor's faith in the loyalty of
Scottish Catholics was rewarded: people visited the parish
church in great numbers during the three days, and from 1 a.m.
to 7 a.m., the men—between fifty and sixty parishioners—
formed a loyal band of courtiers for the vigil. Would detractors
claim that the Eucharistic King was less honoured when the
many worshippers who came to pay their homage to the Son
in the church, crossed the road to pay their respects to His
Mother in the Grotto? The real test lay in the long line of communicants who thronged the altar rails during the Triduum.

Half-a-dozen years prior to these momentous events, the
Grotto had lost one of its most valued friends with the death of
Monsignor Claeys. The first hours of 1935 marked the passing

of its most illustrious, in the person of Cardinal Bourne. As Canon Taylor assisted at the obsequies in London, he could recall how frequently over a span of forty years the Cardinal had played a personal and active role in his own life, and how even to the end, the Cardinal had displayed a deep interest in the progress of the Scottish Lourdes. That same year the Grotto gained a new friend in Monsignor Fulton J. Sheen, universally esteemed American prelate. While visiting Rome and Lourdes, Monsignor Sheen had interrupted his journey in order to preach at Carfin. With typical generosity and good humour, His Lordship has contributed the following anecdote as a tribute to Monsignor Taylor's memory:

Pontifical Mission Organizations,
366 Fifth Avenue,
New York.

October 4, 1966.

" My dear Miss McGhee,

. . . I visited Father Taylor several times at Carfin. The first time I visited him he asked me to preach a sermon in honor of the Little Flower at his shrine, which was opposite the Church of Carfin. I told him I would talk about the Blessed Mother. He insisted on the Little Flower.

We hit upon a compromise. It was this: I would begin by telling a humorous incident about the Blessed Mother and the Little Flower. If the audience laughed, I would talk on the Blessed Mother; if they did not laugh, I would talk on the Little Flower.

The story I told was something that actually happened in Long Beach, California. In this particular church there were two altars immediately adjoining one another, one of the Little Flower and the other of the Blessed Mother. In an earthquake, the statue of the Little Flower fell into the arms of the Blessed Mother unharmed. I said 'If in times of trouble the Little Flower goes to the Blessed Mother, why should we go to anyone else?' I need not tell you that I spoke about the Blessed Mother.

Father Taylor was one of the most spiritual priests I have ever known. It was he who brought to the English-speaking public the life of St. Thérèse, and also fostered her devotion in Scotland. . . . Wishing you every blessing and with the assurance of prayer.

I remain,

Faithfully yours in Christ,

(Sgd.) Fulton J. Sheen,

National Director of Pontifical Mission Organizations."

Apart from Monsignor Fulton Sheen's visits to Carfin, the two mission-minded priests—each National Director of Mission Aid Societies in his respective homeland—renewed acquaintanceship at Rome at the general conferences of the societies.

An incident, with a similar point as that made in the anecdote related above, comes to mind. In 1957, several plane-loads of friends accompanied Monsignor Taylor on a two-day pilgrimage to Lourdes to commemorate the diamond jubilee of his ordination and first Holy Mass. The first coach, carrying Monsignor Taylor and others of the party, developed a mechanical defect. While the driver and a few technically minded men in the coach tinkered with the engine, Monsignor led the rest of us in an urgent S.O.S. to the Little Flower; but to no avail. Now pressed for time, the driver was about to phone for a relief coach when he was asked by Monsignor to delay doing so for a few moments. Turning to the passengers, he remarked: " The Daughter cannot help us; now let us appeal directly to the Mother!" Scarcely had he completed the first few *Aves* when the engine had roared into life. Intercession of the greater Queen had saved the situation and the coach reached the airport without further mishap.

It is but right to add that, contrary to the tone of this tale, Monsignor Taylor did, nevertheless, have his priorities right. The frail and almost blind jubilarian was bent on paying homage for the last time at the hallowed shrine of his blessed Mother without, on this occasion, visiting the Carmel at Lisieux. St. Thérèse was dear to him, but nearer and dearer to his soul were Our Lord Jesus Christ and His Immaculate Mother. This fact is abundantly borne out by his constant practice and preaching: first of all, the Holy Sacrifice of the Mass; next the Rosary— preferably the fifteen decades; next, devotions in honour of the saints, and for Monsignor, St. Thérèse came foremost among the saints.

In 1937, as the Grotto neared its fifteenth anniversary, its revered founder was in his sixty-fourth year of natural life and had been forty years a priest. The death of Canon Hackett left a vacancy in the Archdiocesan Chapter, to which Father Taylor was appointed in September 1937. At the celebration after the new Canon's induction, Mgr. Ritchie, the Grand Old Man of the Glasgow Archdiocese and Provost of the Chapter, spoke these words :

" The elevation of Father Taylor to the Cathedral Chaper is not so much an honour for him, but an honour to the Chapter to have Father Taylor among us."

It was not only the parishioners of Carfin and the Canons of the Chapter who expressed their great joy at the long delayed appointment; all over Scotland, similar sentiments were expressed, for as Monsignor Mullin put it:

> " People outside Carfin could see events more clearly from a distance and they were lost in admiration at what Canon Taylor had done, not only for Carfin, but for the whole of Scotland."

In different terms, Rev. Dr. McEwan of Riddrie said that if it were to be alleged that there was only " one man of faith in Scotland today, then surely that man is Canon Taylor."

Acknowledging his gratitude to his people at the presentation to him of his robes of office, Canon Taylor remarked to his audience that this was the first time in fifteen years that His Grace had said publicly, " I thank you for what you have done." This thanks, Canon Taylor added, goes to the men who stood by him and made it possible. In particular, he named Father John J. Murphy, the hard-working curate at Carfin for eighteen years, and loyal co-operator in the spiritual crusades of the parish; but he had no hesitation in adding that it was the people of Carfin, with their Irish hearts and their arduous labour that made possible the crusade to make the Mother of God known to the people of Scotland.

With due deference to Monsignor Taylor's veracity, the writer would like to add that although over ninety-five per cent of the Grotto volunteers were Irish or of Irish extraction, a small group of Lithuanians also helped with the heavy work in the Grotto; further, from time to time, non-Catholics offered their services to carry out some specialised task at the Shrine. Apart from the heavy labouring jobs in the Grotto, a variety of occupations were always available for those who wished to further Canon Taylor's many crusades. Mr. William Ribchester, M.A., Headmaster of one of the schools in Canon Taylor's parish, often volunteered his services as chauffeur when the busy Canon wished to attend a church function or festival. Mr. Ribchester, who possibly knew Monsignor Taylor better than most, has kindly furnished some reminiscences of his long association with the priest and friend whom he held in the highest esteem. Those of us who are acquainted with Mr. Ribchester will see not only the latter's ebullient character showing through in the stories, but also the sympathy and respect which he had for the Canon.

Mr. Ribchester commences his account of Monsignor Taylor by recalling what was known to all:

" Monsignor Taylor was himself a superb worker and seemed to have the facility of getting others to help him in his work. He expected his assistants to devote all their energies to the task on which they were engaged, to the exclusion of light frivolities which served no essential purpose in life. Life was made by God for God; all man's efforts should be directed towards that end."

Mr. Ribchester, with Dr. McGlynn's connivance, prevailed on Canon Taylor to go on one of his rare " outings." The carrot held up to the Canon was that the destination would be St. Ninian's Cave, near Whithorn. The three voyagers motored down along the West Coast. Mr. Ribchester now tells his own story:

" While driving through the Burns country, I was debating in my own mind whether to burst into a Burns' song or recite a stanza from ' Tam o' Shanter,' when a quiet voice interrupted with, ' I think we'll have the Rosary now.' Before I recovered, the Canon was half-way through the first decade, and I was responding like the best of them. But that was not all; Dr. McGlynn was invited to start the second decade and I, sinner that I am, had no alternative but combine my driving with the effort of leading the third decade in a manner worthy of Our Lady and of my two good passengers.

And that (added Mr. Ribchester) is how the Canon enjoyed a lovely run in the car."

Eventually, the trio arrived at St. Ninian's Cave, where a few prayers were said and a special request made to St. Ninian:

" We asked St. Ninian for permission to ' borrow ' a few stones and boulders from the Cave. As no active objection was made by him—there were no bruised fingers or broken bones as a result— we assumed his permission, especially as the Canon had assured us that the Saint had been the soul of generosity while alive, and so the ' borrowed ' stones were brought back to Carfin and placed at various strategic points in the Grotto."

" Borrowing " seems to have been the operative word when Mr. Ribchester and Canon Taylor went off together, as demonstrated by Mr. Ribchester's next story.

" While I was taking the Canon for a run in the car one day, he complained that some of the more recently built walls in the Grotto looked very bare and new-looking. As if it had been ordained, we passed at that moment the ruins of a long disused church, encircled by a crumbling wall covered with greenery—the very thing we needed! We examined the wall, and soon the boot of the car held a quantity of wall plants, ferns and moss. I was undecided whether the plants of another religion would feel at home in the Grotto. The Canon's misgivings were for another reason, but these were soon allayed by the knowledge that these beautiful plants would be seen and admired by many thousands instead of a disinterested few; and by my assurance that I would not damage anything while picking the plants."

The secret of one of the many subterfuges practised in the Grotto by the ingenious volunteers, in order to produce suitable background effect, is now revealed:

"Canon Taylor was one of the first to make use of artificial Cumberland rock. Earth, rock, stones and pebbles were placed in a suitable pile at the required site. These were covered with concrete, and strong brown paper was pushed and shaped into the concrete at suitable irregular places. When the whole had set and the brown paper removed, the result was Cumberland rock. The Canon was paid many compliments on the rock but few noticed it was artificial. He chuckled when he gleefully told the story to his intimate friends, but to the populace generally Cumberland rock it remained."

The Canon's tact and consideration for children's feelings is next referred to by Mr. Ribchester:

"On one occasion when Our Lady's Grotto was being filled with a colourful array of children from the schools and parishes of the West of Scotland, one group of boys was ill-prepared in rather dull clothes and without sashes. This group was ruining the appearance of the ensemble. Before the children were finally arranged, the Canon asked an usher (Mr. Ribchester) to conduct the group away from the spot where they were, to a high vantage point on the embankments, from where the boys had a lovely view of the proceedings. This satisfied everyone—the Canon was now delighted with the colourful display of the massed groups in regalia, and the leaders of the boys, because of the special privilege shown to them."

Mr. Ribchester claims Canon Taylor related the story of the following incident. It happened, he alleged when the Canon, Dr. McGlynn perhaps and another friend were travelling north:

"The road was slippery, the car skidded, hit the kerb and turned on its side. With the help of passing motorists the car was righted but would not start. Everything was tried without satisfactory result. It was cold and the travellers did not relish staying there while one of them sought help from a distant garage. When they were at their lowest ebb and about to set out for the garage, the Canon suggested that an appeal to the heavenly powers might prove effective. They said a short prayer, tried the car once more, and at the first attempt the car started."

Should one wonder that Monsignor Taylor asked the coach-driver who wished to send for a relief coach to convey the jubilee party of travellers to the airport, not to do so until he had sought supernatural help. Both stories bear a marked similarity; the writer of this biography was on the jubilee coach and most certainly Mr. Ribchester was not aware of the incident, nor was the present writer aware until recently, of Mr. Ribchester's tale, which must have happened over thirty years ago. Other stories which bear the stamp of strange coincidence have been told by reliable witnesses.

Mr. Frank Duff, founder of the Legion of Mary, held Monsignor in the highest esteem, a sentiment which was reciprocated on Monsignor Taylor's part, for he considered that the movement founded and fostered by Mr. Duff was of prime importance in the modern world.

Mr. Duff's first sight of the Grotto was by floodlight in the middle of the night. He had arrived late at Carfin and Monsignor had no hesitation in showing him around the illuminated shrines, a sight which would be expected to rouse admiration even in a hardened unbeliever, and Mr. Duff, as all lovers of Our Lady know, is anything but that. On one occasion, while Mr. Duff was spending a week at Carfin, as Monsignor's guest, it was planned that they should both visit Archbishop McDonald in Edinburgh. Mr. Duff describes the rather remarkable journey in a letter written to the writer in June, 1969.

" On the day on which I was to leave Monsignor Taylor, after my stay in his home, he and I were to make a visit to Archbishop McDonald of Edinburgh. And, you know that you do not miss your appointments with an Archbishop! As you probably are aware, the Monsignor was dilatory in his methods—one cannot be perfect all round—and the result of this was that he left us late for our journey to Holytown Junction where we were to catch the train to Edinburgh. There were no taxis to be got in Carfin, and we had to wait for one to come from Motherwell. In the interval, Monsignor brought me out to the Shrine of the Little Flower and instructed me to pray to her in our emergency. We certainly did that with fervour. The taxi arrived and we set off for the junction— twenty minutes late. As you know, the trains run punctually along that stretch (this station is the first stop the Edinburgh express has after leaving the Central Station, Glasgow), but when we arrived at the junction the train had not yet come in! Indeed, we even had time to purchase our tickets before it came. I regarded this as a veritable little miracle, worked at his request to the Little Flower, and this idea of mine was confirmed by what transpired during the remainder of the journey.

Once on board the train we found ourselves in a compartment with two ladies who ultimately confided their stories to us. One of these was a non-Catholic; she was deeply interested by what the Monsignor said to her and promised to embark on a course of reading. The other lady, a Catholic, was, to put it simply, in immense difficulties. I would say that I was just the very person who fitted into the partial solution of her problem. I would believe that those two persons were, of all the passengers on that train, the two who were most in need of, and at the same time open to spiritual help."

Mr. Duff comments on Monsignor Taylor's spirituality:

"The Monsignor was a man of transcendent faith. It was the whole atmosphere of his life, and it affected those who spoke with him. He carried around with him the feeling of the supernatural.

It was a wonderful compliment to the Legion that he fell so much in love with it. It seemed to reflect all his ideas in the spiritual order . . . He helped the Legion in many ways . . . and in particular he gave great help to the hostels."

Mr. Duff concludes:

"It was bad enough when Monsignor Taylor had to depart from this world, but it would represent unspeakable tragedy if his memory disappeared at once, along with himself . . . That noble person deserves every sort of appreciation which could be lavished on him."

Stories are legion of strange coincidences which occurred to Monsignor Taylor, or to his friends while they were travelling. Two nuns write in a letter to him that they caught a connecting train which " officially did not exist." It seems they had delayed long at Carfin and left too late to catch the normal connection for their convent on the East Coast. They were sceptical at first about Monsignor's assurance that they would arrive at their destination at a reasonable time. When they left the first train the good nuns were assured by a porter that the last train that day had left some time earlier. Disconsolate, they were about to leave the station to seek alternative means of transport, when an official beckoned them and informed them that a train on one of the sidings would be leaving shortly for their destination. The fact that this particular train was not advertised either on time-table or schedule did not worry them unduly. The nuns, as well as Monsignor Taylor, had unbounded belief in the over-riding power of the heavenly guardian of railways.

Another story is told by M. Gerard Dupon of Bruges, and confirmed by Dr. Patrick McGlynn, both of them present when the incident took place. Monsignor and his friend, Dr. McGlynn, had interrupted their return journey from Lourdes to call on M. Dupon. The visit was not merely a social call, for much Grotto business was to be covered in consultation with the Belgian Grotto artist. Dr. McGlynn had an important conference in Glasgow on the Saturday evening and it was necessary that Monsignor Taylor should be back for Sunday Masses and Grotto services on the following day. Unfortunately, on this particular weekend there was a general stoppage of work among transport workers in the Bruges district. Telephone enquiries elicited the information that all aeroplanes had been grounded and coaches to the airport were not running. Nothing daunted, full of faith, the intrepid travellers with their host, made their way to the airport on the back of a cab drawn by a slow-moving old horse. First inspection found the airport as silent as the grave. Need it be said that a few speedy prayers winged their way heavenwards. While they waited, undecided what to do, from a nearby building emerged a tall figure, who unhesitatingly made his way in their direction. As is to be expected, the story had a happy ending. The gentleman was flying in a privately owned plane to Britain, and could he offer the travellers a lift? M. Dupon, who related the story, stated that he, too, if he had wished to leave Bruges, could have travelled with Monsignor Taylor and Dr. McGlynn. Of course, this could have happened to anyone, but the difference lies in that such unusual incidents happened regularly when Monsignor Taylor went a-journeying. It is unfortunate that few of the spiritual coincidences—there have been references made to many such—have not been put on record. One speaks openly of trains and aircraft which turn up at unexpected moments, but the spiritual revival of a soul in distress is rarely a topic for social conversation. And yet the writer has heard of several such stories, the details of which are not sufficiently clear for adequate retelling. A postcard in Monsignor's files briefly tells one. It was sent to him from France bearing the news that the sender, to whom Canon Taylor had once said, " You will become a Catholic," had that day been received into the Church. A number of letters show that his spiritual children, hailing from different parts of Britain, wrote to him regularly, thanking him for what he had done for them over the years.

The installation of the Mass Rock—gifted by an Irish non-Catholic through the good offices of one of Monsignor's Irish clerical friends—and the statue of St. John Bosco were the last important additions to the Grotto until the Second World War and its aftermath had subsided. The mammoth task of building the Holy House in the sunken garden continued right into the war years, until a time when Canon Taylor reported that " Patrick," the last volunteer worker, had been directed to work elsewhere, and the Grotto gardener found himself alone for most of the time. But Our Lady—and Canon Taylor—were not left completely without friends. Just as in the early days of the Grotto, when two Carfin ladies, the late Mrs. Annie McCafferty and her sturdy friend, hurdled a heavy wheelbarrow with the best of the men, during the war years, a few of the lady parishioners took on the task of keeping the areas round the shrine tidy. Periodically, Mrs. B. McDermott—or " Old Mary McDermott," as the villagers referred to her affectionately—with a few friends, saw to it that the statuary was kept clean. Another friend of Monsignor Taylor's could be seen moving around the terracing on either side of Massabieille, as she tended the young plants on crisp spring days. On occasion, too, the scholastics from Craighead offered their help to prepare the shrine for the crowds of visitors who continued to visit the Grotto in spite of war restrictions.

Almost immediately from September 1939, special trains and additional buses were cancelled, and the heartrending tale was always the same, " Sorry, trains—buses—are not available." On the occasion of a Children of Mary rally when it looked as if only sodality members within walking distance would take part in the May procession, half-a-dozen taxis rolled up and close on four dozen excited, blue-mantled figures rushed to join the procession, just then about to commence. And it may be added, a taxi was a costly luxury during the war.

The annual pilgrimage to Lourdes had been suspended in 1940, but the Committee, with the Archbishop's approval, in July 1941, organised the first " Lourdes Day " at Carfin. Restrictions on travel permitted only one special train to be run on that day—all Sunday train services to the Grotto Halt had been suspended " for the duration "—and yet on that July Sunday, well over 25,000 pilgrims congregated in the Grotto to pray for " a swift, just and charitable peace." On this occasion, for the first time, His Grace Archbishop Mackintosh was the celebrant at the Benediction of the Blessed Sacrament, given from an altar above the Madonna's shrine. It was on this Sunday, too, that His

Grace publicly acknowledged in his address to the pilgrims gathered at Our Lady's shrine, that he owed his recovery in health to intercessory prayers to Our Lady of Lourdes and to St. Thérèse to whom he had prayed on the advice of our Holy Father himself.

Referring to this day, Monsignor Taylor wrote in the *Catholic Times* of July 25, 1941:

> "So ends the first chapter of the Grotto story, begun on the September feast of Our Lady of Dolours in 1920, by the cutting of a sod, or more exactly, on the Rosary Sunday of 1922 by the blessing of the statue of the Immaculate. The Lourdes Sunday of 1941, with the Benediction given by His Grace to that marvellous assemblage of Mary's children, Mary's legionaries and Mary's priests, opens a second chapter, destined, with Mary's help, to be still more fruitful in penance, in prayer and in Grace . . ."

Canon Taylor could not have known in 1941 that the second chapter of his own Marian Crusade was to stretch onwards for another twenty-two years; and that during most of this time he would continue to lead Mary's pilgrims in the Rosary, so much loved for centuries in the Church, and advocated so strongly by her, at Lourdes and Fatima.

Although the heavily-laden pilgrimage trains from the East and South were discontinued immediately on the outbreak of war, as were also all Sunday trains to the Grotto Halt, Canon Taylor had the joy of welcoming other pilgrims, men from the Allied services—Army, Navy and Air Force representatives from Newfoundland, from the Antipodes and other far-flung outposts of the United Kingdom. These pilgrims were welcome, as were the Free Forces of France and of massacred Poland.

On the feast of Corpus Christi in May 1940, Carfin was to greet the first large group of the Chasseurs Alpins, those daring little Frenchmen who fled their native land rather than yield to the Swastika. On the eve of the Feast, Canon Taylor received a telephone communication requesting permission for a Communion Mass in the Grotto on the following morning. This was to be followed after breakfast by High Mass, procession and a solemn consecration to Our Lady and the Little Flower of the battalion of 500 men. Canon Taylor did not require to be told that chaplains in the armed services enjoyed the privilege of celebrating Holy Mass in any convenient place. Several telephone calls procured permission for the religious services, but how were 500 men to be fed from the empty larders of the Lourdes Institute? What happened comes down in Carfin history as the little miracle

of the Multiplication of the Loaves. Wednesday was a tradesmen's holiday in Lanarkshire, and stocks in the shops would be
low until the following day. The Legionaries who had charge
of the catering were at their wits' end. Canon Taylor reported
the result in the Catholic press of the following week-end:

" The problem was confided to Our Lady of Massabieille and
St. Thérèse. An S.O.S. was sent out at both Little Flower services
—at 6 and 7.30 p.m. The result was a veritable miracle of generosity. From Motherwell and Mossend, as well as from Carfin, gifts
of every kind of food poured in. By midnight, over 1,000 slices
of bread lay ready. It was the story of the five loaves, the two
little fishes, and even of the twelve baskets, for forty-five loaves
lay as yet uncut, while there was a surplus of seven pounds of
butter. In addition, tea, sugar, cheese, ham, meat, milk, cakes and
other eatables arrived to stock the larder for the morrow—and
all this in a time of strict rationing. Willing helpers laid the tables,
realising as they did so, that the cupboards of many a household
had been stripped bare.

After the open-air confessions and the early Communion Mass,
the grateful men sat down to an excellent repast, affectionately
prepared."

One cannot wonder that some of these exiled men were
reduced to tears at the welcome offered to them in a foreign
land.

Equally striking, though better prepared for, was the pilgrimage made by 400 Polish soldiers who, with Army Bishop
Gawlina, a dozen chaplains, a general and two colonels, " captured " the village of Carfin, at 7.30 one Sunday morn in
September 1940. Their Communion Mass at 9.30 gave the
villagers an indication of the treat in store for them at the 10.30
High Mass sung by Bishop Gawlina and the famous Polish choir.
A further assembly in the Grotto at 2 p.m. when the Rosary and
the Litany of the Holy Name were recited in lusty unison by the
soldiers, made other pilgrims regret that the 1,000 soldiers who
had originally planned to come, had been prevented from doing
so because of an urgent " stand-by," the result of Hitler's
" blitzkrieg " on London.

This first visit by the exiled Polish forces in 1940 set the precedent for an annual rally which has taken place regularly since.
During the commemoration of the millenium of Polish Christianity, a marble plaque in honour of Our Lady of Chestochowa
was erected in the parish church of Carfin, marking, not only
the Polish people's 1,000 years of Christianity, but the twenty-
five years of regular pilgrimage to Our Lady's shrine at Carfin.

The Lithuanians have an even longer tradition of loyalty to
Our Lady of Carfin. Inspired by their faithful chaplain, Father
Petrauskas of Holy Family, Mossend, Lithuanian pilgrims have
from the early days of the Grotto paid their respect to their
Queen and Mother. No pilgrims were made more welcome by
Monsignor Taylor than the exiles from the countries of Eastern
Europe, so long held in bondage by Communist domination.

Father Taylor's crusade to increase Marian devotion in Scotland added to his heavy burden of duties outwith the precincts
of his own parish. His name had popular appeal, not only
because it was associated with the cult of Our Lady of Lourdes
and St. Thérèse of Lisieux, but perhaps even more so because
he was recognised as a man of faith and personal sanctity. The
sincerity of his words, the directness of his eloquence guaranteed
a well-filled hall or church when he was billed as speaker. Hence
he was a popular guest speaker throughout Britain. In season
and out of season, whenever his many duties made it possible,
he spoke wherever there was an ear to listen.

In the early years of the Grotto story he made several four- or
five-day lecture tours in the Midlands and North of England,
during which, on one occasion at least, he addressed twenty
audiences in five days. The North and South of Scotland too
welcomed him gladly. Nobility and commoner became Monsignor Taylor's friends. The Stirlings of Keir, the Frasers, the
Lovats and other gentry of an older generation in Scotland,
claimed him as friend. From the South, the Duchess of Norfolk,
with several members of her family and friends, came on pilgrimage to Carfin; men of letters, too, were known to him
personally; Hilaire Belloc, Francis Thomson, Francis Meynell,
Kathleen Tyndal were friends or associates in literary work.
With so wide a circle of friends among the elite and the lowly,
he was in constant demand as speaker for big audiences; Mission
appeals, Catholic Truth Society rallies, Knights of St. Columba
conferences and assemblies of a similar nature.

At times the views he expressed were not too popular: he was
too emotional, they said; he saw danger to the Church when none
was present; he was medieval in his outlook; one must change
with the times. But, never one to yield to popular clamour when
it offended personal conviction, Canon Taylor continued to
pursue his dedicated course. At Carfin, parishioners and pilgrims
to the Grotto were already praying for Spain before the news of
the blood-bath to which the Church in that country had been
subjugated, had broken on the world. One of his most frequent
ejaculations was, " Saviour of the World, save Russia!" His own

faith in prayer convinced him that Russia could and would be saved from Communism if the world returned to the Rosary. For Stalin he held no brief, nor for that matter Roosevelt and Churchill who, he claimed, betrayed Poland to the Eastern bloc at the Yalta Conference. As early as 1936 he spoke of what might happen in Germany. In the presence of a distinguished platform of Lourdes Committee officials, which included the Archbishop of Edinburgh, two Scottish Lords and other dignitaries of Church and State, he addressed a vast Edinburgh audience with these stirring and prophetic words:

> "The time is past for preaching and planning; we must go down on our knees and storm heaven with our prayers . . . It is not true that the Catholics of Germany can be trusted to stand firm against the pagan doctrines of Nazism . . . The Holy Rosary brings us to Mary and through her to the feet of her Son."

How many of the audience listened to the voice of the seer in the month of February 1936? And, alas, how many more of them let his words pass unheeded?

The war and its aftermath temporarily brought people to their knees, but warnings were soon forgotten. Time and again in the Grotto, Monsignor Taylor preached the Message of Lourdes and of Fatima—Penance and Prayer: the Mass and the Rosary. To encourage the faithful in the love of the Eucharist, a statue of St. Pius X—the Pope of the Eucharist—was installed in the Lower Grotto, after his canonisation. Flanked on one side by St. John Bosco, patron of youth, and on the other by St. John Baptist de la Salle, the triad of statues form an arresting display.

Several years prior to the completion of this shrine, another, more ambitious by far, was erected in the far precincts of the Grotto on a raised mound, adjacent to the sunken garden. Here a group of statuary,* comprising Our Lady of Fatima and the three children to whom she appeared, make an outstanding contribution to the aesthetic appeal of the Grotto shrines. It was planned that the work would be completed so that the shrine might be blessed on Rosary Sunday of Marian Year, 1954. So many difficulties ensued in transit and at customs docks that it was touch and go that the statues did arrive in Carfin in time for His Grace Archbishop Campbell of Glasgow to bless them in December of that year.

---

* The marble statues were designed and fashioned in Portugal. Through the good offices of a mutual friend of Monsignor Taylor and the Portuguese sculptor, the design for the Madonna was submitted for approval to Sister Lucia, the last surviving member of the three seers of Fatima. The cost of the statues was defrayed from a sum of money which had been accumulating in the Grotto Fund for this purpose.

Although quite a considerable number of pilgrims were present for the occasion, in spite of the snell winds, relatively, they were few compared to the 50,000 or more who were present in the Grotto on May 2nd, 1948, at a rally organised by the chaplains, staff and students of Glasgow University, as a counterblast to the insidious Communist propaganda which was then creeping through Europe. As the rally was to be an act of reparation, it was placed under the patronage of the Immaculate Heart of Our Lady of Fatima. At that time, when the restrictions of war were still in force, only pictures and small images of Our Lady of Fatima could be purchased in this country, and this, thought Canon Taylor, was an impasse that could be remedied only by a higher power. The following is an abridged account of what took place.

" On April 13th, 1948, two members of the Grail set out from Edinburgh on a pilgrimage of reparation to Fatima. They landed in Lisbon without any money because of the existing currency regulations, but friends helped them on their way to Fatima. They had been asked before they left Scotland to try and get a statue for Canon Taylor for the Carfin Shrine. This was mentioned in the Portuguese newspapers in which anything connected with Fatima is front-page news . . ."

How the two penniless ladies of the Grail eventually came by a three-foot statue is not made clear in the report, but their story continues with the *fait accompli*:

" The simplicity and goodness of these people greatly impressed the pilgrims. Finally, they were taken to the Bishop of Leiria and when they asked him if he would bless the statue they intended taking back to Carfin for Canon Taylor, with great regret he replied he could not do so in the circumstances, since it was made of plaster, and in danger of breakage en route."

But the good Bishop, on hearing of the details of the forth-coming rally, had an alternative plan. He had in his possession a newly completed wooden statue of Our Lady of Fatima, an exact copy of the original one made according to Lucia's instructions, and intended to replace the first one while it was taken out on pilgrimage.

" 'This one,' said the Bishop of Leiria, 'I intend to give you. I send it to the Archbishop of Edinburgh, because he has shown a great devotion to Our Lady of Fatima. I send it for the conversion of Scotland and England.'

Next day the Cardinal Patriarch of Portugal solemnly blessed the statue in the presence of the Bishop of Leiria. Later, it was placed on the pillar which marks the spot of Our Lady's appearance at the Cova da Iria, from which all statues sent on pilgrimage to different countries begin their journey.

At the Bishop's request the statue was shown to Cardinal Griffin on its way north."

All this took place in Portugal and those most interested in the organisation of the rally were unaware of what had happened until the week previous to the 2nd of May, when Canon Taylor learned the glad news that not only was he to have a statue himself—albeit unblessed and of plaster—but the Metropolitan Archbishop who had planned to be present at the rally, would have with him on that day an official Fatima pilgrimage statue. One can overlook his bubbling exuberance in a short article telling how Our Lady of Fatima came to Carfin:

"The incredible has happened and Our Lady of Fatima has brought herself to Scotland and to the humble village of Carfin . . .

On Sunday, 2nd May, 1948, for the first time since the war, the Grotto Halt was re-opened and sixteen special trains arrived in addition to the countless buses from all over the country. Over 50,000 souls, including nearly 200 priests, two bishops, two archbishops and 1,000 scouts, welcomed the Madonna of Fatima in a blaze of sunshine. The previous week, the same plane bore two statues from Portugal: one for Carfin and one, blessed by the Cardinal of Portugal for the Archbishop of Edinburgh. He and his Vicar General conveyed the statue by car from Edinburgh to Carfin for the great rally procession through the Grotto grounds. The Carfin statue had been placed meantime on the great altar of the Christ King, adorned that morning with a profusion of costly flowers . . .

It was thus that Our Lady of Fatima made her triumphal entry into the West of Scotland."

A member of the Grail has the last word in a letter to Canon Taylor:

"I think . . . that it was through your request for a statue of Our Lady of Fatima, that the wooden statue was sent to the Archbishop of Edinburgh for the whole of Scotland; if it had not been through your asking for one, Our Lady of Fatima might not have come to Scotland in the way that she did."

In October, 1946, while Scotland was still suffering from the transport restrictions of the immediate post-war period, the number of pilgrims who attended the Grotto for the annual celebration of its founding was significantly less than that of Fatima Sunday, in May 1948. But among those who did succeed in getting the necessary transport for the journey was a small group from the parish of St. Mary and St. David, Hawick, in Roxburghshire. Neither Canon Taylor, nor the pilgrims who came from Hawick that day to honour Our Lady of Lourdes at her shrine in Carfin, could suspect that the Rev. Gordon Gray, parish priest leader of the Hawick pilgrimage, would be exalted in later years to the eminent dignity of being the first Cardinal of Scotland since the Reformation.

As already stated, a permanent and more worthy shrine of the Madonna of Fatima was erected in the Grotto in 1954. This shrine and that of St. Pius X were the last major shrines installed during Monsignor's lifetime, although lesser shrines in honour of St. John the Baptist de la Salle and Our Lady of Banneux—the Madonna of the Poor, as she has been called—were erected a few years later.

Monsignor Taylor commenced, and ended, his work in the Grotto Shrine by doing honour to the Mother of God. In the thirty-odd years between these events, he erected an enclosed Blessed Sacrament Chapel, majestic shrines to Christ the King, Christ Crucified and the new-born Child of Bethlehem, as well as shrines in honour of St. Thérèse, the patron Saint of Scotland, St. Joseph, and other Saints of popular appeal; he improved and extended the grounds, he constructed arbours and avenues, he laid lawns and flower beds, the beauty of which captivated the eye and captured the soul. The Grotto became for the pilgrim a haven of peace, serving to shelter him from the distractions of a material world. Even when thousands of pilgrims were massed together, or made their way in slow procession round the winding paths, one could not but be impressed by the spirit pervading the Grotto: that spirit which emanated from each and was common to all, and having as its source the time-worn stepping bridge between man and his Maker, the universal bond of prayer.

The story of Carfin Grotto would be incomplete without some reference to the Chapel of All Saints, which enshrines what is undoubtedly the biggest collection of relics in this country. Although this small Reliquary Chapel is built behind the presbytery—a safety precaution enjoined by the many priceless treasures it contains—nevertheless it is closely associated with the Grotto itself. It was from here, on the feast days of the Saints, that the bearers of the reliquaries, with their escort, set out to join the processions of the faithful through the Grotto grounds, across the way.

From the year 1915, when Father Taylor first arrived at Carfin, his small but increasing collection of relics had been reserved in the Madonna room in the presbytery. The idea, originally fostered by Monsignor Claeys, that a variety of spiritual attractions would draw additional pilgrims to Our Lady's Shrine, thereby enhancing devotion to her Son, bore fruit. As the collection of relics at Carfin multiplied in the next twenty years, and the priceless Grotto Missionary Monstrance and the unique Blessed Sacrament canopy had been added, it became increasingly imperative that a small and fitting shrine should be built where the relics might be displayed and venerated. To execute this plan, Monsignor once more called on willing workers: a group of bricklayers from neighbouring parishes, and from Glasgow, set to with a will and, helped by labourers from his own parish, the outer walls were raised within a week. Father Taylor had been pondering long on the interior decoration of the chapel, but the panelling which he envisaged would be costly. This problem, too, was entrusted to his heavenly benefactors. The following is the story, more or less as he related it, how his problem was resolved:

"I came downstairs one morning and glanced at the headlines of the morning paper lying on the hallstand. For no known reason, I skimmed through the advertisements on an inner page. The word 'Columbia' caught my attention and immediately I knew this was what, unknown to myself, I had been waiting for."

It seems that the luxury passenger liner *Columbia* was being dismantled at Bo'ness and all her effects, furnishing, panelling, etc., were being offered for sale by public auction that same afternoon. A few frenzied telephone calls were made, several helpers were collected, and soon the party had set off by car for the Bo'ness docks. On arrival there, an early enquiry elicited the information that the beautiful panels of the stateroom of the *Columbia* had already been sold for the incredibly low sum of £40. The journey at first seemed to have been a waste of time, but once more Monsignor's trust in his heavenly benefactors had its reward in another of the Canon's "little miracles"; the lady who had bought the panelling had been aghast at the result of her purchase; all she had desired was a small panel, and now she was faced with the task of dismantling the stateroom of a liner and having the panels transported from the ship. The worry was soon removed from her shoulders: she was repaid her £40; she received the small panel she wished for; and Father Taylor's party took on the responsibility for everything else. In the course of the following week, the workers from Carfin toiled night and day, while Mr. Roche, a contractor from Baillieston, and one of the Grotto's most valiant friends, transported the carefully dismantled panels from Bo'ness to Carfin. Had Father Taylor been consulted on the interior decoration of the stateroom of the liner, with the view in mind that ultimately the massive surrounds of the fireplace, with its suitably carved adjoining panels, would be adapted eventually to his purpose, he could scarcely have made a more appropriate choice. What could be more fitting for the interior decoration of a chapel sheltering the original and certainly unique Missionary Monstrance destined to enshrine the Blessed Sacrament; the canopy which was to be used in processions along with the Monstrance; and the outstanding ebony reliquary of the True Cross, than the beautiful panels on which were carved an intertwining design of grape, passion flower and lily?

The fitting out of the little chapel and the installation of display cases and tables was a task speedily accomplished by a team of workers, under the direction of the late Mr. Hugh Devlin, the Grotto foreman for many a year; while from Bruges, M. Dupon held a watching brief to ensure that the artistic and aesthetic standards normally associated with the Grotto would be maintained.

A short history of the Missionary Monstrance, written by Father Taylor, was published in the *Glasgow Observer* on May 18, 1935. At that time it was not considered politic to reveal that ecclesiastical opposition to the unorthodox design of the Monstrance, as well as the exorbitant customs dues demanded before entry to this country, had delayed its arrival at Carfin for close on a year.

The story as given below has been confirmed by M. Dupon and — but for the additions referred to above — follows the account published in the Catholic press at the time.

The Monstrance was designed by M. Dupon of Bruges, and executed under his supervision by a leading jeweller in Brussels. To quote Monsignor Taylor's words:

> " The Monstrance was made possible by the innumerable clients of the Carfin Lourdes Grotto—none of them wealthy, some of them in actual want—who parted with their jewels and long treasured gold pieces, in order that the tribute to the Eucharistic King might be worthy and complete. By a happy thought, the blessed gold of the wedding rings was reserved for the lunette—that part of the Monstrance which contains the Sacred Host."

Regularly, little packages reached Carfin presbytery, enclosing gifts—brooches, pendants, rings, treasured gold medals—from known or anonymous friends. One touching Christmas card, inscribed, " My gift to the Holy Child," had attached to it two gold rings, the last and only earthly treasure the sender possessed.

The size of the Monstrance is not unusual: though measuring three and a half feet in height and weighing twenty-one pounds, it was easily carried in Grotto processions by means of a tray, fastened to shoulder straps. The first two priests chosen by Father Taylor to have the honour of carrying the Monstrance in a Blessed Sacrament procession were Rev. Dr. Brown, Chaplain to Glasgow University, and Father Tozzi, Salesian Provincial and one-time pupil of Don Bosco, the founder of the Salesian Order. The occasion was the unveiling of the statue of St. John Bosco, on Palm Sunday, 1935.

If the uniqueness of the Monstrance did not lie in its size, the unorthodoxy of its design gave rise to speculation and definite opposition from not a few Church leaders on the Continent, as well as from several members of the Hierarchy in Scotland, the Archbishop of Glasgow being one of the latter. Faced with this opposition, and with other unexpected difficulties which confronted him before entry into Scotland with his treasured burden, M. Dupon returned to Bruges, where alternative plans were devised. A photograph of the Monstrance was sent to a relation of his in Rome—a Capuchin Father who later became General of that order, and who in this capacity made it possible for a number of relics of Capuchin saints to be gifted to the Chapel of All Saints at Carfin. The good priest showed a photograph of the disputed Missionary Monstrance to the mission-minded Pius XI, who cordially approved the design about which there had been so much dissension. " It is so beautiful," declared His Holiness, " that it deserves to be sent here. If you do this, I will bless it."

The declaration carved on the ball, which forms the lower part of the Monstrance and represents the world, briefly explains the symbolism:

" In honour of the Most Blessed Trinity, invoking the Mother of God, Mary Mediatrix and Queen of Apostles, together with the Patrons of the Missions, St. Francis Xavier and St. Thérèse of the Child Jesus, this Monstrance wrought by Flemish art, from the gifts of gold of the pilgrims who flock to the Sanctuary of the Mother of God at Carfin in Scotland, was blessed and dedicated to Jesus Christ, King of Kings, Eternal Priest, Saving

Victim, Light of the Gentiles, by Our Holy Father, Pope Pius XI, in the Vatican City upon Christmas Day in the Year of Salvation 1934."

A canopy worthy of the Monstrance was now required. In other circumstances it would have taken years to create the elaborate design and execute the detailed intricacies of the work-manship envisaged by the gifted Flemish artist; nor would the astronomical figure which many commercial firms might de-mand, fit into Father Taylor's very limited budget.

But the financial worries were not his; these he entrusted to the heavenly patrons of the Grotto. Our Lady and St. Thérèse chose their own instruments—artists whose dedication to their work was in the tradition of medieval craftsmen whose reward lay in the glory and honour the work of their hands gave to Almighty God. M. Dupon spent twelve months on the design of the canopy; many long hours, too, were spent on suitable texts, which would be illustrated by the designs on the four panels. But his immediate problem was to find a craftsman who might be able to undertake the delicate carvings involved in the work. Monsignor Taylor's pen continues the story:

> "St. Thérèse sent him a lad of nineteen, Albrecht d'Have, of Eeclo, just finished his apprenticeship, and unable to get work, but out of kindness of heart he employed him. He saw immedi-ately that God had sent him a genius. One slip of hammer or chisel would have ruined the canopy. It took Albrecht only eight months to finish it. As each panel was completed, he walked the six miles to Bruges, carrying it under his arm. Madame Dupon did the painting.
>
> The panels are made of tulip-tree wood from the Philippine Islands; perhaps the finest wood in the world for carving. The whole is a masterpiece of delicate open-work carving."

Briefly, the illustrations symbolised on the four panels are as follows: The Front Panel with its text, " Behold the King cometh to thee full of meekness," reveals the vision of St. John with " the Lamb standing as if slain "; also the Book of Seven Seals, the Four Rivers of Paradise and the four winged creatures, symbolic of the Evangelists; and the twenty-four Crowns of the Ancients, cast before the lamb—no two crowns being alike.

The Left Panel symbolises " All the Saints of the Lord." Here we find St. Margaret with Scottish thistle and lion; St. Patrick, with shamrock, Irish harp and snake; all, a fitting testimony to the Irish miners who built the Grotto and All Saints' Chapel. In the centre of the panel is the monogram of Our Blessed Lady

The Shrine of Our Lady of Lourdes, at the Grotto Silver Jubilee, 1947.

Right:
RELIQUARY OF ST. THERESE.

Below:

ALL SAINTS' CHAPEL OF RELICS, *showing in the centre the Missionary Monstrance with canopy used in Grotto Processions.*

surrounded by the Saints she held most dear: St. Joseph and St. Anne of ancient times and her modern apostles, Bernadette and Thérèse. Other saints of the parish and the Grotto were remembered: St. Francis Xavier, St. Francis of Assisi, St. Anthony, St. John Bosco and the virgin martyr Philomena.

The Right Panel, illustrating the text, " Angels of the Lord, bless ye the Lord," depicts a scene borrowed from Chartres Cathedral—nine Choirs of Angels accompanying the Blessed Sacrament.

The Back Panel represents a like theme: " They follow the Lamb whithersoever He goeth." This refers to those following the Blessed Sacrament. The white lilies under foot reflect the purity of the soul; the flight of doves symbolises its innocence.

M. Dupon relates the following story concerning the dating of the Canopy: He had hoped to use a chronogram for 1935, the year in which it was made, rather than use the ordinary Arabic numerals. To do this, a Latin sentence must be composed bearing a distinct allusion to the object dated, and must in the words used, contain the exact number of the Roman numerals in the date, no more and no less. A modern chronogram is unusual in this country, but has been commonly used in earlier ages.

After much effort, M. Dupon was unable to find anyone capable of composing one, nor could Father Taylor help, and hence the whole idea was abandoned. On the Feast of Christ the King, the worthy Belgian artist was reading the Introit of the Mass which begins, " *Dignus est agnus qui occisus est accipere virtutem.*" He realised that this would make a suitable inscription for the Canopy, and decided to inscribe it. Monsignor Taylor's words complete the story:

" A God-given distraction forced M. Dupon to count the Roman numerals in the sentence. To his amazement, they gave the exact number required for the date—1935. This was a million to one chance. God was blessing the monumental work done by him and his young craftsman."

To those who are not familiar with Latin, it may be pointed out that in older Latin texts the letter " V " was used for the modern " U." Hence the text reads:

" DIgnVs est agnVs qVI oCCIsVs est aCCIpere VIrtVteM."

The Roman numerals added together give the total of MDCCCCXXXV, which translated to Arabic numerals is 1,935.

A whole volume might be written about other treasures in the Reliquary Chapel. Many of the Relics of the Saints have been authenticated and come from reliable sources. Others like that of

K

Our Lady's Veil, a small portion of the larger one at Chartres, are hallowed by tradition and by the prayers in honour of those saints whom they truly represent. The relic of the True Cross was Monsignor Taylor's most treasured possession and no one accompanied him to the Reliquary Chapel without being guided towards the light which always burned in front of the Reliquary. There, Monsignor would invite his companion to kneel down and three times repeat the ejaculation, " We adore Thee, O Christ, and we praise Thee: because of Thy Holy Cross Thou hast redeemed the world."

Next, Monsignor would direct the visitor to the table on which was displayed the amazing collection of Theresian souvenirs and relics gifted to him by Mother Agnes of Jesus and by others over the years. Perhaps at one time Monsignor Taylor possessed more relics of the Saint than any individual outside of Carmel and Rome. When first-class relics of St. Thérèse became scarce, Monsignor found himself in the happy position of being able to return to Mother Agnes a few relics of her saintly sister. The pride of the Theresian relics is the large relic " ex pedibus " gifted to Monsignor for use in the unique processional reliquary designed by M. Dupon, but in addition, one might see here, several pious objects personal to the Saint, among them a small chaplet of the Immaculate Conception and a copy of her morning offering.

Outstanding and original reliquaries, the masterpieces of the Belgian House of Dupon, are easy to recognise: those of St. Thérèse and the English martyr-saints, Thomas More and Bishop John Fisher; the tower reliquary of St. Barbara, Patroness of miners; the church-shaped one of St. Ursula, containing a relic which was gifted to Canon Taylor by Mother Ursula, a Belgian missionary nun. Others too, bearing authenticated relics of modern saints, as well as those of earlier years. All of these to the number of several hundreds, are displayed on specially made tables ranged around the Chapel, or mounted in glass-fronted cabinets attached to the walls.

On one occasion when Monsignor was with the present writer in the Reliquary Chapel, her attention was drawn to an image of the Infant Mary, a gift, it is thought, from the Mother House of the Dominican Sisters of the Holy Rosary at Rome. The little figurine wrapped in swaddling clothes reminded the writer that Pius X had a special affection for the child Mary, whose picture, a replica of the figurine, had adorned his bedroom in the Sarto family home. This little snippet of information relating to the Pope of the Eucharist was seized upon avidly by the priest apostle of the Eucharist; it was another proof that the human heart has the capacity of loving the Virgin Mary in addition to loving her Divine Son. It may be added in parenthesis, that it was rarely that this writer was in a position to provide Monsignor with information relating to his own favourite saints, which he did not already know.

One other reminiscence of the last visit made to the Chapel of Relics in Monsignor's company remains to be told. For over half-an-hour the gnarled hands of the aged Monsignor groped and clutched at the precious relics, as he related a thumbnail sketch of a saint's outstanding characteristics. Even then, about eighteen months before his death, his interest in his treasures remained alert and clear. As his near-sightless eyes peered at the smaller silver cases and the capable, still supple, spatulate fingers, lovingly touched the treasures to which a lucid memory could still lead him unerringly, one could only wonder at his encyclopaedic knowledge of " the things that are unseen." Nowhere could one find a clearer proof of the doctrine of the Communion of Saints. In joy and sorrow these were the sanctified relics of hallowed friends to whom he had constant recourse. The Chapel of All Saints was built in their honour, and during his lifetime, on the appropriate feast days, the relics were carried in solemn procession. He was proud of the Chapel, lovingly built, but even at this late hour in his own life he was left with one task which he felt he had neglected. Turning his sightless eyes upwards, he pointed to the ceiling. " Tell me, child," he said, " does the ceiling look out of place, against the beautifully panelled walls?"

I did not say so, but the thought did strike me that the timber of the ceiling was inferior. " You see," he continued, " the men were rushed for time, and it was the best we could procure at the time; and, as you know," he continued, " first-class wood is an expensive commodity." The impression lingers that, given the opportunity, even at that late hour, he would have had a ceiling installed in keeping with the side panels, and worthy of the wealth of treasures housed therein. It was not to be. The vibrant spirit was still active and directed to spiritual values, but the body was yielding to the approach of its human destiny and many tasks were left undone.

To conclude the long story of the development of the Grotto during Monsignor Taylor's lifetime, brief mention should be made of the alleged claims of cures and recovery in health made by ailing pilgrims—of spiritual " cures " to troubled souls there was unquestionably an abundance. It is not within the scope of any lay person to pronounce judgment on miracles: these lie within the province of the competent Church authorities, and stringent, well-defined conditions are exacted before they are accepted. The writer wishes to state that as far as she herself knows from personal knowledge or from the written evidence she has examined, on no occasion was a claim to complete recovery in health declared a canonical miracle by the competent Church authorities. This does not infer that the prayers of a sufferer have not been answered; nor does it mean that a pilgrim's claim to a recovery in health is without foundation. What it does mean is that the Church must satisfy herself that all the conditions—and these are many and strict—must be present showing that the miracle was unmistakably an act of supernatural intervention, occurring in such a way that it could not be explained in human terms. During the 'twenties and early 'thirties, claims to recovery in health were reported indiscriminately as miracles or cures in the secular press. Periodically, though less frequently, in later years—for the early novelty had worn off—the press still gave such recoveries front page news. Less attractive, and consequently gaining less coverage, was the news that a person who had claimed to be cured ten or so years previously, continued to enjoy good health and came as a pilgrim to Our Lady's Shrine to offer renewed thanks. Less sensational, too, was the news that as a result of a satisfactory answer to prayer, a grateful client embraced the Catholic faith, as was the case with one lady from Carfin and numerous others from the West of Scotland and beyond.

Dr. Badenoch, Edinburgh medical practitioner, became a Catholic because he, also, believed he had been cured from a chronic affliction in his cheek, after the application of Carfin Grotto water and prayers of intercession had been offered to Our Lady on his behalf. The doctor made a detailed study of the cures alleged to have taken place at the Grotto, and although he himself was convinced that benefits to health had been received by many of the claimants, he felt that for some reason known only to Providence, these cures were not destined to be recognised canonically as miracles. Such, too, was the judgment of the Diocesan Medical Board set up to examine two of the many cures claimed in the early years of the Grotto history. Although medical evidence was supplied attesting to a return of good health, other essential factors were lacking: conclusive evidence of the exact nature of illness before the alleged cure had taken place; absence of prior X-ray evidence; or unanimous medical opinion that the correct diagnosis of the malady had been made and adequate medical treatment provided. Those who know of the strict scrutiny given to claims at Lourdes will realise that, relatively, only a small number of alleged cures are declared " miracles " by the official Medical Bureau. One may not, however, assume from this that only those persons officially recognised as " miraculés " by the medical authorities of Lourdes are the only ones who have benefited from the intercessory mediation of Our Lady of Lourdes.

An article published recently by a national newspaper* treats briefly on the " Power of Prayer " when applied for the benefit of sick humanity:

" Figures which set out to prove that prayer can heal are given in a British medical journal today.

The names of ten out of eighteen children with leukemia (blood cancer) were selected at random and sent to friends who had agreed to organise a prayer group.

The families prayed daily for the ten children without being told of the experiment, says the Practitioner, reporting an American study.

Fifteen months later, seven of the ten children were still alive, compared with only two of the eight children not involved in prayers.

These figures ' support the concept that prayers for the sick are effective,' says Dr. P. P. Collett, the American child specialist who organised the study.

Every doctor prescribes this remedy and nearly every doctor has seen it succeed, he says. Comments the Practitioner: ' He would be a brave man who would dare to deny these conclusions.'

He adds: ' It is more than passing interest that in this so-called scientific age, even the cynics in our midst are beginning to admit that perhaps this is right.' "

True Christians are not cynics: trust and confidence in a loving Father has always been a tenet of their faith. Not all Christians believe, as Catholics do, that our Blessed Mother in heaven has the power of mediation with her Divine Son. Devout pilgrims who travelled to the Carfin Grotto to thank God, through His Divine Mother, were not troubled about profound questions of theology—whether the Son was dishonoured because His Mother received additional honour. To a Catholic of simple, direct Faith the Blessed Virgin was unmistakably aligned with the Blessed Trinity. Their purpose in coming was to pray, and this they did with fervent hearts in each *Pater, Ave,* and *Gloria.* Many came to do homage to their heavenly Mother; others came to seek her

---

* *Scottish Daily Express,* August 1, 1969.

help. Are we to believe Our Lady and her Divine Son turn a deaf ear to those who heed the injunction: " Ask and you shall receive "? Monsignor Taylor certainly believed that if he asked with humility, his prayer would be heard, and so also did the thousands who joined with him in the Lourdes invocations: " Lord, that I may see! Lord, that I may hear! . . ." With equal fervour Monsignor led the pilgrims in a paean of thanksgiving when it was reported that a spiritual or temporal favour had been granted.

In *The Carfin Grotto,* Father Taylor tells how one soul made his peace with God as a result of prayers offered within the Grotto walls; the story of many others, to which he alluded at times might be added to this one:

" Some years ago," wrote a priest in a distant town, " a number of pilgrims from this parish went to Carfin. One good woman's husband had for many a year not darkened the church door, but was never out of the public house.

' We are going to Carfin,' said the wife, ' will you come with us?'

' I'll go to Carfin,' he replied, ' but I'm not going to the Grotto. I'll be a bona-fide traveller and go down to Motherwell.'

He kept his word, and while the wife said her prayers in the Grotto the husband went off in another direction. But the good man never reached Motherwell; Our Lady turned him back. He found himself compelled to return to the Grotto, and the following Saturday he went to Confession. From that time onwards he neither touched drink nor omitted his weekly Communion."

Referring to this story, Monsignor Taylor has said: " This is only one of the many rich and hidden blossoms which the Queen gathers in her northern shrine."

How truly Our Lady's injunction to the little shepherdess at Lourdes was being followed out at Carfin: " Pray for the conversion of sinners!"

In the same pamphlet in which the story related above is published, Father Taylor makes reference to the continued good health of pilgrims reported as cured by the national press. Of Mrs. Holmes' case, which was the first one to be advertised to the world, with the result that the obscure village of Carfin became front page news, Father Taylor comments:

" Year after year, despite her great age, ' my lady of the wrinkles ' was to be seen limping gaily in the chief Grotto processions. She died of bronchitis, in January, 1929."

He also made reference to a Protestant family from Greenock:

"As a result of tubercular meningitis, Hugh Bell, a child of nine, was threatened with complete blindness; a brother had already died from tuberculosis. After a visit to the Grotto, Hugh's tuberculosis disappeared and he fully recovered the sight of one eye and could distinguish things vaguely with the other. The mother, too, a patient in a sanatorium, came to Carfin . . . The cure in her case was immediate and complete. The parents and seven children are now members of the Catholic Church."

This family, at least, was convinced that the recovery in health was attributable to Our Lady's mediation on behalf of the ailing members.

The case of little Peter Illand of Dalkeith, also mentioned in *The Carfin Grotto*, was well known to Grotto pilgrims. Year after year, until war broke out, when he did active service with the R.A.F., Peter accompanied the annual parochial pilgrimage, led by Sister Mary Columba and one of the priests of the parish, from Dalkeith to Carfin. As a twenty-month-old child, having suffered for many months from enteritis, he was brought in a wasted condition to Our Lady's Shrine. Not only did he regain the strength to walk unaided at Carfin, but on the testimony of Sister Mary Columba and others who travelled with him, he was able to retain several cupfuls of water from the Grotto, as well as a solid meal of meat and vegetables, without being sick immediately afterwards.

Ten months later, the two and a half year old boy weighed nearly half-a-stone over the normal. It would have been invidious to remark to Peter's mother, or to the good people of Dalkeith, who with Sister Mary Columba, had witnessed the emaciated form of the twenty-month-old boy take on a new lease of life, that the child had not been cured as a result of prayer. Could the question of hysteria or auto-suggestion have relevance in the case of a child so young? The annual and, at times, more frequent pilgrimages from Dalkeith to Carfin gives the lie to doubting Thomases.

Innumerable cures of startling nature have been claimed and reported by those who returned to give thanks. One can only assume that the pilgrim who received the benefit was personally convinced that the favour was an answer to prayer. Occasionally Monsignor Taylor might well ask, "Where are the other nine?" For others there were, who were often only heard of by chance.

One pilgrim travelled from Ireland to petition Our Lady at Carfin to intercede with her Divine Son, on her behalf; several years earlier, her friend had come to Carfin on pilgrimage, with what she claimed to be satisfactory results. The alleged cure in this instance had not been reported to the priests at Carfin, nor had the favoured one returned to offer thanks at Our Lady's Shrine.

A startling case, witnessed by a number of spectators, was that of Miss Mary Thérèse Traynor of St. Aloysius' parish, Chapelhall. Two years after her recovery in health, Mary Traynor was married, with the permission of her own parish priest, at Carfin. Eleven years ago, Mr. McFarlane, Mary's husband, died, and since that time until her retirement more than four years ago, Mrs. McFarlane devoted her spare time to helping the Irish Sisters of Charity nurse the chronic sick at Assumption House, Airdrie. Shortly before her death in 1970, Mrs. McFarlane stated that she had not at any time since her recovery suffered from the afflictions to which she had been prey for seven years prior to 1934. The following, in substance, is the account written down by Father Taylor and confirmed by Miss Traynor, and not differing greatly in detail from evidence supplied by other witnesses, or from the reports blazoned to the world by the Catholic and secular press:

" Mary Traynor had been ill for seven and a half years prior to 1934, a martyr to several different diseases: rheumatoid arthritis, a malady of the stomach and intestines, and a heart condition. The trouble in the abdomen had caused a constant vomiting which had reduced her weight, four years earlier, to six stones, and to much less as her illness progressed. Twice she had spent periods of three or four weeks in hospital, and on each occasion she was returned home as incurable.

In spite of careful nursing by her relatives and almost daily visits from nurse or doctor, Mary's condition deteriorated and on several occasions she had been on the point of death, the most recent relapse being a three week spell of unconsciousness at the beginning of 1934. Bed sores had added to the gnawing pain of arthritic joints, and for twelve months the fingers of the left hand had been so tightly clenched that the nurse could insert cotton wool between them only with the aid of a knife. In four years her doctor had allowed her to leave her home once only, and on this occasion she was carried outside that she might see her native village again.

Her medical attendant had refused permission for her to travel with the sick pilgrims to Lourdes. She was too weak, he said. But Mary, with the connivance of her own family and the non-Catholic nurse who had attended her for some time, had alternative plans. While the doctor was on holiday, she determined to visit the Grotto, where she had not been since her illness began, more than seven years before.

On Sunday, 29th July, Mary, propped up in a taxi, was taken to Carfin, where she drank some water from the Grotto well. One immediate result was that the sufferer was able to retain the water and from then on there was a complete cessation of the vomiting which had tortured and weakened her frame for so long. Later on that afternoon, Father Taylor blessed the invalid with the relic of the Little Flower.

Having heard that on the following Sunday, 5th August—feast of Our Lady of the Snows—Benediction of the Most Blessed Sacrament was to be given in the Grotto by Monsignor O'Brien of Liverpool, to the sick pilgrims of three English pilgrimages as well as to others from Lanarkshire and Glasgow, Mary decided to make the trying journey once more.

Again, propped up with pillows in a taxi, and transferred on arrival to an invalid chair, Mary prayed before Our Lady's statue and drank the Grotto water. During the blessing with the Sacred Host, she experienced an extraordinary feeling of calm, but neither the special blessing with the Sacred Host nor the application of water had any effect on the ankalysed joints. It appeared, as someone remarked, somewhat of an anti-climax to turn to St. Thérèse when Christ and His Mother seemed to have passed the sufferer by.

'But the marvellous consequences of this final appeal,' commented Father Taylor, 'shows the affection of those Two for her who loved them so much.'

After Benediction, those awaiting the blessing with the Relic of St. Thérèse lined up in the Portiuncula in the Lower Grotto. When it came Mary's turn to be blessed, Father Taylor applied the Relic to her aching joints. The effect was immediate: suddenly a warm glow passed through the sufferer's body, 'like a thread of fire '—to use her own vivid expression. In the space of a moment, Father Taylor saw the seeming impossible happen. The clenched fingers slowly uncurled as they were held in the priest's hands, and the packing of cotton wool fell away, leaving the fingers supple and flexible. The unconscious prayer of thanksgiving that left Mary's lips, 'My God and my all,' told the spectators of this drama, that something unusual was taking place.

While the Relic was being applied to the legs and the customary invocations to the Little Flower said, the trembling in the limbs became so severe that it was with difficulty that the Relic was kept in place. While these strange happenings were taking place, the spectators began a fervent Rosary of thanksgiving, and Mary herself suddenly announced that she could walk. This, Father Taylor did not permit. He advised that she should be removed to her waiting car and return a little later for a final blessing.

On Mary's return to the Portiuncula, Father Taylor could see that the left arm was in perfect condition, with no stiffness apparent. During the second blessing with the Relic and the invocations to the Saint, the same violent trembling seized the lower limbs and once more Mary expressed the wish to walk. Assisted by her relatives, she walked round the car, to the joy of all who looked on.

Inside the car, on the journey home, Mary discarded the pillows used to prop her up, and without support, sat upright beside her mother. She had been carried out of her home a helpless invalid; three or four hours later, she walked into her home unaided.

The following Sunday found Mary back—without her invalid chair—on a thanksgiving pilgrimage; and to the joy of all who beheld her and who had read of her recovery in the press, they could watch while with unexpected energy, Mary helped the Legionaries, for a while, to serve refreshments to the sick pilgrims present that day.

A few Sundays later, the congregation of St. Aloysius', Mary's home parish, came on pilgrimage to Carfin to thank Almighty God for the singular blessing granted to one of their number. Further, Father Taylor was asked by them to arrange for a number of Masses of Thanksgiving, and to accept the residue of the donations subscribed by the pilgrims from Chapelhall, as a gift towards the upkeep of the Grotto."

What more can a lay person add to the evidence provided here? Mrs. McFarlane's case has been given in great detail since the one who writes this account has had ample opportunity of speaking with her, with a number of her friends, and with the Sisters of Assumption House where Mrs. McFarlane has given devoted service since her husband's death. There has not been a scrap of evidence produced from any of these sources to suggest that the testimony given by Mary Traynor in 1934, and by Father Taylor, who actually saw the fingers unclench and the helpless legs pulsate violently with renewed energy, is anything other than the truth. And yet in spite of this evidence, Mrs. McFarlane's case would not, and rightly so, be considered by a Diocesan Medical Board for further investigation. Too many of the stringent conditions required by Mother Church were wanting. Mrs. McFarlane's family doctor, while admitting that the symptoms which had been hitherto apparent, had now disappeared, refused to commit his opinion to writing; the medical attendants who had the patient under observation on the two occasions while she was in hospital were not fully convinced that the malady from which she had suffered was rheumatoid arthritis. In the absence of medical authentication of this nature, the Church of necessity refrains from judgment. To the sufferer who knows that his or her prayers of intercession have been answered in some wonderful way, the quibblings of doctors or even the guarded reticence of Mother Church are of no great consequence. Mrs. McFarlane, better than anyone else, knew she had been an invalid for seven years; that she had been gravely ill on more than one occasion; and that she had been restored to good health in two stages after having been brought on pilgrimage to the Grotto at Carfin. She was not even greatly concerned whether her recovery was to be attributed to the intercession of Our Lady or of St. Thérèse. Her first words of thanksgiving—" My God and my all "—made it abundantly clear that she was fully conscious that Almighty God is the giver of all gifts, whether the request is directed to Him, through Our Blessed Mother, St. Thérèse, or any one of the Saints.

Until her death two years ago, Mrs. McFarlane lived in her own home in her native village of Chapelhall, enjoying the average good health of many women of her age. She survived her husband and all the relations who accompanied her to Carfin on these two momentous Sundays in 1934. On being questioned shortly before her death about visiting the Grotto Shrine, with great humility Mrs. McFarlane replied, " I never miss making a pilgrimage of thanksgiving on the 5th of August, the feast day of Our Lady of the Snows."

While allowing for the exaggerated enthusiasm with which each alleged recovery in health was reported in the press, and for the child-like, trusting faith with which Monsignor Taylor invariably saw the Hand of God operating in all material affairs, nevertheless the writer of these lines offers it as her personal opinion—others may disagree if they will—that many occurrences and coincidences, which cannot be explained satisfactorily in a natural manner, have taken place at the Carfin Shrine, and according to recent reports are alleged to be happening there still.

This having been said, the question posed by His Eminence Cardinal Bourne in 1926 remains unanswered: Why Carfin? To this question may be added another: Why have some people received a favourable answer to prayers and others not? The answer to this, too, lies beyond our ken. Almighty God is not subject to any rule or standard; the profundity of His wisdom is outwith the scope of our limited understanding. In stating this, it is not implied that God does not hearken to our prayers. That indeed would be a negation of Christ's message to us. All that we may conjecture is that God in His omnipotence does permit the unexplainable to happen—a special sign of His favour—to occur in certain circumstances. The benefit may be the result of deep, unshakeable faith; it may come as an unasked for favour to one who is deserving of God's beneficence; or again the benefitee, himself quite unworthy, may have been favoured because of the intercessory prayers of others and because of the ultimate spiritual effect on the wayward soul.

It might be assumed that the inexplicable occurrences— spiritual and temporal—claimed to have taken place at the Carfin Grotto Shrine throughout the years, were the result of the overflow of faith in Divine Providence, shown by the countless thousands of pilgrims assembled in prayer. This fervour was increased and deepened by the priest whose humility and unbounded faith in the mercy of God instilled in each pilgrim a great measure of his own love for Almighty God and for Mary, the Mother of Christ.

There have been, and there will always remain, the dissenters who question temporal favours received by pilgrims to Carfin Grotto. But one indisputable spiritual benefit gained by the parish is beyond question: and this is the striking increase in the hearts of the parishioners of the love of Our Lord in the Eucharist. In May 1938, Canon Taylor wrote:

> " Whereas less than thirty years ago not a child assisted at daily Mass, recently during the seven weeks of the summer holidays in this parish of 3,600 souls, nearly 400 children were present each morning at the Holy Sacrifice. Throughout the subsequent Christmas vacation, despite the inclemency of the season, some 200 little souls attended Mass each day. More than once the yearly Holy Communions of the parish have surpassed the gratifying number of 120,000 . . . Indeed the total for children and adults during a space of three weeks (on the occasion of a Mission) reached 21,000! Thus it is that the saints lead us to their Queen, and Mary is ever the surest guide to her Eucharistic Son . . .
>
> The motto of Carfin might well be that of Lourdes: ' Per Mariam ad Jesum: Through Mary to Jesus.' "

Monsignor was to continue uninterrupted the spiritual crusade he preached in honour of Our Blessed Lady for another two decades or more, after he wrote these lines. During the last three or four years before his death in 1963, his vital energy had slowed down, and during diocesan rallies and other important pilgrimages another cleric was deputed to lead the assembly in prayer. Regular pilgrims who had known and loved Monsignor Taylor for many years missed his presence on the rostrum in front of the Blessed Sacrament Chapel. Many indeed have asserted that it was Monsignor's own faith and personal sanctity which was the magnet which drew many pilgrims to Carfin. In his humility he would have scoffed at such an idea. But the fact remains that in addition to paying homage to Our Lady and the Saints in the Grotto precincts, not a few visitors sought and found consolation and renewed spiritual strength after having met the humble and saintly priest who had founded the Grotto, and administered it for forty years.

CHAPTER XII

CULT OF ST. THERESE

It has been said, and few would disagree, that since her canonisation, St. Thérèse has had a marked influence on Monsignor Taylor's spiritual life. During the first two decades of the present century he did much to further the process leading to her beatification and canonisation. He studied—and practised—her " Little Way " of spiritual childhood and, to this end, the research and study of her autobiography and private writings provided him with a deep and intimate understanding of her philosophy and way of life. His close kinship with the Saint's three sisters in Carmel, and especially with Mother Agnes of Jesus—Pauline, the elder sister, whom Thérèse adopted as her "little Mother" after Madame Martin's death—forged a personal link between Father Taylor and Carmel, which in human terms caused him to look to Sister Thérèse as to a well-loved younger sister. In addition to these factors was the familiarity he could claim with the history of all the striking spiritual and temporal " roses " let fall from her hands on those who begged for her intercession. But overriding all these factors, that which influenced him most was Sister Thérèse's absolute submission to the Will of God; her constant and total love of the Child Jesus and His Blessed Mother; and her complete trust in the fortifying strength of the Holy Spirit. Father Taylor had helped to bring greater honour to her name on earth; now that the Church recognised Sister Thérèse as a canonised saint in heaven, he had no hesitation in reminding HER—he used the familiar pronoun frequently—of the promise she had made: " I will spend my heaven doing good upon earth."

On various occasions, by spoken word or in print, Monsignor Taylor has told how a seemingly inconsequential introduction to the Saint's autobiography was for him the origin of a cult to which he dedicated the remaining sixty years of his sacerdotal life.

Monsignor Taylor had been ordained priest in June, 1897, just a little over three months later, in the same year, the sheltered and secluded Carmelite nun entered eternity. Four years later Father Taylor heard of Sister Thérèse for the first time, when seemingly by chance he was urged to read an abridged translation of her autobiography. And yet although unknown to each other the Scottish priest and French nun had much in common: Thérèse Martin was almost a year old when Thomas Taylor was born at Greenock, but both shared the same date of Baptism, 4th January; Thérèse in 1873, Thomas in 1874. On April 9th, 1888, the youngest daughter of Monsieur and Madame Martin after a year's delay, entered the Carmel of Lisieux at the age of fifteen. Four days earlier, on April 5th of the same year, Father P. J. Chandlery, S.J., of St. Aloysius' College, had written to Mr. Taylor at Greenock to make arrangements for his son Thomas's admission to St. Mary's Seminary, Blairs. As we have already learned elsewhere, through no fault of his own, Thomas was compelled to delay entry to the seminary for another year. Both St. Thérèse and Monsignor Taylor had wished to serve on the Mission fields, a privilege which was denied them. As a canonised saint, the former is honoured as the Patroness of the Missions; in much more humble fashion Monsignor Taylor has been referred to in his time as " the most mission-minded priest in Scotland." Nor did they differ in the deep love they had for our Blessed Mother. Monsignor Taylor's favourite church in Paris—even while he was a seminarian—was that of Our Lady of Victories, the church in which he celebrated his second Mass after ordination; this too, was the church visited by Thérèse Martin at the outset of her pilgrimage to Rome, and of which she said when referring to the wonders of Paris, " . . . for me the sole attraction was the church of Our Lady of Victories." But most important of all was the inordinate love that that each had for Our Lord in the Blessed Sacrament of the Altar. A great sorrow in the Saint's life was that she was not permitted to receive her first Holy Communion until she was eleven years of age. The Church in Scotland, less hide-bound by Jansenistic tendencies, allowed her children to approach the Communion rails at least a year earlier. Monsignor Taylor received Holy Communion for the first time shortly after his ninth birthday. Saint Thérèse foretold, that in heaven, she would help to alter the restricting conditions which caused her so much grief; for his part, Father Taylor, even while a seminarian, was a lay member of the Eucharistic League, instituted by the Blessed Sacrament Fathers with the same object as the Saint's in view. As a young priest he became National Director of the League in Scotland and in this capacity, as mentioned elsewhere in this book, he devoted much time, energy and prayer to encouraging the faithful in the more frequent reception of the Eucharist, in addition to his endeavours to make Its earlier reception by children possible.

With so much in common in their lives, it is not surprising that to a certain degree Monsignor Taylor's writing should reveal some of the spiritual aims expressed by the Saint. Years before their lives crossed Monsignor Taylor's spiritual target had been set and the route to it planned: " O Heart of Jesus," he prayed as a seminarian, " give me a Heart like Thine, that I may be another Christ whose life is hidden in Thee!"

On the day of her Profession, Sister Thérèse had written, " I offer myself to Thee, O my beloved, that Thou may ever accomplish in me Thy Holy Will, without let or hindrance from creatures."

With souls attuned to like aims, it is not to be wondered at that Father Taylor once having acquired intimate knowledge of the Saint's way of spiritual childhood, should seek to model his philosophy on hers.

How he first came to hear of her has been related often. The Saint's autobiography — *L'Histoire d'une Ame* — had been translated into English by a Polish professor, Michael Dziwicki, in thanksgiving for a conversion received through her intercession. In the summer of 1901, within four years of the Saint's death, Father Taylor, at that time attached to St. Peter's Seminary was urged by a personal friend, Father Bernard Lynch, to read the book entitled *The Little Flower* in the English translation, during his forthcoming retreat at the Redemptorist Monastery, Perth. Father Lynch, we are told, was so impressed with the autobiography that he himself had read it five times in succession during a retreat. Father Taylor followed his friend's advice and to quote his own words, " The first perusal was a revelation."

Thus, it came about inadvertently that the seeds were sown whereby two years later, prompted undoubtedly by the Holy Spirit, Father Taylor suggested to Mother Mary of Gonzaga, then Prioress at Lisieux, and to the three sisters of Sister Thérèse who were present at the interview, that the initial investigation leading to the process of canonisation should be commenced.

Immediately on his return from Perth in 1901, Father Taylor wrote to the Carmel of Liseux asking for a copy of Sister Thérèse's autobiography in French, a language with which he was well-acquainted. Again from his own writings we learn that before long several dozen copies of the book were sent to fellow-students of St. Sulpice, scattered in various countries—in Great Britain and Ireland, in France itself, in Germany and Italy, in Canada as well as the United States, in Africa and South America, in Asia even and in distant Australia.

Never one to exaggerate or embroider his own achievements, Father Taylor records very briefly and succinctly the action which followed:

"... The next step was the publication of pictures and leaflets through the generous labours of the Brothers of Charity at their Orphans' Press, Rochdale. These were distributed throughout the English-speaking world."*

A series of cryptic entries in diaries from 1902 to 1912 adds further information to the bare outlines of his published writings. In January, 1902, the convert Presbyterian minister, Mr. Charleson set out for the major seminary at the Scots College, Rome armed with a copy of *L'Histoire d'une Ame* given to him by Father Taylor. Less than two months later the seminarian reports on the growing cult of the Little Flower at the College. This was undoubtedly due to the propaganda disseminated not only by Mr. Charleson but also by Alexander Taylor, Father Taylor's younger brother, then in his second year of senior study at that College. Father Taylor, as we know, was already corresponding with the sisters of St. Thérèse in 1902, but on a higher spiritual level his actions are what one might have expected from one whose central devotion was the Sacrifice of the Mass. At his request two Masses were celebrated at the Carmel of Lisieux: the first in thanksgiving to the Blessed Trinity, Jesus and Mary; the second a thanksgiving Mass in honour of Sister Thérèse. Frequently too, in the ensuing years, Father Taylor's Mass list records the memento, "Thérèse" or alternatively "P.F.." (Petite Fleur). The day of her death, September, 30th, was reserved annually for a thanksgiving Mass.

His interest in the life of the young Carmelite nun was deeply appreciated by her three sisters. During 1902 Father Taylor received a number of small relics from Lisieux; these he distributed among his friends. From Mother Marie of the Sacred Heart, Thérèse's eldest sister, he received the symbolic rose petals from the grave; but the greatest treasure of all arrived in early October from Mother Agnes of Jesus: this was a small chaplet used daily in her private devotions by Sister Thérèse. It is one of the important souvenirs of St. Thérèse, still on view in the Reliquary Chapel at Carfin.

An interesting letter, still extant, is that sent in December, 1902, by Mother Agnes to Alexander Taylor in Rome. As well as referring to Alexander's forthcoming ordination, she assured

---

* Taken from his personal writings, some of which were published in *St. Peter's College Magazine*, December, 1947; and in an early issue of *Sicut Parvuli*, date unknown.

him that he, like his brother, Father Taylor, was held in high esteem, at Carmel. On his part, Father Taylor claimed Thérèse's three sisters in Carmel as " mes trois soeurs " (my three sisters). It may be relevant to note that St. Thérèse's brothers died in infancy, as did Father Taylor's only sister. In later years, when speaking of St. Thérèse to anyone who sought his prayers, he would answer in familiar terms: " Don't ask me. Ask HER. She will help you."

In view of the additional work he had assumed during the preceding eighteen months, it is not surprising to learn that during Mass, on December 16, 1902—his twenty-eighth birthday —Father Taylor fainted at the Altar. It would seem he had not then acquired the physical stamina so characteristic of his health during the many years he was to spend at Carfin. The birthday prayer which he recorded that day in his diary was: " During this year may all things be for, with, and in God, through the hands of Mary."

His New Year resolution a fortnight later was a plea of a similar nature, directed this time towards a wider range of heavenly patrons, Thérèse now being added to his list:

". . . May this year be one of advancement towards Jesus by the royal way of the Immaculate Heart of Mary! O Mother, protect your child! O Child of Mary, have pity on me, your slave! St. Thomas, Thérèse, and you, O Glorious Joseph, help me always in the work of this life . . . My holy patrons, help me to be as you— a saint!"

The incoming year 1903, promised to be a busy one and indeed turned out to be a momentous one for Father Taylor. Easter found him and his youngest brother James Bede travelling to Rome with the National Pilgrimage in honour of the Jubilee of the venerable pontiff, Leo XIII. While in Rome the two brothers spent some time with their third brother, Alexander, due for ordination a few months later. On the way home Father Taylor interrupted his journey on the 15th and 16th May to visit the Carmel at Lisieux and the little cemetery where the young Carmelite nun, Sister Thérèse had been buried in 1897. Somewhere in his notes Father Taylor records that he was the first pilgrim from Britain to make a pilgrimage to her grave; and that the priest from the town, who escorted him to it, did not know the location of the grave nor had he read her autobiography.

Also, it is recorded in Father Taylor's diary, though the writing is well-nigh illegible, that on each day he had conversations with Thérèse's three sisters. This must have been the occasion on which the Scottish priest broached the subject of setting in motion the initial arrangements whereby the Cause of Sister Thérèse of the Child Jesus should be forwarded to the Congregation of Rites at Rome. This surmise is confirmed by Rev. R. P. Stephane-Joseph Piat, O.F.M., in an article on Monsignor Taylor, which was published in *Les Annales de Sainte Thérèse* in the year following Monsignor's death.*

An excerpt from the article entitled, " A promoter of the Cult of St. Thérèse in English speaking lands," follows :

". . . It was due to him, too, that she, who across the Channel is known by the endearing name of the ' Little Flower,' has become known throughout the English-speaking lands. It was about 1901 that Father Taylor was captivated by *L'Histoire d'une Ame* . . . In the following year he wrote an abridged life of the French nun . . . Likewise, at the beginning of the century, he presented himself in the Carmel at Lisieux where he had the privilege of conversing with the three sisters of Sister Thérèse, with her cousin Marie Guerin and with Mother Marie de Gonzague. All of them were convinced of the eminent sanctity of the young religious; but when Father Taylor suggested that her Cause should be introduced to the Courts of Rome, the sisters showed some reticence. The Prioress replied that a life showing nothing of the extraordinary did not merit the crown of the Saint."

Father Taylor's persuasion subsequently won the nuns to his view and as a result, a secretariate was set up to which Father Piat also refers :

" In order to record favours of every kind, which were being multiplied daily—in the Dominions and in the United States—a secretariate was set up which would act in liaison with Lisieux. Father Taylor—at the beginning at least—took on his own shoulders this task. He assumed responsibility for the affairs of our Carmelite Sister."

One might easily imagine a degree of presumption on Father Taylor's part in undertaking such an onerous charge after only two years of acquaintanceship with her life story. This characteristic is entirely in keeping with his character. Convinced of the worthiness of a cause, and having examined it from a spiritual angle he devoted to it all his energy. Throughout his life he initiated and propagated many causes: the Eucharistic crusade in this country to promote a greater love of the Blessed Sacrament; the restoration of Our Lady to an honoured place in Presbyterian Scotland; the zealous drive to make this country a

---

* *Les Annales de Ste. Thérèse*, Nov. 1964.

Mission-minded land, to mention but a few.* He associated himself with many others and supplied the initial drive to establish them firmly and thereafter he resigned the reins of office to those with the interest and ability to carry on. Not every cause in which he was interested bore fruit: for a time he devoted himself to the interests of the little Irish girl, popularly known as " Little Nellie of Holy God." The story of this child attracted Father Taylor's interest because of her inordinate love of the Holy Eucharist. Rather than accept the story of the child's sanctity from hearsay, he visited the Good Shepherd Convent in Cork where she had died, in order to investigate for himself the circumstances of her early reception of First Holy Communion. But apart from this, and using her name to propagate the ideal for the early reception of Communion for children, he took no further action in promoting the cult of the little Irish girl. What is significant is that he did acquaint himself with the relevant facts of her short life but for some reason he did not proceed further with his investigations. It was, therefore, quite in keeping with his character and temperament that having visited Carmel and been assured of the saintliness of Sister Thérèse of Lisieux, he would take whatever action his conscience convinced him was the right one in the circumstances. In matters such as these Father Taylor's methods were not those of the majority: he approached his task, not lightly nor in half-hearted fashion. When he was engaged on serious work, all his friends knew about it; all were besought to pray for his intention. And more important still was the fact that Monsignor Taylor himself was one to whom prayer was always a necessary accompaniment to all his actions.

This prayerful aspect of his character was occasionally a source of amusement, as in the case of Mr. Ribchester, who was absorbed with the atmosphere of the Burns country when his blissful reverie was interrupted by Monsignor's invitation to recite the Rosary; or indeed of irritation when on one occasion Monsignor's companion expected a few free moments for conversation. It happened that in the early 'fifties Monsignor Taylor was in hospital having treatment for a painful affliction in his foot. When the immediate danger was over he pleaded with his doctor to be allowed to return to his own parish for a few hours. A Jesuit Father visiting Monsignor in hospital

---

* In a letter to a friend Mgr. Taylor remarked that had he been a younger man he would have investigated the life of Teresa Neumann, the alleged stigmatist. His interest in the German girl was two-fold: first, the only food the girl had eaten for many years was the Consecrated Host; second, Teresa claimed she had been cured through the intercession of Sister Thérèse of the Child Jesus.

volunteered to accompany him in the taxi to Carfin, thinking that this would be a splendid opportunity to have a long chat with the prelate whom he had admired so long. No sooner had the car left the hospital grounds than the good Father was sadly disillusioned. " Forty-five minutes run! Yes, we can manage the Fifteen decades and a few trimmings." That certainly obviated the long confidential chat. The instances quoted are not rare occasions. It would be well-nigh impossible for a Catholic to converse for more than a few minutes with Father Taylor without becoming aware of his devotion to the Rosary of the Blessed Virgin. A parish-priest of the Vincentian Order at St. Mary's, Lanark, the lately deceased Father Sweeney, remarked that one of the most edifying Rosaries he had ever recited was on an occasion when he was spending the night at the presbytery at Carfin. Monsignor invited him to the Chapel to say night prayers, and there, in the darkness and stillness of the sanctuary, the two priests offered up their *Paters* and *Aves* together.

How many Rosaries were offered up on behalf of the Carmelite nun whose Cause Father Taylor had espoused, is a secret which he carried with him to the grave. We have an indication of the number of Masses he celebrated in her honour from the scanty notes which survive in the few diaries still extant. The practice, too, seems to have been established of paying a visit to the Saint's grave on his return journey from a pilgrimage to the Shrine of Our Lady at Lourdes; also the 30th September, from about 1905, was reserved in his diary as a " Memento " of St. Thérèse. No evidence exists to suggest that during these early years the Cause of Sister Thérèse suffered in any way because of competition resulting from his many other duties. What is more probable is that Father Taylor had to forget some of his activities to further the Cause of the Saint, but most assuredly he did not neglect Eucharistic devotion, nor devotion to the Mother of God.

The initial English translation of the autobiography of Saint Thérèse, by a Polish professor, had more than served its purpose by introducing the Saint to Britain, in the spring of 1901. Within a few months Father Taylor had entered on what was to be a major preoccupation until the end of his life. Did Father Bernard Lynch envisage the effects of his advice when he urged the reading of the book on his friend, Father Taylor, who was perhaps the only priest in Britain with the ability and enthusiasm, the spirituality as well as the fortitude to assume the responsibility of furthering the Cause of a Saint.

With the approval of Professor Dziewicki and the blessings of the Carmel at Lisieux, in the summer of 1903, Father Taylor commenced a short brochure of Sister Thérèse's life. His diary records that on January 26th, 1904, he " finished the MS." which he " sent to Archbishop Bourne " on the same day. Three months later, he paid a visit to His Grace at St. Edmund's College, Ware, but what took place at this meeting is not recorded, although it is known that not too long afterwards His Grace accepted from Father Taylor a small relic of the Carmelite nun. Soon he, too, became one of the early pilgrims to her grave. In 1912, Cardinal Bourne was to express in the Preface he wrote for Father Taylor's translation of Sister Thérèse's autobiography — *Soeur Thérèse of Lisieux* — words which fully express the sentiments of many when they first became acquainted with her life story :

". . . To many, on reading for the first time the story of Sister Teresa of the Child Jesus and of the Holy Face, it came almost as a shock to find a very youthful member of an austere Order, strictly retired from the world, engaged in hidden prayer and mortification, appearing before us to reveal to the whole world the wonders of the close intimacy of friendship to which her Divine Spouse had been pleased to call her . . ."

The MS. of 1904, referred to above was published under the title *As Little Children*, and this brief sketch of Sister Thérèse's life very soon ran into 100,000 copies, all of which were quickly dispersed, the profits being set aside for the new full-length translation of the autobiography which was eventually to appear in 1912 as *Soeur Thérèse of Lisieux*.

Thanks chiefly to the popularity of *As Little Children* and the dissemination of literature—leaflets and pictures—from the " Orphans' Press " the cult of the Little Flower became widespread in Britain and Ireland as well as in more distant English-speaking continents. Favours received through her intercession were numerous, and it was Father Taylor's self-imposed task to have these favours, or " Roses " as they were called, collated and recorded at Lisieux. Not all the " Roses " bore the stamp of supernatural intervention, but their number indicated an increasing devotion to the Carmelite of Lisieux.

In reviewing these years in *Soeur Thérèse of Lisieux*, Father Taylor relates how the cult of the Saint received a tremendous impetus in 1908 :

" The genesis of the devotion in these countries is in a large measure traceable to the month of November, 1908. On the fourth of that month, a young Good Shepherd novice at Finchley,

London, found her foot suddenly cured during the night. For months it had baffled the doctors; and she was to have returned home that very morning to Glasgow. The circumstances of the cure were deeply interesting, including as they did a visit from the Little Flower of Jesus; the miracle caused a sensation. It was narrated in various periodicals, and roused a strong public interest in the Servant of God."

A little colour is added to the impersonal account quoted above, by a few comments entered in Mr. James Taylor's diary between November, 1908 and January, 1909:

"November 27th, 1908:   T.N.'s letter about a visitor coming to stay.

November 28th, 1908:   Visitor (C. Clarke) arrived at mid-day.

November 30th, 1908:   Miss Clarke came from Finchley Convent, London, to recruit her health. Through a fall, her ankle ligaments were broken; she was miraculously cured after having been nearly four and a half months laid up.

January 2nd, 1909:   Visit of Father Clarke of Wishaw to see his sister, who is improved so much.

January 22nd, 1909:   Miss Clarke left for G.S. Convent, Finchley, at 8.50.

Mr. Taylor does not indicate whether he shares his son's enthusiasm for Sister Thérèse, Servant of God; nor does he mention that the cure was attributed to the Carmelite nun's intercession. There can be little doubt however that Miss Clarke, the novice from Finchley, was the "genesis of the devotion" to the Saint in Britain. It is worth noting, too, that Father Taylor arranged with Mother Superior of the Good Shepherd, at Finchley, to have the favoured novice under observation in his parent's home at Greenock. Also, it must be remembered that almost from the beginning of the century Father Taylor had been a welcome visitor in the parlour of the Good Shepherd Convent not only in Glasgow, but also in London and Liverpool. Moreover it is not outwith the bounds of conjecture to believe that he had already known Miss Clarke, the sister of a clerical colleague in the Archdiocese, before she had left Glasgow to join the Congregation of the Good Shepherd. At any rate it is more than probable that Father Taylor was directly associated with whatever novenas or prayers were offered to Sister Thérése on Miss Clarke's behalf.

Eight months later, on August 27th, 1909, Glasgow was again favoured; this time the cure was well authenticated by the invalid's family physician; and by Professor Gemmell, surgeon of Glasgow Western Infirmary. The latter certified that his patient, Mrs. Dorans (from the Parish of Our Lady and St. Margaret, Glasgow) had suffered, before her cure, from a " Carcinoma of the sigmoid flexure of the colon . . ."—in lay terms, a malignant tumour in the intestines. On May 17th, 1912, Mrs. Dorans was again examined and the following certificate was issued:

> " We hereby certify, on soul and conscience, that we have carefully examined Mrs. Dorans, and find her in good health, and able to go about and perform her household duties. There is no evidence of a tumour in her abdomen. Two facts about her impressed us. One was the truthfulness and constancy of her statements of her illness under cross-examination, and the other was that she had the facial expression, or ' cancerous cachexy,' of one who had suffered from a grave, malignant disease.
>
> > Signed: Alexander Rankin.
> > George Carmichael.
> > Thomas Colvin."

Of the three signatories the third, Dr. Thomas Colvin alone was a Catholic. In a paper read at Plymouth by Dr. Colvin, at the Annual Conference of the Young Men's Society, on the subject of " Miracles and a modern Glasgow Miracle," the case of Mrs. Dorans was described at great length and the fact was made public that Mrs. Dorans had been summoned, in August 1912, " before the Ecclesiastical Tribunal convened by His Lordship the Bishop of Bayeux and Lisieux, in view of the Beatification of Sister Thérèse, ' The Little Flower of Jesus.' A searching physical examination of Mrs. Dorans was made . . . but the doctors reported that the abdomen was normal."

Monsignor Taylor's account of the cure, appeared briefly in an article entitled " St. Teresa and Scotland," which was published in St. Peter's College Magazine, in December, 1947.

> " Mrs. Dorans of Glasgow had returned from hospital to her home, suffering from the last stage of cancer. Mother Mary Teresa, a Sister of Mercy, had suggested a novena to the Little Flower for her recovery. After a long demur, caused by her love for Our Lady, Mrs. Dorans grudgingly consented to a joint Novena. The answer came quickly. One night the invalid felt a hand pressing on the tumour, which slowly contracted, and completely disappeared. Later on, this startling cure was confirmed at Lisieux itself for the Process of Beatification."

In this case, also, it has not been stated what part, if any, Father Taylor played in instigating the Novena in honour of the Servant of God. What is known is that Father Taylor had been acquainted with several of the Sisters from the Convent of Mercy, since the years when he himself had been a student at nearby St. Aloysius' College. Moreover there was scarcely a convent in Scotland, which had not received from him pictures and leaflets in his efforts to promote the Saint's Cause. It is more than likely that Mother Mary Teresa had joined with the many others in a determined effort of united prayer to procure one of the first class miracles necessary in the Process of Beatification. In the appendix of Father Taylor's translation of the Saint's autobiography—the 1912 edition—we are given an indication of the thoroughness of his investigation of every aspect of this cure, and indeed of every favour brought to his notice.

The third important cure destined to rouse the faithful in the West of Scotland to an even greater love of the Little Flower was that experienced in Our Lady of Good Aid Church, Motherwell, by Margaret Malone, on February 25th, 1911. Five months earlier she had become a postulant in the Convent of the Little Sisters of the Poor, Glasgow. Towards the end of 1910, after a minor accident the sight in her left eye, which had been dim for some time, disappeared entirely. On January 5th, the Community doctor diagnosed a cataract. About the same time all the Sisters joined in a Novena to the Little Flower, but seemingly to no avail. Margaret returned home in order that she might visit the Eye Infirmary. Dr. David Jones, her family doctor gave it as his opinion that the sight was completely gone in the left eye and that there was danger to the right eye. This opinion was confirmed by professors in the West Regent Street Ophthalmic Institution and in the Glasgow Eye Infirmary; the condition was incurable, they declared—not even worth an operation.

Undaunted by the news, Margaret started a novena of Communions in honour of Sister Thérèse. The novena ended on a Friday and Margaret was still blind. The next morning, Saturday, found her again receiving Holy Communion and praying with great fervour. Suddenly, when leaving the church, she found she could see with her left eye. She had been cured!

The family doctor issued a certificate to this effect on August 19th, 1911, and His Lordship Bishop H. G. Graham (then assistant curate at Our Lady of Good Aid Church) verified Margaret's story that " she had been cured after making her novena of Communions, and using a relic of the Little Flower."

In this case there is undisputed evidence that Father Taylor
was a close friend of the Little Sisters and of the old people
they tended. Undoubtedly he would have given them a relic of
the Saint, just as he gave one to his friend Bishop Graham.
Also it is on record that he visited the girl in her home
at Motherwell. Margaret eventually emigrated to New York
where she married, and in course of time one of her daughters,
Mrs. Theresa Brady, of New York, returned to Scotland for a
short visit, some time in the early 'fifties. This good lady sent
to the present writer a somewhat lengthy written account of her
meeting with Monsignor Taylor and the impressions he made
on her at the time of the visit. The whole article is so typical
of Monsignor's words and actions that regretfully the decision
was made to omit or summarise parts of it. Apart from these
alterations the words which follow are the visitor's own personal
account written from notes made after her visit to Carfin:

"On the day I arrived at the Grotto I was directed to the
Church where, I was told, one could always find Monsignor
Taylor. The Church is a small one, and at first glance there seemed
to be no one there. Then I heard low voices and off to the left in
front of the altar of Our Lady of Fatima I saw him. He had his
arms around three boys; their mother stood in the shadows
nearby . . . Whatever he was telling the boys about Our Lady of
Fatima was making a deep impression.

I went quietly down the aisle and entered a seat where his
quaint Scottish brogue reached me. I could hear him saying,
'That's what Our Lady said at Fatima, boys. Just imagine! All
we have to do to stop another terrible war is just to do what is
expected of each one of us every day—to do our daily tasks as
well as we know how, and to say the Rosary. Now, isn't that
easy? And you know, there's somebody else who did just that
and nothing else, and SHE is one of our greatest saints. There
she is!'

And as he walked the boys over to the statue of the Little
Flower, I could hear him earnestly telling her story and how easy
it was to imitate her. It was not what he said that held his listeners;
it was the tone of his voice and the look on his face as he spoke
of his little Saint. To him she was not one far removed from us:
she was real; she shared his everyday life as a very real part of it.
As I listened, I realised how much he loved Thérèse and how
close she was to him. When the boys' mother asked for his
blessing before they left, he said, 'Not my blessing . . . but Hers.'

Then while they knelt, he fumbled in his well-worn cassock, and, producing the relic of St. Thérèse, he held it over the head of each and whispered:

'Dear Little Flower, through the love you had for the Child Jesus, through the love you had for Our Blessed Mother, through the love you had for the Holy Face and the Blessed Trinity, bless me and mine and make me holy.'

Then slowly and very reverently he traced the Sign of the Cross with her relic and handed it to each of them to kiss."

While the American was engrossed in this little scene she had failed to notice the line of people who had quietly entered the Church and were now seated in rows near the sacristy door. When Monsignor Taylor entered the sacristy and the line began to move, it dawned on her that she, too, must join the queue if she wished to meet him. An hour or so went by and then it was her turn. He beckoned her in, closed the door and he himself took a seat on a wooden bench, which faced the statue of Thérèse and a portrait of Pope Pius X. Mrs. Brady now continues:

"When I told him who I was and why I was there, it seemed to make no impression on him. He listened to me politely with one ear cocked. Then I mentioned my mother's maiden name, Margaret Malone, the name by which he had known her. He looked at me as if he could not believe his eyes after all these years (forty years or more). Nothing would do but I should tell my whole life story and give an account of my mother's death which had taken place three years previously on the feast day of the Canonisation of the Little Flower. In the course of the conversation, I mentioned that on the following day I hoped to leave for Lisieux and speak to the Little Flower's sister, Céline. He smiled at that and replied, 'I think you should!'"

Well might Monsignor Taylor smile, for the visitor's statement had provided him with an unexpected opportunity. For some time he had been waiting to hear of someone who intended travelling to France and who might be willing to deliver a personal gift from him to Céline, St. Thérèse's sole surviving sister, at Lisieux. Would Mrs. Brady be willing to do this? Her words show that she was eager to do so.

"Monsignor did not have to wait for my answer. He must have known that Margaret Malone's daughter would consider it a privilege to do this little thing for the Saint who had cured her mother more than forty years earlier . . .

From the church, Monsignor took me upstairs to his study, where we were free to talk. However, our conversation was interrupted frequently, when he would suddenly dash out of the room and disappear downstairs, his periods of absence varying from fifteen minutes to an hour. During these intervals he was in the Confessional or reciting the Rosary with a group of pilgrims, or merely speaking to pilgrims who had travelled a distance to seek his blessing."

Left to herself, the visitor had ample opportunity to examine the treasures of Monsignor's study and bedroom. Wherever her glance fell she could see reminders of St. Thérèse: photographs of the Saint at every age could be seen, while on the mantelpiece stood a small glass case, containing a tiny tress of her lovely hair; nearby on the desk stood a photograph of Mother Agnes of Jesus, signed by herself. On extended shelves about the room were displayed almost every known book written about her, including Monsignor Taylor's own translations of the Saint's autobiography going back to the first editions.

In the bedroom across the passage-way, the visitor could again see portraits of Thérèse and Pius X as they looked down from their place beside the Crucified Saviour and Our Lady of Carfin.* And as she moved around the large room fingering those mementoes so dear to Monsignor Taylor, she realised how fortunate she had been in meeting him. Had she arrived later she would have found him gone: he had planned to travel north to visit an invalid nun, who had just returned from India, where she had been for many years since Monsignor had first directed her there to join a Missionary Order.

The visitor concludes her account.

" At nine o'clock that night Monsignor finally sat down for a few uninterrupted moments before the fire in his study. Throughout the afternoon and evening, he had not taken time off to eat a meal, although he had seen to it that I was well looked after. Turning to me with the wonder and sincerity of a child, he remarked: ' Isn't it strange? She wanted you here today to keep me from going out, for if I had left the Grotto today I would not have met you; but, more than that, all those souls down there that I've been running to all day—some who haven't been to Confession in many years—might have gone away and never returned. See how SHE looks after souls!'

It gave me a queer feeling to think that the Little Flower had used me to accomplish her mission for souls. And indeed how good she had been to me in providing me with the opportunity of doing her, and Monsignor Taylor, a favour.

As we went up the garden path to the street, the rain was coming down in torrents, and still there were people waiting patiently in

---

* The latter was the title popularly applied to the " Stella Maris " in the Grotto.

the rain, at that hour, to see him. His day was not yet done. As I entered the taxi, I turned and looked back; I could not help but think how much like the Curé of Ars he was, in his great zeal for souls and in his humility and simplicity. No wonder the Little Flower loved him so much!"

More than half-a-lifetime before the visit described above took place, Father Taylor was fully engaged compiling evidence on the strange and wondrous results evinced as a result of the intercession of Sister Thérèse, the Servant of God.

On September 6th, 1910, her remains had been exhumed. Only her bones had remained incorrupt, a wish often expressed by her during her last illness. Another wish, too, seemed to have been granted: the palm which had been placed within her coffin on her chaste remains on October 4th, 1897, had remained as fresh and green as ever. " Was not this symbolic of her words: ' I desire at all costs to win the palm of Agnes; if not by the shedding of blood, it must be by love ' ? "*

From 1910 onwards the torrents of miracles claimed, in the words of the Vice-Postulator, " became a deluge." From all over the world reports of favours received came fast and steady. Britain too, and particularly Scotland, claimed its share.

In 1911 Father Taylor was summoned before the Tribunal to testify concerning her FAMA SANCTITATIS, the amazing and world-wide devotion towards the Little Flower. A short account of Father Taylor's evidence survives in manuscript form, among his personal papers, part of an article which, the present writer presumes, was written at the request of the late Monsignor Vernon Johnson for the periodical *Sicut Parvuli*:

" The Congregation of Rites was overwhelmed by the catalogue of well-attested cures which Monsignor de Teil (the Vice-Postulator of the Cause) had presented. Without delay, the Diocesan Process was begun.

After Mother Agnes of Jesus, sister of the Servant of God, had testified, I had the honour of next putting forward the evidence of the English-speaking peoples in favour of her reputation for holiness. That from Scotland was particularly effective. It happened that for over three years, Mr. Diamond, then editor of the *Glasgow Observer*, had printed weekly in his paper, thanksgivings and petitions to the Little Flower of Jesus. Sometimes they reached a column in length. These had been cut out carefully and were now produced.

---

* *Soeur Thérèse of Lisieux*, by T. N. Taylor.

Although not all were certainly supernatural, a devotion wide-spread, ardent and persistent, was easily proved. Indeed the testimony when completed was so cogent that—on the authority of the Vice-Postulator himself—Pope Benedict XVI was deeply impressed. 'I am not surprised at the enthusiasm of the French over their country-woman, but the extraordinary devotion of the English-speaking nations is to me the Finger of God. HIC MIHI EST DIGITUS DEI. I shall canonize her as speedily as possible.'

This pleasure, however, God reserved for his successor, Pius XI, a yet more ardent admirer of the little Carmelite of Lisieux."

Thus in a few short paragraphs, Father Taylor, the second most important witness of the forty-five invited to give evidence before the Tribunal at Lisieux, describes the part he played in the Process leading to the Beatification of the greatest Saint of modern times. This impersonal account makes no reference to the long vigils spent examining and compiling evidence; nor to the hundreds of letters written to clients of the Little Flower in America and Australia, as well as to those nearer home; neither does it mention the careful translation into French of the important testimonies for the benefit of the French-speaking Tribunal. A scanty reference in his own, or in his father's diary, gives us a slight idea of the long journeys made in the evenings or at week-ends in order to satisfy himself of the validity of claims, made by the grateful devotees of the Servant of God.

The case which perhaps attracted most public interest in Scotland at the time under consideration, was the conversion on April 20th, 1911, of a Scottish Presbyterian minister, the Rev. Alexander Grant. Evidence of Sister Thérèse's intervention on his behalf was so conclusive that he, as well as Mrs. Dorans, was invited to give his personal testimony before the Episcopal Tribunal at Lisieux.

The information which follows is taken from a biographical sketch of Mrs. Grant's life which was published in *Les Annales de Sainte Thérèse* in April, 1956, a few months after her death. Of her husband's conversion Mrs. Grant had earlier written:

" He had been summoned on purpose from Scotland to give evidence, and he was examined on August 8th, 1911. He declared on oath:

' It is to the reading of the Autobiography of Sister Thérèse that I owe my conversion . . . All that I had read (earlier), and all my studies had no other result than to attach me more strongly to my Protestant faith . . .' "

When he was requested to relate the story of his conversion, Mr. Grant spoke as follows:

" I had read as if by mere chance in the *Catholic Herald,* which my wife received every week, a short biographical sketch written by the Rev. Father Taylor; the latter mentions in it that the full edition of the History of Sister Thérèse would be published soon. I was deeply interested in this article. I cut out the advertisement, which I carried about in my pocket for almost a year, often enquiring whether the complete biography had yet come out. A friend of my wife's borrowed the older edition from some Catholic nuns. At Christmastide in 1909, on returning home from preaching a mission, I was compelled to keep to my bed with the 'flu; I found this book lying on my table and read it eagerly.

. . . I realised that the work of a genius, a theologian as well as a first-class poet had fallen into my hands. I cannot convey the extraordinary impression that the reading of this life had made on me . . ."

The Rev. Alexander Grant had not realised in December, 1909, that the chances of his remaining a Presbyterian minister for the remainder of his life were slowly receding. Sister Thérèse's " back-room " forces were already at work. His wife, Mrs. Ethel Grant had become a Catholic in July, 1908, and because of this, he was required to resign from his church at Lochranza and move to Edinburgh. Mrs. Grant, worried about her husband's difficulties, had discussed her problems with Mother Mary Teresa of the Convent of Mercy, Glasgow. This nun, it may be recalled, was the one who six months earlier (August, 1909) had urged Mrs. Dorans to make a novena to the Little Flower for a cure of cancer; and as we know, the result was a canonically approved miracle. May one question who was in her thoughts when she said to Mrs. Grant, " We must pray for your husband's conversion."

Naively Mrs. Grant admits in her own writings, " I did not know what ' The Little Flower " was; I thought is was some kind of Catholic badge to be worn in the lapel, and when Mother Teresa later wrote and promised to send me two pictures of the Little Flower, I was no wiser." One must remember that Mrs. Grant had lived since 1900 in a remote village with no Catholic Church, and few if any Catholic inhabitants: the spiritual furore caused in Catholic circles, by the Autobiography of St. Thérèse had not as yet touched her. When, however, she read in the *Catholic Herald* the short biographical sketch written by Father Taylor on, " Sister Thérèse, the Little Flower of Jesus," all the pieces fell into place and she recognised the significance of Mother Teresa's "Little Flower." She admits that she deliberately left the paper 'lying about" in her husband's library, so that he might "by mere chance" read the article. Mr. Grant went further and put the press cutting in his pocket; and stranger still for a man of strong religious convictions he was pleased to accept the little picture of the Carmelite nun which he treasured during the long months of darkness and turmoil which followed.

At which stage Father Taylor became acquainted with Mr. and Mrs. Grant is not clear. The priest's diary records that he visited them at least twice at the beginning of 1911, three months before Mr. Grant decided that he could accept the doctrines of the Catholic Church in their entirety; also Father Taylor was present when Mr. Grant was received into the Catholic Church, by Father Widdowson, S.J., of the Sacred Heart Parish, Edinburgh. Mr. Grant, on Father Taylor's advice, sent a written account of his determined resistance to the doctrines of the Catholic Church, to Mother Agnes at Lisieux; and of how throughout it all he was conscious of the permeating presence of the Carmelite Nun.

At the conclusion of the Episcopal Tribunal in 1911, through the good offices of Father Taylor, the officials responsible for Sister Thérèse's affairs invited Mr. and Mrs. Grant to take charge of the birthplace of their benefactress, at 42, Rue St. Blaise, Alençon. The couple left Edinburgh in May 1912 to take up their duties, but Mr. Grant died five years later at the age of 65. A few hours before his death he was heard to whisper, "Little Thérèse, come and fetch me, if it is God's will, and take me with you."

After Mr. Grant's death in July, 1917, Mrs. Grant continued her mission as custodian of the Saint's early home. Her quiet charm and warm welcome gained her great popularity with the pilgrims who came to Alençon, especially those who were seeking God. Soon it became apparent that Mrs. Grant was directing those of little faith, or no faith at all, to an interview with a Catholic priest. In a little bundle of letters which Father Taylor received from her over the years, invariably there was a request for a Mass or prayers for the conversion of someone in whom she was interested at the time. Until her death in 1956 Monsignor Taylor, who had remained one of her closest friends, shared with her the common interest of a "thirst for souls."

On a number of occasions Mrs. Grant spent a short holiday at Carfin, and all her letters show how keenly interested she was in the success of Father Taylor's apostolate to give greater honour to Almighty God, by increasing in the faithful a deeper

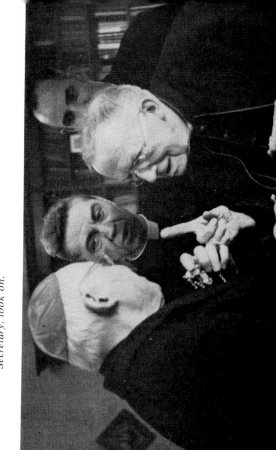

Left: DIAMOND JUBILEE OF ORDINATION.
*Monsignor Taylor celebrates Mass at Our Lady's Shrine
at Lourdes, 12th June, 1957.*

Below: "BUT, SEE WHAT I HAVE!"
*Monsignor Taylor shows Cardinal Tien the Relic of
St. Thérèse. Monsignor J. Conroy, V.G., Motherwell
Diocese (centre), and Rev. B. Schmitz, S.V.D., Cardinal's
Secretary, look on.*

A LAST VISIT TO THE GROTTO.

The late Fathers L. Connelly and M. B. Maher, former parishioners, walk in front of coffin bearing Monsignor Taylor's last remains.

THE FUNERAL PROCESSION LEAVES ST. FRANCIS XAVIER'S CHURCH.

REQUIEM MASS IN OUR LADY OF GOOD AID CATHEDRAL, MOTHERWELL.

love of the Virgin Mary and the saints. Between the two friends there existed a spiritual reciprocity whereby Monsignor Taylor introduced interested clients to Mrs. Grant; and she in turn recommended tourists to Britain to visit Father Taylor at Carfin. More than one of his " spiritual children " had been sent to him in the first instance by his " dear old friend " at Alençon.

In 1939, Monsignor Taylor agreed to manage Mrs. Grant's financial affairs in Scotland, at first through the offices of Mr. Kilpatrick, a close friend; but following the death of the latter, he transacted the business himself. The sum involved was not great, but after necessary deductions had been made for charities nominated by Mrs. Grant personally, the small remainder was to be disbursed at Monsignor's discretion. Like Monsignor himself, in his last years, Mrs. Grant was almost totally blind. From 1951, onwards, her writing was illegible and although a friend overwrote her wandering scrawl there was always the plea, " When are you coming to see your child at Alençon? " For over forty years they were friends and for this time and longer, both strove for the same aim—to increase in those with whom they came in contact a more ardent love of God. If one of the mansions of heaven should be a meeting place for old and dear friends, surely Monsignor Taylor and Mrs. Grant would have many reminiscences to recall, and undoubtedly St. Thérèse, too, would be present at the reunion.

Scarcely had the Episcopal Tribunal, to which Father Taylor had contributed such important evidence in 1910 and 1911, concluded its final session when the busy little priest found himself immersed in the task of seeing his long promised translation of the Saint's autobiography, through the hands of the publisher—and on to the market. A copy of a letter written by Canon Taylor on December 7th, 1942, and presumably sent to his publishers, indicates that the nascent pangs of his brain child caused him not a little unease. It seems that as early as 1908 he had enquired from Burns & Oates, a publishing firm, if a cheap edition of the autobiography at a shilling a copy could be printed. The firm considered the proposition but must have found it uneconomical.

Father Taylor's letter follows :

" Through the sale of pamphlets and leaflets printed by the Orphans' Press, I had in hand a sum of over £200. Meanwhile, the Cause of Beatification began, and I spent in 1910 almost a week before the Tribunal. On my return home, I set to work on a new translation. On account of other duties, it cost two years of unremitting labour. Quite aware that the book was not for a

L

generation, but for centuries, every effort was made to produce a correct, idiomatic and smooth-flowing translation. Hilaire Belloc and Professor Phillimore (of Glasgow University) kindly revised the proofs, but the greatest help was given by the late Sister Aimée of Notre Dame Training College, Glasgow, and Notre Dame, Oxford.

When all was ready, in the summer of 1912, I saw Messrs. Wilfrid and Francis Meynell of Messrs. Burns & Oates, at Orchard Street, London. They informed me that there was no room for a new translation. They had sold 5,000 copies of the first edition, a record sale for a 6/- book of that class, and in addition, a large number of the cheaper impression at 2/6d. The market, they said, was glutted. My reply was that they spoke from a commercial standpoint; this book was to be judged from a supernatural standpoint. I asked, would they print 10,000 copies at 5/-? It was my intention to hand over all profits to Carmel to aid the process of Canonization.

On September 12th, Francis Meynell wrote, ' If you don't sell your edition, we stand to suffer with you. We should be willing, however, to make an exception to the usual procedure and accept £200 at Christmas and £50 by Mid-Summer—the remainder to be discharged out of the sales—towards the cost of production. If the sales show no signs of clearing off the debt we shall, of course, have to issue warrants against you—the Bishop's approval having first been obtained.' "

The mis-judgment of the publishing firm on the prospects of selling a new translation turned out to be a blessing in disguise; since Father Taylor had contracted to pay the cost of publication, the copyright of the translation remained in his own hands and not in those of the publishers. The success of his venture justified his expectations as shown in the paragraph which follows :

" The book was magnificently brought out in the finest paper, type and cover available . . . By a miracle the first copies were in the hands of their subscribers on Christmas Day (1912). Long before the following Christmas, the entire edition (9,050) was sold out. This volume was entitled *Soeur Thérèse of Lisieux*. Later, the complete text of the Autobiography without letters, counsels or ' Roses ' was published at 3/6d. and finally an edition of the same in paper covers at 1/."

A brief summary of the history of the Autobiography until 1942 follows next :

" Shortly before the Beatification it was discovered that the French edition differed slightly from the actual manuscript of the Saint, and it was decided to publish a fresh edition giving the exact text as written by St. Thérèse. After the Canonization in 1925, I spent a full year revising once more the precious text, and at the same time inserting changes from the new French edition. For the present (i.e. in 1942) this is the final text of the Auto-biography."

At this stage he makes reference to various plans he had in mind for the recasting of the chapters dealing with the Saint's striking interventions in more recent years: this he would hope to do when hostilities in Europe had ceased. The final paragraph of his letter explains what he did with the profits from the Autobiography.

" The profits duly passed to the Carmel of Lisieux to assist the process of Canonization. When this was complete I gave over £1,000 to Pope Pius XI for St. Peter's Pontifical Society for Native Priests, of which she is patroness. When her basilica at Lisieux had begun, the income from the book returned to Mother Agnes of the Carmel at Lisieux. That is one reason why this English translation of the Autobiography has been such a success. The book, however, remains my own personal property so that no one, not even in France, could tamper with the text. I have always given freely and without charge permission to quote from *St. Thérèse of Lisieux* . . .

' My main object is propaganda of the book itself; financial considerations are secondary matters. From time to time I had an uneasy feeling of not being fairly dealt with, but that is now past. For the present I am content to leave in the hands of those con-cerned any arrangements that have to be made. I think it would be well to discuss changes in price before settling them. This has been rarely done in the past."

In the concluding paragraph of the letter to the firm Canon Taylor stated that he was enclosing early correspondence which he had received from them, including a letter dated 5th Septem-ber, 1912, and the first statement of account of January 2nd, 1913. It seems a pity he had not retained a copy of these as he did of the letter, excerpts of which are given above.

The long association between Monsignor Taylor and his publishers continued on an amicable footing until about 1947, when by a strange mishap a dispute arose between them. Some years earlier, as a temporary expedient, Canon Taylor had agreed to relinquish personal control of the book for two years. Finding it impossible to secure copies from London when the two years had expired, he asked a Glasgow firm, John S. Burns & Sons—this firm has no connection with the London publishers—

to print a Jubilee edition entitled, *A Little White Flower.** The legality of this undertaking was questioned by the London firm; there was not, the firm claimed, a specified time limit to the agreement Canon Taylor had made. What added further to the confusion was that neither Monsignor's nor the firm's copy of the contract could be found; nor could the publishing firm's legal representative at Glasgow remember the clause of a two year limit to the contract. Some months later while making an exhaustive search of the Company's files, the Glasgow representative not only discovered, in a mislaid file, a forgotten letter he himself had written to the offices of the firm in London, but also a letter written by an official accepting the two year limit on behalf of the company.

The wrangle had caused Monsignor Taylor and his closest friends much anxiety until the mislaid letters were unearthed. By that time conditions obtaining for fifty years were changing; in 1948 the copyright of St. Thérèse's autobiography had expired and writers were free to make their own translations, although Mother Agnes of Jesus still retained control of that part of the book which had been added by Carmel and of which Monsignor Taylor alone held the copyright in Britain. Eventually Monsignor Ronald Knox made another translation; some readers, Monsignor Taylor being one of these, did not entirely favour the modernistic idiom of the new translation. They preferred the style of writing employed by the Saint, with all its poetic imagery. As far as this was possible in good literary English, Monsignor Taylor preserved the style used by Sister Thérèse: this is the hall-mark of Monsignor Taylor's translation. This may be the reason why a number of Saint Thérèse's clients maintain that they prefer the original translation which stood the test of time for close on half-a-century, and of which well over 100,000 copies have been sold.

The spiritual effects of St. Thérèse's autobiography cannot be enumerated in human terms. Father Taylor himself was one of the first in Britain to experience its effects. The number since then who have come under the Saint's thrall may be assessed only by the rapid progress of the Cause which led to her beatification and canonisation. We already know how the Rev. Alexander Grant, in spite of strong resistance on his own part, succumbed to the Saint's influence. The late Monsignor Vernon Johnson, an Anglican clergyman, owed his conversion to having

---

* The firm of John S. Burns & Sons continued to publish for Monsignor Taylor until his death in 1963. As a tribute to him, they have undertaken the publication of this volume also. The American publishing firm, Kenedy of New York, looked after his interests in the U.S.A. until about 1954.

read Monsignor Taylor's book in a college library. A strikingly similar story to that of Monsignor Johnson's, was told by a young Anglican student who arrived at the Carfin presbytery the day before he was due to take up service in one of His Majesty's torpedo boats. Some months earlier, the young man had been browsing through the shelves of his college library when his eye caught Monsignor Taylor's book, *St. Thérèse of Lisieux.* As he scanned the pages a Dean approached, and glancing over the student's shoulder, he remarked, " You had better not read that book; that's the one that caused us to lose Vernon Johnson."

The young man did read the book and as a result he came to Carfin to meet Father Taylor, its author. Although Monsignor Taylor did not meet the young sailor again, he was greatly impressed by the sincerity of his faith as he blessed him with the relic of the Little Flower, before he set out for an unspecified theatre of war.

Tales in abundance have been told by others and still remain to be told of favours received through the hands of the Saint of Lisieux, but those of particular interest here are those relating in some fashion to Father Taylor. In January, 1902, John M. Charleson, a former Presbyterian minister, about to commence his studies for the priesthood, at the Scots College, Rome, received as a parting gift from Father Taylor a copy of *L'Histoire d'une Ame.* After ordination Father Charleson returned to Scotland and eventually was appointed priest in charge of Holy Cross, Croy. Here he was responsible for the elaborate Corpus Christi processions for which the village was at one time noted. Also, Father Charleson was noted for his strong devotion to Our Lady and the assiduous practice of meditating devoutly on the decades of the Rosary, a practice recommended to him by Father Taylor, shortly after the former's reception into the Church. Were it not for the following story, one would scarcely think there was room left in Father Charleson's heart for St. Thérèse.

During the Second World War he retired from parochial work and went to live in England. Here he became seriously ill and was removed to hospital, where he was told that he would not recover from his malady. Later he informed Monsignor Taylor, in confidence, that the Little Flower had appeared to him during his illness and had told him he would recover, although for a while he would retain some of the symptoms of his illness. A letter he sent to Monsignor Taylor towards the end of the war confirms that what St. Thérèse had foretold actually did take place, and to quote Father Charleson, " to prevent me suffering from pride I still have mild attacks but they are becoming less severe and less frequent as time goes on."

Until the present time Father Charleson's confidence has been respected. But now both priests are gone to their heavenly reward, which surely cannot be any the less happy because both could venerate their favourite saint, without this devotion in any way detracting from the worship due to Almighty God and the honour they owed to their heavenly Mother.

As the 'twenties approached the spade work leading to the beatification of the venerable Thérèse had been completed, and other hands taking over from Father Taylor, helped to make the furrows smooth. Although relieved of much of the correspondence by the Central Office set up at Lisieux he remained in close contact with Mother Agnes and with Monsignor de Teil, Vice-Postulator of the Cause. A series of invitations among his letters show that during the remaining years of his life he was a welcome guest at Carmel's deliberations and celebrations. This was so at the beatification ceremony on April 29th, 1923, and again on May 17th of the following year when he was invited to join the official Lisieux party which travelled to Rome for the canonisation ceremony. A full account of the process of St. Thérèse's canonisation and the Papal documents dealing with it, is given by him in the canonisation edition of *St. Thérèse of Lisieux.*"

The ceremonies at Rome completed, Father Taylor hastened home to assist at Carfin's solemnities in honour of the new Saint. Fortified, the previous year, by the assurance of Thérèse's sisters at Carmel that she who loved Our Blessed Lady so dearly while on earth, would continue to do so in Heaven; and that she would draw people to the Shrine at Carfin, so that through Mary, souls would come to know and love Jesus, Father Taylor had made plans to procure a life-size Carrara marble statue made to a design and specification approved by Mother Agnes at Lisieux. The statue, the cost of which was defrayed by pilgrims to the Grotto, was initially set up on a raised cairn. As the years passed, the shrine of the Little Flower was improved several times until eventually it became a mound-shaped, raised rockery on which the roses, which the saint loved so well, became an outstanding feature.

The order of processions in the Grotto remained always the same: Processions commenced at Massabieille with the Rosary and when the processionists had wound their way round the precincts of the Grotto, Benediction of the Blessed Sacrament was given and the Lourdes invocations recited. After the address pilgrims were invited to turn towards the Shrine of the Little Flower and Father Taylor led them in the well-known prayer in the Saint's honour. The ceremony of the " Blessing of the Roses " followed—a colourful ceremony indeed on the feast day of the Saint when the massed thousands held aloft roses of every hue during the blessing. It has been claimed that these roses blessed by the Church's prayer have been efficacious when devotees of Saint Thérèse have called on her help. The claim has been made, too, that an inexplicable perfume has been given off from an artificial rose blessed by the Church. Monsignor Taylor has told that on one occasion, he himself has smelt the perfume emanating from one of these flowers. Others from many parts of the world have claimed a like experience, the result being that roses blessed at Carfin have been carried away in their thousands and venerated in honour of the Saint.

Processions in the Grotto normally ended by a general blessing with the relic of St. Thérèse, after which a short prayer of thanksgiving was recited before the multitudes dispersed. Those who desired an individual blessing were invited to adjourn to the Lower Grotto, where Monsignor would be in attendance. Fervour was not lacking, as these pilgrims waited sometimes for hours on end, while the tireless little priest spoke to each individually— the scene at times was reminiscent of Lourdes when pilgrims were waiting their turn to go into the baths. Here at Carfin could be found the bodily sick or the mentally ill; the maimed and the blind; those heavy of heart or burdened with a troubled conscience. Canon Taylor first of all ministered to those who were seriously ill, as they sat propped up in their invalid chairs, displaying the patience and resignation typical of most sick people. Nor did the Canon rush his ministrations: he gave each his undivided attention as he leaned over, and while placing the relic on the sightless eyes or maimed limb, would urge the sufferer to recite with him the invocation: " Dear Little Flower, through the love you had for the Child Jesus . . ."

The invocations were altered to suit individual conditions, but always the prayer was directed to God, through St. Thérèse.

Less patient and calm than those who suffered from a physical malady were those afflicted by spiritual malaise. It has been known occasionally that such a pilgrim would blurt out his troubles before Father Taylor had time to bless him. When a pent-up pilgrim unloaded his conscience with, " I have been away from the Church for such-and-such number of years," the priest would bless him quietly and take him aside for a moment or two; thereafter, the penitent would be invited to remain behind and make a formal confession and receive absolution. It is impossible to say how often incidents such as these took place; occasionally Father Taylor would say publicly that he had received permission from a pilgrim to make known that a Prodigal Son had returned to the Church after a long absence of many years.

The temporal favours attributed to the blessing with the relic of the Little Flower were varied and numerous; as her intercessory powers are generally recognised, a few only of those alleged to be granted during Father Taylor's blessing with the relic will be referred to here. A pilgrimage train had brought a number of the faithful from somewhere in the east of Scotland. One man, deaf for six or seven years, had remained behind for the special blessing. The blessing and invocations over, the pilgrim, with his wife, made his way slowly towards the waiting train. Unknown to his wife, the deaf man was experiencing alarming sensations in his ears—the crunching of gravel underfoot, a perfectly normal sound to those accustomed to hearing it, but to one who had not heard it for many years the sound was disturbing. Other sounds, too, he heard, but afraid to trust his own ears, he did not say anything to his wife until they had boarded the train, when his first words were, " This train is very noisy." Father Taylor learned of the man's recovery from deafness in the press on the following morning, a recovery which was confirmed by the priest-in-charge of the pilgrim's parish in due course. Could this cure from deafness be explained by a psycho-analyst as the result of the excitement of the moment? Or was it a special favour granted through St. Thérèse in answer to the deaf man's prayers; or Father Taylor's great faith in the efficacy of his own prayers? It might well be the result of a combination of all three, for the ways of Providence are not open to human explanation. Many examples of a similar nature might be given of the wonderful effects resulting from the application of the relic of the Saint after Father Taylor's blessing. These incidents did not always occur at Carfin. Wherever Father Taylor went, he carried with him a relic of his patroness, and it is not then surprising to hear of favours being granted through the Saint in many parts of Scotland and England. In the years following the canonisation of St. Thérèse, Father Taylor was a favourite speaker at the ceremonies of unveiling or blessing of her statue in churches and convents up and down the land. An account of one such blessing of a Shrine in St. Thomas Aquinas' School, attached to St. Catherine's Convent, Lauriston, Edinburgh, is one of interest because St. Thérèse seems to have chosen this occasion as an opportunity for letting fall several of her " Roses."

The blessing ceremony, which took place at 3 p.m., was attended by the children of the school and a number of their parents and friends; this over, Father Taylor addressed the gathering. The ceremony concluded with the veneration of the relic of the Saint. Within a few days, Father Taylor was to learn of three little favours granted during his visit. The account of these is taken from Father Taylor's notes, which may have been a draft of the " Grotto Notes " prepared for the Catholic week-end press:

> " Among those present were a husband and wife. Despairing of finding employment in Scotland, they had decided to go to London, and had already taken their seats and tickets for a train due to go south that evening.
>
> While venerating the relic, they made their needs known to the Little Saint. As they came out of the hall, a lady, not knowing why she did so, suggested they should apply for a post which she believed to be vacant. They cancelled their tickets to London, applied for the situation the following day, and got it: the man to be chauffeur, the wife to attend to the Lodge, etc. An ideal post! They could not have wished for better."

Coincidence, the reader may suggest! If so, another small one follows:

> " Another ' Rose ' was the healing of a heart-breaking difference in a family. As the mother of the family came away from the ceremony, she was radiant with joy, for she felt that now all was going to be right. A few days later word came that the sorrow was at an end."

The article concludes with a third " coincidence " which occurred an hour or so later:

> " The most brilliant ' Rose ' of all was reserved for the evening, when Father Taylor gave an address to the Sisters in the Convent. Among those present was a nun who had for some time suffered from what is called ' Double Vision,' the result of a strain which had caused paralysis of a muscle in the left eye. The only way of rectifying the vision was to wear, for an extended period, special glasses; the glass for the left eye, almost opaque, allowed the wearer to see objects but not distinguish what they were.
>
> During the course of the lecture, the Sister in question suddenly realised that she saw the speaker and everything in the room clearly; and more than that, she was looking at Father Taylor with her left eye and through the thickened glass! Fearing a delusion, she said nothing to those around her.
>
> The lecture over, the Sister removed her glasses and found her sight perfect. Still, she waited to give the matter a perfect test:

she tried the stairs, and found she could go down without spectacles, a thing quite impossible before . . . When Sunday came, two days after the recovery, she found she was able to carry out her normal duties of attending to upwards of a hundred children at the Children's Mass. By this time, she felt there was no mistake and it was time to make known the 'Rose' which St. Thérèse had let fall in St. Catherine's Convent.

Since then, she has completely discarded spectacles and now she can even read her Office daily without them, something she has not been able to do for many years. The non-Catholic doctor's verdict: 'The eye is perfectly normal and,' he added, 'this is none of our doing. We did not expect it in this case.'"

Referring to this latter "striking favour granted by the Little Flower to a distinguished member of the Convent of Mercy, Lauriston," Father Taylor continues:

"A point to be noted is that no one, not even the favoured one, was asking for this "Rose.' Instead, nuns, pupils, and the one who is cured, were storming heaven for the recovery of another member of the community who was seriously ill . . . Already the fortunate recipient had come to Carfin to return thanks to the Little Flower . . ."

Variety is not wanting in the manner in which Heaven grants an answer to prayers. A prematurely born baby girl was seriously ill. The mother had been given permission to visit her infant daughter in hospital at any time, so seriously ill was the child. One evening, the mother was met by the Ward Sister, who told her the baby was dying. Turning on her heel without visiting the baby, the mother went straight to Carfin (about five miles distant from the hospital) and told the sad news to Canon Taylor, who had been acquainted with the family for a number of years. The distressed mother assured the Canon that she was resigned to God's will should He wish to take the infant to Himself, but her prayers were that the little life would be spared should God find her worthy of this grace. Canon Taylor's reply was—and the lady clearly recalled his words: "Go over there (i.e. to the Little Flower Shrine in the Grotto) and *tell her* that I say she must cure your baby, if it is His will."

The mother followed the Canon's instruction and thereafter returned to the hospital after two hours' absence. She did not require to ask the Ward Sister about her baby: the joy in the nurse's face told its own story. The baby had revived from her moribund condition and was already well on her way to recovery. Little baby Thérèse is now a fine young woman, and apart from one minor handicap she has recovered completely from the paralysis which brought her to death's door in the first weeks of her life. An answer to prayer? The parents of the child certainly thought so, as did the nursing and medical staff who were in attendance and who had already given up all hope of saving the child's life.

The following incident, the last dealing with favours to be related here, throws some light on how Monsignor Taylor sometimes reacted when a pilgrim asked for his blessing and prayers. During the 'fifties, when this incident took place, Monsignor Taylor already knew that his own eyesight was failing and that one day, if he lived long enough, he would be blind. He knew, therefore, what the feelings would be of the nun who was threatened with blindness and who came on pilgrimage to Carfin to seek the help of Our Lady and St. Thérèse in her dilemma. The sight in one eye was almost gone, and there was danger that the good one might be affected. When the nun met Monsignor she begged him to pray for her recovery; this he refused to do unless the sufferer, on her part, showed that she was resigned to God's will and willingly made the sacrifice of offering her sight to Him if it was His will that she should go blind. The distressed Sister resisted for a long time, and only after much persuasion did she make her sacrifice. " Now," said Monsignor Taylor, " we shall ask for the Little Flower's help on your behalf," and he proceeded with the blessing and the customary ejaculations.

The following little story serves to cap the incidents just recounted. In a certain church in Lanarkshire, some time in the 'thirties, a statue of the Little Flower had been installed. The venerable old sacristan, as was his custom, set out on the night after the unveiling to lock up all the doors and windows. Very reverently and with creaking joints he genuflected before the Blessed Sacrament altar; from there he moved on, and as he passed the statues of the Sacred Heart, of Our Lady and of St. Joseph, he inclined his head in silent prayer before each. Eventually, he reached the statue of the young French Saint. No prayers here! A grunted " Ugh!" a slight lift of the bent old shoulders, and he moved on. The story, they say, was related by a young curate of the parish, who was sitting in the darkened church saying his night prayers. The curate in question is now in charge of his own parish, and if by chance he reads this, he may be interested to hear the reaction of the Carfin priest, who had in all probability unveiled the statue referred to, as well as the majority of the statues in honour of St. Thérèse, in Lanarkshire. Monsignor Taylor gave his usual little chuckle when he heard the tale—he enjoyed a good story as well as the next—and then came his rejoinder: " You may love the Little Flower; you may even hate her; but you cannot ignore her."

In 1926, Father Taylor attended the International Eucharistic Congress, held that year in Chicago. This visit was combined with a lecture tour in the populous areas of the United States, along the Atlantic seaboard; the main object of the lecture tour was to spread devotion to St. Thérèse. Among his papers is a typed copy of an article written for an unspecified magazine, entitled, " St. Thérèse in the United States." The tenor of the opening paragraphs, excerpts from which are given below, suggests the article may have been published the year following Father Taylor's visit to the States:

" It may interest the readers of this magazine on either side of the Atlantic to learn of the marvellous devotion displayed towards St. Thérèse of Lisieux, throughout the New World, from Alaska to Brazil . . .

On my arrival in the United States last year, the Supreme Secretary of the Knights of St. Columba, to whom I carried a cordial introduction, and Mr. Kenedy, the American publisher of *Saint Thérèse of Lisieux,* assured me that the lecture season had ended, as owing to the warm weather all those who could, would be making their way to the hills or the sea. I was thus left to my own resources. I knew, however, that since her death the Saint had said she desired to be made known; so I was not surprised when doors began to open in fairylike fashion.

Within ten weeks I was summoned to speak upon her life over one hundred and twenty times; and before the close of the lecture tour, in spite of my manoeuvres to escape the unsought ordeal, I found myself in the hands of Senator Cameron, presenting President Coolidge with a copy of the Saint's autobiography . . ."

The 3,000 word article ranges over many reminiscences and varied personalities, all of which have this in common: each person and incident was in some degree associated with St. Thérèse. The first reminiscence—only a few are given here—is chosen because it gives a slight indication of the power-pressure of the hectic ten-week lecture tour; and also because for three or four years the name of Father Quinn has intrigued the present writer, since first she discovered a signed photograph of the American priest among Monsignor Taylor's souvenirs. Only very recently, when revising information for the present chapter, did the separate pieces of the jigsaw fall into place; hence the following excerpt:

" For some time I stayed in Brooklyn with one of St. Thérèse's apostles, Father Bernard Quinn. Formerly an army chaplain, he had the privilege of being the first, during the war, to offer Holy Mass in the house of St. Thérèse at Alençon. Bringing back the devotion to Brooklyn, he asked her to aid him in his labours among the negroes, a work he had specially asked the Bishop to be allowed to undertake. In her usual generous fashion, she blessed his efforts both materially and spiritually. St. Peter Claver's is now the centre of devotion to her in Brooklyn, and in addition to the Sunday services in her honour, seven services are held there every successive Monday, the evening services being crowded in a way that was good to see.

During my sojourn he organised a Little Flower Day and arranged that I was to speak at all the services. A Friday was chosen, and though a mere handful knew the speaker's name (i.e. Father Taylor), and despite the crowds on the previous Monday, once more the sanctuary and porch were filled."

Seven public addresses on one day to large congregations in the overpowering heat of a New York summer! And although Father Taylor does not say so, it is scarcely likely that he would miss the opportunity of speaking individually to many, and of blessing each with the relic of St. Thérèse.

In Hartford, Connecticut, Father Taylor had the privilege of assisting at the consecration of Bishop MacAuliffe, a former fellow-student in Paris. Through the good offices of the latter and of Father Kelly, a priest of the diocese, Father Taylor was given a warm welcome and invited to give a large number of lectures in and around Hartford, where he saw for himself something of the warm affection the Little Flower had gained in New England. Through Father Kelly, also, the Scottish visitor gained a strong footing in Philadelphia, where he met a kindred spirit in the person of Father Lyng of St. Paul's in that city. The work this priest accomplished in his Italian settlement seemed incredible to Father Taylor until he learned the secret of Father Lyng's success: his reliance on the power of St. Thérèse. Father Lyng did all that he could to assist Father Taylor, even to arranging an interview with Cardinal Dougherty, who was one of America's most outstanding clients of St. Thérèse.

The full narrative of this visit and of the favours which the Cardinal received from the Little Flower while he was a missionary bishop in the Philippines, may be read in *Saint Thérèse of Lisieux*.

Wherever Father Taylor went on his whistle-stop tour in the United States, he received a warm welcome. In spite of the oppressive heat, he was enabled to speak in churches, colleges, convents and seminaries; and in the capital city itself he was privileged to address an audience in the Catholic University. Here, too, as earlier in Brooklyn, he was invited to address a distinguished gathering of the Federated Catholic Alumni of the United States:

To continue in Father Taylor's own words:

"But the experience in Washington, which overshadowed all others, was that of the interview at the White House. It entailed much preparatory labour on the part of my genial host, Mr. John J. Noonan, a friend of Father Lyng of Philadelphia. In various ways the Little Flower had come to his aid, and he resolved to find her an entrance into the President's quarters . . .

. . . I heaved a sigh of relief when the first negotiations broke down. Senator Cameron, a Protestant, stepped into the breach, however, and Mr. Noonan came all the way to Chicago to persuade the recalcitrant to return to Washington for twenty-four hours . . . The interview took place under the guidance of the Reverend John J. Burke, C.S.P., the capable and courteous Paulist Father who is the secretary of the National Catholic Welfare Council. Once more St. Thérèse had succeeded in securing for herself an excellent advertisement, as Father Burke took care that the President's gracious hearing of the short address on the autobiography and its Carmelite author, was transmitted to the world's Catholic press, and indeed to much of the secular press as well, through the Council's famous news service."

In the following excerpt, taken from the concluding chapter of the manuscript, Father Taylor gives the palm to the Catholics of the United States for their devotion to St. Thérèse.

"I had gone with the hope of encouraging devotion towards the one who had promised to strew Roses from Heaven until the last soul should have entered Paradise. Instead, I found it was I who had to learn from the youthful Church of the West what was meant by love of the Little Flower of Jesus. Certainly we in this part of the Old World have but a faint conception of how largely she enters into the life of the Catholics in the New . . ."

In conclusion, it may be added here that during his American lecture tour Father Taylor succeeded in collecting a generous sum of money, which was banked towards the time when a new votive church should be built at Carfin. This did not take place during his own lifetime, although Father G. Mullen, the present parish priest, has high hopes that a new church, already under construction in the Grotto precincts, will be completed by spring, 1973.

One aspect of devotion in honour of St. Thérèse still remains to be discussed. This is a private devotion known to those who

practise it as the " Twenty-five Glorias," or more familiarly,
" The Twenty-five Glory Be's." Fortunately, for anyone who
may be interested in this particular form of devotion, copies of
several letters exist—answers which were sent to people who had
enquired for further information. The following, in substance, is
the history of the development of the devotion as explained by
Monsignor Taylor at different times and to different people:

"This form of devotion came to me from America. When I
consulted the Carmel of Lisieux, the reply was that they, too, had
heard of it being used there.

During my six years at St. Sulpice, Paris, I became friendly with
a Sulpician postulant from the seminary in Baltimore. Later, this
Father Harig returned to his old college as a Professor. On my
way to the Eucharistic Congress, held at Chicago in 1926, I
called to see my friend and, frankly, I was shocked at his appearance. He had just been discharged from a mental hospital and
was still feeling far from well. Sorrowfully, I left him. Several
months later, I had a letter from him telling me he had been
compelled to return to the mental institution for further treatment.
While there, one of the staff, a religious and a devotee of the
Little Flower, had strongly urged him to say twenty-five times
daily for life the ' Glory be to the Father, and to the Son, and to
the Holy Ghost, through the Hearts of Jesus, Mary and Joseph.
Amen "—this as a thanksgiving to the Blessed Trinity for the
graces conferred on St. Thérèse during her twenty-five years on
earth. Father Harig faithfully promised to do so, and as a result,
he assured me, he was cured.

My reaction was not favourable. I neither adopted nor recommended the pious practice. It seemed impossible to concentrate
on this form of prayer.

Some years ago a lady in Paisley had—what I now believe to
be—an inspiration to make little cords with twenty-five knots for
the purpose of keeping count of the *Glorias*. She has made them
in many thousands, of which at least 2,000 went to America.
Curiously, she has never had to purchase a pennyworth of cord.
St. Thérèse sees to it. She buys, however, Little Flower medals
and attaches them to the cords. They have always been distributed
gratuitously.*

I gave away those she sent me, but remained unconvinced until
the following extraordinary incident occurred. Dear old Canon
Grant of St. Peter's, Aberdeen, was called to the Infirmary to
attend a woman at the point of death. A motor had passed right
across the body. After anointing her, the Canon placed under her
pillow a Little Flower cord. He did not think he would see her

alive again. Next morning, however, she was actually able to receive Holy Communion. Then, to the amazement of the staff, she recovered. But, what was most extraordinary was that, though she was pregnant at the time of the accident, a few months later the fortunate and grateful lady gave birth to a healthy child.

The sequel was that I accepted the devotion and have frequently recommended its practice. In at least five cases of child-birth, when the doctors demand craniotomy, stating that otherwise the mother would certainly die—the results were quite as inexplicable as in the case of the Aberdeen mother . . . I would be delighted to describe them in detail if you could find time to visit Carfin.

I enclose a cord, already blessed, made by the lady to whom I have referred."

As the readers of this composite account may have guessed from its tone, the last paragraphs have been taken from a copy of a letter sent to a Glasgow medical practitioner who has always been keenly interested in all aspects of Monsignor Taylor's apostolic crusade.

Additional information on the Twenty-five Gloria devotion is found in a circular letter, copies of which Monsignor sent to devotees of Our Lady and St. Thérèse of the Child Jesus:

" My dear friend,
    You have asked for a favour from our Immaculate Mother and her wonderful daughter, the Little Flower of Jesus.

At Lourdes, Fatima and elsewhere, Our Lady has demanded prayer and penance that she may save the world. The Holy Father has said: ' Next to the Holy Mass, the Rosary is the most powerful of prayers.' You will see, therefore, how absolutely necessary it is that the Rosary be said every evening with your children. So emphatically did Our Lady request it, that without the family Rosary I could not guarantee any favour at her hands . . .

With regard to the Little Flower, many of her clients have adopted the practice of saying twenty-five times daily the " Glory be to the Father . . ." to thank God for the spiritual graces *He* lavished on *her* during her twenty-five years on earth. This devotion has obtained the most extraordinary results. *You* help to pay *her* debt: she *must* pay you back—and believe me—she pays like a princess!

As there is grave danger of the recitation becoming merely a mechanical process, it were better to omit the words: ' as it was in the beginning . . . without end. Amen.' Children do not understand them. Adults do not often think on them. It has been found most helpful to say in their stead, the three Holy Names, thus: ' Glory be to the Father, and to the Son, and to the Holy Ghost, through Jesus, Mary and Joseph. Amen.'

In this connection it is well to remember that an indulgence has been granted for each time the Holy Names are recited— either verbally or mentally—and is applicable to the Holy Souls. One valuable consequence will be that the Holy Souls, as well as St. Thérèse, will pray for your intentions.

There is no doubt that it will also help should you promise to spread this devotion to the Blessed Trinity, the Holy Family and the Holy Souls. The 'Twenty-five Glorias' may be said either on the special Little Flower Cord with its twenty-five knots, on twenty-five beads of the Rosary or, and this is greatly preferred where there are children, by reciting five *Glorias* after each decade of the family Rosary.

Assuring you of my prayers and wishing you every blessing.

Yours sincerely in Our Lord,

(Sgd.) Thomas N. Taylor."

In several letters Monsignor makes it quite clear that this version of the *Gloria* is not meant to be used, except when the twenty-five *Glorias* are said in thanksgiving to God for the graces bestowed on the Little Flower during her twenty-five years on earth.

Monsignor Taylor, conceivably, may have been one of the first in Britain to learn of this devotion, but conclusive evidence shows that others in addition to Canon Grant of Aberdeen had been practising it for many years before Monsignor Taylor was converted to its use. Mrs. Margaret Blane, the maker of the cords, with ten of her children had done so since 1934; others, too, had of their own accord, been saying *twenty-four Glorias* of thanksgiving on behalf of the Carmelite nun, unaware that they were not alone in following this practice. An unedited account of how Mrs. Blane commenced making the Little Flower Cords seems to have been written down, but it survives only in fragments, the relevant parts of which are reproduced here:

26th January, 1934.

"I had been saying my twenty-four *Glorias* on my beads and on my fingers, but my attempts were proving unsuccessful. The front door bell kept ringing that day, and each time I answered the door there was no one there. I was puzzled but kept coming back to my duties in the house.

In the afternoon there was a loud ring at the door-bell; I answered again, and still there was no one there; as I made to close the door, a funeral was passing . . . I came in and fell on my knees, praying for the soul of the deceased. I then asked God how I could say the twenty-four *Glorias* in His honour, through the Little Flower. That evening I was handed a parcel, which I opened later in the evening. The parcel contained three balls of cord! Without thinking too much about it, I made the first cord with twenty-four knots. My daughter said to me, ' Give me that one, Mother, and make another for yourself. I made thirteen cords that night.

Next day, I told my Confessor what I had done without his permission; he (Father Little) said that God had received thirteen cords of twenty-four *Glorias* which He might never have got but for me.

From then on, every parcel that came into the house had double string . . ."

At this stage, the sequence of the story, which seems to have been transcribed from notes taken during a conversation, is interrupted. The pages are unnumbered and the correct order is not clear.

" The cords had been going on from January until the middle of August; there were so many things happening that I began to be afraid, and I determined when my stock of cord was exhausted I would stop making the knots. I woke up in the middle of one night and saw the Little Flower. I thought I was dreaming and fell asleep again; I wakened and saw her again. This time I was sure and I sat up in bed, but as far as I can remember, nothing was said, although I felt sure I was to continue my task. I then went to Canon Taylor . . ."

" I made the twenty-four knots for four years, until Canon Taylor told me I ought to add another knot for the twenty-four years *and nine months* of St. Thérèse's life. I was terribly worried over making the knots, as I had so many request letters and cord coming to me. I had one letter in particular asking me to send 1,000 cords to New York. Later on, Canon Lawton (R.I.P.) came down to see me and asked me for my story."

" I have nothing whatever to do with what has happened. I only tie the knots in Honour of God through the Little Flower. If I am hurt or worried, I have only to tell St. Thérèse and everything gets sorted out.

I don't really need lay people to ask for cords, as there are so many priests and convents to whom I send them and they pass them on.

On my honour, I have never bought a ball of cord since I started: I have even got it lying on my door-step and from where it came I really do not know. I promised the Little Flower that if she got the cord for me, I would get the medals, and make no charge, and so it is even up till now."

Although the account given above is prefixed by the date, 26th January, 1934, it may be safely assumed that this refers to the time when Mrs. Blane commenced making Little Flower Cords. Scribbled notes, partly shorthand, attached to the sheets, are dated 16th December, 1951; this indicates that the good lady had been making the cords for seventeen years. In May, 1962, she was still continuing with the good work. In a letter written to Monsignor Taylor on May 22nd, she states that for nearly forty years she had made these cords and that St. Thérèse had seen to it that she was always provided with a sufficient supply. She cites an example:

"I told the Little Flower that I had no string and she was to help me. Shortly afterwards, a man came in and gave me bundles of string which took two days to unravel. This provided me with sufficient to make 800 cords. The next day I received from a lady in Glasgow enough string to make 1,000 cords . . . Our little Saint does not want me to be idle. I think she must be afraid of me when she answers me so quickly. I am quite happy to make my cords as long as God is pleased with my work . . . I will be sending you a bundle this week.

I could go on with much more that has happened at this end, but my business is to tie the knots and nothing more . . .

I remain,

Yours most humbly,

(Sgd.) (Mrs.) Margaret Blane."

The humble mother of eleven children played her part in propagating a devotion—officially a private devotion, but unofficially practised all over the world by many thousands. She made the cords, Father Taylor blessed—and sometimes provided —the medals, and without propaganda the " Twenty-five Glorias " in honour of the Blessed Trinity gained its clientele. Since Monsignor's death, enquiries have elicited the fact that in Scotland, in England, in distant Australia, as well as in the United States, Asia and Africa, this devotion remains a firm favourite. It is surprising, in view of the widespread practice and the enquiries that have been made to the present writer herself, that so far it has not been granted any approval by episcopal authority.

Praying and preaching, important as they may be, did not mark the confines of Monsignor Taylor's crusade to increase devotion to the little Saint who, it seems, had taken him and all his ventures under her wing. Passing reference has been made to one contribution of £1,000 which he presented to His Holiness for the Native Priest Society, over which St. Thérèse is patroness;

in addition to this, over the years, profits from his own translation of the Saint's autobiography have been directed to the use of the Carmel of Lisieux and to the Missionary Sisters sent from there to work in the vineyards of the Far East—this over and above what he gave to the Mission fields from other resources. He who had already done so much for St. Thérèse was not at any time content to rest on his laurels: one mission accomplished was the signal for another to commence. The contents of the letter reproduced below indicate Canon Taylor's next move:

> 19, Golden Sq.,
> Aberdeen.
>
> Oct. 15, 1938.

"Dear Canon Taylor,

At the Bishops' meeting, held at Blairs last Tuesday, the Archbishop of Glasgow submitted a letter from you and a statement regarding a proposal to raise £3,000 for a Scottish Memorial Chapel in the Basilica at Lisieux.

To this proposal, the Bishops gave hearty and unanimous approval, and they decided to leave it to you to take any steps that you like, to raise the money throughout the country. Carfin has its devotees everywhere, and you will know best how to get at the charitable faithful.

I enclose £5 as an offering from myself. It is not much, but I suppose every little helps. I may be able to do more later if the money does not come in as fast as I hope it will . . .

> Yours very sincerely,
>
> (Sgd.) ✠ George H. Bennett."

Seven months later, with some joy, Canon Taylor was in a position to give to the Bishops an account of his stewardship. At the time of writing the letter which follows, he had been convalescing with the Blue Nuns at St. Leonards-on-Sea, after an attack of bronchitis:

> St. John's Villa,
> 23 Church Rd.,
> St. Leonards-on-Sea.
>
> May 6, 1939.

"To the Rt. Rev. Bishop Bennett,
Bishop of Aberdeen.

My Lord Bishop,

. . . The purpose of this letter is to report progress regarding the collection which the Bishops at their autumn meeting decided to organise . . . on behalf of the Scottish Memorial Chapel in the Little Flower Basilica, one of the sixteen national chapels being erected within its walls.

According to the official letter received from Your Lordship, I was authorised to take any steps I might deem opportune for obtaining the required sum. Mgr. Kelly, of Dumbarton, suggested a national collection during Advent, using the envelope system ... The two Archbishops, on being consulted, warmly approved.

By the end of November, 200,000 circulars had been inserted into specially printed envelopes. One was sent to all priests-in-charge, as also a letter, announcing the wish of the Bishops and outlining the method of the collection. A week later, a supply of envelopes, together with a striking poster, was despatched to every parish or mission throughout Scotland ...

The Memorial Fund was also widely advertised in the Catholic press. It seemed a golden opportunity of propagating devotion to the Saint whom the Holy Father was anxious to honour, and whose basilica he desired to see completed 'as beautifully and speedily as possible.' Finally, with the approval of the Bishops, a personal appeal was made during Advent in the cathedrals of the various dioceses. The circular had already informed subscribers how fitting it would be if the gift—£3,000 if possible—could be presented to Mother Agnes of Jesus, sister of St. Thérèse, on Christmas Day.

As Your Lordship remarked on the telephone, Scotland's answer was nothing short of a miracle. By Christmas, the collection had reached £4,000 ... I handed that very afternoon to the Prioress of the Carmel of Lisieux a cheque for that generous amount.

Mgr. Germain, who has charge of the basilica ... has said it was the biggest cheque he had as yet received. When he learned that other donations from Scotland would be forthcoming, he decided that—should our Bishops approve—the surplus would be devoted to the erection of a Lady Altar in the transept, facing the shrine given by our late Holy Father himself. The High Altar, it may be mentioned, is being presented by Cardinal Dougherty, while the nations of the world are sponsoring the sixteen side-chapels. It should be emphasized that previously there was no question of an altar to the Blessed Virgin. Scotland, therefore, will put Our Lady in the basilica.

Mgr. Germain's suggestion was accepted by the Archbishops of Glasgow and Edinburgh, provided the extra £2,000 required were secured without any further appeal. By the middle of February, £5,000 had been deposited in the Bank in Lisieux ... and £68, the first instalment of the last £1,000, lies in the National Bank, Motherwell. The balance is assured, since the profits of *St. Thérèse of Lisieux* will be earmarked for the Lady Altar in the measure required. It may be added that each of the 103 Glasgow missions answered the appeal—Dumbarton, Partick,

Carfin, Pollokshaws and Port Glasgow contributing individually over £100. But for sheer generosity Argyll and the Isles have eclipsed the rest of Scotland . . .

(Sgd.) Thomas N. Taylor."

Further donations continued to come, and slowly the remaining balance on the final £1,000 lessened. As he had guaranteed to do, Monsignor Taylor himself cleared the final dues from the proceeds of his book, *St. Thérèse of Lisieux*. The appreciation of the episcopacy of Scotland was conveyed to the originator and organiser of the whole plan:

". . . I was asked to convey to you the hearty congratulations of the Bishops on the great success of your efforts to raise funds for Lisieux. Surely the Little Flower will send down many Roses on Scotland, and truly we need them in these evil days . . .

I hope that the short rest you have been taking has quite set you up in health and given you a fresh supply of strength and vigour to carry on your great work . . .

(Sgd.) ✠ George H. Bennett."

Canon Taylor's health did improve, though slowly, for periodically he suffered from bronchial colds. The wonder was that his health remained so good in view of the long hours he spent in the Grotto during inclement weather. The so-called convalescent period was but a temporary withdrawal from the hurly-burly, which was his normal life at Carfin—a short spell which gave him the opportunity of working undisturbed, in tranquil surroundings, at whichever tasks were more pressing. In 1939, he stayed at St. Leonards-on-Sea, with the Blue Nuns; on a few occasions before and during the war, he withdrew to St. Joseph's Convent at Woodchester, in Gloucester, where he was treated most regally by the Franciscan Nuns. Not only was he able to work there in peace on the revised translation of the autobiography of St. Thérèse, but also, without constant interruption, he was enabled to compose important letters which from time to time he sent to Lisieux. Advantageously, one of the community was able to help with his secretarial work. Faircopies, in writing other than Monsignor's, are extant, showing that at Woodchester, too, the talents of each of his friends were put to use.

A fishy tale—a true one—is verified by an old and trusted friend of Monsignor, who is a religious at Woodchester. As was his wont, Canon Taylor sent to the convent, where he had been a guest, a small gift to mark his appreciation. Fish, fresh from the angler's rod, had been much appreciated on several occasions by the Sisters at Woodchester. But sad to relate, Sister Teresa Joseph, as Monsignor's life-long friend, was asked to undertake the writing of a very embarrassing letter. Her unpleasant task was to inform Monsignor that the fish on this occasion had arrived at the convent, safe—but not sound. The unpleasant odour of decayed salmon, permeating the precincts of the convent kitchen, put an end to that particular choice of gift from Canon Taylor. This apart, and it was the subject for jest for many a year, the community's memory of him is one recalled with joy: his deep humility, his spirituality, his kindness and courtesy were qualities which made a lasting impression on those who knew him.

If the names of those who held Monsignor in high esteem throughout the years of his sacerdotal ministry, were to be enumerated, the list would include admirers from the four corners of the earth. Especially strong was the respect he commanded in the Mission fields, where, at one time among missionary priests and nuns from the English-speaking lands, his name was known to all as the one who had made known to them through his books and his letters the effective help they might expect from their Patroness, St. Thérèse, if they imitated her philosophy of the " Little Way of Spiritual Childhood."

The surface only has been scratched of Monsignor Taylor's apostolate to increase devotion to the Carmelite Saint of Lisieux. Although much of the information provided here has been gleaned from his own writings and from old correspondence, covering a period of more than half-a-century, it is, nevertheless, but a truism to state that there are many still alive who recall his name with gratitude and affection. Few, if any of these, would deny that they owe to his teaching and example, a deeper love of God and of Our Blessed Lady, as well as a stronger devotion to her, whom he honoured as the " Little Queen." There are others, also—while according to Our Lady and St. Thérèse the honour and gratitude due to them—nevertheless, make the claim that favours received from Almighty God were, at times, largely the reward of the transcendent faith and firm confidence in prayer which were so manifest an aspect of Monsignor Taylor's own character; and which, by his humility and sincerity and his prayerful example, he transmitted to those who sought his counsel and consolation.

Chapter XIII

NUNC DIMITTIS

In June 1957, Monsignor Taylor celebrated the Diamond Jubilee of his ordination to the priesthood. Although now in the winter of his days, having reached his eighty-fourth year, physically he was vigorous and mentally remarkably alert. But for his deteriorating eyesight, a condition which his doctors assured him would end in complete loss of sight, he might have been taken for a man of ten to fifteen years younger. What his inmost thoughts on the prospect of blindness may have been are known only to Almighty God; outwardly he accepted his cross calmly and with resignation, asking of God two things only: first that he should be granted the privilege of celebrating Mass right to the end; and secondly, that those who followed in his footsteps at Carfin would have, not only a deep and constant love of God, but also a steadfast and sincere devotion to the two Patronesses of the Grotto, Our Lady and St. Thérèse of the Child Jesus.

In material terms personal ambition had never been a trait of Monsignor Taylor's character; but in the realms of spirituality his aims and ambitions reached remarkable heights, not only for his own spiritual welfare but for that of all his brethren. In sixty years of priesthood he had not faltered in these aims; nor had he deviated from the vow he had made on the eve of his diaconate to practise the teachings embodied in St. Louis-Marie de Montfort's treatise on " True Devotion to the Blessed Virgin."

A dozen years before Monsignor Taylor was born, Father F. W. Faber, that great lover of the Blessed Sacrament and of Our Lady, wrote the following words, words which might well have been uttered by Monsignor himself, for they express sentiments which were very dear to his heart:

" Jesus is obscured because Mary is kept in the background. Thousands of souls perish because Mary is withheld from them . . . If Mary were but known, there would be no coldness to Jesus then! If Mary were but known, how much more wonderful would be our faith, and how different would our Communions be! If Mary were but known, how much happier, how much holier . . . and how much more should we be living images of our sole Lord and Saviour, her dearest and most Blessed Son! "

Evidence suggests that if in Scotland, during the first half of the twentieth century, Mary's name became better known much of the credit for this must go to Canon Taylor, who never tired of singing her praise. For him Mary was the stepping stone which led directly to her Son, Our Lord Jesus Christ, the Divine Mediator with the Almighty Father; through Mary the way to Jesus was made more direct; and through Jesus entry to the Father's Kingdom was made possible.

In the spring of 1957, the parishioners of St. Francis Xavier learned that their venerable Parish Priest did not wish lavish expenditure on rejoicing for the occasion of his Jubilee celebration on the 12th and 13th June, the commemoration dates of ordination and of the celebration of his first Mass. His expressed wish was for a quick two-day pilgrimage to the Shrine of Our Lady at Lourdes, and anyone who was free to accompany him was invited to do so. Initially the plan was for one charter plane to accommodate the party, for the dates were so close to the annual summer vacation it was anticipated that few would be free from work. The contrary proved to be the case and a second plane, which catered for some, but not all who wished to go, was chartered.

As was usual with a party leaving the village to go on pilgrimage to Lourdes, the pilgrims assisted at early Mass in the village church. This was followed by a light breakfast and a quick visit to Our Lady's Shrine at Carfin and then having been safely labelled and tabbed by the efficient organiser, the late Rev. Peter Murphy, at that time Monsignor Taylor's senior assistant curate, the special coaches set off. The flight to Lourdes, punctuated as one might guess by the Fifteen Decades of the Rosary, was completed without serious mishap, and in spite of his eighty-three years and his impaired vision, Monsignor Taylor was in excellent spirits and at that stage completely relaxed.

After supper on the night of arrival the whole party visited the Grotto for night prayers; those who were less tired accompanied the tireless old jubilarian along the Gave river as far as the Statue of St. Margaret of Scotland. Around midnight Monsignor led his little flock homewards, this time reciting the Litany of Loreto—he never let slip an opportunity to offer up additional prayers. It would be impossible even to hazard a guess at the number of times Monsignor Taylor has recited the Litany of Loreto without notes or reference book, often in front of large multitudes congregated in the Grotto. And yet on this occasion, while surrounded by a little group of his closest friends, his memory failed him completely and he was unable to continue. Fortunately a few of his friends could take over and the embarrassing moment passed. The thought did strike some of those who were present that the excitement of the occasion and the exhausting journey were having their effect on our spry little octogenarian.

The memory of the two Masses on June 12th and 13th—the Jubilee days—is a confused one, of great joy mixed with much sadness: joy that those of us who loved and respected him were enabled to share with him in a thanksgiving commemoration of sixty years of dedicated and loyal service in the sacerdotal ministry; sadness that the parish priest who had been our counsellor and guide for so many years was now nearing the end of his days. This became increasingly obvious as the pilgrims from Carfin watched their venerable jubilarian move with faltering steps on to the altar in the Grotto niche; the tension mounted among his people when they realised that on this morning when he celebrated the Golden Jubilee of his ordination, Monsignor Taylor was quite unable to read even the large print in the special missal which he always used. Fortunately his assistant curate, Father Murphy, was in close attendance and, during the Consecration of the Mass, came to the altar to assist his parish priest. Monsignor was to reproach himself bitterly for not knowing the Mass of Our Lady " by heart." " If I had given the matter some thought," he remarked later to the writer of these lines, "I could have learned the Mass of Our Lady while my sight was strong enough to do so. Such foresight would have saved me endless trouble now."

Even when in good health, as a younger priest Monsignor Taylor took a much longer time to celebrate Mass than does the average priest: during the Jubilee Masses he seemed to ponder over each word as if he were using it for the last time. One could not but have sympathy for the vested prelate who stood nearby patiently waiting his turn to commence his own Mass, which was already much overdue, long before Monsignor Taylor reached the words of Consecration at his Jubilee Mass.

The tension of the morning soon passed, for Monsignor did not permit what he could not prevent, to distress him. With full vigour he took part in all the religious exercises; accompanied his people on a coach run to Bartrès; and listened eagerly to all that the guides had to say. He, the maestro, who had known Bernadette's brother and many of the well-known miraculés of the Grotto, listened with great humility to accounts being retold; perhaps even those which may have had their origin in the handbook Monsignor himself had compiled close on half-a-century earlier.

The forty-eight hour visit was soon over—the last visit which Monsignor Taylor was to make to Lourdes—and without delay the party set out on the return journey to Scotland, Monsignor Taylor's travel bag being noticeably heavier and bulkier than it was when he left home, due partly to the large number of greetings cards and telegrams he had received at Lourdes. Numerous as these were, their number was infinitesimal compared to what reached him at Carfin.

When the party arrived back at Glasgow and Monsignor was about to board the coach waiting there, to his great surprise he was whisked off in a high-powered car on the last lap of the journey home. When the more slow-moving coaches eventually reached Carfin cross-roads, the reason for Monsignor's abduction became very obvious. During his absence the people of Carfin had not been idle. Literally the village was " en fête." What a welcome home for their Canon—the priest who had guided their spiritual destiny for forty-two years! Not only did his own people crowd the streets and entrance to the Grotto, as his car crawled slowly along, but those not of his own religious persuasion were there also to welcome him, as well as many from neighbouring parishes. Carfin had seen much excitement since 1922 and had welcomed not a few dignitaries of church and state to the village, but it is safe to say that never was anyone welcomed with such emotion as was the smiling little priest who was part and parcel of the daily life of the community at Carfin.

The exciting days of commemoration over, Monsignor Taylor settled into his normal routine, pursuing his labours in the parish and in the Grotto. His health remained reasonably good, but his sight deteriorated rapidly over the next few years. But, although he could neither read nor write by the beginning of the sixties, his activities were not too greatly curtailed. He was a frequent and welcome visitor at Bazaars and Garden Fêtes and when he rattled his little bag of coins, and turned his pockets out " For the Missions " his generous example was followed by equally generous action from those who listened to him; also he could still preach retreats and draw large audiences at distinguished gatherings. Life had slowed down but there was still much activity and movement in Monsignor's life, although undoubtedly at this time his greatest worry was the celebration of Mass. In spite of powerful spotlights on the large letters of the special-print missal, the tired old eyes were finding it difficult to focus on the words. Occasionally the older acolytes, who now invariably served his Mass had to prompt him with the opening words on each fresh page. He remarked once that he thought the devil was putting difficulties in his way during Mass, for his mind went blank at parts which he could repeat without hesitation on other occasions. Even up to a few years before his death Monsignor still preferred to say the early Mass; the recitation of the Rosary before first Mass and the Stations of the Cross during Lent—practices initiated by Monsignor during his life-time—remained a feature of the devotional life of Carfin, for some time after his death.

When Father Peter Murphy was transferred to other duties in 1959, Father James Comerford assumed the duties of senior curate. His was to be a testing and trying time in the parish, especially as he had been ordained only as recently as 1952 and now as a curate of only seven years parochial experience he had the difficult task of running a busy parish and administering the Grotto, as well as organising the life of an independent eighty-eight-year-old, who was unwilling to accept that he could no longer undertake all the duties and responsibilities he had assumed at an earlier age. Dealing with the elderly requires much tact and understanding; Monsignor Taylor was fortunate in having around him in his later years young curates who were tolerant and kind and whose zeal in their priestly duties provided them with a good measure of Christian charity, a virtue which at times may be taxed to the utmost by the whims and vagaries of the aged. The strain is all the more difficult when the ageing person remains mentally alert, as in Monsignor Taylor's case; but physically the machine that was his body was slowing down and he was finding it difficult to synchronise the slower tempo of his body with that of his energetic mind. Hence his spirit drove him on to tasks he was unequal to physically, the result being, as happens with many old people, his friends had to take on the duties of friendly watch-dogs over his movements. Especially was this so when he moved from the church grounds, to the Grotto across the way, for scarcely a day passed without a walk around the Grotto and a discussion with the gardeners on the condition and upkeep of the many shrines.

It must have been sometime in the late fifties during one of these jaunts around the grounds that Monsignor informed one of his men that his wish was that after his death his body should be buried in the Grotto. This was not a momentary whim for the matter was referred to on several occasions. Indeed the exact spot was indicated and the gardener, an old friend, was finally convinced that Monsignor Taylor really did wish to be buried on the small grassy spot, in front of the Shrine of Our Lady of the Rosary and St. Dominic. The tomb was to remain unmarked and without headstone or other mark of identification. In case the reader may think this was but the mental aberration of an old man, it would be well to state that many years earlier when Canon Taylor had envisaged the Grotto precincts being bounded on four sides by two railways and two highways, his hopes were that the outer perimeter stretching from Chapelknowe, should be marked by a series of graves where deceased Grotto workers might be interred.

It must be confessed however that the present writer had certain reservations with regard to many of the rumours that were current about Monsignor's wish that he should be buried in the Grotto; and it was not until quite recently when she unearthed a copy of an instruction addressed to his trustees and executors that she was finally convinced that the stories she had heard from various persons had a basis in reality, and that Monsignor's wish had been that the final resting place of his earthly remains should be the Grotto which he had built in honour of Our Lady of Lourdes and Saint Thérèse of the Child Jesus. The text of the instruction follows;

St. Francis Xavier's,
Carfin,
Motherwell.
April, 1937.

"TO MY TRUSTEES AND EXECUTORS

It is my earnest desire that I should be buried in the Grotto at Carfin. I therefore request my Trustees to take whatever steps are necessary to obtain the requisite permissions for this purpose, including the consent of my Ecclesiastical Superiors and the Local Authority in which the Grotto is situated."

The typed copy was not signed but along the top were inscribed the words: "Father Taylor, T/6," in writing which might well have been the Monsignor's own.

The hope that he might be interred in the Grotto, like that for a grand votive church in his own lifetime, was not realised. The nearest he and the Grotto workers came to being interred in the Grotto was when their mortal remains, as a mark of respect, were carried into the Grotto Shrine, before burial in the diocesan cemetery at New Stevenston. The last and the greatest worker of all to receive this honour was Monsignor himself. On the eve of his funeral, lovingly the passkeepers of his church carried his coffin into the Grotto where the Rosary was recited while his parishioners followed his earthly remains in procession through the Grotto grounds, for the last time.

It is unlikely that this thought was in Monsignor's mind when on a Sunday morning in 1961 he announced from the pulpit that he was resigning from his office as priest-in-charge of St. Francis Xavier's parish; and that henceforth the Grotto and parish would be administered by the senior curate, the Rev. James Comerford. " But," added Monsignor, to the obvious joy of his people, " I will not be leaving you until they carry me out in a box."

For some time the people had feared that their parish priest would be leaving the village altogether and would spend his last days away from the parish he had known and loved for close on half-a-century. At no time did Monsignor comment publicly on this matter; nevertheless, his closest friends were aware that the problem was causing him grave anxiety, not so much because of his own future but because of the welfare of the Grotto of Our Lady of Lourdes and St. Thérèse. A letter, which seems to reflect on Monsignor's problem (or on one of a similar nature), has been found in Monsignor's files. His name is not stated, nor are the surnames of the recipient and sender of the letter. In deference therefore to the people concerned, whose identity is unknown to the present writer, their christian names too will be withheld here. The text of the letter follows:

> Convento Dei Cappuccini,
> San Giovanni Rotonda,
> Italia.
>
> 26th July, 1960.

" Dear X.,

      . . . I talked to Padre Pio this afternoon about the case, and he said that the only possible thing to do was to set aside human feelings and co-operate to the full in the wishes of the Bishop. He realises it seems a hard and unsympathetic thing to say, but feels that to do so can have no other result than to bring down the blessing of God both on the work and on the individual. He will pray that everything will work out smoothly and that there will be no hurt done to the feelings of anyone.

All best wishes, etc.,

Y."

All things considered, therefore, it was with much relief that the people of Carfin learned from Monsignor's lips that permission had been granted by His Lordship, the Bishop of Motherwell, for him to remain at Carfin, after retirement.

The decision seemed a wise one especially as the Centenary of the parish was already looming up on the horizon. A century earlier, Rev. John McCay, priest-in-charge of St. Ignatius' Catholic parish, Wishaw, considering Carfin, which was one of the outlying villages which made up his parish, wrote:

> " Carfin: A school-house is much required here. An application for school accommodation for the Catholic children, who attend no school at present, was lately refused on the grounds that in Catholic schools ' idolatrous superstition and damning delusion ' is inculcated. With the small sum of £150, a school house, having the Government requirements for 100 Children, can be built. A Protestant has promised £10 with a site. Will any Catholic lend a helping hand?"

Without waiting for a school, in the year 1862, Canon McCay set up a Mass centre at Carfin. In the following year, 1863, a chapel-school was built in the village; this building was to serve Carfin and the adjoining villages until the present church of St. Francis Xavier was built in 1882. From the original Mass centre, held in the home of the O'Neill family in " The Bellerophon Row," (about 200 yards from the spot where the parish church now stands), developed the titular parish of St. Francis Xavier, where Monsignor Taylor guided the spiritual destiny of the faithful for almost half of the century of its existence.

It would not be correct to say that Monsignor Taylor himself anticipated the centenary year of 1962 with excitement or great emotion: the pendulum does not swing to extremes for the old and in any case he was not personally responsible for whichever arrangements were being contemplated. Indeed it seemed, at times, as the centenary year approached that the condition of his health would prevent him from participating in any of the celebrations. Nevertheless the opening of the year found him with renewed vigour and so it remained throughout the summer. One could see him move about within the perimeter of his own small world: Church, Grotto and presbytery. Within this limited triangle he was independent and could move at ease; beyond this area he had to rely on the assistance of others. It was not unusual to find a tiny tot leading his parish-priest to the home of an elderly parishioner who might be ill: his old friends he never forgot. Nor was it uncommon to find him huddled in a front seat of the church during the normal devotional services of the parish; or in the quiet church during the day, forever fingering his beads, or with sightless eyes gazing at the Tabernacle.

The Centenary Brochure of 1962 had this to say about the opening months of the year: —

> " The deep spiritual life and the strong community spirit of this one hundred year old parish of St. Francis Xavier at Carfin seem to increase with the years . . . The parishioners have entered on this important year in the life of their parish as a time of spiritual renewal and as a family celebration in which all are anxious to participate.
>
> The parish church of St. Francis Xavier was crowded for a Holy Hour at 11 p.m. on the 31st December, 1961, to ask God's blessing on the very special New Year which was approaching and, as midnight struck, the parish choir welcomed the Centenary Year in, to the strains of Handel's Halleluiah Chorus, while the church bell announced to the whole village that the year of thanksgiving and rejoicing had begun. The Parochial Reunion, held a few days later on the 3rd January, had to be repeated on the 10th because of the numbers who wished to take part . . . A Mission was preached in the parish during the first fortnight of April, and it is calculated that ninety-five per cent of the adult population of the parish attended this Mission, and during the Mission fortnight there were 14,000 Holy Communions . . ."

Monsignor Taylor was no longer the nominal shepherd of his flock, but it was apparent to all that plans and arrangements were made with his spirit pervading. True to his principles and practice the villagers sent three invalids to Lourdes and although Monsignor himself would not be there, a goodly number from Carfin would remember his intentions at Our Lady's Shrine at Lourdes

One highlight of this crowded Centenary Year which captivated public interest and provided Monsignor Taylor with a few hours of happiness and joy was the visit to Carfin of Monsignor's friend for many years, His Eminence Cardinal Tien Ken-Sin, the exiled Archbishop of Peking. The visit on the afternoon of March 27 was completely informal, stripped of pomp and ceremony. Protocol demanded that representatives of higher authority should be present, but these apart, the meeting was between two Christians each holding the other in high respect. There was a homely and friendly dignity about the meeting: two old priests, each nearing the end of his day; neither able to see the other clearly and yet both happy and at ease in the other's company. Nearby stood a number of the villagers, rejoicing in their hearts that a Prince of the Church from distant Formosa should think so highly of their parish priest that he would interrupt his journey to the Eternal City to visit him at his home parish at Carfin. It may well be that the visit of His Eminence gave Monsignor Taylor a greater measure of personal joy than did any other happening of his final years. The charity which Monsignor Taylor disbursed did not demand, nor did it expect, positive appreciation: but he was human enough to be overwhelmed with happiness when Cardinal Tien went to some trouble to express his gratitude personally.

Four years after his visit to Carfin, Cardinal Tien's condition of health compelled him to retire. In July of the following year 1967, His Eminence, Thomas Cardinal Tien, the first Cardinal of the Catholic Church from the vast area of the Orient, passed to his heavenly reward. After his death his successor the Most Rev. Stanislaus Lokvang, D.D., Archbishop of Taipei, and his faithful secretary Rev. Bartley F. Schmitz, S.V.D., made it their major concern to further the various causes and welfare schemes so dear to the heart of His Eminence Cardinal Tien. Of these perhaps the chief is the memorial to Cardinal Tien, in the form of the hospital which he founded and which is recognised as the " Tien Medical Centre of Taipei, Taiwan."

On an evening about this time Monsignor Taylor narrowly missed being knocked down by a passing car. He had been standing at the edge of the pavement near the Grotto entrance, when without the least warning he shot like an arrow across the road, in front of an oncoming car, which providentially managed to skid on to the pavement he had just left. By the time the present writer, who was approaching the church gates just then, reached Monsignor, he was expostulating noisily against all car drivers. To put an end to his tirade, shock tactics were necessary. Hence, instead of receiving the sympathy he might normally have expected to the remark, " He might have killed me!" Monsignor was momentarily taken aback by the unexpected retort, " But, Father, what a grand funeral you would have! "

His mood changed immediately and his sense of humour came to the fore. " I suppose you're right, child. They would all turn out for my funeral—even those who never set a foot inside the Grotto."

This was a sore point with him. He could not understand why some priests were apathetic about visiting the Grotto, except when they were more or less expected to do so, on those occasions when the Bishop was present. Only now and again did he let his guard slip and let the fact be known that their non-attendance was a source of worry to him. No doubt many

M

had their own reasons; some may have felt ill-at-ease in Monsignor's company for he was very direct in his approach and it was difficult to evade his searching questions. Whatever the reasons it was known generally that in spite of the example set by the laity in their love for Our Blessed Lady, many pastors lagged behind their parishioners.

Another little incident which took place in June of the Centenary year is worth relating because it sheds some light not only on Monsignor's devotion to the Holy Souls, but on an aspect of his character which was recognised by all his friends: this was a sensitivity to what he might consider a rebuff from someone to whom he was attached.

In June 1962, one of the oldest residents of the village had just died and his corpse had been brought to the church on the eve of the day of burial. The deceased, just a few months older than Monsignor himself, had at one time been a close friend and loyal Grotto worker. Some years earlier when the old man's wife had died, Monsignor Taylor had asked his friend to give up the job on which he was then occupied and take on the job of gardener in the Grotto. This was work he knew well, for during thirty years he had spent much of his spare time working there. Voluntary work, yes! But full-time employment, definitely not! When asked to give reasons, he could not provide Monsignor Taylor with a logical answer, except that he did not wish a " paid " job in the Grotto. What Canon Taylor did not realise was that his old friend felt he would never be able to work in a regular job under him; as a volunteer worker the independent old man reserved to himself the right to walk off the job whenever he did not agree with " the Canon's flights of fancy," something he would not be able to do as a paid employee. But how could a prospective employee convey this to a would-be employer who was also a friend? Neither succeeded in making his views clear to the other, with the result that the barriers of formality were raised and never lowered between the two old friends—each with his share of pride and both with their share of stubbornness. As far as the writer knows, the most engrossing conversation which took place between the two erstwhile friends for over a decade of years was a polite, "Good morning, Father," or a civil, " Good evening, Cormac."

The practice in Carfin for many a year had been to recite after the Absolution over the corpse, not just one decade of the Rosary as in other parishes, but Five Decades. On this occasion in June, 1962, when the remains of his friend lay in state in the church, Monsignor Taylor made up for lost time. Not satisfied with Five Decades, he went on to finish the complete Fifteen. The church was packed, for the deceased had been the eldest resident of the village and a large number of Protestants as well as Catholics were present. Fortunately, many of the former knew Monsignor Taylor almost as well as did his parishioners and were quick to take advantage of a soft whisper, " You had better go now or you'll be here all night."

What Monsignor's inmost thoughts were on this occasion the writer does not know; nor did she ever hear him refer to the rift except when Monsignor had asked her in 1951 to use her powers of persuasion to prevail on the second party in the dispute to reconsider his decision. This she declined to do for she knew better than Monsignor Taylor did, that Cormac was a grand old man but as stubborn as a mule and just as sensitive as was Monsignor Taylor himself in certain circumstances. Hence for a decade of years she watched two old men treating each other with great respect and courtesy, but without the camaraderie of former years. One of them was her parish priest and the other—her father. And in case anyone decides to sit in judgment on their behaviour, the writer, a very interested spectator of this mini-drama, hastens to add that the childish dispute remained restricted to the two: there were no divisions or dissensions in the parish because of it; nor was a dutiful daughter embroiled in a triangular pull of loyalties—daughter-parent-parish priest. Two old friends had had a difference and only death bridged the chasm between them.

In an effort to build up information on the century that had passed, several attempts were made to direct Monsignor's mind back to a particular point on which information was sought, but for the most part, the results were unavailing. On one occasion only was Monsignor prevailed upon to express his views on a past happening; when the writer of these lines asked him if he recalled the Eucharistic Congress of 1908, and the Blessed Sacrament procession which had been cancelled at the last moment by Archbishop Bourne, at the suggestion of Prime Minister Asquith, Monsignor's eyes lit up and the words bubbled over.

" If I had been the Archbishop I would not have cancelled that procession. The Prime Minister at that time yielded to the wishes of a minority faction and for the sake of peace His Grace acquiesced."

To the further remark that in 1924 he himself yielded to the demands of a minority, when he arranged for the Blessed Sacrament Procession, which had been declared illegal, to be diverted from the main street of the village to private grounds, he replied: " I did indeed. But I was a Parish Priest only, not an Archbishop." And then the light of battle faded from the old eyes and with emotions once more under control, he became again the man of peace, whose conduct throughout had been commended by Government officials in the House of Commons. " I suppose," he added thoughtfully, " it all worked out for the best in the end. Justice was done and it was seen to be done with the removal of the Penal Laws from the Statute Book."

Thus spoke the old priest who had been present in London when the Eucharistic Procession of 1908 had been forbidden; and who fifteen years later was the organiser of a Blessed Sacrament Procession in the streets of his own parish at Carfin, a procession which like the one in 1908, was diverted from the public streets because the charge was made that such a procession contravened the clauses of the 1829 Act of Emancipation. Archbishop Bourne (later Cardinal Bourne) was the central figure in 1908; Father Taylor in 1924. One wonders what the Cardinal Primate of England said to the Scottish country priest, when he visited him at Carfin, three weeks after the incident of the " banned " procession. We do know that he watched with interest, the progress of the ensuing Catholic Relief Bill, introduced to the House initially on the instigation of Father Taylor, and supported throughout by members from both sides of the House, most of whom held His Eminence Cardinal Bourne in high esteem. In this case, as in so many others throughout his life, Father Taylor set the ball a-rolling; his friends in influential places, in this instance the Knights of St. Columba kept it going on course for the next two years; finally the wisdom of the Mother of Parliaments saw to it that the injustice of obsolete laws would never again be used against a minority group of citizens in the kingdom.

When in 1962, Father Taylor referred to Archbishop Bourne's action in 1908, it is doubtful whether in his humility he even thought of himself as the one who had set in motion the proceedings which had culminated in the passing of the Catholic Relief Bill of 1926.

When eventually in the late spring of 1962, the news was released that Sunday, 23rd September, 1962, was the day chosen for the official celebration of the Centenary of St. Francis Xavier's Parish; and that The Right Rev. James Donald Scanlan, D.C.L., B.L., Bishop of Motherwell,* had graciously

---

* Translated to the See of Glasgow, 1964.

consented to celebrate Solemn Pontifical Mass on that day, the parishioners were agog with excitement. The older ones especially enjoyed the next few months, for in recounting tales of the earlier years of the parish for the pages of the Centenary Brochure, they relived their youthful glory and were delighted that in spite of their advanced years they could contribute a little to the success of the Centenary celebration. It was a matter of regret that Monsignor Taylor was not well enough to contribute something to the Brochure from his own wide experience. With hindsight comes wisdom; twenty years earlier the present writer might have " brainwashed " Monsignor Taylor while he enjoyed good health and the full use of his faculties.

During July and August of Centenary year, he pursued his limited activities with unusual zest for a man approaching his ninetieth birthday. Visitors he had in plenty, and often these came from distant places; exiles home from distant continents on holiday; priests and nuns from the Mission fields; and visitors too, of different creed and colour all intent on seeing the Grotto at Carfin, and meeting Monsignor Taylor who was so intimately associated with it. One evening during the summer months the present writer was walking along the avenues of the Lower Grotto with her terrier walking at her heels. Unexpectedly, a large limousine drew up and Monsignor Taylor's voice was heard enquiring, "Who is this leading a little white dog? "

As soon as he heard her voice, Monsignor turned to the driver of the car, an American prelate, and explained who the speaker was, adding with an impish grin, " She used to help me, but I think she has been on a prolonged strike for years."

Before his " helper " could retaliate in suitable vein, for Monsignor enjoyed a little back-chat on occasion, the conversation was terminated rather abruptly. The long-suffering terrier decided she had been on her best behaviour long enough, and blind as she too, was, she recognised the voice of the kind-hearted human who had once given her a crunchy peppermint sweet. Such a kindly action must not go unrecorded, especially if there was the slightest chance of a repeat performance. When Monsignor heard the staccato " Woof! Woof! " he stretched down his gnarled old hand and patted the shaggy head of the old terrier. The priest was quite sure the dog had remembered him: the writer was equally sure that her terrier had a much better memory for sweets than for priests, however saintly. And during all this an American Bishop sat back in the driver's seat of the limousine and smiled benignly at the obvious affection Monsignor Taylor showed for animals.

On Sunday, 23rd September, Centenary Celebration day commenced in the parish with General Communion for all at early Masses, in preparation for Solemn Pontifical Mass, which His Lordship, Bishop James Donald Scanlan of Motherwell, would celebrate at 12 noon. As the size of the church put a limit on the number who could assist at this Mass, admission was by ticket only. At 11.15 a.m. Bishop Scanlan and his official party were met at Carfin Cross by a group of parishioners who, preceded by a local band, led His Lordship's party along the main street to St. Francis Xavier's Church.

The church was crowded to full capacity, as the celebrant, the Bishop of Motherwell, assisted by Rev. Gerard Hart (Deacon) and Rev. Peter J. Murphy (Sub-Deacon) both former curates of the Parish, entered the sanctuary. Monsignor Taylor's lifelong friend, the late Rt. Rev. Mgr. Alexander Canon Hamilton was assistant priest to His Lordship, and the Very Rev. Canons Rooney and McCrory were assistant Deacons at the Throne. The Master of Ceremonies was Rev. John J. Burns, assisted by Rev. John F. Breslin, S.T.L., the latter a native of the parish of Carfin.

In the sanctuary, sitting apart, a lonesome figure, was Monsignor Taylor, bearing his years with dignity. Although he was a non-active participant in the official ceremonies, yet on this, as on other days, he was the cynosure of all eyes. It was obvious that he was deeply interested in and fully alert to all that was going on around him; especially did he listen to the scholarly address delivered by His Lordship, Bishop Scanlan. In reviewing the proceedings on the following day, Monsignor had only one little word of criticism, and that was that sufficient praise had not been given to the one who was responsible for the success of the Grotto. " Only once," he pointed out, " was St. Thérèse's name mentioned for the role she played. She was the one who was responsible for bringing people to Our Lady's Shrine."

If up to this point the readers of these lines have believed that Father Taylor himself could claim some credit for the Grotto at Carfin, let them now be disillusioned. On his own words St. Thérèse is the " back-room " saint who ensured its success. At the risk of being accused of facetiousness, one might question who or what inspired in Father Taylor the great love and devotion he had for the Blessed Virgin when in 1893 he made his first pilgrimage to her shrine at Lourdes; this visit took place four years before his ordination and four years before the death of Sister Thérèse, the Carmelite nun. He claimed he

owed much to St. Thérèse; it might be said with great respect—
and no irreverence is implied or intended—that *She* also owed
much to him.

In the evening of the 23rd September, the Centenary celebrations ended for the day, with Solemn Benediction at 6 p.m.
Unlike the morning, this service was less formal, more like a
family gathering. Monsignor Taylor himself was the celebrant
and assisting him as deacon and sub-deacon were two of his
own " boys ": Very Rev. Patrick Donnelly, W.F., and the late
Rev. Lawrence Connelly. The preacher on this occasion was
another friend, the Very Rev. John Canon McCrory from a
neighbouring parish. In spite of all the excitement of the morning and afternoon Monsignor fulfilled this last service of the
Centenary day satisfactorily and with evident happiness
although, he must have been conscious, as were his people,
that his days for the celebration of momentous occasions had
almost ended; few indeed would have expected, a year or so
earlier, least of all Monsignor himself, that he would have been
strong enough to play an active part in the solemn centenary
celebrations of 1962.

On the day following the celebrations the one who writes
these lines was invited to the presbytery to go over the Centenary
Brochure with Monsignor Taylor. It was sad to watch him peer
at the illustrated cover of the booklet in a vain endeavour to
make out the images of Our Lady, St. Francis Xavier and St.
Thérèse, which were part of the design. He listened with avid
interest as excerpts of the history of the parish were read to him
and the accompanying illustrations explained. His reader made
an unwarranted " faux pas " while explaining the telegram of
filial homage which had been sent to His Holiness, Pope John,
on the occasion of the Centenary. When Monsignor asked who
had signed it he was told it had been sent off in his name. With
an unexpected touch of asperity he remarked: " If I had been
asked I would have been more than delighted to associate
myself with the message that was sent in my name. But I was
not consulted." The pique—a justified one—did not last long
for he added almost immediately, " And yet does it matter very
much now? After all, the pledge of loyalty is primarily from
the parish and clergy as a body." And with that the subject was
dropped.

The official Centenary Celebrations safely over, Monsignor
pursued his normal routine in and about the church and Grotto.
On 30th September, 1962, the Grotto was particularly busy and

there is little doubt that many who came to commemorate the sixty-fifth anniversary of the death of the Little Flower of Jesus were anxious also to see Monsignor Taylor who had been sixty-five years a priest and whose parish had just celebrated its Centenary celebrations.

Other important matters were now to capture the imagination and push lesser affairs into the background. On Tuesday, October 11th, Feast of the Maternity of the Blessed Virgin Mary, the opening of the much talked-of Vatican Council was due to take place in Rome. The whole Christian world joined in the Novena to the Holy Spirit for God's blessing on the Council's deliberation. Monsignor Taylor, too, joined in the Church's prayer, but his people were aware that his spirit and drive were weakening. For close on fifty years he had led them—at times drove them—now he had no choice but to leave to others what he could no longer do himself. As far as it was possible, Father Comerford, the Adminstrator of the Parish, followed the routine normally practised in former years. Hence on the evening of Sunday, December 9th, 1962, a torchlight procession in honour of the Immaculate Conception of the Blessed Virgin Mary, wended its way along the village streets, where the windows of the houses, as in former years, were illuminated and decorated in Our Lady's honour. Monsignor himself sat in a car which accompanied the processionists round the village, all of them reciting the Fifteen Decades of the Rosary before a final assembly in the Grotto.

Monsignor would have opportunity to visit the Grotto on other occasions, but never again would he take part in a procession through the streets of the village, nor indeed in a public service in the Grotto. Two days later, on Tuesday, 11th December, 1962, he was to celebrate Mass for the last time. Shortly afterwards he was admitted to the McAlpin Nursing Home where he was to remain until after the New Year. The privilege he had been praying for was to be denied him during the last year of his life; for a year he was unable to offer up the Sacrifice of the Mass, the heaviest cross of all to be laid on his shoulders towards the end of his life. His friends were aware of the serious condition of his health and one can well believe that he himself was, also. A week after he entered hospital, Canon McCrory, Secretary to the Cathedral Chapter, wrote to Monsignor Taylor to express the sympathy of his colleagues. An excerpt of this letter follows :

St. Bridget's Presbytery,
Baillieston.

20/12/62.

" Dear Monsignor Taylor,

. . . I write to convey to you the sympathy of all of us in your present illness. I write to assure you that you are in our minds, and in our prayers.

In the conventional way this will be a quiet Christmas, perhaps even a lonely Christmas; but we know, dear Monsignor, that your spiritual values go much deeper than that. So we pray God to give you the happiest Christmas of all—a Christmas full of His Grace and peace . . .

(Sgd.) John McCrory,
(Secretary to Chapter of Canons,
Diocese of Motherwell).

For a week or so Monsignor Taylor's condition was considered serious, but thereafter he improved, and if the decision had been left to him, he would have been home for the close of the Centenary Year of the parish. Wiser counsels prevailed and he was compelled to remain in the nursing home for another week. A small compensation was offered in the promise that he would be home in time to attend the parish reunion which was to be held a week later. The news that Monsignor would be present was sufficient to boost the sale of tickets for the parish gathering to such an extent that St. Bride's Hall in Motherwell had to be hired for the occasion. All Motherwell must have resounded to the applause when Father Comerford led the very frail Monsignor into the hall, half-way through the festivities. Not only did he spend several hours sitting among his people in the body of the hall but he mounted the platform and with amazing vigour gave a sparkling ten minute talk which left many with the opinion that their venerable parish priest had taken a new lease on life.

While he was seated in the hall he could not see the dancers, but he could hear the whoops of merriment from young and old alike; for this was a parish reunion, and dignity and formality had been left at home. The band had struck up a " Twist " and Monsignor Taylor, who in his hey-day had frowned on many of the modern ballroom dances, was entranced by the music and intrigued by the description of the knee-creaking, trunk-twisting antics of his flock as they gyrated and twirled in

front of him. The writer was well aware, though Monsignor was
not, that the " Twist," also, as performed under certain conditions in certain halls, received much criticism; but in a parish
gathering such as this there was so much fun and hilarity that
even Father Taylor, at his most prudish could not have found
anything to criticise in the form of the dance, although forty
years earlier he might have objected to the manner in which
the ladies dressed.

In earlier years, objection was anticipated by those ladies who
attended formal dances in sleeveless evening gowns, and boleros
or evening stoles were always worn when Father Taylor was
present in the hall. As soon as he left, these were discarded. For
the most part, however, modern ballroom dancing except for
the occasions of Staff or Parochial reunions was frowned on in
the parish. Several letters from the Vicariate make it clear that
Monsignor Taylor had been acting on the principles set down by
his ecclesiastical superiors in not allowing weekly dancing in
any of his halls, for the purpose of raising funds for the parish.
He might, too, have raised a disapproving eyebrow at Bingo, a
modern equivalent to dancing as a fund raiser, if it were shown
that the practice had in any respect proved harmful to the individual. Canon Taylor's maxim seems to have been that however
worthy the cause, a law governing ethical or moral conduct
should not be bent to fit individual circumstance.

Monsignor's premature outing after discharge from hospital
must have overtaxed his strength, for he was confined to his
room for the next four or five weeks. His non-appearance
among them disturbed his parishioners until a public pronouncement from the pulpit assured them that he was being
nursed in the chapel house and that he was making a slow
recovery. Just how slow the recovery was became apparent to all
during the annual Forty Hours' Exposition of the Blessed
Sacrament which took place in the parish on the 17th, 18th and
19th February, 1963. After Rev. P. Montgomery, S.J., Monsignor's friend and confessor had preached the Holy Hour, before
the close of Exposition, Monsignor slowly entered the church
from the presbytery. He looked neither to right nor left as
escorted by Father Comerford, with slow faltering steps he
walked towards the Sanctuary and knelt at the altar rail, while
Benediction of the Blessed Sacrament was given. His face was
waxen, drained of all colour and at that moment he looked a
very frail man. He no longer wore spectacles, for nothing could
help his sight now; he was a blind man. Physically, too, there
was a marked deterioration during the last six weeks; those who

gazed at him could see that their parish priest was a dying man. He was to regain a litle vigour during the next month or so but for all that his people knew that their beloved Canon was nearing the end of his days.

On Passion Sunday, 31st March it was announced at all Masses that Monsignor Taylor was making steady progress; all were invited to remember him constantly in their prayers. He was not again prayed for publicly until near the end of May; during these spring days he could be seen occasionally being wheeled on an invalid chair into the Grotto or church by one of the curates or the workmen in the Grotto. Those who were in attendance state that he was mentally very alert during this time, even up to the end. Certainly he recognised the present writer on the only occasion that she saw him outside the presbytery in his invalid chair. One of the curates wheeled him into the church and as he passed by the Statue of St. Thérèse he bowed his head momentarily in prayer. When passing the Blessed Sacrament Altar he could be heard murmuring his favourite ejaculation, " O Sacrament Most Holy, O Sacrament Divine, all praise and all thanksgiving be every moment Thine."

From June onwards until his death on December 1st, Monsignor Taylor was prayed for publicly at all services in the church. He was still able to move around a little and receive visitors in his own room. The great difficulty was that so many people wished to meet him that his small reserves of energy would have been entirely dissipated had all who called been allowed to speak to him. Left to himself of course he would have refused nobody. One day an Irish lady arrived at the presbytery and asked if Monsignor Taylor was fit to bless a beautiful bundle of roses she had with her. It was with some reluctance that one of the staff attending Monsignor accepted the flowers for it was known he had not been too well that morning. However, the roses were brought to him and his joy at smelling their fragrance, and of blessing the flowers with the special blessing used by the Order of Carmel in honour of St. Thérèse seemed to act as a tonic to him that day. On this day the roses were fresh flowers, having their own fragrance. Monsignor Taylor related that on one occasion he was privileged to smell the perfume given off by an artificial rose, which had been blessed during an official " Blessing of Roses " ceremony. Most faithfully had he performed this ceremony in the church and Grotto for many years.

The present writer was to see him on two other occasions before his death. Some time in the late autumn she spent about

twenty minutes with him. Although he was sitting huddled in
an armchair in his bedroom he was obviously very weak. On
this occasion she was conscious that Monsignor's interests were
no longer of this earth. Visibly he was detaching himself from
what bound him to earth. He talked quite openly of his coming
death; he was not afraid to die, he said; he was ready and
willing to go whenever God called him. But it seemed that God
must wish him to do more penance before he left this earth.
That he did not mind at all for himself; his great worry, he said,
was that he was giving a lot of trouble to those who nursed him.
In particular, he referred to the staff and the curates who were
so kind and patient to a " cross old man."

As his visitor took her leave of him, tired as he was, he
insisted that they say together one *Pater, Ave* and *Gloria* before
she left him. For the last time he gave her his blessing and as
he half raised his hand she felt she was in the presence of one
who was very close to God. This, too, was the impression held
by those who tended him. One lady asserts that as she went
round his room tidying or laying things by, very often she sang
hymns and Monsignor occasionally joined in. This routine was
varied by some prayers or a decade of the Rosary and on his
good days Monsignor was always pleased to take part. He liked
to have people he knew around him; long standing friends or
those parishioners whom he had known well for many decades.
A favourite visitor, one of his own parishioners, was the late
Father Lawrence Connelly. Monsignor had baptized Father
Lawrence, he had given him his First Holy Communion, he had
attended his ordination; and now the young priest who as a
child had often served the Canon's Mass was serving him in a
different way, by giving him his companionship in the evening
of his life. Father Connelly who had proved so faithful to his
aged parish priest was himself to follow Monsignor Taylor into
eternity just ten months later, on 3rd October, 1964, feast-day
of Saint Thérèse of the Child Jesus, great patroness of both
priests. Lines taken from Father Connelly's Obituary read as
follows:

> " The saintly Canon (Taylor) was to leave his mark on a most
> pliable soul, for all Father Connelly's life-long devotion to Saint
> Theresa and Saint Francis Xavier can be traced to the influence
> of his parish priest."

One of the most treasured possessions in the Connelly home
is the relic of Saint Thérèse which Monsignor Taylor gave to

Lawrence before he set out for Blairs College to commence his studies for the priesthood.

On Wednesday, September 25th, a special novena in honour of the Little Flower was started for Monsignor Taylor, the last three days, from 1st to 3rd October, being a special triduum of Masses, Holy Communions and evening devotions. His curates did not forget him, nor did his parishioners. During the last weeks of November he was confined to bed, sometimes very much against his will. He was still mentally alert and although he could not see, he usually recognised the voices of those around him. Because his heart was now weakening, and the severe abdominal complaint from which he was suffering, was worsening, someone had to be with or near him day and night during the last few months of his life. Mostly, the night nursing was done by religious, chiefly by the Irish Sisters of Charity from Assumption House, Airdrie.

The latter, like all the others who had attended Monsignor Taylor during his last illness, remarked on his patience. There were moments when he suffered great distress, and strong demands were made on his self control and powers of restraint; at these times all he wished was to be left alone. He was known at one time to become completely exasperated and utter a most ungentlemanly " Shut up! " at one of his helpers who was doing her best to make him comfortable. She was so amused at such an unusual expression coming from the saintly old Monsignor that she could not prevent herself from chuckling all day.

To the question, was he afraid to die he invariably gave the same answer. No, he was not afraid to die. Would he go straight to Heaven? Of that he was not sure, but he relied on God's mercy to get him to Heaven sometime. When one of the Sisters who nursed him asked what would the Little Flower do when she learned he was coming, he chuckled and replied instantly, " She will drop everything and come running to meet me."

One lady who attended him daily, with the utmost sincerity related the following story, which she says she had never understood, although Monsignor gave her some sort of explanation. She gave Monsignor his breakfast tray with a dish of porridge on it, something he could manage to take as a rule without any help. She left him for a few minutes and on her return she found the tray had been removed from the bed and was placed on a small table on the other side of the bedroom. She knew Monsignor, a blind invalid of near ninety years, could not possibly have risen from the bed and carried the tray across to the other side and then returned to bed during the short interval in which she was absent from the room. Quite taken aback, she stood for a while without saying anything; then Monsignor's voice broke the silence, " My Mother did this for me. She lifted the tray from the bed and placed it over there."

On being questioned as to Monsignor's mental condition the morning on which the incident is alleged to have taken place, the lady was quite definite that he knew exactly what he was saying at the time. She was the one who was so startled by his statement that she did not even question him further about the incident. She assumed he was talking about Our Lady and not his earthly mother; he often referred to Our Lady as " My " or " Our " Mother. Had the tray not been removed from the bed she might have thought that he was imagining things; but the tray had been removed and it was almost an impossibility for Monsignor to have removed it; and certainly no one had entered his room during the minute or so she was absent. The incident is related here exactly as told to the writer of these lines. The one who told the story was telling the truth as far as she knew it : the one thing she regrets is not having asked Monsignor to explain more clearly what had happened.

Towards the end of November, the present writer saw Monsignor Taylor alive for the last time. This was within four or five days of his death, and on this day he was in a comatose condition completely unaware of what was happening around him. He was to regain consciousness within the last days but it was clear that he would not recover. On Sunday, 1st December, 1963, a Triduum of prayers was started in honour of St. Francis Xavier, the titular Saint of the parish, the Saint whose motto— " For Jesus and Souls! "—the seminarian Thomas Nimmo Taylor had accepted as his own on his twenty-first birthday, over sixty-eight years earlier. But the three days of prayer were not to be completed during Monsignor Taylor's life-time: he died on the evening of the first day just after 8 p.m. on Sunday, 1st December, 1963, in the ninetieth year of his life and the sixty-sixth year of his priesthood; forty-eight of these years were spent in the Parish of St. Francis Xavier's at Carfin, to which he had come in July 1915.

All that Sunday his death had been expected hourly and when the church bells tolled mournfully just before 8.30 p.m. the people of Carfin knew they had lost the spiritual father who had directed their lives for almost half-a-century. The country learned of Monsignor's death from the news bulletin broadcast by the B.B.C. at ten o'clock, and although he had withdrawn greatly from public life within the last three years or so prior to his death, it is unlikely that there would be many Catholic homes in Scotland, nor for that matter much further afield, where his name would not still be well-known and where his death would not be mourned.

Monsignor Taylor suffered much distress and, at times, severe pain during the last years of his life; but this suffering he accepted with resignation and offered up for his missionary brethren. " Now that I am no longer able to work for the missions," he told a reporter from the *Glasgow Observer*, " I will offer my suffering for them." And undoubtedly he had full opportunity to make this offering on many occasions. The abdominal malady from which he suffered should have been treated much earlier; in this respect while caring for others he had neglected himself. Also his life had been a strenuous one with little rest and less sleep, while irregular and frequently skimped meals formed the normal pattern of his eating habits. Throughout his life he had been hard on himself, never succumbing to unnecessary luxuries or creature comforts, until his last illness became so advanced that others were compelled to re-order the severe routine of his life; not by their own choice, but because the routine times for meals were regulated to the temperate needs of the parish priest, rather than to that of his vigorous curates. More widely held was the view that St. Francis Xavier's parish was not one where a number of curates, given the choice, would choose to go. Monsignor Taylor's demands, not only on his assistant priests, but indeed on all his friends, were often exacting. In justice it must be added that never, at any time, did he spare himself; nor did he ever expect others to do what he himself was unwilling to do. On many an occasion he met with opposition to his plans, from his curates as well as from his friends. But generally it was accepted that Monsignor's wishes were for the greater good, however inconvenient or irritating these might be to others. Some of his friends, on reading this, will recall how on occasion they themselves were compelled to yield to his insistent demands, and how in exasperation they gave their grudging assent to his appeal: " All right, Canon, but remember, I am not doing this for you. I am doing it for Our Lady."

Since the whole of his priestly life had been directed towards fostering in his people a greater love for God and His saints, he could not have asked for a better reply.

During the days following Monsignor Taylor's death the intensely Catholic village of Carfin was a village of silent mourning. From early morning until late at night countless visitors thronged to the little village church and to the Grotto across the way to pay their tribute of respect to one of the best known and best loved priests in the country. On the morning after his death a growing disquiet and tension became apparent among the villagers. This may have been primarily due to delay in the release of formal instructions with regard to funeral arrangements; many of the villagers were aware that Monsignor Taylor's wishes were that he should be buried in the Grotto, in front of the Dominican shrine of Our Lady of the Rosary. It had been rumoured, too, with how much truth the writer of these lines is unable to say, that routine inquiries had earlier been made and the civic authorities had not raised any objections to the suggestion. In the circumstances the villagers of Carfin felt that His Lordship the Bishop of Motherwell was the only one who could resolve the difficulty; but His Lordship was attending the closing session of the Vatican Council and it was unlikely that he would be able to return home in time for the funeral.

It must be admitted that few of the Carfin folk were convinced that Monsignor's wish for a final resting place in the Grotto would be granted; what caused them much greater concern was that all during Monday and up to Tuesday evening it was not known whether permission had been granted for his remains to be borne around the Grotto. The one who writes these lines clearly recalls that it was not until about tea-time on Tuesday evening that the Administrator informed her that a number of boys had just been sent round the village to warn people that before the evening service at 7.30, Monsignor Taylor's body would be carried round the many shrines of the Grotto. This would be the last occasion within the precincts of the Grotto which he and they had built together, that his own people would have the opportunity of giving honour to this great-hearted little man, this priest of extraordinary simplicity and sanctity, who had worked with them and for them for almost half-a-century.

After the return of the cortege to the church, the people of the parish said their final farewell to their spiritual father as they filed slowly past the open coffin, where his body lay. In spite of strict instructions that no one was to touch the embalmed body, several people attempted, unsuccessfully, to do so. As soon as the service was completed that evening the coffin was sealed and was to be opened again only temporarily when Monsignor's nephew would arrive from England the following day.

On Wednesday evening Requiem Mass was celebrated and the solemn dirges were sung in his own Church of St. Francis

Xavier. On Thursday morning, the day of the funeral, in slow
and solemn procession the cortege moved away from the church
at Carfin through the village streets, accompanied by the hundreds of his people who would assist at the Solemn Requiem
Mass in Our Lady of Good Aid Cathedral, Motherwell. An
assurance had been given to the Administrator of Carfin parish
that, apart from priests and nuns, lay people would not gain
admittance until the Carfin contingent had arrived. This arrangement was strictly adhered to and in spite of their fears all those
who had travelled in the official coaches from Carfin found
seats reserved for them. Others unable to travel by the funeral
coaches, where admission tickets had been issued, were less
fortunate, although most of them found standing room at the
back of the cathedral.

As His Lordship, Bishop Scanlan, had not yet returned from
the Council, Solemn Requiem Mass was celebrated by his Vicar
General, Monsignor John Conroy, D.D.; he was assisted at the
altar by the Revs. James Comerford and Peter Murphy.

Every diocese in Scotland was represented in the congregation;
prelates, clergy, heads of religious orders, and a cross-section of
lay folk from far and near, packed the cathedral. On the streets
outside, along the funeral route, crowds of mourners standing
two or three deep prayed silently, or waited respectfully until
the cortege had left the cathedral, on the last lap of the journey
to St. Patrick's cemetery, at New Stevenston.

Below are excerpts from the panegyric preached during the
obsequies in the cathedral, by the Right Rev. Monsignor
Alexander Canon Hamilton, late parish priest of St. Mary's,
Hamilton, and a lifelong friend of Monsignor Taylor.

*" Here was a great priest whose life was acceptable to God
and proved ever faithful to Him."*

" There lie before the altar the mortal remains of one of
our best known and most beloved priests. He was indeed a
great priest, great not merely because of the wonderful things he
accomplished, but because he was the embodiment of full priestly
dedication. At his ordination he gave himself wholeheartedly to
God. He seemed to have ever before him the words which St.
Teresa of Lisieux wrote to the priest she called her brother missionary—words which I found written in the fly-leaf of one of
Monsignor's books:

' I am about to go before God and I understand more than ever
that one thing only is necessary—to work for Him *alone* and do

nothing for self or creatures. Jesus wishes to own your heart completely. Before this can be, you will have much to suffer. But, oh! what joy when comes the happy hour of going home!'

Jesus wishes to own your heart *completely*—there is the motif of all the sixty-six years of Monsignor Taylor's priestly life. All he wrote and said and did was simply the overflowing of his love of God."

Monsignor Hamilton dealt with Monsignor Taylor's education, ordination and his early years as a curate, after which he was appointed to the senior Seminary at Bearsden. Since Monsignor Hamilton himself was a student under Professor Taylor at St. Peter's College, the paragraphs dealing with this period of Father Taylor's life are reproduced almost in their entirety, although much of the information has already been given elsewhere in this book:

". . . Some three years after his ordination, in 1897, he was appointed to the Chairs of Sacred Scripture and Church History in St. Peter's College, Bearsden. But, besides the work entailed by these and other subsidiary subjects, Father Taylor was engaged in many other activities. In 1893, he had made a pilgrimage to Lourdes and this was the beginning of his extraordinary love for that shrine of Our Lady in the Pyrenees. While in the College at Bearsden, he gave numerous lantern lectures on the apparitions and in 1911, he published a short book entitled *Lourdes and its Miracles.* Lourdes was little known in Scotland at that time, and it may be said that the devotion of our people to Our Lady of Lourdes derives in no small measure from his lectures and writings. But the most famous book that came from his pen during these college years was his translation of *L'Histoire d'une Ame,* the autobiography of St. Teresa, published under the title of *Soeur Thérèse of Lisieux* . . . The book was given a tremendous reception throughout the English-speaking world, and the same is true of its successor, *A Little White Flower,* reprint following reprint, till the name of the Little Flower of Jesus and devotion to her and her " Little Way " spread wheresoever English was spoken. Surely this is the crowning point of Monsignor Taylor's life. Under Divine Providence he was chosen to be the promoter of the spirituality of St. Teresa, who was called by Pope Pius XI, 'The Darling of the World.' Well may we be proud to acclaim one of our own Scottish priests the apostle of such a cause. When the preliminary investigation for her canonisation was held at Lisieux in 1911, Father Taylor was one of the principal witnesses to the widespread devotion to her, in English-speaking lands.

Father Taylor left St. Peter's College in the year 1915. In a farewell speech the Rector said that the 'piety and earnest love of things unseen which have always been characteristic of our late professor, will doubtless accompany him to St. Francis Xavier's, Carfin.'

.   .   .   .

We are here to pray for him. It is all he would ask of us now. The good people of St. Francis Xavier's will cherish his memory and ever thank God for having given them such a devoted father in Christ."

The words used by the Rector in his farewell speech to Father Taylor in 1915 might well have been given as the theme of this biography. Stripped of his " piety and earnest love of things unseen," Monsignor Taylor appears before us as an average priest, an earnest priest, a human priest showing the strengths and human frailties which are the lot of those who follow in their Master's footsteps. But his life reveals all these qualities and more—much more. With greater intensity he aimed at the heights although at times the common inheritance of our weak human nature dragged him downwards. He knew and understood his own faults; his unpunctuality worried him endlessly and the thoughtless word which at times escaped his lips reminded him that constant guard must be kept on a wayward tongue. Honest and open criticism he accepted and welcomed but impatience mounted and at times erupted against those who attacked in the dark. There was no limit to the ends he would go in his " thirst for souls," and in this he may have fallen foul of a few of his clerical colleagues and his ecclesiastical superiors. But this book is not the biography of a man, whose life is distinguished from that of others, because of his many faults. Rather, this is an account of the life of a great priest, whose faults and feelings were the outcome, it has been claimed by his friend, Monsignor Hamilton, of the exuberant enthusiasm which carried him along without let or hindrance on the path which led ever closer to God.